A
TRIBUTE
TO
GEZA VERMES

Essays on Jewish and Christian Literature and History

edited by
Philip R. Davies
&
Richard T. White

Journal for the Study of the Old Testament
Supplement Series 100

Copyright © 1990 Sheffield Academic Press

Published by JSOT Press
JSOT Press is an imprint of
Sheffield Academic Press Ltd
The University of Sheffield
343 Fulwood Road
Sheffield S10 3BP
England

Typeset by Sheffield Academic Press
and
Printed on acid-free paper in Great Britain
by Billing & Sons Ltd
Worcester

British Library Cataloguing in Publication Data

A tribute to Geza Vermes: essays on Jewish and Christian
    literature and history.
    1. Christianity, history   2. Judaism, history
    I. Davies, Philip R.   II. Vermes, Geza *1924-*   III. Series
    209

    ISSN 0309-0787
    ISBN 1-85075-253-2

JOURNAL FOR THE STUDY OF THE OLD TESTAMENT SUPPLEMENT SERIES

100

Editors
David J A Clines
Philip R Davies

JSOT Press
Sheffield

CONTENTS

EDITORS' PREFACE

We owe thanks to all the contributors for their scholarship and for their patience with our prolonged labours. It has been a pleasure to bring together in a single volume a wealth of first-rate scholarship. But we also wish to record our appreciation of the many other friends, students and colleagues of Geza Vermes who would like to have participated in this tribute, but whose generosity we were unable to accommodate. The large number of scholars upon whom we could have called is a testimony to the esteem and affection in which Geza is held; while we have enjoyed the task of editing this volume, we have felt a very keen regret at the inevitable exclusions which our responsibilities have imposed. Our particular thanks are due to David Clines, whose editorial labours beyond the call of duty removed many blemishes from the final proofs. David Neale cheerfully completed the onerous task of indexing.

Finally, let this volume express our personal thanks to a much-loved teacher and colleague. We are grateful for the privilege of preparing for Geza Vermes this well-deserved tribute, which we hope respresents a measure of the range and quality of his own contribution not only to our understanding of the world of classical Judaism and Christianity, its history and literature, but also to the contemporary climate of Jewish and Christian scholarship whose amicable yet critical cooperation he has done so much to foster.

Philip R. Davies
Richard T. White

Geza Vermes, Professor of Jewish Studies in the University of Oxford and Fellow of the British Academy, was born on 22nd June 1924 and educated at the University of Budapest and the University of Louvain. He edited *Cahiers Sioniens* from 1953-55 and then worked at the Centre National de Recherche Scientifique in Paris, before his appointment in 1957 to a lectureship in Divinity at Newcastle University. In 1965 he became Reader in Jewish Studies at the University of Oxford, where he has remained. He lists in *Who's Who* as his recreations watching wild life and correcting proofs.

ABBREVIATIONS

AB	Anchor Bible
ANRW	*Aufstieg und Niedergang der römischen Welt*
BAR	*Biblical Archaeology Review*
BASOR	*Bulletin of the American Schools of Oriental Research*
BDB	Brown-Driver-Briggs, *Hebrew and English Lexicon*
BMC	G.F. Hill, *A Catalogue of the Greek Coins in the British Museum*
BWANT	Beiträge zur Wissenschaft vom Alten und Neuen Testament
CBQ	*Catholic Biblical Quarterly*
CBQMS	CBQ Monograph Series
CIL	*Corpus Inscriptionum Latinarum*
CPJ	*Corpus Papyrum Judaicorum*
DJD	*Discoveries in the Judean Desert (of Jordan)*
EI	*Eretz Israel*
EJ	*Encyclopaedia Judaica*
HSM	Harvard Semitic Monographs
HTR	*Harvard Theological Review*
HUCA	*Hebrew Union College Annual*
ICC	International Critical Commentary
IDB	*Interpreter's Dictionary of the Bible*
IEJ	*Israel Exploration Journal*
JANES	*Journal of Ancient Near Eastern Studies*
JBL	Journal of Biblical Literature
JJS	Journal of Jewish Studies
JRA	*Journal of Roman Archaeology*
JRS	*Journal of Roman Studies*
JSNT	*Journal for the Study of the New Testament*
JTS	*Journal of Theological Studies*
JQR	*Jewish Quarterly Review*
KB	Köhler-Baumgartner, *Lexicon in Veteris Testamenti Libros*
NT	*Novum Testamentum*
NTS	*New Testament Studies*
NTSupp.	Supplements to Novum Testamentum
PAAJR	*Proceedings of the American Academy of Jewish Research*
Payne-Smith	R. Payne Smith, *Thesaurus Syriacus*
PEFQS	*Palestine Exploration Fund Quarterly Statement*
PEQ	*Palestine Exploration Quarterly*

PG	Migne, Patrologia Graeca
PW	Pauly-Wissowa, *Real-Encyclopädie der classischen Altertumswissenschaft*
RB	*Revue biblique*
RGG	*Die Religion in Geschichte und Gegenwart*
REJ	*Revue des études juives*
RHR	*Revue de l'histoire des religions*
RQ	*Revue de Qumrân*
RTP	*Revue de théologie et de philosophie*
RSR	*Recherches de science religieuse*
SEG	*Supplementum Epigraphicum Graecum*
SJLA	Studies in Judaism in Late Antiquity
Strack-Billerbeck	H. Strack and P. Billerbeck, *Kommentar zum neuen Testament aus Talmud und Midrasch*
SVTP	Studia in Veteris Testamenti Pseudepigrapha
THAT	Theologisches Handkommentar zum alten Testament
THKNT	Theologisches Handkommentar zum neuen Testament
ThR	*Theologische Rundschau*
TU	Texte und Untersuchungen zur Geschichte der altchristlichen Literatur
TDNT	*Theological Dictionary of the New Testament*
TWNT	*Theologisches Wörterbuch zum neuen Testament*
TSAJ	Texte und Studien zum antiken Judentum
WdO	*Die Welt des Orients*
ZPE	*Zeitschrift für Papyrologie und Epigraphik*
WUNT	Wissenschaftliche Untersuchungen zum Neuen Testament
WMANT	Wissenschaftliche Monographien zum Alten und Neuen Testament

Ancient Texts

Philo
Flacc.	*In Flaccum*
Leg. All.	*Legum Allegoriae*
Spec. Leg.	*De specialibus Legibus*
Quaest. in Gen.	*Quaestiones et Solutiones in Genesim*
De Plant.	*De Plantatione*
Vit. Mos.	*De Vita Mosis*

Josephus
Ant.	*Antiquitates Judaicae*
BJ	*Bellum Judaicum*
C. Ap.	*Contra Apionem*

Patristic

CCL	*Corpus Christianorum, Series Latina*
GCS	*Die Griechischen Christlichen Schriftsteller*
Adv. Haer.	Epiphanius, *Adversus Haereses*
Apol.	Justin Martyr, *Apology*
Barn.	*The Epistle of Barnabas*
Ben. Jac.	Jerome, *De Benedictibus Jacob Patriarchae*
Adv. Marc.	Tertullian, *Adversus Marcionem*
Adv. Jud.	Tertullian, *Adversus Judaeos*
Did.	*Didache*
Hom.	*Clementine Homilies*
1 Clem.	*1 Clement*
Panarion Haer.	Epiphanius, *Panarion (Haereses)*

Classical

Hist. Romana	Dio Cassius, *Historia Romana*
De Inv.	Hermogenes, *De Inventione*
Pap. Lips.	Papyrus Lipsius (Griechische Urkunden der Papyrus-sammlung zur Leipzig, I)

Rabbinic

ARN	*Aboth deRabbi Nathan*
b.	*Babylonian Talmud*
Deut., Eccl. R.	*Deuteronomy, Ecclesiastes Rabbah*
FT	*Fragment(ary) Targum*
Gen. R.	*Genesis Rabbah*
M. Teh.	*Midrash Tehillim (Psalms)*
MHG	*Midrash ha-Gadol*
Pes. R.	*Pesiqta Rabbati*
PR	*Pesiqta Rabbati*
PRE	*Pirqe deRabbi Eliezer*
PsJ(on)	*Targum Pseudo-Jonathan*
t.	*Tosefta*
Tan.	*Tanḥuma*
(T)N	*Targum Neofiti*
(T)O	*Targum Onqelos*
y.	*Jerusalem (Palestinian) Talmud*

PART I

SEMITICA

THE LION OF THE TRIBE OF JUDAH HATH PREVAILED

Edward Ullendorff

School of Oriental and African Studies
University of London

In August 1988 the Countess of Avon (the widow of Anthony Eden, the Earl of Avon) was kind enough to draw my attention to a framed inscription in the Emperor Suite of the Grand Hotel, Eastbourne, whose text is reproduced in this short article.[1] The inscription contains a number of oddities, in particular the assumption that the late Emperor Haile Sellassie's 'brave heart' had earned him 'the title throughout the world of "The Lion of Judah"'. It is this element to which the present note is principally addressed. But before I turn to this point, I need to refer briefly to the conundrum of the date and to the somewhat unusual signature.

The Grand Hotel's text gives the date of the visit as 1936, and one would imagine that they ought to know the date from their guest register. The 1936 date also tallies with the description 'shortly after fleeing his own country' at the time when the Fascist forces occupied the capital Addis Ababa in May 1936. Yet the Emperor's dating, in his own hand, is 1930 of the Ethiopian era (i.e. September 1937 to September 1938). We know from his own autobiography and countless other sources that he left Addis Ababa on Friday 23rd Miyazya 1928 (= 1st May 1936). The remainder of the Gregorian year 1936 corresponds to the Ethiopian year 1928 up to September, and from September to the end of December to the Ethiopian calendar 1929. Since Emperor Haile Sellassie was obviously aware of the date on which he appended his signature, one can only assume that this document was prepared and signed about a year after his stay at the Grand Hotel, and in any event not before September 1937. Unfortunately, there is no reference to the Emperor's Eastbourne visit in the second volume of his autobiography, nor in

EMPEROR SUITE

This suite was named in memory of Emperor Haile Selasse of Ethiopia, who stayed at the Grand Hotel in 1936 shortly after fleeing his own country, following the invasion of Mussolini's Italian forces.

He was a small man in stature, but a fine soldier with a brave heart, which reputation earned him the title throughout the world of "The Lion of Judah".

Haile Selasse I R.R.

Inscription kept in the Emperor Suite of the Grand Hotel, Eastbourne, published by kind permission of the General Manager any other relevant source known to me. One further detail deserves a brief mention: the curious and, in my experience, unprecedented omission of the second element (*M*) identifying the Ethiopian calendar, i.e. '*A*(*mätä*) *M*(*əhrät*) 'Year of Mercy'—probably no more than a *lapsus calami*. The signature is penned in Latin and Ethiopic characters. Both show a practised hand. The Latin spelling (transcription) of the name is that adopted by him in the past. In later years, on the very rare occasions when he added a foreign transcription to the Ethiopian original, there was usually an *i* before the final *e* of Selasse. The appending of R.R. (*Regum Rex*) is distinctly unusual, though I myself possess a specimen of this kind where the R.R. follows not the Latin transcription of his name but the Ethiopian original. In the Eastbourne signature the Ethiopic version of the name consists of initials only: *Qä*(*damawi*) *Ḥa*(*ylä*) *Sə*(*lasse*) *nə*(*gusä*) *nä*(*gäst*), the last two words being, of course, the Ethiopic equivalent of R.R., 'King of Kings'. I have never before seen the initialled form of the Emperor's name as a signature, though I recall one or two instances where these initials are penned along the margins of documents. Both the Latin and Ethiopic characters are unmistakably written in Haile Sellassie's own hand.[2]

I now turn to the main object of these lines. The Eastbourne inscription is, of course, in error in assuming that it was Haile Sellassie's brave stand in the face of brutal aggression in 1935-6 that 'earned him the title . . . of "The Lion of Judah"'. Neither is this phrase a title nor has it any connexion with any event in the last Emperor's life. What is a venial fault in the Eastbourne document must be reckoned an unforgivable solecism in the Minority Rights Group's Report No. 67, 1985 (*The Falashas: The Jews of Ethiopia*), where Haile Sellassie is described as 'the self-styled Conquering Lion of the Tribe of Judah' (p. 6). This statement is tantamount to referring to Queen Elizabeth II as 'the self-styled *Fidei Defensor*'. The latter is a (originally) papal conferment of the 16th century, while the former is a long-established motto or emblem attached not to the person of the Emperor but to the Ethiopian polity as such. It is the merit of Sven Rubenson to have dealt with this matter in detail and conclusively (*Journal of Ethiopian Studies*, III, 2, 1965, pp. 75-85), while the present writer has endeavoured to elucidate the problem in the context of his *Ethiopia and the Bible* (The Schweich Lectures of the British Academy, Oxford University Press, 1968).

The Lion of the tribe of Judah, the Root of David, is derived from Rev. 5.5 and in that context refers, of course, to Christ who will 'open the book and loosen the seven seals thereof'. The idea of the lion of Judah goes back to Gen. 49.9 גור אריה יהודה 'Judah is a lion's whelp', while the root of David relates to Isaiah 11.1. These expressions underline the Biblical attachment of Ethiopia and its dynasty and in particular the remarkable *imitatio Veteris Testamenti*. 'King of Zion' or 'Israelitish Kings' are the ways in which Ethiopian Emperors have traditionally referred to themselves. This tradition, established well over a millennium ago, has now been broken—or at any rate interrupted—by the advent, since 1974, of alien ideologies imposed upon this ancient realm—until the day of *perestroika* dawns also in this part of the Horn of Africa.

NOTES

1. I am very grateful to Lady Avon for copying the text for me and to the General Manager of the Grand Hotel for letting me have the photograph of the inscription here reproduced.

2. In a work by Ryszard Kapuscinski, entitled *The Emperor: the Downfall of an Autocrat* (London, 1983), which has enjoyed a, to my mind undeserved, vogue as a book and a play, it is averred that the 'monarch not only never used his ability to read, but he also never wrote anything and never signed anything in his own hand. Though he ruled for half a century, not even those closest to him knew what his signature looked like' (p. 8). This statement, like countless others in the book, is entirely fictitious (Richard Pankhurst, in a letter to the *Times Literary Supplement* of 17 April 1987, has rightly pointed out that Kapuscinski's work which has been accorded a Library of Congress (and indeed British Library) classification for 'history' cannot, in fact, be accepted as having a basis in history). Every literate Ethiopian will have seen the late Emperor's signature in newspapers and books. I myself possess many examples of his signature and his writing. This slur on the reputation of Haile Sellassie is of a piece with so much current meretricious scribbling, notably by those who neither knew the man nor possess any real acquaintance with historic Ethiopia—or indeed knowledge of its languages.

PART II

DEAD SEA SCROLLS

TWO BIBLICAL HEBREW ADVERBS
IN THE DIALECT OF THE DEAD SEA SCROLLS

P. Wernberg-Møller

Oriental Institute
University of Oxford

I i

One of the linguistic peculiarities of the Dead Sea Scrolls is the form
in which the Hebrew adverb for 'exceedingly, greatly, very' (מאד)
appears, both in the biblical and non-biblical documents. The root of
the word is Common-Semitic and is attested in nouns and verbs in
widely scattered Semitic languages, including the Canaanite dialects.
The originally substantival character of the common adverb is
clearly attested in Biblical Hebrew, not only in Deut. 6.5, cf. 2 Kings
23.25, but also in the prepositional expressions עד־מאד, במאד, מאד
and עד־למאד,[1] and the adverbial use of the word is correctly described
as an adverbial accusative.[2] The same usage can be seen also in
Ugaritic.[3] The form of the word in the Scrolls varies in two respects
from the standard form attested in the Masoretic Text.

Firstly, in the *plene* spelling of the word,[4] the *waw* appears some
times *before* the *aleph*; cf. 1QIsa[a] 16.6, 56.12 (מואד), and 47.6, 9; 52.13;
64.8, 11, attesting to the far more frequent form מואדה which occurs
also in 11QT (56.19),[5] and 11QPs[a] (104.1; 119.41, 43, 96, 107, 138;
139.14; 142.7; 145.3);[6] in a few cases, however, the *waw* is 'correctly'
placed *after* the *aleph* (cf. e.g. מאודה in 1QIsa[a] 38.17), reflecting
presumably the scribe's knowledge of the etymologically correct
form of the word. The measure of inconsistency appearing in these
orthographic variations is best explained by assuming that the *aleph*
was not, in fact, pronounced in this and a number of similar words in
which the glottal stop appears in medial position. מואד was therefore
probably pronounced /mōd/, and מואדה and מאודה were realized orally
by the speakers of the DSS dialect as /mōdā/. The fact that the word

is occasionally spelt without *aleph* (see below) points in the same direction, and so does the circumstance that an etymological *aleph* in medial position (after *shewa*, and between vowels) is fairly frequently omitted in writing from a number of other words in our documents.[7]

Secondly, the adverb is spelt with a final ח which cannot be the consonantal element of a pronominal suffix and must be a *mater lectionis* marking a vocalic ending which is likely to have been /ā/. That this is not the feminine ending is, I believe, generally accepted by now, although throughout the 1950s, 1960s and even into the 1970s it appears to have been taken for granted by some scholars that the longer form of the noun was a feminine form of the biblical Hebrew masculine form.[8] However, there is no sound basis for such a view if examined etymologically and comparatively. Walter Baumgartner's outstanding reputation as a careful scholar, whose judgment could be trusted, may have been responsible for the popularity of this mistake. It appears to have been Israeli scholars who, rather than actually demonstrating the impossibility of the now largely discarded view, propounded an alternative suggestion for which there is a sound philological basis. Kutscher appears to have been the first to take the ח as the adverbial ending /ā/. The Hebrew original of his analysis of 1QIsaᵃ was published in 1959, a year after Baumgartner's article in the *Eissfeldt Festschrift*; however, Baumgartner was unable to take account of Kutscher's view which was not published in English until 1974, the same year in which part II of the revised version of Koehler's *Lexikon* was published.

ii

The most significant change in the linguistic analysis of the DSS since the 1950s has come about by the effort to understand the orthography and phonology in terms of phonetics of modern linguistics. However, Kutscher and Qimron, in their important publications already referred to, differ from each other in some important respects.[9] In spite of regarding the special orthographic features as reflecting an oral tradition, Kutscher does not actually see the DSS language as a spoken language, but as a *literary* vehicle modelled as closely as possible on late BH, as attested e.g. in Chronicles. According to Kutscher the Jews of Palestine did not speak Hebrew during the last centuries BCE, although Hebrew continued to be written and served largely as a literary language.[10]

Kutscher does, however, allow for the possibility that archaic forms survive in the DSS language which, he suggests, reflects the lingusitic situation in Palestine during the last pre-Christian centuries during which the Jews spoke Greek and Aramaic and BH was known in at least three different reading traditions (Tiberian, Babylonian and Samaritan). The orthography, with variants like ריאש, רוש, רואש and ראוש (cf. מאדה, מודה, מוארה and מאודה) is accounted for by Kutscher and Qimron along identical lines: they both assume that the glottal stop in medial position (i.e. after *shwa* and between vowels) was not pronounced at the public reading of the sacred texts; but Qimron regards the DSS as attesting to an actually spoken Hebrew dialect and plays down the Aramaic influence which Kutscher tends to regard as all-pervading. On their own, separate premises, these two scholars are, of course, totally consistent, for with Kutscher's view of Hebrew becoming largely a dead language in late post-exilic times and Aramaic becoming the commonly spoken language goes, of course, an emphasis on the Aramaic elements in DSS language; and Qimron's insistence on the survival of Hebrew as a spoken language among circles outside the mainstream of Judaism carries with it the view of the special features of DSS language (whether attested in biblical or non-biblical documents) as *Hebrew* dialectal features. The main point of this quite important difference between Kutscher and Qimron, which has a bearing on our present concern, is that, to Qimron, the special features of DSS Hebrew such as *mōdā* 'very', and the presence in the vocabulary of that language of words known neither from other Hebrew sources nor from Aramaic, can be explained only by assuming that DSS Hebrew is based on and reflects a dialect which was actually spoken by the copyists of the biblical DSS and by the authors and scribes responsible for the non-biblical DSS.[11] Although combining late-biblical, and post-biblical Hebrew lingusitic elements with a sprinkling of Aramaic influence, the Dead Sea Scrolls were copied and composed by writers who spoke a Hebrew dialect with its own characteristic features, some of which have come down to us in their writings. As has been said above, the special vocabulary is important for Qimron's argument— and so is the fact that the special linguistic features of the DSS dialect are found both in the biblical and non-biblical documents. On Kutscher's premises (that Aramaic was universally spoken by the Jews of Palestine in late post-exilic times and that the DSS language was a literary language only) the impact of the language of the non-biblical documents on the biblical ones is hard to explain: what would be the point of introducing features of a late *literary* language into a biblical text like the Book of Isaiah composed hundreds of years before? If BH became a dead language in the course of the post-exilic era and remained the language of the learned only, there would have been no need for re-writing (or 'up-dating') the sacred texts. In fact, any attempt to do such a thing would have been firmly resisted, and the idea might not even have occurred to anyone. It is more likely that there were Hebrew speakers throughout the period in question and that some of these (religious) circles, whose language was a Hebrew dialect, with a certain amount of Aramaic influence, produced their own copies of the sacred texts. In official Jewish circles such a procedure would, of course, not have been tolerated. The kind of direct interference with the Hebrew text of a biblical book, which we encounter in 1QIsaᵃ, would not have been tolerated within the mainstream of Judaism.

iii

The longer form *mōdā*, with a final, unstressed /ā/, unknown in Hebrew outside the DSS dialect, is a small, but distinct feature of the language spoken in the circles which produced the DSS. The older view that the ה is a marker of the feminine gender has been dealt with above. Qimron regards the ending as a locative termination which in this and other adverbs has lost its original, locative function.[12] He does not, however, distinguish clearly between the originally *consonantal*, local-terminative (or directional) ה, and the adverbial ending /ā/, the latter being the ancient Common-Semitic accusative marker, widely used as an adverbial case ending. Kutscher is more precise on this point,[13] as he rightly distinguishes between the directional ה and the adverbial ending, although he fails to describe *mōdā* as an adverbial accusative pure and simple. It is clearly unsatisfactory to regard the ending in *mōdā* as a *locative* ending when a much simpler explanation (as a noun in the accusative, functioning as an adverb) is available. The form is structurally similar to Arab *jiddan* and there is nothing inherently unlikely in a Hebrew dialect preserving in its spoken and written form a linguistic element which has disappeared from the standard language, *after* the dropping of short, final vowels (including case ending). Indeed, the chance survival of isolated linguistic featues in a dialect spoken by a group of people cut off from the mainstream of Jewry because of their religious convictions, is very likely; some such theory would account for some of the peculiarities of DSS Hebrew, found in both biblical and non-biblical documents. Kutscher's cautious acknowledgement of the possible survival of archaic features in DSS Hebrew[14] is, of course, consistent with his view that Hebrew died out as a spoken language in late post-exilic times and so was not spoken by the circles behind the Scrolls in any shape or form. However, on his premises, the special features, (including archaic elements), in the DSS dialect are difficult to account for. The common word *mōdā* 'very' which, with one or two exceptions, is used throughout the texts, whether prose or poetry, must reflect a peculiarity in the spoken language which, together with other linguistic features (archaic and/or dialectal), by a happy chance has come down to us.

iv

The spelling of the word מאד without the *aleph* occurs in an apocryphal Zion psalm from Cave 11.[15] The word is clearly the same as BH מאד, the *masculine* noun, and the suffixed form מודי supports the view that the longer form *mōdā*, common in the DSS Hebrew, is not a feminine form.

C. Rabin, in a note on CD 9.11, suggested over thirty years ago that מאד 'power' perhaps occurs in מודה in 1QS 10.16.[16] The phrase there, of which מודה forms a part (בהפלא מודה), is a little unusual and has been dealt with in several different ways. In my edition of 1QS I suggested (wrongly) that בהפלא was a defectively written infinitive *construct* hiphil and that מודה (= תודה) was the object of that verb;[17] the result was a rather unsatisfactory translation. G. Vermes's rendering ('I will bless Him for his exceeding wonderful deeds'[18] presupposes the taking of מודה as the noun מוד (= מאד) plus the suffix for 3 masc. sing., as Rabin had already suggested (cf. above). The last mentioned scholar regarded מודה as parallel with the following גבורתו; however, as Vermes has seen, the poetic structure of the context suggests that מודה is not balanced by גבורתו; besides, the variations in the spelling of the suffix in close proximity, although not impossible, would appear to be rather striking. Vermes's free rendering makes good sense and reads well; it is a compromise solution which combines Rabin's insight with the requirements of the context. But a preferable solution emerges if מודה (= מאודה) (read as *mōdā*) is taken as the adverbial accusative of מאד and translated 'very', qualifying the preceding הפלא(ב) (infinitive *absolute*), functioning as an indeclinable noun and, with the preposition ב meaning 'wondrously', as T. Leahy has suggested.[19] The line is then to be rendered as follows:

> I will bless Him very wondrously (or: in a quite extraordinary[20] way), I will meditate upon His power, and upon His mercy I will lean the whole day.

The phrase הפלא מודה (= הפלא מאד), although not occurring in BH, is structurally similar to הרבה מאד. It could be yet another feature peculiar to the DSS dialect. The phrase occurs in 1QH.

The ending of *mōdā*, etymologically a fossilized accusative which remained in the DSS dialect long after the disappearance of case endings from the spoken language, at some point lost its status and function as a case ending and could, as a result, quite naturally be construed with a preposition, e.g. in the phrase עד מואדה (1QIsa[a] 64.8, 11; 11QPs[a] 119.43, 107). This would, of course, have been impossible if the case system had been fully operative in the spoken language.

II i

The BH adverbs שם and שמה are both used in the meanings 'there' and 'thither', although the former is mostly employed in the locative and the latter in the local-terminative sense. The purpose of the following observations is to suggest that the two forms were originally variants and that the longer form, in the course of the historical development of BH, became structurally similar to, and so came to be identified with, שם plus the final unstressed /ā/ of direction commonly known as the *hē locale*. The varied use of שם and שמה in BH is to be explained in terms of historical linguistics, and the apparent inconsistencies in the biblical books (sometimes even within the same verse) should be seen as variations which were available to the biblical writers who made use of these alternative forms as they saw fit. Usage is likely to have varied in the dialects of spoken Hebrew during and after the biblical period; that this is so is suggested by the evidence of the DSS in which the functions of שם and שמה, although overlapping in meaning with each other in that dialect also, differ from BH usage in a significant way. This points to yet another linguistic feature characteristic of the DSS dialect.

ii

In order to understand the etymology of שמה it is necessary to refer briefly to Ugaritic and classical Aramaic.[21] In Ugaritic both the shorter form *ṯm* and the longer form *ṯmt* are found, clearly corresponding to שם and שמה of BH; both words are used in the locative sense 'there'.[22] The form *ṯmt* shows that the vocalic ending of שמה originally had nothing to do with the *hē locale* which has a different history. A suffix /ta/ is known from classical Arabic where *ṯumma-ta* is a variant of *ṯumma* 'then' (related to *ṯamma* 'there', derived from the same root and of kindred meaning). Evidence of this indeclinable, Proto-Semitic suffix, probably functioning originally as a deictic element, is restricted to the West-Semitic speech area within which the vocalization and function of the adverb, or adverbs, formed from the root *ṯmm* varied dialectally, expressing a point in time and/or space, and vocalized either with /u/ or /a/, or both; and Hebrew שמה can be seen to have evolved neither from *šámma* (= Arab. *ṯmma*), nor from *šámmaha* but from *šámmata* > *šámmat* > *šámma*. The original short vowel of the second syllable (to be seen most clearly in the Arabic forms), though lost in שם, was preserved in שמה; it is best described as the adverbial accusative case ending (rather than simply a connecting vowel), a well-attested function of the accusative in classical Arabic to indicate time and place, among other things.[23] The old etymology of שמה as שם plus *hē locale* is therefore wrong and can safely be discarded. The particular history of שמה became obscured, partly by the structural similarity of the word with the *hē locale* formations, and partly by BH usage in which שמה is overwhelmingly used in the local-terminative sense. However, in its original form שמה (>*šámmata*) did not exclusively, or even commonly, indicate the movement or direction towards somewhere, as the suffix /ta/ never had that specific function; in this respect it differs markedly from the originally consonantal *hē locale* suffix /ha/ whose function was originally to indicate movement and direction. The locative function of שמה (attested in BH in 18 passages),[24] should therefore not be explained as due to the *hē locale* having lost its original, directional sense, but as an original semantic feature.

iii

The (admittedly sparse) evidence of שם and שמה from North-West Semitic inscriptions is as follows: Phoenician and Old Aramaic testify to שם in the locative sense, whereas in Moabite (closely similar to Hebrew), שם, apart from its locative function, also functions in the local-terminative sense after a verb of motion נשא.[25] In these dialects, as far as we know, the longer variant was not found, and שם functioned in the locative, as well as in the local-terminative sense, at least in Moabite. שמה used in the local-terminative sense occurs in the Lachish ostrakon no. 4, after a verb of motion (שלח),[26] and in the Arad inscription no. 24.20, also after a verb of motion (בוא);[27] this is in accordance with BH which reflects linguistic usage in standard Hebrew of the late monarchic period. The longer form retained its locative function, at least in the literary language, as may be seen also from BH.

The linguistic situation, as regards שם and שמה and their equivalents in West and North-West Semitic, may be summarized as follows: *The shorter form* in the locative sense is attested in Arabic, Ugaritic, Phoenician, Old Aramaic, and BH; in the local-terminative sense it is found in Moabite and BH. *The longer form* in the *locative* sense is attested in Arabic, Ugaritic, and BH; cf. also Biblical Aramaic תמה (with the stress on the final syllable); in the local-terminative sense it is found in BH, and in non-biblical Hebrew of the late monarchic period.

Of the languages and dialects listed, BH alone appears four times, i.e. under both headings and in all sub-divisions. BH is therefore by far our fullest source of information about the varied functions of שם and שמה with the related Semitic dialects affording valuable additional background evidence, however scant; and in its frequent use of שמה in the local-terminative sense Hebrew stands alone. There is enough evidence to conclude that שמה originally was a variant of שם and that the two forms originally shared the same semantic fields, with some regional and dialectal variations which we are unable to trace in detail for lack of evidence.

iv

As has been said above, the usage of שם and שמה in BH varies within the same book, and sometimes even within the same verse, as e.g. in Jer. 22.27; Isa. 34.15.[28] The general impression is one of considerable, apparently random use of the two adverbs.

Of special interest in the present context are the cases where שם and שמה occur in the meanings 'thither' and 'there' respectively, contrary to common usage in BH. The material is complex and deserves a fuller treatment than can be given here; for lack of space, only a few examples and some general remarks can be offered here.

שם is used with a verb of motion (as e.g. in Jud. 19.15; 21.10; 2 Sam. 2.2; 17.18; 1 Kings 19.9), and is construed with verbs like נחת (2 Kings 6.9), ירה (2 Kings 19.32), הריח (Jer. 29.14); in this *local-terminative* sense the adverb occurs fairly frequently in Jeremiah and Ezekiel.[29] In Deut. 1.37 MT has שם and SamP. שמה, elsewhere MT has שמה and SamP. שם as e.g. in Num. 33.54 (with יצא) and Deut. 31.16 (with בוא).

שמה is commonly used with verbs of motion, and with some verbs the high degree of consistency may reflect idiomatic usage. נום, for instance, is always (except in Isa. 20.6, see below) construed with שמה and the same applies to נתן which, in the sense of 'putting something *into* something' (as opposed to 'putting something somewhere'), is always construed with שמה except Exod. 40.7.[30] In the locative sense שמה is attested with verbs like שכב (Josh. 2.1)[31] חבה (= חבא, Josh. 2.16), קטר (2 Kings 23.8), בכה (Gen. 43.30). היה (Jer. 27.22; Ruth 1.7). These instances suffice to illustrate the locative function of שמה in BH, and J. Hoftijzer is mistaken in his efforts to argue that constructions with שמה in MT almost always imply an element of movement.[32] The BH material is too complex to be dealt with synchronically, and it is only through a historical and comparative study of the evidence that its variety in the usage of שם and שמה becomes clear.

The BH evidence suggests that in the course of time (i.e. within the biblical period and later) שמה, because of its formal similarity to the *hē locale* constructions, came to be used *largely* in the local-terminative sense, and שם *largely* in the locative sense. Hebrew dialects may well have varied in this respect; indeed, individual speakers may, outside idiomatic usage, have had the choice to select the one or the other of these variants according to personal preference. To express emphasis שמה, for example, may have been felt to be particularly effective rhetorically at the beginning of an utterance; for examples of such possible emphatic use of שמה and ושמה see Isa. 22.18; Jer. 27.22 and several other passages. Some degree of variability in the spoken DSS dialect is suggested by evidence from the biblical and non-biblical documents from Caves 1, 4, and 11 which in their usage of שם and שמה differ significantly from BH, although overlapping with the latter to some extent and sharing with it the dual (locative and local-terminative) function of these adverbs.

V

שם and שמה are both attested in the DSS although it is an interesting linguistic fact that the longer form is not found at all in 1QS, 1QM,[33] 1QpHab and 1QH. שם occurs frequently in these documents, always in the locative sense. שמה in the locative sense is well attested in 11QT,[34] 1QIsa[a] (see below), fragments from Cave 4, and 11QPs[a]. It is not possible, in the present state of knowledge, to explain why the longer form does not occur in the texts from Cave 1 mentioned above. The frequent use of שמה in the locative sense in the other documents is a salient linguistic feature which points to a common usage in the DSS dialect which can be seen to have affected the linguistic shape of biblical passages and phrases, in biblical documents (like 1QIsa[a]) and in a non-biblical document containing a biblical tag or allusion; and this usage of שמה is found in non-biblical contexts as well. In biblical or quasi-biblical contexts locative שם, although often copied as שמה,[35] at times appears in its masoretic form; this is the case in several passages in 1QIsa[a] (7.23; 13.20, 21; 23.12; 27.10).[36] The same manuscript confirms the local-terminative use of שם in two passages (37.33; 57.7), although generally שם of MT is replaced by שמה.[37] In a biblical quotation, or allusion to a biblical passage, שם of MT is copied unchanged (see *DJD* VII, 504 1-2, VI.13-14, after a [reconstructed] verb of motion), but changed to שמה in the same text (*DJD* VII, 504 1-2, V.12, after the same verb (הריח) which is construed with either שם or שמה in MT. The DSS copyists were well aware of the biblical usage of שם and שמה in their dual sense of 'there' and 'thither' and so, when copying or quoting Scripture, would at times leave a שם (locative or local-terminative) of MT unchanged, although in their spoken dialect they probably mostly tended to use שמה in both senses. We can only guess at the precise extent to which usage of שם was reduced in the spoken language. The shorter form of the adverb may have been used in idioms and certain verbal combinations, like e.g. נגש שם (*DJD* VII, 492, 1.10) and רבץ שם (Isa. 13.21; 27.10, copied unchanged in 1QIsa[a]). Other fixed phrases, attested both in MT and 1QIsa[a], are עלה שם (Isa. 57.7) and ירה שם (Isa. 33.33); cf. above, under iv. Where MT varies, e.g. in constructions with בוא, הלך and ירד, the DSS dialect prefers שמה; the same tendency can be seen to be the case even with a stative verb like שכן; cf. Isa. 13.21, 65.9 in both of which passages 1QIsaᵃ has שמה whereas MT reads שם in the former and שמה in the latter (see n. 31 above). Where MT uses שמה (locative), 1QIsaᵃ confirms the longer form: it is never changed to שם; and where MT has שם (locative) 1QIsaᵃ has שמה in four cases (13.21, 34.12, 14, 15). שמה with היה appears to have been a common construction in the DSS dialect; cf. 1QIsaᵃ 35.8, 9; 48.16 (the same construction is not unknown in MT, see Jer. 27.22; Ruth 1.7); similarly, instead of אין שם of MT, אין שמה sems to have been preferred (1QIsaᵃ 34.12), although אין שם also occurs (*DJD* I, 27 1, I.7).

As compared with BH the DSS testify to an extended usage of שמה in the *locative* sense, with the retention of its local-terminative sense. Both functions of שמה can be seen in *DJD* VII, 491 10, I.19 (שמה [...נותמה](כול הו[דרות המלחמה יסּפרו שמה ואחר ישובו אל מח where the adverb occurs twice, once as a locative, and once (with a verb of motion) as a local-terminative. This extension of שמה in the locative sense is a feature of the spoken DSS dialect, on a par with the archaic preservation of the accusative ending in /mōdā/ dealt with earlier. However, שם was also part of the spoken dialect, as we have seen, although its local-terminative function (attested in a fairly substantial number of cases in BH) appears to have been severely reduced and it functioned largely as a locative adverb. In addition to the instances already mentioned, the combination ברך שם may be mentioned; the phrase (clearly echoing biblical phraseology) appears consistently in this form only: the verb is never, in any of the texts published so far, construed with שמה, see 1QM 14.3; 18.6, and *DJD* VII, 512, VII.5; *DJD* V, 158 1-2.7. Familiar to copyists and speakers alike from the Bible, the phrase was always copied in its biblical form and likely to have been used thus in the spoken language also. Another instance of locative שם occurs in *DJD* V, 174, 1-2.4, in the phrase קדושי שם 'my holy ones are there'; although unlikely to have been part of the spoken dialect, this case is nevertheless worth mentioning as another example of שם in the locative sense, because it occurs in a text found together with other texts in which שמה (locative) was the rule rather than the exception; perhaps שם was used in preference to שמה in certain phrases, like e.g. אשר יהיה שם שם (1QS 6.3, 6; 8.13, cf. also Isa. 7.23 MT and 1QIsaᵃ), and there may well have been cases in the spoken language where a significant distinction could only be upheld and ambiguity be avoided, by using שם and not שמה and vice versa, as

e.g. the difference between נפל שם (1QM 19.11) 'to fall in that place'
and נפל שמה (cf. Gen. 14.10; Exod. 21.33) 'to fall *into* that place'.
With the locative שם and the local-terminative שמה at their disposal
the DSS dialect speakers were presumably able to distinguish
between שם (locative) and שמה (local-terminative), in spite of the
marked increase in the usage of שמה as a locative adverb, especially
in idioms where the distinction would be semantically significant.

However that may be, it was the greatly increased usage of שמה in
the locative sense that made the (otherwise unknown) expression
משמה 'from there' possible. One could, of course, conjecture that this
expression arose by analogy with מחוצה (Ezek. 40.40, 44). I prefer,
however, to see in this unique formation a dialectal variant of משם,[38]
mainly because of the history of שמה in the locative sense within the
DSS dialect; in my view it should be seen as yet another linguistic
structure peculiar to the DSS dialect which came about when the
vocalic ending was no longer regarded as a case ending. In that sense
it is a secondary formation, presupposing (a) the loss of the case
system and (b) the spread of שמה as a locative adverb. In this respect
the DSS dialect differed significantly from BH. The DSS dialect, by
its common usage of שמה as a locative, preserved an original feature
of the adverb which prevented its large-scale identification as a *hē
locale* structure (to be seen in BH). In this respect the DSS dialect
was 'archaic' and 'conservative' as compared with BH in which the
original locative function of שמה (as a variant of שם) was largely
(though not wholly) lost, due to the formal similarity of the word to
the *hē locale* structures.

The linguistic diversity among the speakers of Hebrew in post-
exilic times naturally extended beyond the characteristic usage of a
couple of adverbs like those dealt with above. However, the wider
implications of this important fact for the study of the history of the
religious circles that produced, or copied, the DSS lie outside the
scope of the present article.[39]

NOTES

1. See Gesenius/Buhl's *Handwörterbuch* (1921), p. 392, and Brown/
Driver/Briggs' *Lexicon*, 1952, p. 547.
2. Cf. BDB, *loc. cit.*
3. Cf. Cyrus H. Gordon, *Ugaritic Textbook*, 1965, p. 430. For the use of

the accusative case to form adverbs in classical Arabic, see W. Wright, *A Grammar of the Arabic Language*, I (1874), pp. 321f. As for BH, see Gesenius/Kautzsch/Cowley, *Hebrew Grammar* (1910) (=G K), pp. 372-75.

4. The word is spelt without a *waw* once in 1QM (12.12); see Y. Yadin, *The Scroll of the War of the Sons of Light against the Sons of Darkness*, Oxford, 1962, p. 252, and once in 1QIsaᵃ (31.1).

5. Cf. Y. Yadin, *The Temple Scroll*, vol. I, Jerusalem, 1983, p. 30. In the following TS stands for Yadin's edition.

6. Cf. *DJD* IV and J.A. Sanders, *The Dead Sea Psalms Scroll*, 1967, and Y. Yadin, 'Another Fragment (E) of the Psalms Scroll from Qumran Cave 11 (11QPsᵃ)', *Textus* 5 (1966), p. 4.

7. See E.Y. Kutscher, *The Language and Linguistic Background of the Isaiah Scroll*, 1974, pp. 167ff., 498ff. Apart from Kutscher's authoritative work the excellent descriptive treatment of the orthography, phonology, morphology and syntax of the dialect of the Qumran documents by Elisha Qimron (*The Hebrew of the Dead Sea Scrolls*, Harvard Semitic Studies 29) 1986 should be consulted; on מורה מאור, מואר מוארה see especially pp. 25, 69, 109, 117.

8. The entry in Koehler–Baumgartner's *Hebräisches und Aramäisches Lexikon*, II, 1974, p. 511, is clearly in need of correction on this point which reflects Baumgartner's erroneous view as expressed by him already in 1958 in *Von Ugarit nach Qumran* (Eissfeldt Festschrift), p. 29.

9. See also Kutscher's article on the language of the DSS in *Encyclopaedia Judaica* 16 (1971), cols. 1583-90.

10. *EJ, vol. cit.*, col. 1584.

11. Cf. Qimron, *op. cit.*, pp. 117f.

12. *Op. cit.*, p. 69.

13. See his *Language and Linguistic Background*, p. 414.

14. In *EJ, loc. cit.*, cols. 1584, 1586, 1587; cf. also E. Tov, *Textus* 13 (1986), p. 43, n. 29, quoting F.M. Cross.

15. *DJD* IV, p. 86, 1.2, and cf. the editor's comment, p. 88.

16. See his edition of *The Zadokite Documents*, Oxford, 1954, p. 46, n. 11. Cf. also Qimron, *op. cit.*, p. 25. The taking of מורה as the adverb 'very' in 1QS 10.16 is confirmed by closely similar phraseology in 1QH where the word is spelt with and without *aleph*; see K.G. Kuhn, *Konkordanz zu den Qumrantexten*, 1960, p. 113.

17. *The Manual of Discipline*, Leiden, 1957, p. 146.

18. See *The Dead Sea Scrolls in English*, Harmondsworth, 1962, p. 90.

19. *Biblica* 41 (1960), p. 144.

20. For this meaning of הפלא, see 2 Chron. 2.8.

21. A.F.L. Beeston, in *A Descriptive Grammar of Epigraphic South Arabian* 1962, p. 52, suggested that South-Arabian *ṯmt* meant 'there', but this view is no longer held by the experts who now favour the interpretation

of the word as a place-name (so Professor Beeston orally). I have therefore omitted the South-Arabian material from the present inquiry.

22. Cf. J. Aistleitner, *Wörterbuch der Ugaritischen Sprache*, 1974, p. 337.
23. Cf. n. 3 above.
24. See *BDB*, p. 1027.
25. For references, see H. Donner and W. Röllig, *Kanaanäische und Aramäische Inschriften*, III, 1964, pp. 24, 43.
26. Cf. Donner and Röllig, *op. cit.*, I (1966), no. 194.8, and II (1968), p. 194. Other readings of this line have been proposed by W.F. Albright and F.M. Cross (for references, see Donner and Röllig, II, p. 195).
27. See Y. Aharoni, *Arad Inscriptions*, 1981, p. 46.
28. In Isa. 34.15 1QIsaᵃ reads שמה... שמה for שם... שמה of MT.
29. Cf. *BDB*, s.v. שם.
30. Similarly, עלה (normally construed with שם) appears to reflect idiomatic usage in the spoken language which has preserved the construction with שם in the local-terminative sense in a much used idiom. It is interesting to note that 1QIsaᵃ 57.7 reproduces שם of MT, without changing it to שמה; on the other hand, for שם in Ps. 122.4 11QPsᵃ reads שמה; see *DJD* IV (1965), p. 24.
31. On the other hand, the verb שכן, in BH construed with a variety of propositions (על־פני, בתוך, תחת ב, בין, על, עם), is normally construed with שם (Num. 9.17; Josh. 22.19; Ex. 43.7), but in Isaiah with שם (13.21) and שמה (65.9); in both passages 1QIsaᵃ reads שמה (see below).
32. See *A Search for Method* (1981), pp. 138ff. A similar view was firmly rejected already by H. Hupfeld, *Die Psalmen*, III, 1860, pp. 329f., n. 66. Hoftijzer does, however, acknowledge the 'rare' use of שמה with locative function in BH, *op. cit.*, p. 139, n. 436; but he ignores the history of the word which alone can explain why the word is used in MT in the locative sense, in both verbal and verbless sentences. T. Nöldeke, although (as we can now see) wrong in the etymology proposed by him, realized the archaic nature of BH שמה in the locative sense; see his *Mandäische Grammatik*, 1875, p. 204, n.2.
33. In a fragment of the War Scroll from Cave 4 שמה occurs in the *locative* sense (see below).
34. שמה in the local-terminative sense occurs only once in 11QT (46.13), after a verb of motion (יצא). For occurrences of שמה in 11QT Yadin's concordance in his edition, vol. II, should be consulted. שם occurs perhaps once (32.10), but the reading is not certain.
35. See e.g. 11QT 63.2; *DJD* VII, 492 1.9, 10; *DJD* V, 174 1-2, 1.3.
36. In 35.9 1QIsaᵃ has לוא יהיה שמה followed by ולוא ימצא שם with the verbs, and not the adverbs, in perfect balance (MT: תמצא); a similar random use of שם and שמה occurs also in MT, as has been said (cf. above, at the beginning of section iv). A special case is 1QIsaᵃ 20.6 where, instead of the unusual נסנו שם of MT, 1QIsaᵃ reads נסמך שם. This reading could have

come about because the copyist, on the basis of his knowledge of BH and his familiarity with the usage in his spoken dialect, suspected that the *verb* was wrong and in need of correction. The reason for the reading שמה in 1QIsaᵃ 13.20 after יהל is uncertain, as we do not know how the copyist interpreted the verb.

37. For references see Kutscher, *op. cit.*, p. 413. שמה occurs with עמד in a non-biblical text from Cave 1 (*DJD* I, 22, I.2). In the Cave 4 material the following additional example occurs: in a biblical paraphrase of Gen. 32.25 שמה was added after the words ויותר יעקוב לברו 'and J. was left by himself *there*' (*DJD* V, 158 1-2.3, as plausibly reconstructed by the editors). In 11QPsᵃ שם צוה (Ps. 133.2) appears as שמה צוה, probably with no difference in meaning although the editor, I think wrongly, takes the reading in the local-terminative sense and finds support for Gunkel's unnecessary emendation here (*DJD* IV, p. 44).

38. Cf. 1QIsaᵃ 52.11; 65.20, and the phrase ויקום משמה in a non-biblical fragment from Cave 4 (*DJD* V, 177. 1-4.13). משם occurs in the commentary part of 1QpHab (10.4), and in a Samuel-Kings apocryphon from Cave 6 (*DJD* III, 9, 33.3).

39. The reader's attention is drawn to the important article by E. Tov referred to in n. 14 above. Dr. Tov, in his wide-ranging survey, deals with the orthography and language of the DSS and their origin and suggests that not all the Scrolls were copied at Qumran; he thinks that, although some of the documents on the evidence at present available to us are linguistically unique, the dialectal peculiarities may not in fact have been confined to the narrow religious circles of Qumran. However this may be, Dr. Tov's main concern is to argue that the Qumran scribes wrote only—or at least primarily—in this particular language and orthography displaying the special dialectal and orthographic features (cf. *art. cit.*, p. 39).

HALAKHAH AT QUMRAN

Philip R. Davies

University of Sheffield

I

I have adapted the title of this article from L. Schiffman's important monograph,[1] conscious that both of its major terms have been problematized in subsequent research. The problems relating to the use of the term 'halakhah' concern orality, application, and relationship to scripture. Baumgarten, for instance, has stressed the importance of the distinction between Qumran *written* law and Pharisaic *oral* law[2] (though the basis of this distinction seems to me irrelevant, since the Mishnah only claims to be oral, but is in fact written; any written code might at one time have been oral[3]). The application of the halakhah is rather more important: rabbinic halakhah is exoteric and explicitly lays claim upon all Israel; the laws in CD or 1QS are, as Schiffman has demonstrated, esoteric, and while they lay claim upon all Israel in theory, actually apply to members of communities only—whether or not these communities claim to be the 'true' or 'real' Israel.

It is the third issue which proves the most productive, however. Rabbinic halakhah, according to the theory of *Aboth*, derives from Sinai like the written law, though some of its content appears to be the result of development of scriptural law and much of it not. There is a similar ambiguity in the Qumran laws, many of which, as Schiffman has shown, are exegetically derived from Scripture, but parts of which, chiefly in the *Community Rule* (1QS), do not appear to be.

Is it useful to speak of 'halakhah' at Qumran? If by 'halakhah' is to be meant only Pharisaic-rabbinic law, the term is not strictly applicable to Qumran. If 'halakhah' be defined as a set of laws governing the behaviour of a Jewish society, the term is appropriate. Definition of the term is a matter of predilection, and I shall exercise that predilection here by defining—purely for the purposes of this

paper—what I shall mean by 'halakhah', which is: a body of law governing Jewish behaviour which in practice or in theory derives from scripture and acquires its authoritative status thereby. This definition may even be implicit in Schiffman's work, since he takes this quality to be the property of all Qumran law. However, I shall argue that Schiffman is not correct, and therefore that some Qumran law is halakhah (in my sense) and some not. I also suggest that the distinction between scripturally-derived and non-scripturally-derived law is either explicit or implicit in the Qumran literature and not a scholarly rationalization, and that the distinction is of fundamental importance in Qumran research.

The topic of law in Qumran research is currently occupying a great deal of attention. It has, of course, had a prominent place even before 1947—since Schechter's publication of 'Fragments of a Zadokite Work';[4] and in particular, the detailed comparisons of its legal materials with Pharisaic/rabbinic halakhah by Ginzberg and later Rabin.[5] More recently, however, the publication of 11QT has reemphasized the importance of the issue in Qumran studies. The history and identity of the authors of the Scrolls is now being increasingly assessed in terms of *legal divergence*. Research (and in addition speculation) presently focusses on the apocryphal (i.e. hidden away and not yet published) *Miqṣat Maʿaseh Ha-Torah* (MMT), also referred to as a 'halakhic letter', a text which promises to confirm legal issues rather than priestly dynastic rivalry as holding the key to the prehistory and/or formation and development of whatever we mean by the 'Qumran sect'. Whether it is a letter remains very debatable; but 'halakhic' it appears to be, on my definition.

II

Mention of the 'Qumran sect' introduces the second problematic term of Schiffman's title. In the present climate, influenced by the assault of N. Golb on the supposition of a 'Qumran sect'[6] and my own suggestion that CD and 1QS (not to mention 1QSª) describe different communities,[7] it remains licit to use 'Qumran' only in respect of the geographical area or the manuscripts found in the caves there, and not the community which has been for a long time, and is still widely, assumed to have lived in what are now the ruins of a settlement. With the presumption of *a* 'Qumran community', the notion of a 'halakhah at Qumran' was meaningful whether or not it was appropriate. But with two or more groups described in the texts, it needs to be *discovered* whether they shared the same 'halakhah', or indeed whether 'halakhah' is the appropriate term for the legal materials of either or both communities. If it is true that law holds the key to the origin and character of what most scholars still call 'the Qumran sect', then it seems worth asking whether it also holds the key to the distinction between different communities which, as I have argued, are reflected in CD and 1QS respectively. Accordingly, I now propose (a) to draw attention to the difficulties which have already been encountered in defining 'the halakhah at Qumran' and (b) to suggest that the theory of two different but related communities, represented respectively by CD and 1QS, offers a better account of the character of the legal materials at Qumran than previous attempts at such an account have managed. More precisely, I want to suggest that the legal (and indeed, social) basis of each community is constituted rather differently, and that the term 'halakhah' is appropriate to the one and not to the other.

(a) *The Problem*
By way of exemplifying the problem encountered in defining 'the halakhah at Qumran', I draw attention to two as yet unresolved disputes. The first was initiated by Y. Yadin in his edition of 11QT.[8] On the basis of some similarities between this and other Qumran texts, he affirmed that 11QT was definitely a product of the Qumran sect. This verdict was subsequently assailed by Levine and Schiffman among several others,[9] who pointed with equal if not superior justification to the differences between 11QT and other Qumran texts. Further contributions to the debate testify to its importance for halakhic research in the Scrolls.[10] The evidence produced on either side needs no rehearsing, nor is the problem amenable to solution by pedantic reexamination of every particular case. Such issues are not resolved by the democratic principle of majority vote, and the fact is that certain *similarities* exist with other Qumran texts and certain *differences* also. To complicate the issue further by resorting to the term 'sectarian' takes us away from a solution, since it implies a notion of orthodoxy, and projects, at least to the naive reader, the idea that somehow all 'sectarian' systems might have a common denominator.

The problem, in fact, lies with the problem, i.e. with the

formulation of the question. The question cannot be *whether* 11QT has any connections with other Qumran texts, but *what sort* of connections and *with which texts*. According to that reformulation, the term 'Qumran' cannot be employed as a blanket designation for a literary corpus; we have to address individual texts without prejudice as to their overall integrity as a corpus. This is no new principle: it has already been well expressed by Schiffman as follows:

> When first unrolled, and in the publications of Professor Yadin, it was assumed that this text 11QT testified to the traditions of the same group usually termed the Qumran sect, identified by most scholars with the Essenes. . . Beginning soon after publication, a series of articles, to which this writer also contributed, took issue with this point, arguing that the Temple Scroll did not accord with various teachings of the better known Dead Sea sect and that it had to be considered as emerging from a closely related, but different group. . . In fact, we are only now realizing the extent to which the library at Qumran was eclectic. . .[11]

The second dispute to which I refer is between Schiffman and Weinfeld. In his *Halakhah at Qumran*, Schiffman had arrived at the following conclusions: all Jewish groups in the Second Temple period tried to assimilate extra-biblical teachings into their way of life. The 'writings of the Dead Sea sect' show that the group achieved this by using the concepts *nigleh* and *nistar*, the former being the simple meaning of Scripture revealed at Sinai and available to all Israel, the latter hidden knowledge of the law, available to the sect only by inspired biblical exegesis. Schiffman goes further in suggesting that these exegetically derived laws were eventually composed into *serakhim*, lists of sectarian laws, and were then redacted into such collections as CD and 4Q159 (the so-called 'Ordinances'). But although Schiffman deals for the most part with materials from CD, he incorporates 1QS and 1QM into his analysis too.

In this analysis, there is one evident omission, namely the considerable amount of material in 1QS which deals with matters of discipline within the *yaḥad*. In a second monograph, which now uses the term 'Sectarian Law' in its title,[12] Schiffman considers this, and similar material in CD, concluding that while the legislation contained herein had no evident basis in Scripture, it nevertheless intended to fulfil the ideals of the Biblical legislation. This is somewhat more than a considerable qualification of his earlier thesis, and certainly invites an analysis of this kind of legislation from a different point of view.

Such a point of view was indeed adopted by Weinfeld, for whom the term *serekh* carries a different meaning in 1QS. It was 'coined intentionally to serve as a substitute for the common Hellenistic term for an association: τάξις'.[13] Examining the 'penal code' (cols. 5-7) of 1QS, he discovers a 'striking similarity to the codes of the various associations of the Greco-Roman period',[14] listing as common concerns infidelity (sc. to the guild), ethics and morality, insolence towards members and leaders, laws of evidence and classes of penalties. Other common features are veneration of the founder of the sect and renewal of the validity of the code. Differences between the codes of non-Jewish guilds and the Qumran Sect are as follows: in the latter, no rules about sacrifices, about funerals, or about payment of dues, but, unlike the former, blessings and curses on entry, religious moralistic rhetoric accompanying the ordinances, hymnic material within the code and the formulation of the code for the ideal future as well as for the present.

In one of his appendices,[15] Weinfeld attacks the thesis of Schiffman's *Sectarian Law*, claiming that the 'organizational rules of the sect' have no basis in Jewish ideals, let alone exegetical processes, but reflect the practices of Hellenistic associations. The character of such legislation is thus rather typical of sectarian communities in general. Specifically in the case of 'judges' and 'reproof', argues Weinfeld, Schiffman has misunderstood the concept.

What are the issues in this dispute? They seem to centre on a particular set of regulations, in which Weinfeld sees parallels with Hellenistic sects generally and Schiffman with the principles of Scriptural law. The problem is that both are construing the problem in essentially the same way. Two examples from the texts will suffice to illustrate this:

> . . . if he kept silent at him from one day to the next, and spoke about him when he got angry with him, it was a capital matter that testified against him, because he did not carry out the commandment of God, who said to him: 'Thou shalt surely reprove thy neighbour and not bear sin because of him' (CD 9.6-8).

This passage is cited by Weinfeld, p. 40, who acknowledges that here 'there is a demand to reprove the accused person on the same day, and it seems that the issue referred to is a sectarian homiletic interpretation of scripture'—Weinfeld is even able to identify the interpretation as a midrash on Numbers 30, noting that CD cites Num. 30.15 in proximity to Lev. 19.17. He fails to acknowledge that Schiffman's theory is actually supported in this case.

On the other hand, stipulations about spitting in the assembly, being improperly dressed, laughing foolishly, gesticulating with the left hand, and similar misdemeanours (1QS 7), may well be in the spirit of the Jewish Scriptures, but only in such a way that virtually any Jewish practice can be so related given sufficient ingenuity. These rules do not either explicitly or implicitly derive from Scriptural authority, and it is improbable that they were arrived at by a process of exegesis. In this case, Weinfeld has the better of the argument.

Again, we see that both sides are right and both are wrong; again the problem lies with the problem. The data and the conceptualization require to be altered so that something other than contradictory answers emerge.

(b) *A Solution*

As I have concluded above, the solution amounts essentially to a reformulation, or a more precise formulation, of the problem represented by the terms 'halakhah' and 'Qumran', in which both terms are provisionally replaced. Instead of 'halakhah', which is a certain kind of law, we address the phenomenon of law and legal authority in general, from scriptural law, through law derived by exegesis of scripture, to law without a scriptural basis. Even when the precise lines of demarcation remain blurred, the essential distinctions between these three kinds remain firm. 'Qumran' (or even 'Qumran community') will be replaced by individual texts, in each of which the status and character of law may be differently presented. After, but only after, this task of *analysis*, the task of *synthesis* will be appropriate.

Of course, a good deal of important and valuable work has been done on the basis of individual documents, as the debate about, for example, the relationship between 11QT on the one hand and Jubilees[16] or CD[17] on the other. There has also been in recent years a considerable change in the climate of opinion on the scrolls. The well-directed and oft-repeated criticism by Golb of most of the fundamental working hypotheses of Qumran scholarship have succeeded in provoking a sort of agnosticism with regard to the provenance of the Scrolls, which provides a much better methodology for the analysis of laws than the earlier assumption of a single 'Qumran community'. However, this agnosticism has a tendency to become dogmatic, perhaps because it has been necessarily also iconoclastic. There is a danger, as I see, that in overturning the foundations of the once prevalent consensus on Qumran all that has been achieved by way of positive comparison between the texts becomes abandoned. But if the coherence of the Qumran texts is not remain as a dogmatic presupposition, then neither is their incoherence.

III

As a point of departure for the present contribution to 'halakhah' in the Qumran scrolls, I take, not surprisingly, my own conclusion that the communities described in CD and in 1QS are different, but related—specifically, that the *yaḥad* was formed by a group owing allegiance to one who claimed the title *moreh ṣedeq*, given in CD 6.11 to an eschatological figure who would terminate the 'age of wrath' and supersede the laws appropriate for that time by 'teaching righteousness'. I suggested that what we find in 1QS, or at least in the core of it attributed to the Teacher, is evidence of the kind of radical revision of legislation that such a claim authorized.[18]

Since my hypothesis has been neither fully adopted nor rejected, I propose to test it further by applying it to the solution of the problem of law in the Dead Sea Scrolls, or at least to the disputes I described earlier. Schiffman's opinion, quoted earlier, can certainly be endorsed:

> the Temple Scroll did not accord with various teachings of the better known Dead Sea sect and ... had to be considered as emerging from a closely related, but different group.

However, it appears that the direction in which Schiffman's halakhic research is leading takes him towards what he calls 'Sadducees';[19] curiously enough, the party with which I. Lévi, R. Leszynsky, G. Margoliouth and R.H. Charles[20] had associated the *Zadokite Fragments*. It seems to me extremely probable, given the parallels between CD and 11QT, that this 'closely related, but different group' is the one I identified as the community of the 'Damascus covenant', the community described in CD, but I shall not develop the argument this far in the present essay.

From my conclusions about the clear distinction between the communities of CD and 1QS, the question of the basis of law in these writings yields a different aspect and indicates a different set of answers. The *Admonition* of CD, as is well known, exploits throughout scriptural texts and episodes from Israel's history as recorded in scripture. Its argument with outsiders is at every point addressed in terms of an appeal to a jointly acknowledged authority— the written scriptural law, an excellent example being the dispute about marrying two wives in one lifetime (CD 4.20-21).[21] Schiffman's conclusion about the hermeneutic of *nigleh* and *nistar* is based almost entirely on this document, and fully borne out by it. The one set of community laws summarized (as I have maintained) in the *Admonition*, CD 6.14b-7.6a, is quite evidently distilled from scriptural law, in particular the Holiness Code (Lev. 17-26).[22] It can be demonstrated, with Schiffman, that the laws which govern the behaviour *of the community of CD* are all derived from scripture—with one or two exceptions. These exceptions occur exclusively in those parts of the *Admonition* which I have concluded (on entirely separate grounds) were not part of the original community's laws, but belong to material which has been added as part of a recension of the text by the *yaḥad*. Thus, in CD 20.2 we find: '...the same is the case with every member of the congregation of the men of perfect holiness who was loth to carry out *the commands of upright men*' (my italics); more significantly, 20.27bff. reads:

> But all they that hold fast to these rules, inasmuch as they go out and go in according to the Law; and listen to the voice of the Teacher of Righteousness ... and who give ear to the Teacher of Righteousness and do not reject the righteous ordinances (*ḥuqqê haṣṣedeq*) when they hear them ...

Obedience to the law is here coupled with obedience to the Teacher, quite unlike the way in which the tradition of legal exegesis of the community is traced back to the 'Interpreter of the Law' in CD 6.7, where is is clear that the process of 'interpreting the law' continues within the community. Accordingly, authoritative exegesis is not vested in any one figure until the 'Teacher' appears.

The *Laws* of CD are also derived from scripture. Sometimes this is explicit, as when the formula *ᵃšer 'āmar* occurs (9.2, 9) or *kî' kātûb* (11.20); sometimes it is a definition of a biblical law, as for example, the precise time when Sabbath begins (10.15), or the amount of water required for purification (10.11). Doubtless several of these rules reflect common Jewish practice and were not exclusive to the community; several parallels with rabbinic legislation can be found, which does not prove that the community was a rabbinic one, or even Pharisaic.

Certainly, a form-critical and source-critical investigation of the *Laws* of CD is much needed. We must not be misled into assuming an entirely coherent and monolithic legislation here, nor a complete corpus. The organization and structure of the material in CD 9-16 remains a problem. We have reference to the *serek môšāb 'ārê yiśrā'ēl* (12.19) and *serek môšāb hammaḥᵃnôt* (12.23), reminding us of the *serek hā'āreṣ* of 7.6. Such references prompt us to ponder the social organization of the community of CD—indeed, to reflect on whether 'communities' is not a better description. If CD itself testifies to a certain homogeneity between different 'orders', it remains a strong possibility that the possible diversity of *serakhim* betrays not only a loose confederation but possibly an amalgamation of related groups. It is worth bearing in mind this possibility, just as we must acknowledge that in the Mishnah different legal opinions are sometimes expressed alongside one another without entailing that its laws point necessarily to different rabbinic communities. The halakhic tradition of the community/communities represented by CD will not have been monolithic (certainly not if some groups contained families and others not)—but as far as the evidence of CD exhibits, it was presented and developed as a derivation by legal exegesis from Scripture, and adhered to both as the law of Moses (CD 5.8) and the will of God (3.13ff.) Although I shall not argue it here, the form of the *Temple Scroll* is very well explained as a codification of this halakhah in the form of divine speech to Moses, a clear indication that for the community which produced it correct interpretation of scripture *was* scripture.

Therefore, what Schiffman says about 'the halakhah at Qumran' applies at least to CD, although we have seen exceptions in CD 20. The centre of the issue between Weinfeld and Schiffman lies, however, in 1QS (as does the nub of the dispute about whether 11QT is a 'product of the Qumran sect') because 1QS has always been seen as the rule *par excellence* of the 'Qumran sect'. Now, no less than CD (indeed, somewhat more), 1QS is a product of redaction. It proves impossible to apply its contents, on the basis of a synchronic approach, to the structure of a single community without a great deal of conjecture and special pleading. (A notorious example is the case of the 'Council of the Community', which has yielded a satisfactory solution only when interpreted diachronically as representing an early stage in the formation of the *yaḥad*.[23])

According to the opening of the *Community Rule* the members of the *yaḥad* are to live according to the *serek hayyaḥad*, 'that they may seek God and do what is good and right before Him, as He commanded by the hand of Moses and all His servants the Prophets . . .' That the aim of entrance into the *yaḥad* is obedience to the will of God, as revealed in law and prophets, is said clearly enough, but it is not said whether the rules within the *serek hayyaḥad* themselves *constitute* the will of God as revealed in scripture, or *enable it to be fulfilled*. The distinction is obvious and crucial; a religious society, for example a monastic order (and I am not implying that this is an appropriate analogy for the *yaḥad* itself, but only for its rules), exists for the service of God, yet its rules are not dictated by God—rather, they derive from a founder and are intended to facilitate the service of God. The Rule of St Bendict, for instance, is not scripture. It is not even halakhah, since its contents do not claim or derive authority from scripture. Similarly, the rules of behaviour for community members contained in 1QS are not derived from scripture and do not claim to be. In many cases even the topics are not prescribed by scripture.

It is true, of course, that in 1QS scripture is cited in support of an attitude or rule, for example in 5.15: 'He shall indeed keep away from him in all things: as it is written, "Keep away from all that is false" (Exod. 23.7)'; cf. Isa. 2.22 cited shortly afterwards. Both texts are cited in support of the command to keep away from outsiders; whether they are used formally to authorize the ruling seems to me doubtful; both biblical texts (and one is not from the Torah) are very general and hardly argue for the specific ruling being given—it seems to me that their citation serves an exhortative role, and not the provision of a basis for halakhic exegesis. Since Schiffman does not use these citations in support of his contention that Qumran law is exegetically derived from scripture, it may be that he concurs with my judgment. Unlike him, however, I find no evidence that the laws governing the behaviour of the *yaḥad* in 1QS are either presented or intended to be understood as derived from scripture.

This is not to say that adherence to scripture, however interpreted, is not taken for granted in 1QS. Certainly, 1QS makes adequate reference to trangression of the 'law of Moses' and the 'precepts of God'. What role do these laws play in the *yaḥad*? On the assumption that this *yaḥad* developed out of the community of CD, it inherited a tradition of legal exegesis as the basis for its communal life. How, if at all, would it have continued that tradition, and how would that tradition have been reconciled with the non-scripturally-derived rules for communal life in the *yaḥad*? Indeed, do we have any evidence from 1QS that such laws were inherited from the 'Damascus' community and functioned also in the *yaḥad*? The evidence of 1QS is tantalizing on this matter. It certainly pays lip-service to scripture, but nowhere delivers an unambiguous statement about the way in which scripture applies within the *yaḥad*. The silence is perhaps not accidental. It may be that a deliberate ambiguity or ambivalence prevails. According to 1QS 6.6-7, 'where there are ten, there shall never lack a man among them who shall study (*drš*) the law continually, day and night, concerning the right conduct of a man with his companion. And the congregation shall watch in community for a third of every night of the year, to read the book and to study law and to pray together.' But what is 'the book'—Scripture? If so, is exegesis an individual matter? We find in 1QS 9.16f. a reference to the 'counsel of the Law (*torah*)' which the *Maskil* shall conceal from the 'men of the Pit'—but the counterpart is that he provides 'knowledge according to the spirit of each', the 'mysteries of marvellous truth' to the members—not interpretation of the law.

The kind of ambivalence to the authority of scripture in the *yaḥad* entails a certain attitude towards the laws of CD. Whether or not, as I have argued, CD was redacted in the *yaḥad*, fragments of its contents are among the materials from caves 4, 5 and 6. What was the status of these contents within the *yaḥad*? On the one hand, the *yaḥad* claimed to be the true heir of that community, while on the other, it believed that with the advent of the 'Teacher' the 'laws for the period of wickedness' were no longer necessarily operative. Was the halakhah of CD operative in the *yaḥad* or not? Or how much?

The answer to this question requires a very close scrutiny of those passages in CD and 1QS (i.e. CD 20 and 1QS 8-9) in which can be seen some overlap in terminology and in historical context. According to CD 20.27ff.: 'All they that hold fast to these rules (*mišpāṭîm*), inasmuch as they "go out and go in" according to the law (*tôrâ*); and listen to the voice of the Teacher. . . and who learn from the former judgments (*mišpāṭîm hāri'šônîm*) by which the men of the *yaḥad* (emending *yhyd*, as also in 20.14) have been judged; and who give ear to the voice of the Teacher of Righteousness . . .' Twice in this passage we have a pairing: first law/voice of the Teacher, then *mišpāṭîm hāri'šônîm*/voice of the Teacher. I suggest that the first element in each pair is matched, and consequently the second too: the *mišpāṭîm hāri'šônîm* are the laws of the community of the Damascus covenant, laws which are derived from Scripture, taken to be the meaning of Scripture, and hence *torah* (the equation explicit in CD 6.4). But this law, says the text, is in some way equivalent to the 'voice of the Teacher'. The status of the Teacher with regard to the *torah* fits very well with what is prescribed for one 'who will teach righteousness at the end of days' in CD 6.11—he will bring to an end the period of wickedness—*and* the laws which apply to it. His voice will replace, supersede, or definitively interpret the law. Which of these is the case only further scrutiny of the texts will show.

1QS 9.9-10 appears to confirm this interpretation of CD 20.27ff.: 'They shall depart from none of the counsels of the law (*torah*) to walk in the stubbornness of their hearts (cf. CD 3!), but shall be ruled by the *mišpāṭîm hāri'šônîm* in which the men of the *yaḥad* were first instructed until the coming of the Prophet and the Messiahs of Aaron and Israel'. Here too there is also a reminiscence of CD 6.11 in the combination of 1. set of laws/rules, 2. the phrase '*ad bô*', and 3. future messianic figure. Another close parallel is with CD 12.23, where the men of the community 'walk in these (?) until the rise of the Messiah of Aaron and Israel'. The key to understanding 1QS 9.9-10 is the identity of those who will walk in the *mišpāṭîm hāri'šônîm*. The explanation generally offered is that these are the men of the *yaḥad*. Their exact identity needs further investigtion. But for the present, the important point is that it was by these *mišpāṭîm hāri'šônîm* that the men of the *yaḥad* were *first* instructed. Does this phrase illuminate for us a period early in the formation of the *yaḥad* when the halakhah of the 'Damascus' community was still being observed as its exclusive law? For where is the voice of the Teacher here? And why are a prophet and Messiahs awaited? This question takes us somewhat farther from the topic of this essay, and I shall develop it elsewhere.[24]

I hope I have here prepared the ground for an examination of the relationship between CD (except for p. 20) and 1QS in terms of the legal authority subsisting in each text. This authority is essentially quite different in each case, for the two communities respectively represented are separated by the presence of an authoritative figure whose 'voice' is treated as in some way equivalent to Torah. This investigation has led to the conclusion that it is precisely the *eclipse* of halakhah that characterizes the *yaḥad* in opposition to its parent. This eclipse may have been gradual, and never total, but it suggests that 'halakhah at Qumran' is a seriously misleading slogan.

NOTES

1. L.H. Schiffman, *The Halakhah at Qumran*, Leiden: Brill, 1975.
2. 'The Unwritten Law in the Pre-Rabbinic Period', in J. Baumgarten, *Studies in Qumran Law*, Leiden: Brill, 1977, pp. 13-35.
3. Cf. also J. Milgrom in respect of the *Temple Scroll*: 'There was only one difference [between the Qumranites and the rabbis], and it made all the difference. It is exemplified by their respective use of the exegetical technique of homogenization/*binyan 'āb*. In the Temple Scroll it produced Scripture. For the rabbis it produced oral law' ('The Qumran Cult: Its Exegetical Principles', in G. Brooke [ed.], *Temple Scroll Studies*, Sheffield: JSOT Press, 1988, pp. 165-80, quoted from p. 178).
4. S. Schechter, 'Fragments of a Zadokite Work', in *Documents of Jewish Sectaries*, Cambridge: CUP, 1910, reprinted with a Prolegomenon by J.A. Fitzmyer, New York, 1970.
5. L. Ginzberg, *Eine unbekannte Jüdische Sekte*, New York, 1922 (ET New York: KTAV, 1970); C. Rabin, *Qumran Studies*, Oxford: Clarendon Press, 1957 (reprinted New York: Schocken, 1975).
6. N. Golb, 'Who Hid the Dead Sea Scrolls?', *Biblical Archaeologist* 48 (1985), pp. 68-82.
7. P.R. Davies, *The Damascus Covenant*, Sheffield: JSOT Press, 1983.
8. Y. Yadin, *The Temple Scroll*, Jerusalem: Israel Exploration Society, 1984 (1987 ET, revised).
9. B.A. Levine, 'The Temple Scroll: Aspects of its Historical Provenance and Literary Character', *BASOR* 232 (1978), pp. 5-23; L.H. Schiffman, 'The Temple Scroll in Literary and Philological Perspective', in W.S. Green (ed.), *Approaches to Ancient Judaism II*, Chico: Scholars Press, 1980, pp. 143-58.
10 See, *inter alios*, B.-Z. Wacholder, *The Dawn of Qumran: The Sectarian Torah and the Teacher of Righteousness*, Cincinnati: HUC, 1983; H. Stegemann, 'The Origins of the Temple Scroll', in *VT Supplements* 40, Leiden: Brill, 1988, pp. 235-56; 'The Literary Composition of the Temple Scroll and its Status at Qumran', *Temple Scroll Studies*, pp. 123-48; Y. Yadin,

'Is the Temple Scroll a Sectarian Document?' in G.M. Tucker and G.A. Knight (eds.), *Humanizing America's Iconic Book*, Chico: Scholars Press, 1980, pp. 153-69; M.R. Lehmann, 'The Temple Scroll as a Source of Sectarian Halakhah', *RQ* 9 (1977-78), pp. 579-87.

11. 'The Temple Scroll and the Systems of Jewish Law of the Second Temple Period', *Temple Scroll Studies*, pp. 239-55, quotation from p. 239.

12. *Sectarian Law in the Dead Sea Scrolls: Courts, Testimony and the Penal Code*, Chico: Scholars Press, 1983.

13. M. Weinfeld, *The Organizational Pattern and the Penal Code of the Qumran Sect*, Fribourg: Editions Universitaires/Göttingen: Vandenhoeck & Ruprecht, 1986, p. 13.

14. *Ibid.*, p. 23.

15. Appendix E: The Recent Monograph of Schiffman, pp. 71-76.

16. L.H. Schiffman, 'The Sacrificial System of the *Temple Scroll* and the Book of Jubilees', in K.H. Richards (ed.), *SBL Seminar Papers 1985*, Atlanta: Scholars Press, pp. 217-33; J.C. VanderKam, 'The Temple Scroll and the Book of Jubilees', in *Temple Scroll Studies*, pp. 211-36.

17. P.R. Davies, 'The Temple Scroll and the Damascus Document', *Temple Scroll Studies*, pp. 201-10; B.-Z. Wacholder, 'Rules of Testimony in Qumranic Jurisprudence', *JJS* 40 (1989), pp. 163-74.

18. *The Damascus Covenant*, pp. 123ff., 203; 'The Teacher of Righteousness and the End of Days', *RQ* 13 (1988), pp. 313-17.

19. The main impetus for this is provided by the still unpublished *4QMMT*; see Schiffman, 'The Systems of Jewish Law' (cited n. 11), pp. 245ff.

20. I. Lévi, 'Un écrit sadducéen antérieur à la destruction du Temple', *REJ* 65 (1913), pp. 24-31; R. Leszynsky, *Die Sadduzäer*, Berlin, 1912 (esp. pp. 142-67); R.H. Charles, 'The Zadokite Fragments', in R.H. Charles (ed.), *Apocrypha and Pseudepigrapha of the Old Testament*, Oxford: Clarendon Press, 1913, II, pp. 785-834.

21. See P.R. Davies, *Behind the Essenes. History and Ideology in the Dead Sea Scrolls*, Atlanta: Scholars Press, 1987, ch. 4 and bibliography cited there.

22. See J. Murphy-O'Connor, 'A Literary Analysis of Damascus Document VI,2-VIII,3', *RB* 78 (1971), pp. 210-32; Davies, *The Damascus Covenant*, pp. 133ff.

23. For arguments in favour of this view, see E.F. Sutcliffe, *The Monks of Qumran*, London: Burns and Oates, 1960, pp. 58ff. and 254ff.; A.R.C. Leaney, *The Rule of Qumran and its Meaning*, London: SCM Press, 1966, p. 211; J. Murphy-O'Connor, 'La genèse littéraire de la Règle de la Communauté', *RB* 76 (1969), pp. 528-49; J. Pouilly, *La Règle de la Communauté de Qumrân*, Paris: Gabalda, 1976, pp. 15-34.

24. In a forthcoming article in *RQ* 5 (1990).

THE TEACHER OF RIGHTEOUSNESS—
A MESSIANIC TITLE?

Michael A. Knibb

King's College
University of London

I

The teacher of righteousness appears to have played an important role in the history of the Qumran community, but despite his importance it is surprising how little precise information we have about him. Explicit references to the teacher are found only in the *Damascus Document* and the biblical commentaries, and none of these writings is very informative. The *Damascus Document* uses the title 'the teacher of righteousness' (מורה צדק) only twice (1.11; 20.32), but refers to the same figure by the titles מורה היחיד (20.1) and יורה היחיד (20.14), i.e. 'the unique teacher' or—reading היחד for היחיד—'the teacher of the community'. A fifth passage (6.11) refers to 'the one who shall teach righteousness at the end of days' (יורה הצדק באחרית הימים), and this will occupy us later. Of the other references, the first occurs in the well-known account of the origins of the community that forms the introduction to the *Admonition* (1.1–2.1) and tells how God 'raised up' the teacher of righteousness at the end of a twenty-year period during which the members of the community had wandered, conscious of their guilt, like blind men; the second occurs in the conclusion to the admonition (20.22b-34) and describes faithful members of the community as those 'who obey the teacher of righteousness'; the third and fourth both occur in a secondary passage concerned with the exclusion of apostates (19.33b-20.22a) and refer to the 'gathering in', i.e. the death, of the teacher. This passage dates from the decades immediately after the death of the teacher and indicates that at the time at which it was written the community was demoralized, and there was a serious risk of a wholesale defection of members to a rival group under the leadership of 'the liar'. In addition, the teacher is apparently also mentioned in the Well Midrash (6.2b-11a) by the title 'the interpreter of the law' (דורש התורה).

The references to the teacher of righteousness in the biblical commentaries are more numerous, but they also are not all that informative. Here the Hebrew expression used is מורה הצדק and once מורה הצדקה (1QpHab 2.2). Several references (4QpPs^a 1-10 3.19; 4.27; 4QpPs^b 1.4; 2.2) occur in contexts that are too damaged for much to be made of them. Apart from these, 4QpPs^a 1-10 3.15b-17a refers to the role of the teacher as the founder of the community: 'Its interpretation concerns the priest, the teacher of [righteousness, whom] God [ch]ose to stand be[fore him, for] he appointed him to build for him a congregation [of. . . '. 1QpMic 10.4-7 (which survives only in fragmentary form) and 1QpHab 8.1-3a mention the teacher in relation to his followers, and the latter passage states that these followers will be saved from judgment 'because of their suffering and their faithfulness (אמנה) to the teacher of righteousness'. In an important passage (1QpHab 7.1-5a) concerning the interpretation of prophecy the teacher is described as the one 'to whom God made known all the mysteries of the words of his servants the prophets', and the role of the teacher as an interpreter of prophecy is also mentioned in 1QpHab 2.7-10a, where the teacher is referred to as 'the priest in whose [heart] God put [understand]ing'. Disputes between the teacher of righteousness and the group led by 'the liar' are mentioned in 1QpHab 5.9b-12a, 2.1b-3a, and in 4QpPs^a 1-10 1.26b-2.1a, where the teacher—in reference to his role as interpreter of scripture—is called 'the interpreter of knowledge'. The biblical commentaries, particularly the *Habakkuk Commentary*, also refer to a figure called 'the wicked priest', but in the commentaries as they now exist the teacher and the wicked priest are mentioned together in only three passages: 1QpHab 11.4-8a states that the wicked priest pursued the teacher to his place of exile in order to 'confuse' him and his followers on the day of atonement, while 1QpHab 9.9-12a—with its parallel in 4QpPs^a 1-10 4.8-10a—refers to God giving the wicked priest into the hand of his enemies 'because of the iniquity committed against the teacher of righteousness and the men of his council'.

The above is the sum total of the explicit references to the teacher of righteousness in the Qumran scrolls, and it will be apparent that the information they provide is relatively limited. The passages listed above centre around a small number of themes: the role of the teacher as founder of the community, and as interpreter of scripture; his disputes with 'the liar' and his followers, and with the wicked priest; the importance of obedience and faithfulness to the teacher; and the demoralization caused by the death of the teacher. The situation is made worse by the fact that the biblical commentaries, which provide a major part of our evidence, date from some time after the death of the teacher, and that in any case many of the comments they contain are exegetically based, and are not motivated by a concern to convey precise information. This is not to say that we have no historical information about the teacher, nor that what is said in the scrolls about the teacher cannot be fitted into a historical framework, and I have indicated elsewhere my general approach to these questions.[1] But it does appear to me that the scrolls tell us much less about the teacher than we sometimes imagine.

The situation would be materially different if we could with confidence assign to the teacher any of the writings which, at one time or another, have been attributed to him: at an early stage in Qumran research, the *Community Rule*, the *Rule of the Congregation*, the *War Scroll*, the *Hymns*,[2] more recently *Jubilees*, the *Temple Scroll*, and *Miqṣat ma'ase ha-torah* (some of the precepts of the Torah).[3] Here the hymns should perhaps be discussed first of all in that they do appear to contain statements of an autobiographical kind.

Many scholars have assumed that the *Hymns*—or at least a number of them, the so-called 'Hymns of the Teacher'[4]—were composed by the teacher of righteousness and are a direct reflection of his experiences, and they have therefore used the *Hymns* to build up a picture of the personality of the teacher and to reconstruct incidents in his life. The article by Lignée in the *Mémorial Jean Carmignac* (1988) is a very recent example of this kind of approach, which goes back to the early stages of Qumran research. Lignée argues that the *Hymns* abundantly reflect the teacher's controversy with 'the liar', whom he identifies with John Hyrcanus,[5] and he quotes a number of passages from the *Hymns* in support of the view that under John Hyrcanus the teacher of righteousness was arrested, imprisoned, tried, and condemned to exile. Thus, for example, 1QH 4.8b-9a, 'They have banished me from my land like a bird from its nest', and 5.7b-8a, 'You have placed me in a dwelling (מגור—Lignée, like Dupont-Sommer, misleadingly translates 'place of exile') with many fishers who spread a net upon the face of the waters and (with) the hunters of the sons of iniquity', are taken to refer literally to an exile of the teacher during the period of office of John Hyrcanus.[6] Both passages have been used in a similar way for biographical purposes by previous scholars.[7] But this kind of approach to the *Hymns* fails to take account of their literary genre. The literary forms used in the Hymns, as Holm-Nielsen demonstrated, represent a continuation and development of the literary forms used in the canonical psalter,[8] and the *Hymns* are cast in the kind of language familiar from the psalter. Furthermore, the vocabulary and imagery employed in the *Hymns* are heavily dependent on the Old Testament. Thus, in the example mentioned, the exile need not be interpreted literally, but may be only a symbol for distress,[9] and in any case the first passage quotes from Prov. 27.8, the second is built up from Jer. 16.16 and Isa. 19.8. In view of these considerations it is difficult to interpret the Qumran *Hymns* as referring to the concrete experiences of a specific individual. It is impossible to say whether the 'Hymns of the Teacher', much less the collection as a whole, were composed by the teacher or not, but they cannot be used to reconstruct details of the career and character of the teacher—any more than the confessions of Jeremiah can be used to do the same for Jeremiah. Nor do I find any evidence for the suggestion made by Philip Davies that, whoever wrote the *Hymns* 'within the Qumran community these hymns—and at the very least the autobiographical ones—were understood to be compositions of the "Teacher"'.[10]

As to the other writings mentioned above, it is of course conceivable that they were written by the teacher of righteousness. This is the kind of thing that it is difficult either to affirm or deny. However, it does seem very unlikely that they can all have been written by him—both because of the different character of the individual writings, and because some of them (the *Community Rule*, the *War Scroll*, the *Temple Scroll*) are clearly composite. It also seems very unlikely that the teacher was the author of Jubilees, which is a work that is not sectarian in character and is addressed to all Israel. In contrast, there is no doubt a case for thinking that the teacher was at least responsible for the composition of the oldest layer in the *Community Rule*, i.e. columns 8-10, the programme for a group that was about to withdraw into the wilderness in order to be able to observe the law exactly in accordance with the group's particular interpretation of it, because it is difficult to dissociate the teacher from the withdrawal to Qumran. Of the other writings, the *Temple Scroll* and *Miqṣat maʿase ha-torah* (*MMT*) deserve further consideration inasmuch as García Martínez has recently suggested—as part of what he has called 'a Groningen Hypothesis'—that the former may have been composed by the teacher, and that both are in any case to be associated with him. He argues that the *Temple Scroll* comes from the formative period before the community led by the teacher broke with the Essenes and withdrew to Qumran and thinks that *MMT* is only slightly later—on the assumption that it was written immediately after the break had occurred.[11]

The oldest manuscript of the *Temple Scroll* dates from about 150, but the work itself may be somewhat older than this. Its composition certainly antedates the formation of the Qumran sect, but it is not clear to me that its contents are sufficiently distinctive to enable us to associate it specifically with the teacher, or to claim more for it than that it is a pre-Qumranic Essene work. The situation is perhaps a little different for *MMT*, which has a marked polemical character.

The editors of this as yet unpublished work have described it in a preliminary study[12] as a halakhic letter which sets out the areas in which the group behind the document differed from its opponents and which had led to its separation from the majority of the Jewish people. The fact of separation is explicitly stated in the epilogue: 'We have separated ourselves from the majority of the peo[ple. . .] from intermingling in these matters and from participating with them in these [matters]'. The main body of the work consists of a cultic calendar (only partially preserved) and a list of halakhot, and the polemical character of the work is indicated by the formula with which each halakhah beings: 'and (also) concerning X we say that'. Of the topics of controversy on which the sect differed from its opponents, the editors draw attention to three: (1) the cultic calendar; (2) ritual purity (especially in connection with the Temple), and the sacrificial cult; (3) laws on marital status. They suggest that '*MMT* is a letter from a leader of the Qumran sect (possibly the teacher of righteousness himself) to the leader of its opponents (possibly Jonathan or Simon)', and that it may be 'the earliest Qumranic work, probably written immediately after the separation of the sect'.[13] In qualification of this view García Martínez thinks that *MMT* was addressed not to the Hasmonaean rulers, but to the religious group from which the sect had separated.[14]

It is only after the extant fragments of *MMT* have been published that it will be possible to make a judgment about where exactly this document belongs in the course of events by which, first, the Essenes emerged as a distinct group within the Jewish community, and then, at a later stage, the teacher-group separated from the Essenes. The problem about doing this is that the beginning of the document, which *might* have given us more information as to its historical context, has not survived. Clearly it is conceivable that the document was written by the teacher, and that it stems from the critical moment at which he and his followers broke away as a separate sect. But other possibilities need to be kept open. Be that as it may, the point I wish to make here is that according to the information we have so far been given, *MMT* gives no indication that the document was written by the teacher of righteousness, and indeed makes no reference to him whatever. The same is also true of the other documents we have been discussing, and were it not for the references to the teacher in the *Damascus Document* and the biblical commentaries we would not be aware of the existence of the teacher of righteousness or of his important role in the history of the Qumran community.

II

It is against this background that I would like to consider the suggestion that 'teacher of righteousness' was a messianic title. This suggestion emanates from Philip Davies and was originally made in his comprehensive study of the *Damascus Document* entitled *The Damascus Covenant*.[15] He has repeated the suggestion elsewhere[16] and recently elaborated it in an article in the *Mémorial Jean Carmignac*.[17] His argument is based on an interpretation of the Well Midrash in CD 6, and it is perhaps worth quoting the passage here in full:

> (5.20) And in the time of the desolation of the land movers of the boundary arose and led Israel astray, (21) and the land was made desolate because they preached rebellion against the commandments of God (given) through Moses and (6.1) through the holy anointed ones; and they prophesied lies to turn Israel away from following (2) God. But God remembered the covenant with the men of former times, and he raised up from Aaron men of understanding, and from Israel (3) men of wisdom, and made them hear (his voice). And they dug the well: the well which the princes dug, which the nobles of the people laid open (4) with the sceptre. The

well is the law, and those who dug it are (5) the converts of Israel who went out from the land of Judah and sojourned in the land of Damascus. (6) God called all of them princes because they sought him, and their [re]nown was not disputed (7) by the mouth of anyone. And the sceptre is the interpreter of the law of whom (8) Isaiah said: 'He produces a tool for his work'. And the nobles of the people are (9) those who come to lay open the well with the staffs with which the ruler decreed (10) that they should walk during all the time of wickedness, and without which they will find nothing, until there appears (11) the one who shall teach righteousness at the end of days.

This passage refers to the founding of the community that lies behind the *Damascus Document*, and to the revelation given by God to that community, and these events are presented as marking the end of Israel's state of exile.[18] The Well Midrash elaborates the theme of the revelation given to the community. Two individuals are mentioned within it: 'the interpreter of the law' (דורש התורה, 6.7) and 'the one who shall teach righteousness at the end of days' (יורה הצדק באחרית הימים, 6.11). The former individual is commonly assumed to be the one elsewhere called 'the teacher of righteousness', the latter is clearly a messianic figure, as is confirmed by the related passage in 12.23b-24a which refers to certain laws being valid 'during the time of wickedness until there appears the messiah of Aaron and Israel'. However, Philip Davies, as part of a much larger theory that the origins of the Essenes are to be traced to the Babylonian exile,[19] argues that 'the interpreter of the law' was the founder of the community described in CD 6, and that 'the one who shall teach righteousness at the end of days' is the figure who in later layers of the *Damascus Document* and in the biblical commentaries is referred to in the past.[20] He bases his argument not only on the obvious similarity between the title יורה הצדק in 6.11 and the title מורה צדק or מורה הצדק, but also on considerations drawn from the two other passages in the *Damascus Document* which refer to the founding of the community, pages 1 and 4. Thus he argues that on page 1 the founding of the community and the arrival of the teacher in it are kept quite distinct, and that the teacher 'cannot therefore be the דורש התורה of 6.7, who is placed at the beginning of the community's foundation'.[21] In CD 4, in which, as he points out, the founding of the community is presented in a very similar way to that of CD 6, no reference is made to either the interpreter of the law or the teacher. But he notes that the idea in CD 4 that the laws established at the

foundation of the community remain valid 'until the completion of
the time' (4.8b-9a, cf. 10b) has a parallel in the idea in CD 6 that the
מחוקקות אשר חקק המחוקק (line 9) remain valid until the arrival of the
יורה הצדק at the end of days. (This last point does confirm the view
that the יורה הצדק is a messianic figure, but does not help his main
point unless one already accepts that CD 6 refers to the historic
teacher.) Philip Davies further believes that his theory regarding the
teacher of righteousness offers an explanation for the founding of the
Qumran sect:

> References to the MWRH ṢDQ as a figure of the past in *CD* and
> the *pešarim* must imply that this figure, or one accepted as this
> figure, had indeed appeared. Accordingly, one may expect his
> followers to anticipate the end of the present era, and to accept any
> abrogation of the laws which the teacher authorised. (We may also
> wonder whether the arrival of this figure was acknowledged by all
> those who expected him.) In the light of these logical deductions,
> what we know of the Qumran community becomes entirely
> plausible. If a community, which apparently preceded the formation
> of the Qumran sect, anticipated a future figure whose arrival that
> sect proclaimed, we have the essential answer to the formation of
> the Qumran sect itself, formulated not in terms of external factors
> such as wicked priests or general desertion of the law, but in terms
> of what can very loosely be called 'messianic pretension'.[22]

This argument has been accepted by Murphy-O'Connor in his
article 'The Damascus Document Revisited' (1985), but he takes it a
stage further in that he assumes that the teacher also appropriated
the messianic title 'Prince of all the Congregation'.

> Not only does [Philip Davies's] interpretation furnish an explanation
> of why the ex-High Priest became known to his followers as the
> Teacher of Righteousness, but it also provides a more adequate
> rationale for his proposal that the Essenes should move to the
> desert. I had suggested that this was essentially a pragmatic
> solution to the problems posed by a hostile environment, but the
> heightened sense of the imminence of the eschaton implicit in the
> ex-High Priest's claim to be the expected Teacher of Righteousness
> is certainly a more adequate motive. Equally, the reaction of the
> Man of Lies should no longer be seen in terms of envy, but as the
> repudiation of an eschatological claim that exhibited no solid
> guarantees. . .
>
> If, as seems highly probable, this personage assumed the title of
> Teacher of Righteousness on the basis of [CD] 6.11, it is likely that

he also appropriated the title Prince of all the Congregation from
7.20. Both are seen as the eschatological counterpart of the
Interpreter of the Law, the founder of the community in Babylon,
and both occur in documents which antedate the conversion of the
ex-High Priest.[23]

If we may for the moment leave on one side the question of 'the
prince of the whole congregation', there are, it seems to me, several
reasons why it is unconvincing to suggest that the teacher of
righteousness was accepted by his followers as the messiah, that is, as
the one who fulfilled the messianic prophecy of CD 6.11. In the first
place, if this were so, we would expect to find some clear reflection of
it in the Qumran scrolls; but there is no evidence of this kind in the
scrolls unless it is assumed that the use of the title 'the teacher of
righteousness' is itself sufficient evidence. In fact, as we have seen,
the teacher is explicitly mentioned in only a limited number of
passages, and in none of these is it in any way suggested that he was
regarded as the messiah.

Secondly, the fact that there is a connection between the title
מורה הצדק that is applied to the messiah in CD 6.11 and the title
מורה הצדק that is given to the founder of the Qumran sect does not
seem particularly significant. The title used for the messiah in CD
6.11 has been taken from Hos. 10.12 (עד־יבוא וירה צדק לכם) and refers
to the teaching functions of the messiah, probably here regarded as a
priest, a function that is also alluded to in the application to the
priestly messiah in 4QTestimonia of Deut. 33.8-11. The use of the
title מורה הצדק to refer to the founder of the Qumran sect is no doubt
likewise based on Hos. 10.12, and also perhaps on Joel 2.23
(כי־נתן לכם את־המורה לצדקה). But the connection between the two
titles ought not to lead us to assume that the historic teacher was
regarded as the messiah in that we have a clear case in the scrolls
where the same title is applied both to a figure of the past and to a
messianic figure. Thus there is no question that the דורש התורה of CD
6.7 is a figure of the past, and that the דורש התורה of 4QFlor 1-3 1.11,
who accompanies 'the branch of David', is a messianic figure.

Thirdly, a major part of Philip Davies's argument against the
identification of the interpreter of the law of CD 6.7 and the teacher
of righteousness of CD 1.11 is that the former is placed 'at the
beginning of the community's foundation', the latter comes to an
already existing community.[24] However, the reference to the
interpreter of the law occurs in the middle of the Well Midrash (CD

6.3b–11a), as part of the explanation of the various elements in Num. 21.18, and it is not at all clear to me that it is possible to conclude from this passage that the interpreter belongs to the very beginning of the community's foundation; his place in the chronological sequence of events depicted in the Well Midrash is uncertain— assuming it is right to think in terms of a sequence. The problem is made more complicated by the fact that it is not clear to which community the Well Midrash refers, the Essene movement or the Qumran sect. The *Damascus Document*, although in origin pre-Qumranic, presupposes the break between the teacher-community and those Essenes who remained loyal to 'the liar'. The Well Midrash refers to the community it describes as sojourning 'in the land of Damascus'. There has been much debate concerning the meaning of 'the Land of Damascus', but it still seems to me most probable that it is a symbolic expression for Qumran. If this is so, the Well Midrash refers to the settlement of the teacher-community at Qumran, and this would confirm the view that the interpreter of the law and the teacher of righteousness are to be identified.

For these reasons it seems to me unconvincing to argue that the teacher of righteousness was accepted by his followers as the messiah. This conclusion, if correct, makes Murphy-O'Connor's suggestion concerning the title 'Prince of all the Congregation' somewhat improbable. A major part of his argument is that if the founder of the Qumran sect assumed the title 'Teacher of Righteousness' from CD 6.11, 'it is likely that he also appropriated the title Prince of all the Congregation from 7.20'.[25] But if the former suggestion seems unconvincing, the latter must seem even more so, and there is in fact no evidence whatever in the scrolls to indicate that the founder of the Qumran sect appropriated the title 'Prince of all the Congregation', or was so regarded by his followers.[26]

III

Part of Philip Davies's argument is the suggestion that the formation of the Qumran sect is to be explained 'not in terms of external factors such as wicked priests or general desertion of the law, but in terms of what can very loosely be called "messianic pretension"'.[27] If the rejection of external factors is correct, the suggestion of 'messianic pretension' is unconvincing, and it is much more likely that the causes of the split of the Qumran sect from its parent community are

to be sought in the teaching given by the teacher. This point has
recently been emphasised by García Martínez in an article entitled
'Qumran Origins and Early History: A Groningen Hypothesis',[28]
and in the final part of this study I would like to consider briefly this
aspect of the 'Groningen Hypothesis'.

Central to the argument presented by García Martínez is the view
that a clear distinction is to be drawn between the origins of the
Essene movement and those of the Qumran group. The origins of the
Essene movement are traced by García Martínez to the Palestinian
apocalyptic tradition of the third century, and the emergence of the
Essenes as a distinct movement is placed at the end of the third or the
very beginning of the second century, before the crisis provoked by
Antiochus Epiphanes. The origins of the Qumran group are traced
by him to a split in the Essene movement caused by the arrival
within it of the teacher of righteousness and by the eschatological
views and the halakhah which he taught; after a formative period of
controversy and ideological development, which lasted throughout
the period of office of Jonathan and Simon and only reached its
culmination during the period of office of John Hyrcanus,[29] those
loyal to the teacher are held to have broken away to form a separate
sect and to have withdrawn to Qumran. According to García
Martínez, it was the halakhah taught by the teacher rather than the
eschatology that was the major source of controversy within the
Essene movement that ultimately led to the separation of the
Qumran group, and he argues that the *Temple Scroll* and *MMT* cast
an important light on the halakhic issues in dispute.[30] As we have
noted, he assigns the *Temple Scroll* to the period of controversy
before the community broke away, but thinks that *MMT* is slightly
later on the assumption that it was written immediately after the
break had occurred. In his view the *Temple Scroll* may have been
composed by the teacher of righteousness, and both works are in any
case to be associated with him. On the evidence provided by these
two documents he maintains that the fundamental disputes within
the Essene movement were centred on the calendar and on halakhot
relating to the temple cult, ritual purity, and, to a lesser extent,
marriage.[31] As he rightly points out, the sectarian *halakhah*
developed within the Qumran group is based on a particular
interpretation of the underlying biblical laws, and he comments:

> How is it possible to explain the emergence within the Essene
> movement of this particular way of interpreting the biblical
> prescriptions laid down by the sectarian halakhah? The answer to
> this question is no other than the Teacher of Righteousness'
> consciousness of having received by divine revelation the correct
> interpretation of the biblical text, an interpretation which is thus
> inspired and prescriptive, and the acceptance by some of the
> members of the community of this interpretation as a revelation.
> The rejection by the rest of the members of the Essene movement
> of this interpretation and of the particular halakhah deriving from
> it would end by making it impossible for them to stay together.[32]

Whether García Martínez is right in his views about the authorship
of the *Temple Scroll* and about the circumstances in which both this
work and *MMT* were composed, or not, on the main point at issue
here, what factors led the Qumran sect to break away from the
Essene movement, the approach of García Martínez seems to be
more plausible, and to be more solidly based in the texts, than the
suggestion of 'messianic pretension'. Thus the texts clearly reflect the
importance attached to the teaching given by the teacher and claim
divine revelation as the justification of the particular interpretation
of the biblical text on which the teaching was based. Negatively, the
importance of the teaching given by the teacher is reflected in what is
said about the false teaching of 'the liar' (4QpPs[a] 1-10 1.26a-2.1a;
1QpHab 10.9-10; cf. CD 1.14b-15a; 8.13). Positively it is inherent in
the titles applied to the teacher: 'teacher of righteousness' (or
'legitimate teacher'), 'interpreter of knowledge' (4QpPs[a] 1-10 1.27),
and 'interpreter of the law' (CD 6.7)—assuming, as seems to me the
case, that the latter title does apply to him. The idea that the teaching
given by the teacher was based on divine revelation is emphasized in
the *Habakkuk Commentary*, both in the well-known passage on the
meaning of prophecy in 7.4-5a: 'Its interpretation concerns the
teacher of righteousness to whom God made known all the mysteries
of the words of his servants the prophets'; and even more in 2.1b-10a:
'[The interpretation of the passage concerns] the traitors with the
liar, for [they did] not [believe the words] of the teacher of
righteousness (which he received) from the mouth of God... And
likewise the interpretation of the passage [concerns the trai]tors at
the end of days. They are those who act ruth[lessly against the
covena]nt, who do not believe when they hear all the things that [are
to come upon] the last generation from the mouth of the priest in
whose [heart] God put [understand]ing that he might interpret all

the words of his servants the prophets, through [whom] God foretold all the things that are to come upon his people and [his congregation]'. It has perhaps not been sufficiently be noticed, however, that the *Habakkuk Commentary* refers only to the interpretation of prophecy, not that of the law. This suggests that at the time at which the commentary was composed, apparently in the early part of the first century BCE, it was the eschatological teaching of the teacher that had become a particular point of issue.

The contribution that Geza Vermes has made by his published writings to our understanding of Judaism, including not least our understanding of the scrolls, has been enormous. This brief study is offered to him in friendship and gratitude for the help he has given his fellow scholars.

NOTES

1. See M. A. Knibb, *The Qumran Community* (Cambridge Commentaries on Writings of the Jewish and Christian World 200 BC to AD 200, 2), Cambridge, 1987; *idem.*, *Jubilees and the Origins of the Qumran Community, An Inaugural Lecture delivered on 17 January 1989*, King's College London, 1989.

2. Cf. e.g. A. Dupont-Sommer, *The Essene Writings from Qumran*, Oxford, 1961, pp. 71-72, 200; J. Carmignac in J. Carmignac et P. Guilbert, *Les Textes de Qumran traduits et annotés*, I, Paris, 1961, pp. 85-86.

3. For Jubilees, see H. Lignée, 'La place du Livre des Jubilés et du Rouleau du Temple dans l'histoire du mouvement Essénien. Ces deux ouvrages ont-ils été écrits par le Maître de Justice?', *Mémorial Jean Carmignac, Revue de Qumran* 13 (1988), pp. 331-45 (here pp. 340-42). For the Temple Scroll, see Y. Yadin, *The Temple Scroll*, Jerusalem, 1983, I, pp. 394-95. For 4QMMT, see E. Qimron and J. Strugnell, 'An Unpublished Halakhic Letter from Qumran', *Biblical Archaeology Today*, Jerusalem, 1985, pp. 400-407 (here p. 400). Cf. recently J.C. Reeves, 'The Meaning of MOREH ṢEDEQ in the Light of 11QTorah', *Mémorial Jean Carmignac*, pp. 287-98 (here pp. 295-98).

4. For the Hymns of the Teacher, see G. Jeremias, *Der Lehrer der Gerechtigkeit* (Studien zur Umwelt des Neuen Testaments, 2), 1963, pp. 168-267.

5. *Mémorial Jean Carmignac*, pp. 332-33.

6. *Mémorial Jean Carmignac*, pp. 334-40.

7. For 1QH 4.8-9a, cf. e.g. Jeremias, *Der Lehrer der Gerechtigkeit*, pp.

211-12, 217. For 1QH 5.7b-8a (see also 5.5), cf. e.g. Dupont-Sommer, *The Essene Writings*, pp. 214, 364; Carmignac in Carmignac et Guilbert, *Les textes de Qumran*, I, pp. 213-14.

8.   S. Holm-Nielsen, *Hodayot: Psalms from Qumran* (Acta Theologica Danica, 2), Aarhus, 1960.

9.   Cf. Holm-Nielsen, *Hodayot*, p. 81.

10. P.R. Davies, *Behind the Essenes: History and Ideology in the Dead Sea Scrolls* (Brown Judaic Studies, 94), Atlanta, 1987, pp. 89-90.

11. F. García Martínez, 'Qumran Origins and Early History: A Groningen Hypothesis', *Folia Orientalia* 25 (1988), pp. 113-36 (here pp. 121-22, 124).

12. Qimron and Strugnell, *Biblical Archaeology Today* (above, note 3), pp. 400-407.

13. *Biblical Archaeology Today*, p. 401.

14. *Folia Orientalia* 25 (1988), p. 122.

15. P.R. Davies, *The Damascus Covenant: An Interpretation of the "Damascus Document"* (JSOT Supplement Series, 25), Sheffield, 1983, pp. 119-25.

16. *Behind the Essenes*, pp. 28-30.

17. 'The Teacher of Righteousness and the "End of Days"', *Mémorial Jean Carmignac*, pp. 313-17.

18. For more details, see Knibb, *The Qumran Community*, pp. 45-50.

19. Cf. *The Damascus Convenant*.

20. Cf. *Mémorial Jean Carmignac*, p. 314.

21. *Mémorial Jean Carmignac*, p. 315.

22. *Mémorial Jean Carmignac*, p. 316.

23. J. Murphy-O'Connor, 'The Damascus Document Revisited', *RB* 92 (1985), pp. 239-44 (here pp. 241, 243).

24. *Mémorial Jean Carmignac*, pp. 314-15.

25. *RB* 92 (1985), p. 243.

26. Murphy-O'Connor's discussion does, however, raise some interesting issues about the relationship between CD 7.96-8.2a and 19.5b-14, which I hope to return to elsewhere.

27. *Mémorial Jean Carmignac*, p. 316.

28. *Folia Orientalia* 25 (1988), pp. 113-36.

29. This aspect of the hypothesis presupposes acceptance of the suggestion by van der Woude that the term 'the wicked priest' in 1QpHab refers not to one particular Hasmonaean high priest, but to the sequence of Hasmonaean high priests from Judas Maccabeus to Alexander Jannaeus, who are referred to in a precise chronological order; cf. A.S. van der Woude, 'Wicked Priest or Wicked Priests? Reflections on the Identification of the Wicked Priest in the Habakkuk Commentary', *JJS* 33 (1982), pp. 349-59. This is an attractive suggestion, but I remain unconvinced that a precise chronological sequence is plausible within the context of 1QpHab.

30. *Folia Orientalia* 25 (1988), pp. 120-23.
31. *Folia Orientalia* 25 (1988), pp. 122-23.
32. *Folia Orientalia* 25 (1988), p. 124.

THE HOUSE OF PELEG IN THE DEAD SEA SCROLLS*

Richard T. White

New York

One of the more perplexing problems of the non-biblical Dead Sea Scrolls is their relationship to the Bible. They use so many words and phrases of biblical origin that they often appear to be pastiches. This is particularly true of the *Damascus Document* where scarcely any completely original phrases seem to have been turned. Comprehension of such a stylistically cumbersome and elusive text is further hampered by the fact that no Dead Sea scroll was written with a twentieth-century readership in mind, for today's understanding of the Bible is completely different from that of the Second Temple period. Any word or phrase will have been understood in terms of ancient exegesis and our modern biblical commentaries are frequently of little help.

Rabbinic interpretations often come to our aid for they are a development of the same exegetical tradition of which the Dead Sea Scrolls are an early offshoot. Despite the fact that the Rabbis and the sectarians differed in their immediate concerns and in the application of their biblical text there is a great deal of similarity between them. Not infrequently a comment in one of the scrolls is identical to a later rabbinic comment, even one made a millennium or more later. This paper is concerned with the implications of looking at one term—the House of Peleg—in the light of rabbinic interpretation.

The House of Peleg (בית פלג) appears twice in the scrolls; in the *Damascus Document* (CD 20.22) and the *Nahum Pesher* (4QpNah 3-4 iii 11—iv 1). The second part of the name probably derives from the Biblical name Peleg which is found in Gen. 10.25. The dictionary etymology of the name—'separation'—was originally thought to be ideal as a designation of the sectarians themselves,[1] but more recently there has been a tendency, using the same etymology, to see the

House of Peleg as a group who have broken away from the Qumran sect proper[2] or as a separate group entirely.[3] Gen.10.25 tells us that Peleg got his name because 'in his days the earth was divided', alluding to the dispersing of the nations after the building of the Tower of Babel in Gen. 11.1-9. The Rabbis called this generation the Generation of the Separation (דור הפלגה) and developed many details not obvious from the Hebrew text of Gen. 11. I contend that the writers of the Dead Sea Scrolls already knew some of the midrashic ideas associated with the Generation of the Separation, and when they wrote about the House of Peleg they had one eye on Gen. 11 and its interpretation and the other on the contemporary group to whom this label is applied.

Damascus Document (CD) 20.22-27

A

1]מבית פלג
2 אשר יצאו מעיר הקדש
3 וישענו על אל
4 בקץ מעל ישראל
5 ויטמאו את המקדש
6 ושבו עד אל
7 וזֹֽיֹשׁ]ך העם בדברים מעטֹ[ים
8 כוֹ]לם איש לפי רוחו ישפטו בעצת הקדש

B

1 וכל אשר פרצו את גבול התורה
2 מבאי הברית
3 בהופע כבוד אל לישראל
4 יכרתו מקֹֽ[רב] המחנה
5 ועמהם כל מרשיעי יהודה
6 בימי מצרפותיו

4QpNah 3-4 iii 11-iv 1

כוש עוצמה ומצרים ואין קצה פוט והלובים היו בעזרתך
פשרו הם רשעֹ[י יהוד]ה בית פלג הנלוים על מנשה

N.B. The lacunae in the quotation from Nah. 3.9 have been filled in from MT.

A. 1.   . . . the House of Peleg
   2.   who went out from the holy city
   3.   and relied on God (or: claimed to rely on God)
   4.   in the period of Israel's sin.
   5.   And they polluted the Temple.
   6.   But they will return to God.
   7.   And the people [will be appe]ased with modest word[s.
   8.   A]ll of them will be judged, each according to his spirit, in the holy council.

B. 1.   And all who have broken the boundary of the law
   2.   among the members of the covenant,
   3.   when the Glory of God appears to Israel,
   4.   they will be cut off from the mid[st] of the camp
   5.   and with them all those who lead Israel astray
   6.   in the days of his purgings.

'Ethiopia and Egypt were her strength and it was infinite. Put and Lubim were thy helpers' (Nah. 3.9). Its interpretation: the evil ones [of Judah], the House of Peleg, who are joined with Manasseh.

CD 20.22-27 is extremely difficult; virtually every phrase contains some problem. As soon as a decision is made on one problem it forces an improbable explanation of another. Some of the difficulties are to be explained by the fact that there are a number of quotations and allusions in the passage. These have not necessarily been fully accommodated to their new context. Further, the writer was often more concerned with the logic and rhetoric of his extremely complicated argument than with its literary flow and cohesion. Finally it is by no means certain that pages one to eight and twenty of the *Damascus Document* (the so-called Admonition) were written by one person[4] or for that matter even whether parts A and B originally belonged together.[5]

There are three places where the readings are problematic. At the beginning of A.1, there is a space where there is no visible text. Furthermore, some read simply בית פלג,[6] others מבית פלג.[7] Hence we do not know whether the text refers to a group who have broken away from the House of Peleg or to the entire house. Nor indeed is it clear whether the House of Peleg is a group or an institution.

In A.6 there is a mark which looks like a *waw* above עד, suggesting a correction to עוד and hence a completely different relationship with

A.7 which itself begins with a word of which only the final *kaph* is clear. With the reading עוד in A.6 this lacuna has been reconstructed to read ושבו עוד אל דרך העם בדברים מעטים, 'and they returned to the way of the people in a few respects'.[8] The disadvantage of reading עוד is that it removes what appears to be a quotation of Isa. 19.22.

Immediately before בית פלג in the *Nahum Pesher* there is a lacuna that is usually filled with מנשה or יהודה, so that 'House of Peleg' is in apposition to one of these groups. Other possibilities have not been tried.

The Departure from the Holy City

On the assumption that the Holy City is Jerusalem (and the *miqdash* is the Jerusalem Temple), the House of Peleg did exactly what the Generation of the Separation did. They went out מקדם (Gen. 11.2), which it is usual to translate as 'from the east'. Syntactic and geographical difficulties notwithstanding, מקדם is the location of the Garden of Eden (Gen. 2.11). Ibn Gikatilla draws attention to the fact that the same expression is used in both verses and makes the obvious deduction that the same place is intended.[9] In this he is anticipated to some extent by Philo.[10] The Garden of Eden (or the spot immediately outside it) is equivalent to the Temple, though the precise understanding of that equivalence varies from commentator to commentator. This was well known to the writers of the scrolls who frequently combined 'garden' imagery with 'temple' imagery. The equation of Garden of Eden = Temple = Jerusalem is standard in rabbinic exegesis and was already used within the Bible itself. In view of the wording of B.4, we should mention another midrashic synonym of these three terms—'camp'. The fact that both Gen. 11.2 and Num. 10.34 contain the phrase בנסעם was noted by Tosafot who link 'as they journeyed from the east' with 'when they went out of the camp'.[11]

Reliance on God

A.3 is a quotation from Mic. 3.11, which Rabin feels is made 'contrary to the context'.[12] I assume he means that in the Biblical text this phrase means 'claimed (falsely) to rely on God', whereas here it is to be taken literally as 'they (actually) relied on God'. There is no disputing that Rabin is correct in his assessment of the biblical text but that was not the way that R. Jose bar Elisha understood it. He commented, 'They were evil, except that they put their trust in him who spoke and the world came into being'.[13] Even if what amounts to the only interpretation of Mic. 3.11 in classical rabbinic literature fits the meaning suggested by Rabin for CD it is still not certain that such meaning is required in CD, for it seems strange that a group who did in fact rely on God should be judged. It seems to me more likely that they claimed (or seemed) to rely on God and this claim was to be examined at a future date by the 'holy council'. As I shall explain later, there are very strong reasons for taking this understanding of the quotation from Micah into consideration.

The Pollution of the Temple
The subject of 'made the *miqdash* unclean' is not clear[14] and the matter is possibly complicated by the fact that we do not know what precedes 'House of Peleg' in the text. Our choices are Israel, the House of Peleg or some members of the House of Peleg. Because of the difficulty of a finite verb co-ordinated with an infinitive construction, the House of Peleg (or some members of it) seems the more likely possibility. But that leaves the problem of whether members or would-be members of the Qumran sect could be Temple-defilers and how they might have defiled the Temple (or *miqdash*) after leaving Jerusalem. The solution has been to suggest that יטמאו means 'declared unclean'. This not only removes the idea that the House of Peleg actually defiled the Temple, it would also put them in the same theological camp as the sect.[15]

Two very late rabbinic sources provide us with an interpretation of Gen. 11 which is intriguing when compared with CD 20.22-27 and which might allow us to follow the more usual understanding of the syntax:

> The Generation of the Separation wished to separate between Yesod and Malkhut, and wished to avail themselves of Malkhut through the forces of uncleanness and by means of the 'filth' with which the infamous serpent inseminated Malkhut through the First Man by means of the secret of the Tree of Knowledge of Good and Evil, since the Temple is prepared for purity, and if so impure individuals would enter it and pollute the Temple, etc. Thus the First Man wished to avail himself[16] of the Temple through the name of uncleanness, i.e. evil, and so too did the Generation of the Separation, and for that reason they were sent into exile.[17]

> When they [the Generation of the Separation] wanted to separate the Shechinah from the building[18] and when it was separated the

forces of uncleanness flowed in it through the 'filth' of the serpent. This is the meaning of 'let us burn them thoroughly (נשרפה לשרפה)' (Gen. 11.3). According to its deeper meaning this is connected with 'our holy and our beautiful house . . . is burned up with fire' (Isa. 64.10) and similarly with 'because he hath defiled the sanctuary of the Lord' (Num. 19.20).[19]

Immediately after its discussion of the Generation of the Flood which it presumably combines with the Generation of the Separation, Jubilees 23.21 mentions a future generation who will pollute the Temple. In many ways the passage in which this prediction occurs is a standard 'intertestamental' description of the horrors of the future, but there are a number of phrases which bring CD to mind and make one wonder if it does not foretell the very time in which the writer of CD sees himself as living.[20]

The 'Punishment'

In the *Manual of Discipline* there is a passage which makes us question the necessity for dividing B from A:

> Every man who enters the Council of Holiness who walk in the way of perfection as commanded by God, and who deliberately or through negligence transgresses one word of the law of Moses, on any point whatever, shall be expelled from the Council of the Community and shall return no more . . .[21]

The sequence of events appears to be the same: entry to, or examination by, the Holy Council, subsequent transgression and expulsion. If A and B were originally separate entities, then the similarity between the *Damascus Document* and 1QS can surely be accounted for only by assuming that 1QS is modelled on CD after A and B have been put together. But there are distinct differences between CD and 1QS. Most noticeable are the more colourful diction and the apparent eschatological intent of CD to which its choice of vocabulary would seem most suited.

In light of the similarity between the two documents we might assume that being 'cut off from the camp' is a circumlocution for being 'expelled from the sect', the more so since so many of the general treatments of Qumran speak of a community dwelling in camps.[22] How then could the same punishment be applied to 'those who lead Judah astray', since they are apparently not members of the sect? Why should expulsion be delayed, albeit for a short time?

Perhaps the answer is to take 'camp' in its Biblical sense of all Israel, of which the sectarians are one element.

All other occurrences of כרת in CD with this meaning are instances of divine punishment; the sons of Noah, the Generation of the Separation (if Rabin's suggestion of dropped copy is correct), the Generation of the Wilderness Wandering and 'their kings' were all extirpated or cut off in their prime by God (albeit at times through human agency).[23] Particularly noteworthy is the Generation of the Wilderness Wandering for the phrase 'will be cut off from the midst of the camp' may be modified from Dt. 2.14 מקרב המחנה עד תם כל הדור אנשי המלחמה. The earlier part of this verse is quoted and similarly modified in CD 20.14f.

Accordingly our phrase would be a prototype of the later rabbinic institution of *karet*.[24] This 'punishment' derives from biblical phrases similar to the one in CD and has come to mean premature death, usually 'at the hands of heaven'. It is not a punishment that could be inflicted by the sectarians themselves; it is not exclusion from the sect nor the death penalty in conventional terms. The statement that 'those who have broken the boundary of the Law will be cut off from the camp' is not a sentence in the legal sense but comes much closer to being a declaration of the state that the guilty party is in or even a curse.

If A and B are connected then there is an element of irony in the choice of 'punishment'. For the historical Generation of the Separation caused the lifespan of the human race to be shortened while here the guilty elements within the House of Peleg are 'condemned' to premature death. Despite the plain meaning of Gen. 11 which informs us that they are scattered abroad, divine punishment of violent death for the Generation of the Separation is also found in the midrashim which explain that לשריפה (Gen. 11.3) indicates that they will be 'burned out of this world'.[25] The Rabbis seem to have searched widely for hints of a more severe punishment for the Generation of the Separation. Another example that fits in well with our text is the idea that שפה אחת (Gen. 11.1) can be interpreted as שפו פורענות under the influence of ישופך ראש (Gen. 3.15).[26]

The statement of the offence, whatever it was, is פרצו גבול התורה. This is probably derived from Eccl. 10.8, פרץ גדר. Rabin notes that in *b. Shab.* 10a, Eccl. 10.8 is 'referred to violation of Rabbinic laws' and also invites comparison with CD 1.16, לסיע גבול.[27] The continuation of the biblical verse reads ישכנו נחש, 'a snake will bite him'.[28] This is a

paradigm example of *karet* in action and was taken as such by the
Rabbis (for example, Rashi, whose first comment is simply 'death at
the hands of heaven'). The phrase פרץ גדר has not then simply
provided lexical inspiration for CD's פרצו גבול. The continuation of
the verse is also present in a highly disguised form; A.3 and 4 are, as
it were, a paraphrase of פרץ גדר ישכנו נחש.
   Two other sentences whose diction[29] falls somewhere between CD
20.25-57 and 1QS 8.21ff. should be compared:

CD 20.3f.   בהופע מעשיו ישולח מערה... עד יום ישוב
CD 20.6-8   ובהופע מעשיו... אל יאות איש... כי אררוחו כל קדושי עליון

We note that the curse can apparently be removed, as can the
condition of *karet* in Rabbinic law.
   The vocabulary of these quotations is mundane and comparatively
colourless with the exception of קדושי עליון which at first glance gives
an eschatological tinge to the passage. The term is derived from בני עליון
in Ps. 82.6,[30] the use of which verse in Rabbinic exegesis and in the
New Testament is vital to the understanding of the term here.[31] The
idea is that Israel who have received and observe the Law can be
called 'eternal' or 'Godlike'. This allusion reminds the reader of the
sect's claim to have the truth. The status of being Holy Ones of the
Most High also means that they are not under threat of *karet*.
   The verse before the one containing the 'sons of the Most High'
which is used in CD 20.8—Ps. 82.5—reads 'They have not known;
they will not understand; they will walk about in darkness'. In the
Psalm there is obviously a contrast between those living with the Law and
those living against. In CD the one verse (82.6) is applied to the sect.
In *Tanhuma* the other is applied to the Generation of the Separation—
the Biblical prototype of the group under criticism in CD.[32]
   Philo, too, contrasts the 'sons of Man/Adam' in Gen. 11.5 with
'sons of God'[33] though none of the biblical texts he cites contains the
word עליון. He is, however, aware of the connection of Dt. 32.8, which
does contain עליון, with the Generation of the Separation.[34]

The Judgment
Because it follows immediately on a paragraph describing a book in
which the deeds of men are recorded, it is tempting to think that the
statement about the House of Peleg being subject to the judgment of
the Holy Council indicates some event equivalent to Judgment Day

in the eschatological future. Some rabbinic texts take the 'scattering' of Gen. 11.4, 8 as indicating that the Generation of the Separation will have no part in the world to come.[35] In this case we could interpret those who have broken the boundary of the law as the sinners and those who have held fast (CD 20.27) as the righteous. This would be a very fitting note on which to end the Admonition. The House of Peleg would thus be a designation of the sectarians themselves. While this interpretation might be attractive, there is a problem: it seems impossible to interpret House of Peleg in the Nahum *pesher* as the sect.[36]

In other passages 'Holy Council' seems to be a label for the sect[37] or a part of them[37] and not an institution in the heavenly or future realm. It seems likely that the House of Peleg are applying for membership[39]—seeking refuge, as CD 20.34 would appear to have it—if A.6 is taken as referring to the past, or are being in some sense invited to apply for membership or return to the fold. They will be examined by the sectarians as individuals and not as a group. This suggestion can be supported by comparison with the *Manual of Discipline* which reads:

> He shall judge every man according to his spirit. He shall admit[40] him with the cleanness of his hands and advance him in accordance with his understanding (1QS 9.15f.).

In CD those judged unworthy will be 'cut off' while those who are found worthy will be admitted ('they will rejoice', CD 20.33) provided they say the confession quoted in lines 28ff. In this light one cannot deny the possibility that 'camp' alludes to the sect.

The Theophany

The phrase בהופע כבוד אל presents a number of problems. It can be taken with B.1-2 as describing the past when the 'boundary of the law' was broken or with B.4 giving the future occasion when the offenders will be punished. On comparison with 20.3-8 (quoted above) future reference would seem more likely and hence something like *karet* would be more appropriate than expulsion.

I assume that the appearance of the glory is intended to be the antithesis of 'he hid his face from Israel and from his sanctuary' (CD 1.13), for 'removing the glory' is the post-biblical synonym of 'hiding the face'. B.3 would then refer to the past or future restoration of Temple worship.

The appearance of the Glory might also indicate the destruction of the House of Peleg, for Gen. 11.5, וירד יהוה לראת, of course, implies a theophany, as is made clear in a number of midrashic texts which observe that this is the second of ten descents of the *shechinah* mentioned in the Pentateuch.[41] Only the Targum in *Neofiti I* mentions 'glory' in the stock phrase 'glory of the *shechinah*'. It is tempting to think that because of A.6 the House of Peleg has already been destroyed, but since we do not know whether the House of Peleg as a whole or merely a part of them is the subject of this clause any deduction to that effect would be premature. Also since ושבו עד אל means 'and they *will* return to God' in Isa. 19.20 we have to take into consideration that it has that meaning here too.

The two events—the destruction of the House of Peleg and the return of the Glory to the Temple—need not be distinct events.

Breaking the Boundary

Breaking boundaries is mentioned only in B.1 but boundary moving is mentioned three times in CD. At 1.16 the phrase לסיע גבול is a reworking of תשיג גבול in Dt. 19.14. It appears to have been altered under the influence of Eccl. 10.9, מסיע אבנים. At this point it is mentioned that this is also one of the crimes that bring on the 'curses of the covenant' (CD 1.17) and is encouraged by the 'man of scoffing' who has arisen to drip waters of falsehood to Israel. The effect is that they look for gaps (פרצות). At 5.20 'boundary movers' (Hos. 5.10) have arisen to lead Israel astray from the commandments of Moses in the period of the destruction of the Land. At 19.15(8.3) there is a fuller quotation of Hos. 5.10—the princes of Judah are like boundary movers.

While Gen. 10.25 and 11.8, 9 imply boundaries, it is the setting up of those boundaries and not their destruction or removal that is intended in the text.

Rabin points out that all the references in CD to boundary moving or breaking are taken from biblical verses which were interpreted by the Rabbis as meaning law breaking rather than literal boundary moving.[42] Yet this appears to be not simply sectarian jargon for criminal behaviour but refers to the activities of a particular group lead astray by the Man of Falsehood or the Man of Scoffing, as is made clear in CD 1.16.[43]

The idea of dripping turns up again in 4.19 where we learn about the Wall-builders who have been caught in Belial's nets.[44] They are the people who went after צו, who, the text explains, is a Dripper.

The proof text offered for dripping is Mic. 2.6, the last words of
which verse are ולא יסג כלמות. Kimchi connects this expression with
ארור מסיג גבול (Dt. 27.17). צו, of course, is taken from Hos. 5.11, the
verse following the source of 'boundary movers' at 5.20 and 19.15. In
the midrashim Hos. 5.11 is connected with Gen. 2.16—those who go
after צו are those who disobey the commandment of Gen. 2.16. In the
biblical text this is the instruction not to eat of the fruit of the tree
but in the midrashim a list of commandments is mentioned. The
precise details of the list vary from Midrash to Midrash.[45] The failure
to observe that commandment results in the condition of being
mortal.

The 'Wall-builders' are mentioned again in 8.12 where it is stated
that 'they did not understand all these things'—the last of which is
the vengeance of the Head of the Asps (Dt. 32.33) and we are again
brought back to Micah 2 with 'dripping'—this time to v. 11. The
term 'Wall-builders' is derived from Ezek. 13.10 where we notice a
great deal of pertinent vocabulary including the only biblical
occurrence of the feminine plural פרצות, the word used in 1.16. They
also appear in 19.31f. where we are told that God abhors them and
his wrath is kindled against them and all who 'go after them'.

B.1 is therefore connected with this complex of phrases through
the rephrasing of פרץ גדר into פרצו גבול and the notion of violent death
implied by the continuation of Eccl. 10.8. Provided that B is the
continuation of A, the House of Peleg must be regarded as at least of
a similar type to the Wall-builders.

In *Gen. R.* 38.7 R. Nehemiah connects the root לוץ with the
Generation of the Separation using Prov. 3.34, אם ללצים הוא יליץ.[46]
This is his explanation of וימצאו בקעה in Gen. 11.3, i.e. R. Nehemiah
may be taking בקעה not in the sense of 'valley' but as 'split' or
'gap'.[47]

His Purgings
There are a number of possibilities for the antecedent of 'his
purgings'—Judah, Israel, House of Peleg, Man of Lies. Suffice it to
say that for the present purpose the purging seems to be the occasion
when those who have broken the boundary of the Law will be sorted
out from those who have adhered to it—a process that in the view of
the writer of CD may or may not be already underway.

Of particular interest as a parallel is the Talmudic passage already
quoted in connection with the statement about reliance on God. The
discussion of Mic. 3.11 continues with:

They are evil except that they put their trust in Him who spoke
and the world came into being. Accordingly the Holy One Blessed
Be He brings three punishments (פורעניות) upon them corresponding to their three transgressions. 'Therefore shall Zion for
your sake be plowed as a field and Jerusalem shall become heaps
and the mountain of the house as the high places (במות) of the
forest' (Mic. 3.12). The Holy One Blessed Be He only places His
Shechinah on Israel when bad judges and officials have ceased
from Israel, as it is said, 'And I will turn my hand upon thee, and
purely purge (ואצרוף) away thy dross (סגיך) and take away all thy
tin' (Isa. 1.25).

In addition to the trust in God, the three transgressions remind us of
the three nets of Belial—fornication, wealth and polluting the
Temple (CD 4.15)—in which the Wall-builders are caught. The
placing of the Shechinah would correspond to the appearance of the
Glory in B.3, the bad judges and officials to the Princes of Judah and
the purging to B.6.

A more explicit connection of this theme with the Generation of
the Separation is found in *Midrash Tanḥuma* (to Gen. 20.1) which
applies to the story of the Tower of Babel Ps. 53.3-4(2-3), 'God looked
down from heaven on Man ... All of them are dross', and then
explains that when they become dross they make idols.

Small Words

The biblical source of דברים מעטים is presumably Eccl. 5.1(2) יהיו דבריך
מעטים, where it is stressed that God is in heaven and humanity on
earth—the natural order of things that the Generation of the
Separation tried to upset.[48] In its biblical context the phrase just
quoted is part of an injunction to be modest in prayer. If, in the
House of Peleg passage, the Temple is, or has been declared to be,
unfit for Temple service, then true believers would have to be content
with a more modest form of worship. We note also that דברים מעטים is
parallel in form and approximately so in meaning with דברים אחרים in
Gen. 11.1.[49]

Peleg had a brother, Yoktan, for whose name the Bible (Gen.
10.25) provides no etymology. The Rabbis produced two. The more
common is שהיה מקטין את עצמו ועסקיו 'he made himself and his affairs
small'. For the present purpose it would not be inappropriate to say
that he was 'modest'.[50] The second is ביומי אתקטעו ימיהון דבני נשא 'in
his days the length of men's lives was cut short'.[51] While this

explanation appears only in later rabbinic texts it is in fact an early interpretation; it is found in Jubilees, Hebrew fragments of which have been found at Qumran. But perhaps more significantly the Hebrew text of Jubilees for this very etymology is quoted in the *Damascus Document* itself where it is used as a proof text for the age limit of judicial service:

> And let no one over sixty years any longer set himself up to judge the congregation; *for when man sinned his days were lessened and when God waxed wroth with the inhabitants of the earth he commanded that their understanding should depart before they complete their days* (CD 10.8-10).

The *material* is the quotation from Jubilees 23.11 in a different recension from the one currently known.[52] The phrasing of the first two clauses is noteworthy: כי במעל האדם מעטו ימו—the words for 'sin' and 'lessened' are identical to 'sin' and 'small' in the House of Peleg passage. The passage in Jubilees from which the quotation is taken makes the sin in question that of the people of the flood and probably the generation of the Tower of Babel, though they are not mentioned explicitly. At least one Rabbinic text also uses the root מעט in its etymological interpretation[53] while others transfer the idea of a shortened lifespan to Peleg, taking the name as equivalent to חצי 'half'.[54]

The statement about the House of Peleg begins with a 'cryptic' epithet derived from the name of one brother and ends with a comment apparently inspired by contemporary interpretation of the name of the other.

The Unity of the Admonition

From the preceding discussion it will be clear that, given the idea that the House of Peleg is in some way connected with the Generation of the Separation, other parts of the *Admonition* are not incompatible with that hypothesis. When applied to CD the rabbinic texts would suggest at least that the House of Peleg and the Wall-builders led by the Dripper of Lies are the same group. But in fact there is very little in the *Admonition* that does not have a parallel in rabbinic comments on the Generation of the Separation. The following is a further illustration.

Tanḥuma, which quotes Ps. 53.4(3) in its discussion of the Generation of the Separation (mentioned above), also quotes the preceding verse: 'to see if there were any that did understand (משכיל)

that did seek (דרש) God.' CD makes a similar statement in a modified quotation from Hos. 3.4 shortly before the House of Peleg passage: 'In that period the wrath of God will be kindled against Israel, as he said, "There will be no king and no ruler and no judge and none to reprove in righteousness"' (CD 20.16f.).

Ibn Gikatilla, building on *Tanḥuma* and other traditions that are demonstrably ancient, provides us with another enigmatic comment:

> For in the days of the First Man the righteous one was gathered in and the people of the Generation of the Separation and the Generation of the Flood rebelled and polluted the rivers and blocked up the springs and all the *sefirot* withdrew ever upward; there was none to seek and none to supplicate.[55]

In CD immediately before the statement about the wrath of God the text reads 'from the day when the unique teacher was gathered in ...' We expect CD to use the term 'Teacher of Righteousness'. The fact that it does not can be explained in light of an association between the Generation of the Separation and the House of Peleg. Abraham was unique in his generation,[56] he did not follow the counsel (עיצה, sic) of the Generation of the Separation. He was righteous in his generation.[57] The same ideas are stated quite straightforwardly in the Wisdom of Solomon[58] and, in a much more elaborate fashion in the *Biblical Antiquities* of Pseudo-Philo.[59]

Whether we take יחיד as the adjective 'unique' or as a dialect form of the noun יחד 'community'[60] it seems likely that the more familiar term has been modified deliberately to bring to mind what was for the writer of CD the historical prototype of his own period.

Nahum Pesher

In interpreting Nah. 3.9, 'Ethiopia and Egypt were her strength and it was infinite. Put and Lubim were thy helpers', the *pesher* explains that they are 'the evil ones [of Judah], the House of Peleg, who joined with Manasseh'.[61] The connection between the bibilical verse and its interpretation is to say the least obscure. However, the nations listed in the biblcal text are virtually identical to the list in Gen. 10.6— Ethiopia, Egypt, Put and Canaan. *Genesis Rabbah* quotes R. Berechiah (A5) as explaining that 'each one said to his fellow' in Gen. 11.3 means 'Egypt said to Ethiopia'.[62] Presumably the writer of the *pesher* could have produced his interpretation only if he was already aware of the association attributed to R. Berechiah.

If in this instance we take Manasseh not simply as the brother of

Ephraim, for it is obvious that in other passages that is one of the
intended associations of the name, but rather as the king Manasseh
whose sins brought on the destruction of the first Temple we can
relate it to the idea of the House of Peleg as Temple pollutors in CD.
Interestingly the three transgressions mentioned in the rabbinic
interpretation of Mic. 3.11 are named as idolatry, immorality and
bloodshed, in a repetition of that interpretation in *b. Yoma* 9b. They
are also specified as being the sins of Manasseh on account of which
the First Temple was destroyed.

Ephraim
Ephraim is mentioned twice in the *Damascus Document* (7.11ff. [A
text] and 14.1), in both cases in a quotation of Isa. 7.17, 'from the day
that Ephraim departed [sic] from Judah'. The Targum to this verse
translates, somewhat unusually, with אתפליגו.

In the midrash Peleg's brother, Yoktan, is compared with the moon
which is less conspicuous than the sun, and, strangely, with Ephraim
who was smaller (i.e. younger) than his brother Manasseh. The
midrash claims that they are all related because each 'made himself
small' (*Gen. R.* 6.4; cf. also 37.7 and 97 on Gen. 48.13). This leads us
to another curiosity in connection with the Nahum *pesher*. In the
midrash Yoktan, the younger brother, is connected with Ephraim,
the younger brother, while in the *pesher* Peleg, the older brother, is
connected with Manasseh, the older brother.

The discussion on דברים אחרים in the midrash also mentions
Ephraim; this time in a proof text:

> Rabbi said, 'Peace is great. Even though Israel were worshipping
> idols there was peace among them. The Holy One Blessed Be He
> said, as it were, "I do not rule over them", as it is said, "Ephraim is
> joined to idols: let him alone" (Hos. 4.17). But if their heart is
> divided, it is written, "Their heart is divided; now shall they be
> found faulty" (Hos. 10.2).'[63]

Rabbi's words form part of a discussion of the difference between the
Generation of the Flood and the Generation of the Separation. The
problem at issue is why the Generation of the Flood was completely
obliterated while the Generation of the Separation was not:

> The Generation of the Flood, because they had taken part in
> violent acts (Some remove the landmarks; they violently take away
> flocks, and feed thereof [Job 24.2]), no remnant was left from them.
> But the [Generation of the Separation], because they loved one

another (And the world was of one language [Gen. 11.1]), a remnant was left from them.

Both the 'removal of landmarks/boundaries' and the use of the term 'remnant' are characteristic of CD.

Mic. 3.10, the verse immediately before the statement about reliance on God, reads 'They built up Zion with blood (בדמים) and Jerusalem with iniquity'. This would surely remind us of the city of blood (עיר הדמים) of Nah. 3.1 which is understood in the *pesher* as the city of Ephraim. In the Habakkuk *pesher* one who builds a city with blood (Hab. 2.12) is interpreted as the 'dripper of lies' (10.9f.). It should also be observed that the harsh conditions, particularly disregard for human life, under which the city of the Generation of the Separation was built is a commonplace in Jewish interpretation from Philo onwards.[64]

This city is further described as a 'city of vanity' (עיר שוו). There may be a play here with צו at 4.19.[65] There is not only a similarity in pronunciation but also the ancient versions appear to have understood צו in Hos. 5.11 as if it were שוא.[66] In one of its comments to Gen. 20.1 *Tanḥuma* explains that Ps. 26.4, 'I have not dwelt with false (שוא) people', refers to the righteous Abraham not joining in the blasphemous enterprise of the people of the Generation of the Separation.

Stegemann[67] and Murphy-O'Connor,[68] using some of the arguments given above, are of the opinion that the two titles Ephraim and House of Peleg apply to the same group who have broken away from the main sect. For Murphy-O'Connor their rejoining the sect is referred to in CD 20.22-27, implied in other parts of the Damascus Document and to be inferred from the fact that buildings of the Qumran site were expanded greatly in the Ib phase.[69] There is, however, no other evidence apart from CD 20.22-27 interpreted with A.6 in the past tense that Ephraim/House of Peleg ever recanted.[70]

Identification

There seems little doubt that the label 'House of Peleg' is used to describe a real group. It would also be a group who left Jerusalem, and who can in some way be associated with the defilement of the Temple. This much we can discover from the *Damascus Document* itself without recourse to any rabbinic parallels. Where the admittedly later rabbinic texts come into play is in establishing the possibility that the label House of Peleg is related in some fashion to the Generation of the Separation and not merely to the name Peleg in Gen. 10.25.

Since the principal fact known about that Generation is that they built a tower, we should be looking for some second Temple group also associated with a tower. There is only one real candidate: the followers of Onias who built a temple in the form of a tower at Leontopolis in Egypt.

Our principal source of information for this temple is Josephus, who unfortunately provides two contradictory accounts. In *War* he informs us that Onias III was the builder and in *Antiquities* Onias IV. The difference could be accounted for by Goldstein's theory that in *Antiquities* Josephus depended on a propaganda document written by Onias IV himself,[71] though this would leave us with the problem of having to decide whether Onias was a reliable eye-witness or a biased partisan. It would be easy to see the importance of the temple as highly overstated (by the partisan Onias, if Goldstein's theory is correct, and then by Josephus with a bias in the opposite direction) were it not for the fact that rabbinic documents imply that it had a great significance in its day.

Onias and his followers can certainly be said to have gone out from Jerusalem when Israel sinned. There was also enough defilement of the Temple, whether through abominations or the service of High Priests improperly elected, for Israel to be accused of defiling the Temple. The construction of the rival Temple at Leontopolis can also be seen as an act of defilement if take the House of Peleg as the subject of A.5. Onias was, as it were, attempting to marry Israel to two Temples at the same time.

Onias also had territory in Egypt to provide revenue and, like the Generation of the Separation, built not merely a temple to rival the Jerusalem Temple but also a city resembling Jerusalem (*War* 1.23). I would suggest that the city of Ephraim in the Nahum *pesher* and the city of vanity built by the Dripper of Lies in the *Habakkuk pesher* are Leontopolis. The disparaging epithets 'Wall-builders' and 'Daubers' would make perfect sense in this context. Furthermore since Leontopolis is outside Israel there may be no real need to emend the text from חרץ to חיץ.[72]

Leontopolis was apparently a military colony.[73] Onias led an army in support of Cleopatra the widow of his patron Ptolemy Philometer against the usurper Ptolemy IX Physcon.[74] In a separate connection Josephus reports that two sons of Onias were appointed generals in charge of Cleopatra's army.[75] CD (20.14) quotes the phrase 'men of war' from Dt. 2.14 in the expression כל אנשי המלחמה אשר שבו עם איש

הכוב. Thus the phrase 'men of war'[76] is associated with 'the Man of the Lie' who would appear to be the leader of the House of Peleg. It would not be inappropriate to remark that the Man of the Lie has done exactly what the *Temple Scroll* specifically prohibited, 'he shall not bring the people back to Egypt for war',[77] but what the Dead Sea Isaiah Scroll may have expressly encouraged or predicted: '. . . and he will send them a saviour who will *go down* and rescue them'.[78]

Onias's activities in Egypt, though not necessarily his temple-building, appear to have started by 164 BCE, for there is a letter dated September 21st of that year sent to one Onias[79] who was apparently of high standing. This would, of course, imply Onias IV not III but would contradict Josephus' report that Onias fled to Egypt only after the appointment of Alcimus as High Priest in 162.[80] The duration of the temple's existence given by Josephus cannot be 343 years,[81] which is impossible if the temple was founded by either Onias III or Onias IV.[82] The emended figure 243[83] or Jerome's 250[84] would be near enough approximations, however, giving us 170 and 177 BCE respectively. This takes us back to the date when the *Damascus Document* informs us that the Teacher of Righteousness was 'raised up'—176 BCE.[85] It was also apparently at this time that the Dripper was active, though it is difficult to tell from CD whether he appeared before or after the Teacher.[86] For the present purpose we will note only that such dates as are available would not be inappropriate for an identification of the Dripper as Onias.[87]

At least as early as 1919 a connection was suggested between CD 20.25, 'all who have broken the boundary of the Law', and Dan. 11.14, 'the sons of the breaches of your people',[88] which appears in a context discussing the division of the people into pro-Seleucid and pro-Ptolemaic factions. Jerome, who appears to have relied on Josephus's account, relates this verse specifically to the time of Antiochus IV Epiphanes. He explains that the phrase להעמיד חזון (*ut impleant visionem*) refers to Onias's attempt to fulfill the prophecy (*vaticinium*)[89] of Isa. 19.19 and that פריצי עמך are those who, in their desire to make sacrifices in a place other than the legal one, forsook divine law.[90]

Sacrifices were apparently made at Onias's temple.[91] It therefore presumably had the status of a *bamah*, 'a high place'—an alternative sacrificial site which could be used when the Jerusalem Temple was unfit for cultic worship. But, naturally, the 'temple' at Elephantine notwithstanding, when the Temple in Jerusalem was available such a *bamah* would have been regarded as illegitimate, i.e. it would have reverted to being a *bamah* in the more familiar biblical sense of a site with the status of an idolatrous shrine. If the temple at Leontopolis was indeed built after the Jerusalem Temple had been desecrated, as Josephus reports,[92] any conventional justification for this temple in Egypt would have been that it was a temporary or convenience measure.

There is therefore little reason to believe that R. Meir's statement that Onias's Temple was intended for idol worship[93] is literally correct. It is rather an expression, albeit a harsh one, of the view that Onias's temple was illegal.[94] It is used in the same metaphorical fashion as the quotation of Ezek. 14.3, 'they have set idols upon their heart', is used in CD 20.9.

The precise nature of that illegality is spelled out in the Mishnah[95] which by quoting 2 Kings 23.9, 'Nevertheless the priests of the high places came not up to the altar . . . in Jerusalem', makes it quite clear that at least for the Mishnah Onias's structure was regarded as a *bamah*. The priests who served at Onias's temple were permitted to eat sacrifices but not offer them. They were classed as 'blemished' (בעלי מומין). CD 8.4 (ms. A) makes a similar statement about the Princes of Judah who, according to ms. B have 'become like those who move the boundary': they will 'hope for healing but the blemish will cleave'.[96] It should also be borne in mind that the first occurrence of 'boundary moving' in the *Damascus Document* (1.16) causes 'the curses of the covenant to cleave'. If the 'boundary movers' are the Oniad party in Egypt, then CD and the Mishnah are speaking about them in the same terms. It is also noteworthy that the same Mishnah regards a vowed sacrifice made in Onias's temple as an acceptable offering but declares that he who makes the offering is subject to *karet* for having made that sacrifice outside the Jerusalem Temple.[97]

Onias's building activities were apparently a symbolic[98] exercise in applied exegesis[99] and his temple may have been intended for the imminent eschatological future. According to Josephus[100] and possibly also the Talmud,[101] he justified his temple construction with the prediction of Isa. 19.19, 'In that day shall there be an altar to the Lord in the midst of the Land of Egypt and a pillar at the border thereof'. The preceding verse would also appear to have something to do with his venture, at least in some of the ancient versions (Symmachus, Vulgate, Targum) and the Dead Sea Isaiah scroll, which specify that one of the five cities speaking Canaanite and swearing by (?) the Lord will be 'the city of the sun'. The Septuagint reads πόλις ἀσεδέκ which is the equivalent of עיר הצדק, an evocative name since Onias was a priest of the Zadokite line. This phrase is found in Isa. 1.26 (עיר הצדק קריה נאמנה), where it refers to the Jerusalem of the future. In this way Heliopolis could be equated with Jerusalem. Isa. 1.26 is itself linked, through 'I will restore thy judges as at the first', with Isa. 19.20 as interpreted in the Septuagint and Targum where Hebrew ורב is translated as 'judge' or 'judging'.[102] These midrashic links come to the surface only in the combination of Hos. 3.4 and 2 Chron. 15.3 quoted in CD 20.16f. (אין מלך ואין שר שופט ואין מוכיח בצדק).[103] However, the midrashic idea that the period of the Generation of the Separation might be characterized as one of bad judges could account for the use of the use of the passage from Jubilees quoted above as a justification for the age-limit imposed on judges.

CD 20.23f. quotes another verse from Isa. 19, וישבו עד אל (v. 22), provided we ignore the *waw*-like stroke above עד, and R. Jose b. Elisha's discussion of Mic. 3.11 (quoted in CD 20.23) involves the use of Isa. 1.25 bringing in the idea of dross and hence of purging as in CD 20.27. The choice of the euphemism 'Holy City' instead of the proper name Jerusalem (which is never used in CD) can then be explained as being a reminder that there is only one Holy City, which is neither that built by the Generation of the Separation nor Heliopolis/Leontopolis. A similarly pointed reminder is found in CD 3.18ff., following a catalogue of Israel's sinful history, 'But God ... "built them a sure house (בית נאמן)" in Israel ... They that hold fast to it are destined for eternal life'. The point is even more obvious in English if we translate as 'immovable house'.[104] The reference to the activities of 'Yoḥane and his brother' in CD 5.18f. seems to fill a similar purpose: the reader is reminded that in the past there was another example of those in the pay of the Egyptian authorities, who under the leadership of one whose name bears a certain resemblance to Onias (Ḥonyo), opposed the true religion. They were ignominiously defeated.[105]

The height of Onias's tower is the same as that given in the Bible for the Second Temple. For Hayward this does more than simply confirm the Temple status of the tower in Leontopolis; it suggests to him that 'Onias copied the height of the Temple built by his Zadokite ancestor Jeshua ben Jozadak'.[106] There is, however, clearly a difference in the two ventures; Jeshua ben Jozadak led his followers *to* Jerusalem while Onias led his followers *from* Jerusalem. It will, of course, be clear that Onias had to adapt himself to his own circumstances but if Onias's aim was to build a new Jerusalem then he too can be said to have led his followers *to* Jerusalem, though for his detractors he will still have gone from Jerusalem to Shinar/Babylon.

Or. Sib. 5.501-3 mentions a temple in Egypt which, it has frequently been suggested, is the one at Leontopolis, not least because there is a strong echo of Isa. 19.19 in line 501:

> Then there will be a great temple in Egypt, and a people fashioned by God will bring sacrifices to it. To them the imperishable God will grant to reside there.[107]

It is also noteworthy that the invitation to build this temple is given by 'a man clad in linen, one of the priests' (l. 492). This may be an allusion to one of the passages in Daniel[108] or Ezekiel[109] that mention a similar priestly figure. Further, the form of his words, 'Come let us erect a sanctuary of the true God', brings Gen. 11 to mind. He goes on to say, 'Come, let us change the terrible custom we have received from our ancestors'. This may be an echo of Dt. 19.14 in a form close to that used in CD 1.16, 'moving the boundary which the forefathers had set up in their inheritance'. The standard rabbinic understanding of 'move' at this verse is 'alter'.[110] The most obvious example to quote which suggests that we have far more than an echo here, one is R. Simeon ben Yohai's comment on Prov. 22.28, 'Any custom that your ancestors established, do not change it'.[111]

Boundaries—international boundaries rather than those around private property—were associated quite naturally with the Generation of the Separation even in Biblical times, as is clear from Dt. 32.8—'When the Most High divided to the nations their inheritance, when he separated the sons of Adam, he set the bounds of the people according to the number of the children of Israel', בהנחל עליון גוים בהפרידו בני אדם יצב גבלת עמים למספר בני ישראל. Philo, without the intermediate step of Prov. 22.28, links this verse with Dt. 19.14, 'Thou shalt not remove thy neighbour's landmark which they of old time have set in thine inheritance'.[112] These are then very likely the boundaries that have been moved by the followers of the Dripper. In view of the fact that the Qumran caves contained a fragment of Dt. 32 that reads בני אלים instead of בני ישראל in v. 8, it is likely that what is intended here is the division of the world into 70 nations corresponding to the 70 angels rather than the division of the Land amongst the twelve tribes of

Israel. This would imply that the boundary broken is not some detail of the Law but an actual boundary between nations, i.e. Onias's Tower is not within the boundaries of Israel.[113]

At first flush Josephus' report of the construction of a tower does not seem particularly Temple-like—at least not Jewish Temple-like. We expect courtyards, altar, holy of holies, etc., but not really a tower. In attempting to show that the idea of a tower has an association with Temple, Hayward points to a number of occurrences in other texts. The nearest contemporary is *1 Enoch* 89. Another of the texts which Hayward cites is the Targum of Isa. 5.2 which interprets MT's 'tower' as 'sanctuary' and Hayward suggests, quite properly, that 'it is not impossible that Onias was familiar with an interpretation of Isaiah's words not unlike that preserved in the Targum'.[114] But we can add that there is another important instance in *Or. Sib.* 5.424, shortly before the apparent reference to Leontopolis:

> For a blessed man came from the expanses of Heaven ... And the city which God desired, this he made more brilliant than stars and sun and moon and he provided ornament and made a holy temple exceedingly beautiful in its fair shrine and he fashioned a great and immense tower over many stadia touching even clouds and visible to all, so that all faithful and all righteous people could see the glory of eternal God, a form desired. ... It is the last time of holy people when God ... founder of the greatest temple, accomplishes these things (*Sib. Or.* 5.414-433).

In the letter purportedly sent by Onias to Ptolemy, the writer asks permission to establish a central place of worship so that the Jews in Egypt might live 'in mutual harmony'. While this phrase might simply be an indication of Onias's political ambitions, it is also possible to interpret it as being another aspect of the symbolic nature of his plans: he wished to turn the clock back to the period before the building of the Tower of Babel when the world was 'of one language and of one purpose' (Gen. 11.1). The idea that there was peace and harmony at that time is brought out in a number of Midrashim, including *Genesis Rabba* quoted above.[115] It is also used in a prediction of the future in the *Testament of Judah* (25.3), 'And you shall be one people of the Lord, with one language'. On this verse Charlesworth remarks succinctly that 'the adoption of one language restores the unity of mankind shattered since the divine judgment at the Tower of Babel confused the language of man'.[116]

Within the 'land of Onias', some forty miles from Leontopolis, or the place now generally regarded as Leontopolis,[117] in the direction of Memphis was another site, also described in the first century CE as a 'camp'[118] which some have thought is the site of ancient Leontopolis. Perhaps remarkably, its ancient name was Babylon.[119]

NOTES

* I am indebted to Moshe Bernstein, Yaakov Elman, Henry Resnick and Eliot Wolfson for all sorts of assistance.

1. L. Ginzberg, *An Unknown Jewish Sect*, 1976, p. 284. Ginzberg quotes the applied etymology of Jubilees 10.18 to the effect that Peleg separated himself from the rest of humanity.

2. A.S. van der Woude, *Die messianischen Vorstellungen der Gemeinde von Qumran*, Assen, 1957, p. 36.

3. J. Murphy-O'Connor, 'The Essenes and their History', *RB* 81 (1974) p. 239.

4. Murphy-O'Connor, *op. cit.* and the literature cited there, and P.R. Davies (*The Damascus Covenant. An Interpretation of the 'Damascus Document'*, Sheffield, 1983).

5. A.-M. Denis, *Les thèmes de connaissance dans le Document de Damas*, Louvain, 1967, p. 175 (discussed by Murphy-O'Connor, 'A Literary Analysis of Damascus Document xix, 33-xx, 34', *RB* 79 [1972], p. 557).

6. C. Rabin, *The Zadokite Documents*, Oxford, 1958, p. 41. The reading of בהתפלג, endorsed by Meyer, 'Die Gemeinde des neuen Bundes im Lande Damaskus: eine jüdische Schrift aus der Seleukidenzeit', *Abhandlungen der preussischen Akademie der Wissenschaften*, phil.-hist. Klasse 9, 1919, p. 43, n. 2 now seems most unlikely in view of the fact that בית פלג is mentioned in the Nahum Pesher.

7. Schechter, *Documents of Jewish Sectaries*, I, Cambridge, 1910, p. xlv (reprinted New York, 1970, p. 77). There is an additional alternative—ובית פלג, cf. van der Woude, p. 35.

8. G. Vermes, *Les manuscrits du désert de Juda*, Tournai, 1954, p. 173.

9. *Shaarei Orah* (quoted in Yalqut Reubeni). Other comments such as 'they traveled from the land of Israel and went down to Babylon' (*Zohar* Gen. 75b) and 'they despised the pleasant land' (*PRE* 24), not to mention 'rejected the First One in the world' (*Gen. R.* 39.7 and parallels), are in the same vein. The more logical point of departure for the journey to Shinar—the site where Noah and his sons reached dry land—leads to the same equation because in the midrashim Noah made his thanksgiving sacrifice on the site of the future Temple (e.g. *PRE* 31).

10. *On the Confusion of Tongues*, 60f.

11. J. Gellis, ed., *Tosafot ha-Shalem*, I, 1982, p. 249. This connection would perhaps explain Rashi's לתור (see Num. 10.33) where other discussions of Gen. 11.2 have למצא.

12. *Op. cit.*, p. 41. See also A. Rubinstein, 'Notes on Some Syntactical Irregularities in Text B of the Zadokite Documents', *VT* 7 (1957), p. 359.

13. *B. Shabbat* 139a.

14. Ginzberg, p. 104; Rubinstein, *loc. cit.*

15. There is another mitigating option that might help explain the fact that there is no outright condemnation of the House of Peleg: they did in fact commit some act in the Temple but that act was in reponse to some other more serious act committed by others. In this connection we have an alternative source for A.5—Ezek. 9.7 where the 'man dressed in linen' and his followers are instructed to defile the temple and fill its courts with corpses. The instructions in Ezek. 9 are preceded by an appearance of the Glory. Ezek 9.4 is quoted in 8.3 but there is no obvious means of relating it to A.5.

16. There is a play here on שמיש‎, 'sexual intercourse'. I am grateful to Dr Eliot Wolfson for helping me with this and other texts of a similar kind.

17. דור הפלגה רצו להפריד בין יסו״ד ומלכו״ת ורצו להשתמש במלכות בכחם הטומאה וע״י הזוהמא שהטיל נחש הידוע במלכו״ת ע״י אדה״ר בסוד עץ הדעת טוב ורע לפי שהמקרש הוא מזומן לטהרה ואם כן יכנסו בו טמאים ומטמאים את המקרש וכו׳. לפיכך רצה אדם הראשון להשתמש במקרש ע״י שם טומאה דהיינו רעה וכן רצו אנשי דור הפלגה ולכן גלו (Ibn Gikatilla, *Shaarei Ṣedeq* quoted in *Yalqut Reubeni*). I hesitate to polish up or annotate this overly straightforward translation. I have not been able to find the text in *Shaarei Ṣedeq* or *Shaarei Orah*. Note also *Shaarei Ṣedeq* 48a2 לשמרה לעשות גדרים וסייגים לשמירת הגן שלא יכנסו כחות הטומאה לפנים אותה where the Garden, like the Temple, symbolises the *shechinah*. The identity of the two places is well established in both Bible and midrash.

18. The building here is both the Temple and the structure of the *sephirot*.

19. כי רצו להפריד השכינה מן הבנין ובהפרדה היו כחות הטומאה שופעין בה מזוהמת הנחש וזהו ונשרפה לשרפה בסוד בית קרשנו היה לשרפת אש ובסוד כי את מקרש הטמא (Recanati).

20. Rabin refers to this prediction four times in his notes to CD.

21. כול הבא בעצת הקורש ההולכים בתמים דרך כאשר צוה כול איש מהמה אשר יעבר דבר מתורת מושה ביד רמה או ברמיה ישלחהו מעצת היחד ולוא ישוב עוד (1QS 8.21-23) 'Returning again' might also be connected with A.6 but I am not taking this into account.

22. Note with reference to this passage O. J. R. Schwartz, *Der erste Teil der Damaskusschrift und das alte Testament*, 1965, p. 159, who derives from the word מחנה confirmation that at least some of the sect lived in camps and yet seems to regard מחנה as an integral part of the extirpation (*Ausrottung*) of both some members of the sect and 'those who lead Judah astray', who for her are outsiders.

23. I am aware that if CD is indeed a composite document it is far from certain that all authors who contributed to it will have used words in the same way.

24. See Ta-Shema, 'Karet', *Encyclopedia Judaica*, X, cols. 788f.

25. *Gen. R.* 38.8. The notes in J. Theodor8-Ch. Albeck *Midrash, Bereshit Rabba. Critical Edition with Notes and Commentary*, Jerusalem, 1965, *ad loc.*, suggest that 'swallowing' rather than burning is intended. To which we may add that according to *PRE* 18 Abraham said בלע יהיה פלג לשונם 'Swallow up, O Lord, divide their language' (Ps. 55.9), on seeing the building activities of the Generation of the Separation. (The same verse is quoted in Tanhuma נח 18 and *M. Tech.* 1.13 on Ps. 1.1 as if the verbs were in the past tense.) Note also the snake in Ibn Gikatilla and Recanati and particularly how it is connected with נשרפה לשרפה in the latter, and the additional ironic element in e.g. Bahya, when epitomizing a great deal of earlier exegesis, that the tower was built 'to save from death' (כדי להנצל מן המיתה).

26. *Tan.* נח 18 with the commentary עץ יוסף, and *Tan.* B נח 24.

27. *Op. cit.*, p. 4. See also *b.A Z* 27b where Eccl. 10:8 is used in connection with alien worship and connected with Lev. 18:5. Note also *Masseketh Semachot deRabbi Chiyya* 4.4 (ed. M. Higger, pp. 227ff.) where the boundary in question would seem to be that between clean and unclean. (Note the text quoted in *Gen. R.* on 11.3 on בקעה.) It is also noteworthy that 4.5 of the same text discusses the book or books in which the names and deeds of the righteous and the wicked are recorded. The House of Peleg passage is preceded in CD by mention of a similar book with a similar function. At least sofar as the rabbinic text is concerned the connection is made through 'distinguishing good and evil' and 'serpent'. Furthermore the snake represents פורענות in *Semachot* 4.4 and brings to mind that CD 8.10-12, in the same vein as rabbinic interpretation but with a characteristically specific twist, understands וראש פתנים ינם as 'the chief king of the Greeks who comes to take vengeance on them'. M. Lehman ('Midrashic Parallels to Selected Qumran Texts', *RQ* 3 [1961], p. 549) mentions another example where rabbinic exegesis has Adam in the Garden while the *pesher* has gentiles.

28. If Rabin's restoration of וישך in A.7 is correct there might be a pun. If so the word play is the same as that in its putative source Num. 17.20 (שכך) which plays off Num. 20.6, 8 (נשך).

29. The difference in usage of בהופע is quite obvious; in ll. 3 and 6 the following genitive is 'deeds' and the context is apparently legal, in l. 25 the genitive is 'Glory' and the context is divine and possibly eschatological. The difference in usage should not be taken as evidence for different authorship for the distinction is probably merely a modern one, and further the virtually synonymous root גלה is used in both applications within the same paragraph in 4QpNah 3-4 iii 3-5 in reference to what seems to be the same group under a different name: באחרית... הקץ יגלו מעשיהם הרעים לכול ישראל... ובהגלות כבוד יהודה ידודו פתאי אפרים מתוך קהלם, 'At the end of time their wicked deeds will be apparent to all Israel ... and when the glory of Judah is revealed the simple ones of Ephraim will flee from the midst of their assembly'.

30. Rabin. Others, e.g. A. Lacocque, *Daniel in his Time*, Columbia, SC, 1988, p. 32, connect with Dan. 7.18 etc.

31. Cf., most recently, J.H. Neyrey, 'I Said "You Are Gods": Psalm 82.6 and John 10', *JBL* 108 (1989), pp. 647-63.

32. It is noteworthy in this connection that one of the commonest associations of 'darkness' is Egypt as, for example, Isa. 9.1, where 'The people walking in darkness' becomes in the Targum 'The people, the children of Israel who were walking in Egypt as if in darkness'.

33. *On the Confusion of Tongues*, 142-46. All referencecs to the text and translation of Philo and Josephus are to the Loeb Classical Library (London and New York, various dates).

34. *On the Posterity of Cain*, 89 (see below).

35. *B. Sanh.* 107a and parallels. Biblical כרת is at times understood as meaning 'deprive of the world to come', e.g. Num. 15.31 in *b. Sanh.* 90b/91a, *Sifre* Numbers 112 and *PsJ ad loc.*

36. This has, however, been attempted by Baumgarten, *Studies in Qumran Law*, Leiden, 1977, p. 72.

37. P. Wernberg-Møller, *The Manual of Discipline*, Leiden, 1957, p. 57, n. 62.

38. Rabin, p. 42.

39. Suggested by P. R. Davies, *op. cit.*, p. 193. For Murphy-O'Connor (*RB* 81, p. 239; cf. *RB* 79, p. 557) the House of Peleg were newcomers to the sect for whom the extensive construction work of period Ib was undertaken. There is, however, no firm evidence that they actually succeeded in joining the sect.

40. See Wernberg-Møller, *op. cit.*, p. 137 n. 37, for the fact that לקרבו means 'admit'.

41. *PRE* 14, 24; *ARN* 34.

42. In the case of Dt. 19.14 the interpretation is in fact based on Prov. 22.28 which contains very similar phrasing. The two verses are frequently equated in Rabbinic literature and apparently also in the Peshitta to Dt. 19.14. It is clear from, amongst other features, the fact that רעיך has not been taken over in the quotation, that there is some leaning in the direction of Prov. 22.28 in CD. See also Ginzberg, p. 7 n. 4, who points out that there is a similarly interpreted use of Dt. 19.14 and Prov. 22.28 in *1 Enoch* 99.2, 14 and *2 Enoch* 52.9. A similar link between Dt. 19.14/Prov. 22.28 and Eccl. 10.8-9 is perhaps made by the Targum to Eccl. 10.8 when it uses the phrase גודא דעלמא 'fence of the world'. Cf. also the phrase מפני שפרצתי גדרו של עולם put into the mouth of the serpent in *Ecc. R.* 10.14 and parallels.

43. For the argument against taking all boundary moving as an allusion to the same group, see Stegemann, *Die Entstehung der Qumrangemeinde*, pp. 166ff. (unavailable to me). Cf. also Davies, p. 120.

44. Note the phrasing of Philo, *On the Confusion of Tongues*, 92: '. . . Israel is imprisoned in the gross material nets of Egypt and submits to do the

bidding of an iron tyranny, to work at brick and every earthy substance with labour painful and unremitting'. Philo here (and apparently also in *On the Posterity of Cain*, 52ff.) compares and contrasts the building of the Tower of Babel with the servitude of the Israelites in Egypt. Cf. also *y. Suk.* 54c for a similar contrast.

45. See the various combinations given in the notes to *Gen. R.* (ed. Theodor Albeck), *ad loc.*

46. See also the texts quoted in *Gen. R.* (ed. Theodor-Albeck), *ad loc.* Note also the idea of mocking combined with the mocker being mocked where the verb is שחק and the prooftext is Ps. 2.4 in *Tan.* נח 28. Note also *M. Teh.* 1.13 to Ps. 1.1 and *b. A.Z.* 18a where the phrase מושב לצים appears later in the same verse (Ps. 1.1).

47. It is presumably such a word play that allows *Midrash Aseret HaDibrot* (quoted in *Torah Shelemah*, II, p. 311) to put in the mouth of the Generation of the Separation 'let us take' hatchets and split (ונבקיע) heaven'. The problem at hand, of course, is why build in a plain (בקעה) when you can have a head start, as it were, by building on a mountain (cf. Rashi to b. Sanh. 109a). A virtually identical statement, which must surely depend on the Hebrew text of Gen. 11, is found in *3 Baruch* 3.7.

48. The Generation of the Separation is mentioned in *Eccl. R.* to the following verse where it is one of a list of blasphemers and other enemies of God.

49. It is noteworthy that *Tan.* ויקרא 7 takes the antithesis of יהיו דבריך מעטים to be 'blasphemy' while in נח 2 דברים אחרים means words of 'blasphemy'.

50. The theme of modesty turns up in connection with the Generation of the Separation, e.g. *b. Hul.* 89a. אתם ממעטים עצמכם; *PR* 12 (on Job 13.12) מה אתם מתעים את הבריות שהם רואים אתכם וסבורים אם צדיקים כאברהם שמשל עצמו באפר . . . כדור המבול

51. Tg and Ps. Rashi to 1 Chron. 1.20.

52. See Rabin, p. 50.

53. *Sefer Ha-Yashar* (to Gen 10.25). The dedicatee of this volume devoted a chapter to enumerating the early features of the Abraham story contained in *Sefer Ha-Yashar* (*Scripture and Tradition in Judaism* [Studia Postbiblica, 4], Leiden, 1961, pp. 67-95). These few words can perhaps be added to that list. There is perhaps an echo of this interpretation in *Midrash Aggadah* (*ad loc.*) which explains that their ears were not shortened by exactly half but to 'two hundred and a bit (מעט)'.

54. *Sefer Ha-Yashar* (*idem*), Recanati, Ibn Gikatilla (quoted in *Yalkut Reubeni*) and R. Shmuel b. Nissim Masnut, *Bereshit Zuta* (ed. Mordechai Ha-Cohen) to Gen. 10.25 (and the references given there by the editor). Cf. also Ibn Ezra.

55. שהרי בימי אדם הראשון נאסף הצדיק והמירו אנשי דור הפלגנה ודור המבול והשחיתו הנהרות וסתמו כל המעיינות ונתלקו כל הספירות למעלה למעלה אין דורש ואין מבקש (*Shaarei Ṣedeq* 42a1). The mention of the First Man

comes about because of the use of the word אדם in Gen 11.5, which allows a midrash to deduce either that Adam was still alive when the Tower was built or that this rebellion is a continuation of that of Adam and Eve.

56. The terms 'righteous' and 'righteousness' in the Dead Sea Documents are problematic, in so far as it is not clear when they are used in a technical sense with echoes of Zadokite (priesthood) and Sadducee and when they are used with no technical sense. See, most recently, P. R. Davies, *Beyond the Essenes. History and Ideology in the Dead Sea Scrolls*, Atlanta, 1987, pp. 51-72. I have deliberately avoided associations of these terms and their equally clichéd opposite 'evil'.

57. *Gen. R.* 38.6 and parallels, but available already in the proof text used there: אחד היה אברהם (Ezek. 33.24).

58. 'It was she (i.e. Wisdom) who, when the nations in their single-minded wickedness were put to confusion, recognized the righteous man and kept him blameless before God' (10.5). Cf. the commentary by Winston (AB, vol. 43, pp. 214f.) who connects the 'single-mindedness' with the rabbinic view that the Generation of the Separation were of 'one עיצה'. Jubilees (10.18, 22) also knows of the idea of the 'counsel' that the Generation of the Separation followed but appears to have regarded Peleg rather than Abraham as the righteous one of the period.

59. 6.1-18.

60. Wernberg-Møller, 'צדק, צדיק and צדוק in the Zadokite Documents (CDC), the Manual of Discipline (DSD) and the Habakkuk-Commentary (DSH)', *VT* 3 (1953), pp. 310-315.

61. The restoration follows that of Stegemann (*op. cit.*, pp. 92f.; cf. also Murphy-O'Connor, *RB* 81, p. 240), despite the objections of Horgan (*Pesharim: Qumran Interpretations of Biblical Books* [CBQMS, 8], 1979, p. 190) that the space may be too small for יהודה and noting the phrase כל מרשיעי יהודה in CD 20.26f.

62. *Gen. R.* with slight variants in later midrashim such as the two recensions of *Tanḥuma*. To some extent this contrasts with the texts that state that Nimrod was the leader of the Separation. That contrast can be pushed too far for the instigators do not have to be the leaders, as is made clear in *PRE* 11, 'They made Nimrod king over them.' Nimrod, it should be noted, was the son of Cush.

63. *Gen. R.* 38.6; cf. also PR 50.6 (a shorter version, omitting the second part and given in the name of R. Eleazar).

64. Note particularly the story recorded in *3 Baruch* 3.5 (Generation of the Separation), *PsJ* Ex. 24.10, *PRE* 48 (Servitude in Egypt). The equation between the two biblical events is found as early as Philo (see n. 44, above). Since it is earlier than the other texts, *3 Baruch* would likely have the original place for this story, but it too alludes to details of the events of Exodus (cf. H.E. Gaylord in James H. Charlesworth, *The Old Testament Pseudepigrapha*, I, 1983, p. 65 n. 3).

65. Cf. Charles, *ad loc.*, and G. Jeremias, *Der Lehrer der Gerechtigkeit*, 1963, p. 88. The latter also notes that the occurrences of שוא in the Hodayot are related to CD and the Habakkuk *pesher*.

66. Rabin to CD 4.19.

67. *Op. cit.*, pp. 69-82, 178.

68. *Op. cit.*, pp. 239-44.

69. *Ibid.* p. 239. Davies (*Beyond the Essenes*, p. 71) speaks of a 'Zadokite infiltration of Qumran' and suggests a possible 'return from Leontopolis'.

70. The only possibility would be to understand the text of 4QpNah 3-5 iii 3-5 (quoted above, n. 29) as a prediction with the benefit of hindsight.

71. Jonathan Goldstein, 'Tales of the Tobiads', in J. Neusner, ed., *Christianity, Judaism and Other Greco-Roman Cults. Studies for Morton Smith at Sixty*, Part 3, Leiden, 1975, pp. 91-121.

72. חוץ seems to be the spelling at 4.19 and in the A text at 8.12, 18.

73. Tcherikover, *Hellenistic Civilization and the Jews*, Philadelphia, 1961, p. 279.

74. *C. Ap.* 2.50-52 and the passing reference in *Ant.* 13.65.

75. *Ant.* 13.285.

76. War is again a frequent motif in rabbinic interpretation of Gen. 11 and is found as early as Philo (*On the Confusion of Tongues*, 44).

77. 56.16. Falk (*Jewish Law Annual* 2 [1979], pp. 34f.) suggests that the Temple Scroll denounces a Jewish presence in Egypt and that 'for war' is a 'reproach to Jewish mercenaries'. It should not be thought that the Temple Scroll's rewriting of Dt. 17.16 is necessarily 'sectarian' exegesis for it is difficult, though not impossible, to explain *m. San.* 2.4 without such an understanding of the biblical text.

78. 1QIsa[a] 19.20 וישלח להם מושיע וירד והצילם for MT וישלח להם מושיע ורב והצילם. Cf. R. Hayward, 'The Jewish Temple at Leontopolis: A Reconsideration', *JJS* 33 (1982), p. 440f.

79. *CPJ* I. The reading is far from clear. See conveniently Tcherikover, *op. cit.*, p. 498.

80. *Ant.* 12.387; 20.235f.

81. *War* 7.436. For the problems of identification see, *inter alios*, M. Delcor, 'Le Temple d'Onias en Égypte', *RB* 75 (1968), pp. 188-205.

82. It is possible that Onias renovated an existing temple (cf. *Ant.* 13.66-71) or took over a military chaplaincy. We note the various reports in the various traditions of patriarchs stopping at Heliopolis and perhaps very significantly the fact that according to Artapanus the forced construction work during the Servitude in Egypt included building the temple at Heliopolis (frag. 3.2). There is every possibility that there was some tradition for the temple at Leontopolis tracing its history back before Onias. Another possibility is the theory advanced by M. A. Beek, 'Relations entre Jérusalem et la Diaspora égyptienne au deuxième siècle avant Jésus-Christ', *Oudtestamentische Studiën* 2 (1943), pp. 119-43.

96   *A Tribute to Geza Vermes*

83. Cf. M. Delcor, *art. cit.*, p. 189.
84. *In Danielem* 11.14.
85. CD 1.5-12. We note that this dating fits well with Rowley's view that Onias III was the Teacher of Righteousness (H.H. Rowley, *The Zadokite Fragments and the Dead Sea Scrolls*, 1952, pp. 67ff.).
86. It is not clear what CD 1.13ff., 'this is the time . . . when the Man of Scoffing who dripped arose . . . ', means.
87. Since *b. Men.* 110 speaks of a rivalry it is distinctly possible that both figures 'appeared' at the same time.
88. Meyer, p. 43. n. 4; similarly, e.g. Montgomery, *ICC*, pp. 438f.; Lacocque, p. 33; Wacholder, *The Dawn of Qumran*, pp. 201f.
89. Interestingly the Septuagint of Daniel 11.14 renders חזון by 'prophecy' (προφητείαν) in contrast to all other occurrences of חזון in Daniel which are rendered more literally, see S. P. Jeansonne, *The Old Greek Translation of Daniel 7-12* (CBQMS, 19), 1988 p. 59. Theodotion's rendering of פריצי by λοιμῶν is also worthy of attention since this is also a translation of Hebrew ליץ. Cf. Montgomery, *loc. cit.*
90. 'Qui dereliquerunt legem Domini, volentes in alio loco praeter iussum erat, Deo victimas immolare . . . ' (*In Danielem* 11.14). In this Jerome seems to be inspired by *Ant.* 13.69ff. It is possible with Marcus (*Josephus*, vol. VII, p. 261) to see Josephus' remarks as directed against the choice of a pagan site for a temple but it seems more likely that Onias is being criticized simply for building a rival temple.
91. Although this is not specifically stated by Josephus it can be inferred from *b. Men.* 109ff. and *t. Men.* 13.12-15, but there was some uncertainty in rabbinic times, for *b. Meg.* 10a contains the statement, 'I have heard that sacrifices were made at Onias' temple'.
92. Cf. Josephus, *War* 1.31-33; 7.421ff.
93. *B. Men.* 110.
94. The Talmud continues with R. Judah's statement that it was not for idol worship but rather לשם שמים, leaving the precise attitude of the Talmud unclear. The standard interpretation that it was 'illegal but not heterodox' seems to have begun with Abraham Geiger (*Urschrift und Übersetzungen der Bibel*, 1928, p. 36), from where it spread unacknowledged through the secondary literature.
95. *M. Men.* 13.10.
96. CD 8.4. The reading of the manuscript is corrupt. ירבק המום is the reconstruction.
97. *B. Men.* 109a.
98. Hayward, *passim.*
99. Vermes, *Postbiblical Jewish Studies*, 1975, pp. 82-85.
100. *War*, 7.432; *Ant.* 13.68.
101. *B. Men.* 110.
102. Likewise the Targum to Hos. 5.11 understands those who went after

צו as 'because their judges turned to go astray after filthy lucre (ממון שקרא)'. The latter phrase is the Aramaic equivalent of CD's הון הרשעה (8.5) in a variant of the description of one of the nets of Belial in which those who go after צו are trapped (cf. also 6.15).

103. The first two phrases represent the MT of Hos. 3.4 which continues with (ואין אפוד ותרפים) ואין זבח ואין מצבה. The second pair of phrases is an interpretation of 2 Chron. 15.3 ללא אלהי אמת וללא כהן מרה. Kimchi's interpretation of the first element as 'judges' is entirely in line with rabbinic interpretation of similar occurrences of אלהים in the Hebrew Bible. The Targum's לית כהן מליף זכו, 'no priest teaching righteousness', may be a last trace of the interpretation preserved in CD. This provides us with a link between the Dead Sea Scrolls' use of 'Teacher of Righteousness' and the medieval phrase 'priest teaching righteousness'. For the latter see M. Bregman, 'Another Reference to "A Teacher of Righteousness" in Midrashic Literature', *RQ* 10 (1979), pp. 97-100. The effect, if not the motive, of CD's phrasing is to remove the cultic elements from the Hosea text or perhaps to suppress any reminiscence of the מזבח and מצבה of Isa. 19.19.

104. See Wernberg-Møller, *VT* 3, p. 313.

105. There does not seem to be great merit in regarding this passage as being a late insertion (contrast J. Duhaime, 'Dualistic Reworking in the Scrolls from Qumran', *CBQ* 49 [1987], pp. 32-56). The observation that it does not at first glance fit with what precedes and what follows (cf. Schechter and Charles) is well taken though perhaps overstated. Furthermore the reference to Jannes and Jambres in 2 Tim. 3.8 would have to be judged as similarly out of place in an identical sequence of catalogue of sins, attribution to ignorance and comparison with Jannes and Jambres. The contrast between the dualism of CD 5.16-19 and the rest of the text is also somewhat overstated; the contrast is surely between the explicit dualism of this passage and the implicit dualism of the text as a whole. We note that in the Koran (2.96[102]) Harut and Marut who are thought by some to be Jannes and Jambres in another guise are present in Babylon.

106. *Art. cit.*, p. 433.

107. Collins in Charlesworth, I, 1983, p. 405.

108. Dan. 10.5; 12.6, 7.

109. Ezek. 9.2, 3, 11; 10.2, 6, 7.

110. See Targumim and commentators, as well as Peshitta. The text continues with 'on account of which they performed processions and rites to gods of stone and earthenware and were devoid of sense'. Could this be an echo of Onias's request (recorded in *Ant.* 13.66-71) to rebuild a ruined pagan Temple?

111. *Midrash Mishle, ad loc.* See also Rashi, *ad loc.*, and *Midrash Aggadah* to Dt. 19.14.

112. *On the Posterity of Cain*, 89. Philo follows the variant reading or midrash of LXX that the number is that of the angels of God.

113. Hans Burgmann ('"The Wicked Woman": der Makkabäer Simon?', *RQ* 9 [1974], pp. 254-8; reprinted in *Zwei lösbare Qumrânprobleme: Die Person des Lügenmannes, Die Interkalation im Kalendar*, Frankfurt, 1986, pp. 64-68) makes a similar interpretation of 'boundary moving' in CD but applies it to the Maccabean conquests.

114. *Art. cit.*, p. 432. Cf. also *b. Suk*. 49a for a close variation of the Targum's interpretation. Also Rashi on Mic. 4.8 suggests that (עדר) מגדל should be interpreted as the Temple, and in so doing he seems to be the first after *1 Enoch* to be on record as making such a connection. It may just be significant here that according to some rabbinic texts David decides on the height of the Temple following an encounter with a giant horned animal that takes place while he is pasturing flocks (cf. *m. Teh.* 22.28, 78.20, 91.1, 92.9).

115. *BR* 38.6. See also *Tan.* נח 24; *ARN* 12.

116. Charlesworth, *op. cit.*, I, p. 801 n. 25a. A similar thought may also be present in *Jub.* 3.28 where it is stated that prior to the Fall the animals had been 'of one speech and one language'.

117. A. Kasher, *The Jews in Hellenistic and Roman Egypt*, pp. 119ff.

118. *CPJ*, II, no. 417 ll.3-4.

119. Babylon was the ancient name for Fustat which eventually became Cairo (see A.J. Butler, *Babylon of Egypt*, Oxford, 1914); and this is of course where the Cairo Geniza, which contained the first known manuscripts of the Damascus Document, is located. Could it be that that Geniza held copies of the version actually sent to Onias from Qumran?

PART III

TARGUMS AND RABBINICA

QUID ATHENIS ET HIEROSOLYMIS? RABBINIC MIDRASH AND HERMENEUTICS IN THE GRAECO-ROMAN WORLD*

Philip S. Alexander

University of Manchester

Athens or Jerusalem

The idea that Christian European civilization has two main historical roots, one going back to classical Greece, the other to ancient Israel, is one of the oldest and most pervasive tenets of western thought. These two traditions—the Hellenic and the Hebraic—to which the West is heir have usually been seen as fundamentally different, and, indeed, as opposed—a view often expressed through Tertullian's famous question, *Quid Athenis et Hierosolymis?*, 'What has Athens in common with Jerusalem?', to which the implied answer has normally been a resounding, 'Nothing!'[1] Historians have tended to see western civilization as existing in the interval of tension between 'Athens' and 'Jerusalem', like an electromagnetic field between the poles of a magnet. Attempts are made periodically to discover the distinctive essences of the two traditions, and movements of thought arise which claim to promote one against the other—Hellenism against Hebraism, and vice versa.[2]

Usually the differences between 'Athens' and 'Jerusalem' have been defined in terms of concrete beliefs or ideas. For example, the Hebraic doctrine of creation has been contrasted with the Hellenic doctrine of the eternity of the world. Some, however, have argued that the differences can be defined more radically in terms of hermeneutics: 'Athens' differs from 'Jerusalem' in its whole approach to reality in general, and to the interpretation of texts in particular. This notion that there is a distinctively Hebraic as opposed to

Hellenic hermeneutics surfaces in the work of the influential contemporary literary critic Harold Bloom. Bloom has developed an elaborate theory of criticism which sees all creative writing (whether poetry or prose) as an implicit reading of a precursor text. To understand any given text one must identify its precursor and analyse the inter-relationship of the two texts. Bloom sees the relationship in Freudian terms as essentially Oedipal: the strong, younger writer will use every means in his power—including 'Oedipal trespass'—to escape the dominating influence of the older. Bloom construes the role of literary criticism in very similar terms— save that in literary criticism (unlike 'creative' writing) the precursor text is explicit, being the text at hand which the critic is setting out to explain. Though Jewish, Bloom formulated the broad outlines of his theory before he became aware of possible Jewish antecedents to his ideas.[3] Then he discovered the Qabbalah, and he was struck by the thought that its strong reading of the Biblical text is a striking illustration—perhaps, one might say, vindication—of his theories.[4] Increasingly he seems eager to emphasize the Jewish parallels to his thought, and to present his theories as an attack from a Hebraic standpoint on the Hellenism of the New Critics who dominated American literary criticism in the thirties and forties—Ransom, Tate, Warren and Cleanth Brooks. This is certainly how Susan Handelman sees Bloom's work, and she has attempted (as Bloom has not) to justify this judgment historically by analysing the nature of classic Jewish Bible exegesis, and so demonstrating the essentially Rabbinic character of Bloom's criticism.[5]

José Faur is another writer who has argued recently that there is a Hebraic as opposed to a Hellenic way of reading texts.[6] Faur is particularly interesting for our purposes, because, unlike Handelman and Bloom, he is an expert in Rabbinic literature who unquestionably knows the sources at first hand. Faur's central thesis is that the Rabbis' theory of textuality is more or less the same as that found in modern semiotics, so much so that one can talk of 'Rabbinic semiotics'. He sets up a binary opposition between Greek and Judaic thought: the former is ontological, visual and geometrical, the latter is semiological, auditory and algebraic. Greek categories of thought, he argues, have dominated European civilization with the result that Rabbinic modes of thought, especially as expressed in Rabbinic Bible hermeneutics, have remained outside of, and opposed to, the cultural code of the West. Recently, however, the situation has begun to

change. In structuralism and post-structuralism ideas close to those
of the Rabbis have emerged within the western tradition:

> Contemporary critical theory is now challenging many of the
> premisses and categories separating western from rabbinic literary
> theory. Structural and post-structural criticism ... has resulted in
> a common ground sufficient to permit exploring some of the
> fundamental principles underlying rabbinic interpretative and
> literary theory in terms of contemporary critical analysis.[7]

A line runs from Rabbi Aqiba to Jacques Derrida—Reb Derrida as he
once playfully called himself: Benei Beraq has more in common with
Paris than one might have thought:

> The object of *derasha* is liberation from conventional reading. As
> did Jacques Derrida, the rabbis sought 'a freeplay', amounting to a
> 'methodical craziness' whose purpose is the 'dissemination' of
> texts; this craziness, though 'endless and treacherous and terrifying,
> liberates us to an *errance joyeuse*'.[8]

Behind these breathtaking generalizations appears to lie a simple
historical claim which it is the aim of this paper to investigate. The
claim is that Rabbinic hermeneutics as exemplified in classic
Rabbinic midrash is fundamentally different from Greek hermeneutics
as exemplified in the interpretation of texts in the Graeco-Roman
world. Evidence will be brought which at least *prima facie* suggests
that this is not the case: the hermeneutics of the Rabbis can be
paralleled in all essentials from the hermeneutics of the Graeco-
Roman world. Rabbinic hermeneutics is thoroughly of its time and
place: it is a form of the hermeneutical code which prevailed
throughout the world of late antiquity.

Midrash

Before turning to hermeneutics in the Graeco-Roman world it is
necessary to say something about the vexed question of the nature
and definition of midrash, which embodies Rabbinic hermeneutics.[9]
For the purposes of the present analysis I shall restrict the
phenomenon of midrash within early Jewish literature to the corpus
of classic Rabbinic midrashim—works such as *Sifre*, *Sifra*, *Mekhilta
deRabbi Ishmael*, and *Genesis Rabbah*. I shall, consequently, side-
step the controversy over whether or not the Qumran *pesharim*,
Philo, apocalyptic, the so-called 'rewritten Bible' texts (*Jubilees*,

Genesis Apocryphon, Liber Antiquitatum Biblicarum), and the Targumim should be classified as midrash.

Even with such a restricted reference midrash is still a highly complex phenomenon which can be analysed as process, artefact, and form. As process, midrash describes the application of certain Rabbinic exegetical techniques to Scripture. Some of those techniques (though by no means all) are defined in the Rabbinic lists of hermeneutical norms—the Seven *Middot* of Hillel, the Thirteen of Ishmael and the Thirty-Two of Yose ha-Gelili.[10] As artefact, midrash denotes the end-product of the application of such a hermeneutical system to Scripture—a midrashic text, which may range in length from a short pericope expounding a single word or verse (a microtext), to an extensive document such as *Genesis Rabbah* which expounds a whole Biblical book (a macrotext). Midrash, finally, denotes the form or forms of such a midrashic text. There are a number of distinctive literary forms—both simple and composite—embodied in midrashic texts. Simple forms are forms which cannot meaningfully be reduced to other forms; composite forms are constellations of simple forms. The former tend, naturally, to correlate with microtexts, the latter with macrotexts. The fundamental and all pervasive form of midrash is Biblical Lemma + Comment. Form is fundamental to the definition of midrash: any text which does not display the Lemma + Comment form is not, strictly speaking, a midrash, however much it may appear to reflect the application of midrashic methods of exegesis. A midrash should display all three aspects of the phenomenon—process, artefact and form. Form is fundamental to midrash because it is the base-form of Lemma + Comment which make possible the expression of some of the basic principles of midrash: to a degree form determines the nature of the process. First, it allows a polyvalent reading of Scripture. Midrash (unlike Targum and 'rewritten Bible') regularly gives multiple and sometimes contradictory interpretations of the text, introduced by such formulae as *davar aher*, 'another interpretation'. Second, it allows named authorities to be quoted—Rabbi Ishmael, Rabbi Aqiba and so forth. Midrash goes out of its way to quote the scholars by name, to create the impression of an on-going tradition of interpretation which is a collective enterprise. Third, the Lemma + Comment form allows the exegetical reasoning to be made explicit. In particular it allows Scripture to be linked explicitly with Scripture and other verses to be quoted (introduced by formulae such as *šene'emar*, 'as it is said').

So much for midrash. The problem now to be addressed is whether or not midrash, and the Rabbinic hermeneutical system it expresses, can be paralleled from the Graeco-Roman world. The Graeco-Roman evidence will be briefly surveyed under four heads: (1) the exegesis of Homer and the classics; (2) the interpretation of law; (3) rhetorical elaboration of argument; and (4) the interpretation of dreams (oneirocritica).

Homer and the Classics

In surveying the activity of commentating in the Graeco-Roman world it is appropriate to begin with Homer. Homer, the 'prophet of all', held pride of place in the canon of Greek literature, and his was probably the earliest text to generate commentaries—*hypomnemata*.[11] As the name *hypomnemata* suggests, these commentaries originated in lectures on Homer within the Hellenistic schools. The majority of the commentaries belong to what Schulz calls the 'lemmatic type',[12] i.e. like Rabbinic midrash and Qumran *pesher* they are genuine commentaries in the Lemma + Comment form. Text and commentary were normally written on separate scrolls, the commentary and the text being related in two main ways: (1) by means of lemmata, i.e., as the Greek word suggests, by words or phrases 'taken' from the original, and (2) by means of critical signs which correspond to similar signs in the original text. The use of these critical signs reminds us that the basic aim of many of the commentaries was textual: they were concerned with the preservation of the original text from corruption, and, indeed, where it was felt necessary, with its emendation. An edition of the original was prepared in which certain problematic words or verses were obelized. These were then discussed at length in the commentary, and solutions propounded. Lieberman claims that in the whole of Rabbinic midrash there is not a single case of a genuine emendation of the original text of the kind so beloved of the Alexandrian grammarians.[13] In a narrow sense this is true, but the motive of preserving the original from corruption was surely not unknown to the rabbis. An apparatus for preserving the original Hebrew only comes to full flowering in the Massorah of the early Middle Ages, but it must have been present in a number of more elementary forms already in the Talmudic period. It should be noted, moreover, that the use of the obelus in Homer actually argues a certain *respect* for the received text. The Greek scholars show a tendency to leave the standard text intact, and to confine their suggested improvements to the accompanying notes. The lemma is normally of the abbreviated type, i.e., only catchwords or a caption are quoted. Sometimes, however, the lemmata give the full text, in which case the work can be regarded as containing both an edition of the text, as well as a commentary. The lemma is often made easy to find by being written outside the text (ἔκθεσις), usually protruding into the margin, or by the use of special symbols (colons and dashes), or by spacing. The content of the commentaries is diverse. P.Oxy 1086 (1st cent.

BCE), on Iliad II, explains less obvious words and phrases, glosses geographical and mythological names, and discusses at length Aristarchus's reasons for condemning lines 791-5. P.Oxy 221 (1st cent. CE), attributed to the scholar Ammonius, comments on Iliad XXI: it quotes authorities by name, discusses athetized passages, unusual words (e.g. the name Achelous), and the accentuation. The separate mention of eels and fish at line 203 becomes the occasion for a disquisition on natural history. This tendency to learned disquisition is evident also in P.Oxy 1087 (1st cent. BCE), which comments on Iliad VII.[14]

K. Lehrs, in an important essay first published in 1833,[15] distinguished two groups of grammarians who commented on Homer. One group, the ἐνστατικοί, brought various charges (κατηγορίαι) against the writings of Homer, the other group, the λυτικοί, attempted to refute the accusations and to offer a defence (ἀπολογία) of the poet. Athenaeus, *Deipnosophistae* XI, 493d, gives an example of how this worked. The problem concerned Iliad XI 636f.:

ἄλλος μὲν μογέων ἀποκινήσασκε τραπέζης
πλεῖον ἐόν, Νέστωρ δ᾽ ὁ γέρων ἀμογητὶ ἄειρεν.

Another man could hardly move the cup from the table
When it was full, but Nestor, that old man, raised it easily.

Sosibius, the λυτικός, reports Athenaeus, commented on this couplet as follows: 'Today the charge is brought against the Poet that, whereas he said all others raised the cup with difficulty, Nestor alone did it without difficulty. And it does seem unreasonable (ἄλογον) that, in the presence of Diomedes and Ajax, to say nothing of Achilles, Nestor should be represented as more vigorous than they, though he was more advanced in years. From these charges we can absolve the Poet by assuming the figure called *anastrophe* (τούτων τοίνυν οὕτως κατηγορουμένων τῇ ἀναστροφῇ χρησάμενοι ἀπολύομεν τὸν ποιητήν). That is, from the second line, πλεῖον ἐόν, Νέστωρ δ᾽ ὁ γέρων ἀμογητὶ ἄειρεν, we should remove the word γέρων from the middle of the verse and place it at the beginning of the first line after ἄλλος, and construe the words at the beginning thus: ἄλλος μὲν γέρων μογέων ἀποκινήσασκε τραπέζης/ πλεῖον ἐόν, ὁ δὲ Νέστωρ ἀμογητὶ ἄειρεν ('Another old man could hardly move the cup from the table/ When it was full, but Nestor raised it easily'). With the words in this order, it is clear that Nestor is the only one of the old men, no matter who they were, who raised the cup without difficulty'.[16]

This approach to commentating by way of offering solutions (λύσεις) to difficulties (ἀπορίαι) in the text generated a whole body of 'problematic' literature, like the Ὁμηρικὰ προβλήματα of Heraclitus, and the Ὁμηρικὰ ζητήματα of Porphyrius. The word ζήτηματα here recalls the technical use of the verb ζητέω, 'to inquire', in this literature. The problems are often introduced by the formula: ζητεῖται, διὰ τί ..., or simply by διὰ τί ... This sort of problematic literature extends far beyond Homer. Note, for example, the Πλατωνικὰ ζητήματα of Pseudo-Plutarch.

The similarities between this kind of Homeric commentary and Rabbinic midrash (in respect of form, content and general approach) do not need labouring. There is a great deal of midrash concerned with philological matters (e.g. the explanation of rare words and even grammatical forms), with realia, and with the identification of place-names. The sort of learned disquisition on natural history which we noted in P.Oxy 221 can also be paralleled in midrash. For example, natural history comes into discussion of the laws of kashrut, not to mention 'cosmology' and 'science' into midrash of the story of creation. The Rabbis were nothing if they were not scholars. The Rabbis also elaborate their discourses (both in Talmud and midrash) through posing and solving problems. These units of discourse, which are traditionally known as be'ayot (= προβλήματα/ ἀπορίαι) often begin with the formula *mippene mah*, 'on account of what ....?' (= διὰ τί). Note also the semantic overlap of the verb ζητέω used in Greek exegetical literature, and the verb *daraš* used in Rabbinic.[17] Of particular interest is the fact that both the Rabbinic midrashim and the Greek *hypomnemata* cite authorities by name, since this is not a feature of other types of early Jewish Bible commentary, e.g. the Qumran *pesharim*.

108

A Tribute to Geza Vermes

The commentaries we have considered so far are antiquarian in character, that is to say, they are concerned essentially with academic, scholarly matters. Homer, however, was subjected to interpretation from another angle. Homer, and to a lesser extent Hesiod, functioned as central *religious* texts in Greek culture: they were the two primary sources of Greek theology. But from a moral and religious viewpoint Homer and Hesiod came to be seen as posing problems: they report the Olympian gods as indulging in all sorts of immorality and vice, as being, to sophisticated perceptions, rather unsavoury characters. Already in the sixth century BCE Xenophanes of Colophon was complaining that 'Homer and Hesiod have attributed to the gods all that is shameful and a reproach among men, theft, adultery and mutual deception'.[18] The only way to save the text was by a radical reinterpretation, by treating it as allegory, i.e., as saying something different from what it appeared to be saying. Greek tradition has it that this allegorizing of Homer began with Xenophanes' contemporary, Theagenes of Rhegium, who began to look for 'hidden meanings' (ὑπόνοιαι) in the works of Homer. In the late fifth century BCE Metrodorus of Lampsacus, a pupil of Anaxagoras (who may have taught that Homer in his poems treats 'of virtue and justice' [περὶ ἀρετῆς καὶ δικαιοσύνης][19]), developed a full-blown allegorical reading of Homer. The Stoics did much to popularize this allegorizing by systematically reading their philosophy and cosmology into Homer.

Again the parallels with midrash do not need to be spelled out at length. The Rabbis, too, inherited a sacred text which, to a significant degree, was out of step with their morality, and their world-view. They too looked for the hidden sense of Scripture and 'saved' it by subjecting it to allegorical reinterpretation, i.e., they made it say something different from what it appeared to say. Porphyry's Platonic allegorizing of Homer is most obviously paralleled in Jewish literature in Philo's Platonic allegorizing of the Torah, but it should be remembered that such philosophical allegory is not unknown in midrash: note, e.g., Rabbi Hoshaiah's famous midrash at the beginning of *Genesis Rabbah* (1.1).

Homer may have been the first to attract commentaries, but he was by no means the last; other classics were also subjected to glossing. Greek commentaries are extant on Aristotle's *Topica*, on some of the plays of Aristophanes, on Plato's *Theaetetus*, on the speeches of Demosthenes (by Didymus the grammarian), on parts of the Hippocratic corpus (by Galen)—to mention but a few examples. And in Latin we have Asconius on Cicero's speeches (from the time of Nero); Servius on Vergil (4th cent.); Aelius Donatus on Vergil (c. 350); Tiberius Claudius Donatus on the Aeneid (c. 400); and Boethius on the *Topics of Cicero* (6th cent.).

In addition to the lemmatic commentary we should note in passing the genre of epitome in the Graeco-Roman world. The basic purpose of the epitomist was to shorten a longer work by extracting from it what seemed to him essential. This was done in a variety of ways, ranging from excerpting of selected passages to independent summarizing of contents. When the epitomist adds observations of his own, or material drawn from other sources, we have what Schulz calls 'commenting epitome'.[20] There are obvious similarities between 'commenting epitome' and the 'rewritten Bible' texts of early Judaism. It is interesting to note that in Greek culture epitomizing was rather looked on as hack work, and not real scholarship.

Interpretation of Law

Commentary played a central role also in the sphere of law. Here, too, the same basic situation pertained: an authoritative text was in need of interpretation and application. The situation may be illustrated from Roman law, which provides a more unified and better documented tradition than Greek law.[21]

In Rome *interpretatio* (= 'the explanation of the significance of a legal norm or term'[22]) originally fell exclusively within the province of the pontiffs and of the other priestly colleges. In the third century BCE, however, beginning probably with Appius Claudius Caecus (cos. 307 and 296 BCE), lay experts in the law (called *iurisprudentes*, or, more commonly, *prudentes*) began to come to the fore. These lay jurists appear to have been men of high social position who had the time and the inclination to devote themselves to the study of law. They were 'amateurs' in the strict sense of the term: though some of them doubtless held magistracies at various points in their careers, 'jurist' was not as such a recognized public office at this time. Any individual jurist's authority depended on his social standing, on the public offices he had filled, and, above all, on the reputation he had acquired for legal knowledge and expertise. His reputation rested on public perception of the quality of his legal opinions and the cogency of his legal reasoning.

Despite their unofficial status the jurists played a central role in Roman legal history. They acted as jurisconsults (*iurisconsulti*) whose opinions were sought, in the form of *responsa*, by private individuals, by advocates and orators, and by judges. They appear to have assisted the *praetor urbanus* in drafting the Edict which he issued on entering his term of office. They drew up wills, contracts and other forms of legal document. And, although they did not, strictly speaking, teach school, they did allow suitable young men of good family to study informally with them and to observe how they dealt with legal problems in the forum or at home. Pomponius credits these jurists with laying the foundations of the civil law. He writes: 'After the enactment of these laws [i.e. of the XII Tables] there arose a necessity for forensic debate, as it is the normal and natural outcome that problems of interpretation should make it desirable to have guidance from learned persons (. . . *ut naturaliter evenire solet, ut interpretatio desidaret prudentium auctoritatem*). Forensic debate, and jurisprudence which without formal writing emerges as expounded by learned men (*hoc ius, quod sine scripto venit compositum a prudentibus*), has no special name of its own like other subdivisions of the law designated by name (there being names given to these other subdivisions); it is called by the name "civil law" (*ius civile*)' (*Digest* 1.2.2.5). Elsewhere Pomponius designates as one of the main sources of Roman law 'our own *ius civile* which is grounded without formal writing in nothing more than interpretation by learned jurists (*proprium ius civile, quod sine scripto in sola prudentium interpretatione consistit*)' (*Digest* 1.2.2.12).

In post-Republican times jurists continued to play an important part in the interpretation and administration of law. It is, perhaps, a testimony to their influence (both actual and potential) that the State increasingly tried to institutionalize and bureaucratize their role. Augustus authorized certain jurists to give responsa *ex auctoritate principis* (though he did not suppress the right of 'unauthorized' jurists to give responsa, in Republican fashion, on their own private authority). Hadrian abandoned this scheme of authorization; instead he entrusted his *consilium*, which included some of the leading lawyers of his day, with the task of 'policing' the administration and practice of the law. And by the time of Hadrian it had become standard for all magistrates to be advised by jurists (known as *adsessores*) who were appointed and paid by the State. It seems that in many cases the magistrates wielded very little power but merely 'rubber-stamped' the decisions made by their assessors. Legal training in Rome began to be formalized in the time of Augustus. The two earliest Roman law-schools, founded according to Pomponius by Labeo and Capito (*Digest* 1.2.2.47-53), belong to this period. They were probably organized along Hellenistic lines, and doubtless like the Roman schools of grammar, rhetoric and medicine, were recognized in due course as corporations by the State. The bureaucratization of legal training reached its acme in the fourth-sixth centuries CE. By then a State-controlled legal profession had emerged. All advocates had to have completed a five-year course of study in a State law-school, where they were taught by professional, salaried teachers. Justinian limited the teaching of law to the three imperial schools of Rome, Berytus and Constantinople, and laid down in considerable detail the syllabus they were to follow. Juristic training and jurisprudence in this period becomes strongly classicizing, i.e., it consists largely of the elucidation and adaptation of a small canon of authoritative, classic legal texts. The political purpose of this bureaucratization is clear: it was aimed at limiting the freedom of the jurists to give their own interpretation of the law. Justinian bluntly makes the point that just as the emperor alone has the right to enact laws, so he alone has the right to interpret them: 'If ... anything should appear doubtful it is to be referred by judges to the very summit of the empire and made clear by the imperial authority, to which alone it is granted both to create laws and interpret them (*hoc ad imperiale culmen per iudices referatur et ex auctoritate Augusta manifestetur, cui soli concessum est leges et condere et interpretari*)' (*Tanta* 21).

It is within the broad context of the need for interpretation that we should place the Roman legal commentaries. These are found both in lemmatic form and as epitomes, the former being rather more numerous than the latter. Ulpian's commentary *Ad Edictum* in eighty-three books, extensive portions of which survive,[23] illustrates the type. 'A strict scheme of exposition is adhered to. The commentary on each title begins with a general consideration of its heading which provides an introductory orientation in regard to the individual Edicts of the title. The commentary on the individual Edict gives (1) the text of the Edict; (2) a close interpretation of its clauses, in which the clauses serve as lemmata or captions, and the commentary follows; (3) the text of the *formula* offered by the Edict; (4) any necessary interpretation of the *formula*, also in lemmatic form' (Schulz[24]). The following fragment of Gaius's commentary on the XII Tables may give something of the flavour of these commentaries. The lemma was a law which forbade killing an enemy, if you find him within your house, 'unless he defends himself with a weapon' (*nisi se telo defendit*).[25] Gaius discusses what is meant here by 'a weapon' (*telum*):

> *Telum*, indeed, is commonly the name given to that which is launched from a bow, but it equally signifies anything which is launched by hand; so it follows that stone, wood and iron are included in this noun. And it is so called from the fact that it is launched into the distance, having been derived from the Greek τηλοῦ ('afar'). We can find the same sense also in a Greek noun, for what we call *telum* they call βέλος ('missile'), from βάλλεσθαι ('to be thrown'). Xenophon reminds us of this, for thus he writes: 'The missiles (τὰ βέλη) were hurled together—spears, arrows, sling-stones, and very many rocks as well'.[26] That which is launched from a bow is designated by the Greeks with the specific noun τοξεύματα, but is designated by us with the general noun *telum*.[27]

Clearly Gaius is making a serious legal point here: he wants *telum* to be taken in its widest possible sense (against what he seems to concede is 'common usage'), presumably to prevent anyone from arguing that the law applied only to someone defending himself with an arrow. But his reasoning is surprisingly philological. He tries to prove that by etymology *telum* is a general term meaning anything that is launched into the distance, and that its semantic range is exactly equivalent to the Greek βέλος, which, as the quotation from Xenophon shows, includes spears, arrows, sling-stones and ordinary pieces of rock. A more obviously legal way of reasoning would have been to accept the restricted common usage, but to argue that *telum* was only for the sake of example: it is hard to make a significant distinction between an enemy defending himself with an arrow, and one who uses a sword, or a club, or a stone. This philological interest reminds us that the natural setting for these commentaries is the law schools. The relationship between the commentaries and *interpretatio* of law in the courts was oblique. The judges, at least in the later empire, would have been trained on commentaries such as Gaius's, but it is unlikely that in giving a judgment in court on some moot legal point they would have gone off into a philological disquisition such as we find here. In the later empire there was, arguably, a widening gulf between the academic jurists who taught law in the schools and the great jurists of the imperial *consilium* who actually influenced the development of law. The relationship between the academic lawyers and the real bureaucrats was probably not dissimilar to that between the judiciary and the study of law in the universities today.

There is a marked absence in Roman legal literature of extended theoretical discussion of the principles to be applied in the interpretation of legal texts. Principles are, indeed, enunciated as *obiter dicta*, as when the jurist Servius states in the course of an argument that 'the meaning of words ought to be established by common usage, not by the judgments of individuals' (*non ex opinionibus singulorum, sed ex communi usu nomina exaudiri debere*) (*Digest* 33.10.7.2). The *Digest* collects a large number of these *obiter dicta* in two chapters at the end, the first of which (50.16) is entitled *De verborum significatione* ('The Meaning of Expressions'), and the second (50.17), *De diversis regulis iuris antiqui* ('Various Rules of Early Law'). It is not always clear how a rule for determining the meaning of a legal expression differs from a *regula iuris*, but broadly speaking these two chapters give hermeneutical norms for the interpreting of legal texts. For example, *Digest* 50.16.6: 'The expression "according to the law" is to be understood as referring to the intention of the laws as well as their express statements'. 50.16.102: 'A law may suffer "derogation" or "abrogation". Derogation affects a law when part of it is removed, abrogation when it is entirely abolished'. 50.16.124: 'The words "one or another" are not only disjunctive, but also belong to subdisjunctive speech.' 50.16.195: 'The use of a word in the masculine gender is usually extended to cover both genders'. 50.17.9: 'In matters that are obscure we always adopt the least difficult view'. 50.17.56: 'In doubtful cases the more generous view is always to be preferred'. 50.17.147: 'The special is always included in the general' (*semper specialia generalibus insunt*). The absence of theoretical discussion is probably not accidental. Like most other lawyers, Roman jurists tended to learn law not from theory, but from practice and from the analysis of concrete laws and cases. The limitations of rules of law are clearly stated at *Digest* 50.17.1: 'A rule is something which briefly describes how a thing is. The law may not be derived from a rule, but a rule must arise from the law as it is. By means of a rule, therefore, a brief description of things is handed down and, as Sabinus says, is, as it were, the element of a case, which loses its force as soon as it becomes in any way defective.'

There is much in the development of Roman jurisprudence, as we have sketched it, which runs parallel to the development of Rabbinic halakhah. The parallelism cannot be explored fully here; all we can do is to indicate the lines along which it may be pursued. The role of the Rabbis (the 'Sages', *ḥakhamim*) is similar to that of the Roman jurists (the *prudentes*, or 'learned men'). The Rabbis were the heirs of the scribes (*soferim*), who increasingly in the post-exilic period had taken over from the priests the task of interpreting the law. Like the early Roman jurists, the Rabbis appear initially to have had no official standing in society: their influence and authority rested on the respect they earned from the general public for their knowledge of the law and their ability at solving legal problems. They performed all the functions of the early jurisconsults: they advised judges, plaintiffs and defendants; they gave legal counsel in the form of responsa; they drafted contracts, testaments and other legal documents; and they took pupils to whom they passed on their interpretations of the law. Their interpretation of the law became a major source of Jewish law, and was known as the 'Oral Torah' (*torah še-be'al peh*), in contrast to the 'Written Torah' (*torah še-bikhtav*) of the Pentateuch. In like manner, as we have seen, the *interpretatio prudentium* in Rome came to constitute a *ius civile* which was designated as 'unwritten' (*sine scripto*), to distinguish it from written texts such as the XII Tables and the praetorian Edict.

Just as jurisprudence in Rome became more institutionalized as time went on, so the Rabbinate became more institutionalized within Jewish society. This point may be illustrated succinctly from the development of Rabbinic ordination (*semikhah*). According to the Palestinian Talmud (*y. Sanhedrin* 1.2), the scholars originally ordained their own pupils after a suitable period of training; later the approval of a *bet din* was required; finally, however, ordination could only take place with the approval of the *Nasi*, the Jewish Patriarch. The picture that emerges from Talmudic sources is of an increasingly centralized bureaucracy (cf. *y. Yebamot* 12.6 and *Ḥagigah* 1.7). In the third century CE we find the Rabbis functioning as judges in a well-regulated system of Jewish courts spread throughout the Jewish towns and villages of Palestine, supervised by the *Nasi*, who was recognized by the Romans as the political head of the Jewish community. They adjudicate cases involving property, bailments, torts, damages, contracts, wills, marriage and divorce, and questions of personal status, all largely according to Rabbinic halakhah as contained in the Mishnah. And for the first time we get hints of money being paid for the teaching of the Mishnah (*y. Nedarim* 4.3). The *Nasi* functioned within Jewish society rather like the Emperor in Roman society, and, like the Emperor, he had his *consilium* (known as the 'House of the Nasi'), which doubtless included jurists who advised him on matters of law. It was due to one of these Jewish Patriarchs (Judah ha-Nasi) that in the early third century CE the Mishnah, the Jewish analogue to Justinian's *Digest*, was promulgated and made the basic textbook in the Rabbinic schools.

Like the Roman jurists, the Rabbis seem rather reluctant to elaborate any theories of legal hermeneutics or to draw up general principles of interpretation. Maxims of the *regulae iuris* type are found scattered throughout Rabbinic literature: e.g. *dibberah torah kilšon bene adam* (*b. Berakhot* 31b)—'Torah speaks in ordinary human language' (cf. Servius's dictum quoted above: *non ex opinionibus singulorum, sed ex communi usu nomina exaudiri debere*). The Rabbis, as we noted earlier, did draw up lists of hermeneutical norms (*middot*) which have a certain similarity to the norms collected at the end of the *Digest*: compare, e.g., the Rabbinic rule *mipperat ukhelal—hakkelal mosif 'al happerat umerabbinan hakkol*[28] with the Roman legal norm *semper specialia generalibus insunt*. However, as we shall presently see, the real analogies to the *middot* are to be found in the rhetorical handbooks.

These comparisons must be treated with great caution. It is not intended to imply that there are no substantial differences between Roman and Rabbinic jurisprudence. Clearly we are dealing with two vastly complex legal systems and much more detailed analysis is required in order to discover whether the parallels are real and significant. However, we have established a *prima facie* case for seeing Rabbinic and Roman interpretation of law as broadly similar. The function of interpretation in the development of the law, the role of the jurists, the literary forms of commentary and their *Sitz im Leben*, and the techniques and methods of interpretation, all appear to be broadly the same in both systems. We have failed to identify any fundamental differences in the hermeneutic codes of Roman and Rabbinic legal science. Though some of the content of Rabbinic law would have seemed strange to a Roman jurist, he would have found little difficulty in understanding the role of the Rabbi as an interpreter of the law, or in appreciating his legal modus operandi. Rabbinic halakhah is thoroughly at home in the legal world of late antiquity.

Rhetorical Elaboration of Argument

Though the orbits of the jurists and the rhetoricians overlapped, for our purposes it is important to stress the differences between the two professions. Rhetoric claimed to teach men how to speak effectively in public, including the law courts. It was concerned not so much with the interpretation of texts as with the persuasive elaboration of arguments.[29] The parallels between Rabbinic midrash and rhetoric which have most caught the attention of scholars have largely to do with ways of developing an argument.[30] The closest analogies to the Rabbinic lists of *middot*[31] are to be found not in the works of jurisprudence, but in the rhetorical handbooks. Three examples will suffice to make the point. Quintillian, *Institutio Oratoria* VII 8.3, divides the syllogism, by which he means deduction 'from the letter of the law that which is uncertain' (*ex eo quod scriptum est id quod incertum est*), into the following five species of question: (1) 'If it is right to do a thing once, is it right to do it often?' (*an, quod semel ius est, idem et saepius*). (2) 'If the law grants a privilege with reference to one thing, does it grant it with reference to a number?' (*an, quod in uno, et in pluribus*). (3) 'If a thing is legal before a certain occurrence, is it legal after it?' (*an, quod ante, et postea*). (4) 'Is that which is lawful with regard to the whole, lawful with regard to the part?' (*an, quod in toto, idem in parte*). (5) 'Is that which is lawful with regard to a part, lawful with regard to the whole?' (*an, quod in parte, idem in toto*). Fortunatianus, *Ars Rhetorica* I 25 (ed. Halm, *Rhetores Latini Minores*, p. 100), similarly states that the *collectio* (= the syllogism) can be eiaborated in five ways: *Collectio quot modis fit? Quinque: a simili, a consequenti, a contrario, a maiore ad minus, a minore ad maius*. Hermogenes, *De Inventione*, distinguishes five arguments (ἐπιχειρήματα) that can be derived from the circumstances of a case, viz. the arguments from place, time, manner, person, cause and act,[32] and he argues that, in principle, each one of those arguments can be developed in six ways: ἐργάζεται δὲ πᾶν ἐπιχείρημα . . . ἀπὸ παραβολῆς, ἀπὸ παραδείγματος, ἀπὸ μικροτέρου, ἀπὸ μείζονος, ἀπὸ ἴσου, ἀπὸ ἐναντίου.[33] The general parallelism between these lists and the Rabbinic lists of *middot* is obvious and may have been noticed as early as the mediaeval Qaraite scholar Judah Hadassi (see his *Eshkol ha-Kofer* §§155-62). Hillel's List of seven *middot* demonstrates the similarities: 'Hillel the Elder expounded seven norms before the Bene Bathyra, and these are they: (1) *qal vaḥomer* (2) *gezerah šavah* (3) *binyan av n̄ikkatuv eḥad uvinyan av miššene ketuvim* (4) *mikkelal uferat* (5) *mipperat ukelcl* (6) *kayyoṣe bo bemaqom aḥer* (7) *davar hallamed meʿinyano*.[34] Quintilian and Fortunatianus even give brief examples of their norms, very much in the manner of the Rabbinic glossators of the *middot*. (Fortunatianus introduces his examples with *quem ad modum*, just as the Rabbinic glossators introduce theirs by *keṣad*.) It is true that a problem noted elsewhere with regard to the Rabbinic *middot*[35] seems to apply equally to the rhetorical norms: the rhetorical norms are both prescriptive and descriptive; they state not only what was done, but what, in the view of their formulators, ought to have been done, and as an account of the actual methods of elaborating arguments or of exegeting texts they are rather defective. However, the parallelism is not without interest or significance. It is not necessary here to claim that the Rabbinic *middot* were derived from Greek (though some borrowing is possible, and, indeed, likely). For present purposes it is sufficient to note that the parallelism suggests that the Rabbis and the rhetors subscribe to a broadly similar hermeneutical code, and that the way in which the Rabbis develop their arguments is not fundamentally alien to the Graeco-Roman world in which they lived.

Oneirocritica

As Lieberman has rightly noted there is a final context in which the parallelism between Rabbinic midrash and Graeco-Roman hermeneutics should be considered, viz. *oneirocritica* (the interpretation of dreams).[36] Once again we have the basic situation of an enigmatic text (the dream), which is in some sense regarded as authoritative (a message from the gods) and stands in need of interpretation.

Freud distinguishes two traditional methods of dream-interpretation: (1) the symbolic method which 'considers the content of the dream as a whole and seeks to replace it by another content which is intelligible and in certain respects analogous to the original one'; this approach is holistic and treats the dream as a coherent allegory; and (2) the cipher method which 'treats dreams as a kind of cryptography in which each sign can be translated into another sign having a known meaning, in accordance with a fixed key'; this approach is atomistic and regards the dream as a series of discrete, even confused and contradictory signs.[37] The Greek *oneirocritica*, as represented by Artemidorus Daldianus,[38] follows the cipher method and uses a variety of devices, such as punning, numerical equivalence and *notarikon* (νοταρικόν), to establish a correspondence between the dream image and its interpretation. Artemidorus III.28 gives a simple example of numerical equivalence (ἰσόψηφα):

> A weasel signifies a cunning treacherous woman and a lawsuit. For the word δίκη [lawsuit] is equal in numerical value to the word γαλῆ [weasel]— ἔστι γὰρ ἰσόψηφος δίκη καὶ γαλῆ.

Artemidorus IV.24 illustrates *notarikon*:

> A certain military commander dreamt that the letters ι,κ,θ were written on his sword. The Jewish war was being waged in Cyrene and the dreamer gained the highest distinction in that war. This was just what I predicted. For *iota* signified the Jews [Ἰουδαίοις], the *kappa* signified the Cyrenaeans [Κυρηναίοις], and the theta signified death [θάνατος]. Before the actual event, the dream was impossible to interpret, but once it actually came true, the interpretation was quite obvious.

In other words the sword contained the coded message θάνατος Ἰουδαίοις [καὶ] Κυρηναίοις—'Death to the Jews and the Cyrenaeans'. There can be no doubt that the Rabbis were well acquainted with this kind of *oneirocritica*. The 'dreambook' in *b. Berakhot* 55a-57b employs the cipher method in the interpretation of dreams (in marked contrast, it should be noted, to the Bible, which generally employs the symbolic method), and shows many striking and detailed parallels to Artemidorus.[39] Take the following oft-quoted example (56b):

> A certain heretic said to Rabbi Ishmael: I dreamt that people told me, Your father has left you money in Cappadocia. He said to him: Have you any money in Cappadocia? No, he replied. Did your father ever go to Cappadocia? No, he replied. In that case, said he, *kappa* means a beam and *dika* means ten. Go and examine the beam that is the head of ten, for it is full of coins. He went and found it full of coins.[40]

The Rabbis applied at least two of the techniques of *oneirocritica* to the interpretation of the aggadic portions of Scripture, viz. *notarikon* (for which they used the Greek term), and numerical equivalence (which they called *gematria*). They are respectively norms 29 and 30 in the list of thirty-two *middot* attributed to Yose ha-Gelili.[41] The application of the methods of the *oneirocritica* to the Bible suggests that the Rabbis saw some similarity between the text of the dream and the text of Scripture. They were probably not the first Jewish exegetes to see this analogy. Earlier the Qumran sect had applied to Scripture the *pesher* style of exegesis which appears to have been associated traditionally with the interpretation of dreams. Once again, we need not involve ourselves in the question of borrowings. It is sufficient for our present purposes to note that in this final hermeneutical context, as in the other three, the Rabbis appear to have followed a hermeneutical code similar to that prevailing in the Graeco-Roman world of their day.[42]

Rabbanism as a Phenomenon of Late Antiquity

How are the parallels between Rabbinic hermeneutics and the hermeneutics of the Graeco-Roman world to be explained? In general, not in terms of direct borrowings and influences, though *some* borrowing is clearly attested. Lieberman rightly says: 'The early Jewish interpreters of Scripture did not have to embark for Alexandria in order to learn there the rudimentary methods of linguistic research. To make them travel to Egypt for this purpose would be a cruel injustice to the intelligence and acumen of the Palestinian Sages.'[43] What we are dealing with are basically parallel social structures producing similar historical effects.

The Rabbinic and Graeco-Roman cultures in late antiquity were parallel in two very significant respects. First, both cultures were 'classicizing', i.e. they were largely based on a body of canonic texts.[44] This is obviously true of Rabbanism, but it was true to an important degree of Graeco-Roman culture as well. Graeco-Roman culture canonized a body of literature as the standard of excellence: its traditions were, like the education of most European gentlemen till recent times, based on classics. Teaching and knowledge tended to be imparted in conjunction with the study of classical, canonic texts. If students learned geography it was through exposition of the wanderings of Odysseus, or through commentary on the Catalogue of Ships. If they were taught astronomy, it was through reading a literary text, Aratus's *Phainomena*. If they were taught Latin as a foreign language, it was through reading Vergil with the help of a Greek crib.

A second significant parallel between Rabbanism and Graeco-Roman culture is in the role of the schools. There are interesting similarities between the structure and functions of the Graeco-

Roman schools and the Rabbinic *yeshivot*. They are strongest, not between the *yeshivot* and the *gymnasia*, but between the *yeshivot* and the Graeco-Roman technical schools which taught, for example, engineering law, medicine and other practical subjects. Much of the literature of late antiquity, outside the revered 'classics', may be described as 'school literature'. The schools saw themselves as passing on a tradition, often from a 'founder', and they preserved lists of tradents through whom the doctrine was passed down. Within the schools, in teaching and transmission, there was a strong emphasis on orality, and a distrust of the written word, outside the corpus of the great classics recognized as canonic by the school. It was necessary to sit at the feet of the master, to hear and observe him as an apprentice, and to learn by the living voice.[45] This emphasis on orality led to a school literature which was often rather amorphous, and represented a snapshot of the ongoing and evolving tradition at a moment of historical time. Much of the school literature was anonymous: it was a collective effort, and, if it was attributed, tended to be attributed pseudepigraphically to leading scholars of the school, or to the 'founder'.

These two factors—the centrality of canonic texts and the role of the schools—largely defined the framework of hermeneutics both in Rabbinic and in Graeco-Roman culture. Our preliminary investigations strongly suggest that they led to the evolution of broadly similar hermeneutical codes in both cultures. Rabbanism at this level at least is a typical phenomenon of late antiquity, and 'Jerusalem' has a great deal in common with 'Athens'.

NOTES

*This paper, in different forms, has been presented during the past two years in Oxford, Dublin and Manchester, and has benefited from comments by a number of colleagues. I would particularly like to record my thanks to Professors John Dillon and George Huxley who made valuable and constructive criticisms which saved me from some of the pitfalls of such a wide-ranging investigation.

1. Tertullian, *De praescriptione haereticorum* VII: *Quid ergo Athenis et Hierosolymis? quid academiae et ecclesiae? quid haereticis et Christianis? Nostra institutio de porticu Solomonis est, qui et ipse tradiderat dominum in simplicitate cordis esse quaerendum.* For a discussion of what Tertullian himself might have meant by this see C.N. Cochrane, *Christianity and*

Classical Culture, New York: OUP, 1957, pp. 213-60. Cochrane, presumably retroverting from the English, gives the question as *Quid Athenae Hierosolymis?*, 'What is Athens to Jerusalem?' *Quid Athenis et Hierosolymis?*, however, has a rather different nuance: 'What do Athens and Jerusalem have in common?'

2. Note how the Athens/Jerusalem dichotomy forms part of the intellectual framework of Stephen Clark's highly original study *From Athens to Jerusalem: The Love of Wisdom and the Love of God*, Oxford: Clarendon Press, 1984. See esp. p. 79: 'Tertullian's mocking question, "What business has Jerusalem with Athens?" is the thought from which I began . . .'. Thorlief Boman's attempt to distinguish Hebraism from Hellenism, *Hebrew Thought Compared with Greek*, London: SCM Press, 1960, was rightly severely criticized by James Barr in *The Semantics of Biblical Language*, London: OUP, 1961.

3. See *The Anxiety of Influence*, New York: OUP, 1973.

4. See *Kabbalah and Criticism*, New York: Seabury Press, 1975; *The Breaking of the Vessels*, Chicago and London: University of Chicago Press, 1982.

5. Susan A. Handelman, *The Slayers of Moses: The Emergence of Rabbinic Interpretation in Modern Literary Theory*, New York: SUNY Press, 1982.

6. José Faur, *Golden Doves with Silver Dots: Semiotics and Textuality in Rabbinic Tradition*, Bloomington: Indiana University Press, 1986.

7. Faur, *Golden Doves*, p. xxix.

8. Faur, *Golden Doves*, p. xviii.

9. I attempted at some length to define midrash in my unpublished Speaker's Lectures, Oxford 1986-88, on 'Midrash and the New Testament: The Use of the Bible in the Early Synagogue and in the Primitive Church'. For preliminary statements of my views see 'Midrash and the Gospels' in C.M. Tuckett (ed.), *Synoptic Studies*, Sheffield: JSOT Press, 1984, pp. 1-18; 'Jewish Aramaic Translations' in M.J. Mulder (ed.), *Mikra* (*Compendia Rerum Iudaicarum ad Novum Testamentum II/1*), Maastricht: Van Gorcum, 1988, pp. 225-41; 'Retelling the Old Testament' in D.A. Carson and H.G.M. Williamson (eds.), *It is Written: Scripture Citing Scripture, Essays in Honour of Barnabas Lindars*, Cambridge: CUP, 1988, pp. 99-121. It is a pleasure to note that Geza Vermes's pioneering study *Scripture and Tradition in Judaism*, Leiden: Brill, 1961; 1973, has deservedly become a classic definition of midrash.

10. *T. Sanhedrin* 7.11 (ed. Zuckermandel, p. 427); *ARN* Recension A,37 (ed. Schechter, p. 110); *Sifra*, Introduction (ed. Friedmann, p. 27); *Mishnat Rabbi Eliezer* I-II (ed. Enelow, pp. 10-41); *Midrash ha-Gadol, Bereshit*, Introduction (ed. Margaliot, pp. 22-40). Further, P.S. Alexander, 'The Rabbinic Hermeneutical Rules and the Problem of the Definition of Midrash', *Proceedings of the Irish Biblical Association* 8 (1984), pp. 97-125.

11. On the early Homeric scholia see R. Pfeiffer, *History of Classical*

Scholarship: From the Beginnings to the End of the Hellenistic Age, Oxford: Clarendon Press, 1968; E.G. Turner, *Greek Papyri: An Introduction*, Oxford: Clarendon Press, 1968, pp. 100-24; P.M. Fraser, *Ptolemaic Alexandria*, Oxford: Clarendon Press, 1972, Vol. I, pp. 447-79; Vol. II, pp. 647-92.

12.   F. Schulz, *History of Roman Legal Science*, Oxford: Clarendon Press, 1946, pp. 183f.

13.   S. Lieberman, *Hellenism in Jewish Palestine*, 2nd edn, New York: Jewish Theological Seminary of America, 1962, p. 47; *Yevanit ve-Yavnut be-Ereş Yiśrael*, Jerusalem: Bialik Institute, 1962, p. 185. Lieberman's work is fundamental to our subject, but needs to be set in a broader context.

14.   Turner, *Greek Papyri*, pp. 118f.

15.   *De grammaticis, qui* ἐνστατικοί *et* λυτικοί *dicti sunt*, in his *De Aristarchi Studiis Homericis,* 3rd edn, Leipzig: S. Hirzel, 1882, pp. 197-221.

16.   Further, Lieberman, *Hellenism*, pp. 47ff.; *Yavnut*, pp. 198ff.

17.   For the equivalence of *daraš* and ζητέω see, e.g., Deut. 4.29 in the Hebrew and in the LXX.

18.   Xenophanes Frag. 11 in H. Diels and W. Kranz, *Die Fragmente der Vorsokratiker*, Berlin and Zurich: Weidmannsche Verlagsbuchhandlung, 1964, Vol. I, p. 11.

19.   Diels-Kranz, *Vorsokratiker* 59 A 1 and 61 A 2.

20.   Schulz, *Legal Science*, p. 184.

21.   I follow the standard accounts of Roman jurisprudence, notably Schulz's classic monograph, *History of Roman Legal Science*. Clear and useful is A. Watson, *Law Making in the Later Roman Republic*, Oxford: Clarendon Press, 1974. Quotations from the *Digest* are taken from *The Digest of Justinian*, Latin text edited by Th. Mommsen, with the aid of P. Krueger; English translation edited by A. Watson, Vols. 1-4, Philadelphia: University of Pennsylvania Press, 1985.

22.   A. Berger, *Encyclopedic Dictionary of Roman Law*, Philadelphia: American Philosophical Society, 1953, p. 513.

23.   The remains may be found in O. Lenel, *Palingenesia Iuris Civilis*, vol. 2, Graz: Akademische Druck- u. Verlagsanstalt, 1889; reprinted with Supplement, 1960.

24.   Schulz, *Legal Science*, pp. 197f.

25.   The content of the law from the XII Tables may be deduced from Cicero, *Pro M. Tullio* 21.50. See further S. Riccobono, *Fontes Iuris Romani Antejustiniani: I. Leges*, Florence: S.A.G. Barbèra, 1941, p. 58.

26.   The quotation is from *Anabasis* 5.2.14. Gaius possibly quotes the text from memory. Marchant's edition in the Oxford Classical Texts reads: καὶ τὰ βέλη ὁμοῦ ἐφέρετο, λόγχαι, τοξεύματα, σφενδόναι, πλεῖστοι δ᾽ ἐκ τῶν χειρῶν λίθοι.

27.   Lenel, *Palingenesia Iuris Civilis*, I, p. 243.

28.   This may be paraphrased as follows: 'When a specific term is followed by a general term the general adds to the specific and we include everything

[contained in the general]'. This is the fifth of the so-called Thirteen Principles of Rabbi Ishmael. See further note 10 above.

29. For a comprehensive account of Graeco-Roman rhetoric see J. Martin, *Antike Rhetorik: Technik und Methode*, Munich: C.H. Beck'sche Verlagsbuchhandlung, 1974.

30. See, e.g., D. Daube, 'Rabbinic Methods of Interpretation and Hellenistic Rhetoric', *HUCA* 22 (1949), pp. 239-65. Further bibliography in Alexander, 'Rabbinic Hermeneutical Rules', p. 116 note 2.

31. Further, Alexander, 'Rabbinic Hermeneutical Rules', p. 119 note 16.

32. Hermogenes, *De Inv.* III.5 (ed. Rabe, p. 140): εὑρίσκεται τοίνυν πᾶν ἐπιχείρημα γινόμενον ἀπὸ τῆς περιστάσεως. περίστασις δέ ἐστι τὸ πᾶν ἐν ἡμῖν καὶ λόγοις καὶ πράγμασι καὶ δίκαις καὶ ὑποθέσεσι καὶ βίῳ, τόπος, χρόνος, τρόπος, πρόσωπον, αἰτία, πρᾶγμα. προστιθέασι δὲ οἱ φιλόσοφοι καὶ ἕβδομόν τι, τὴν ὕλην, ἣν ὁ ῥήτωρ οὐκ ἰδίᾳ χωρίσας ἔχει, πιθανῶς δὲ ἐπιμερίζει τῶν ἄλλων ἑκάστῳ, ὅτῳ ἂν καὶ δύνηται.

33. Hermogenes, *De Inv.* III.7 (ed. Rabe p. 148). Hermogenes concedes that it will not always be possible to elaborate every argument in all six ways: οἷον τὸ ἐπιχείρημα ἔστω εἰ τύχοι ἀπὸ προσώπου· πολλάκις μὲν εἰς κατασκευὴν τοῦ ἐπιχειρήματος τοῦ ἀπὸ τοῦ προσώπου εὕρηται ἐργασία ἐκ παραδείγματος μόνον, πολλάκις δὲ καὶ ἐκ παραδείγματος καὶ ἐκ παραβολῆς, πολλάκις δὲ καὶ ἐκ τούτων καὶ ἐκ τοῦ ἐναντίου, πολλάκις δὲ καὶ ἐκ πλειόνων.

34. *ARN*, Recension A,37 (ed. Schechter, p. 110). Further, Alexander, 'Rabbinic Hermeneutical Rules', pp. 99ff.

35. Alexander, 'Rabbinic Hermeneutical Rules', pp. 114f.

36. Lieberman, *Hellenism*, pp. 70-76; *Yavnut*, pp. 202-12.

37. Sigmund Freud, *The Interpretation of Dreams*, trans. J. Strachey, The Pelican Freud Library, vol. 4, Harmondsworth, Middlesex: Penguin Books, 1986, pp. 170ff.

38. Ed. R.A. Pack in the Teubner series (Leipzig, 1963). I follow the translation of R.J. White, *The Interpretation of Dreams: Oneirocritica by Artemidorus*, Park Ridge, NJ: Noyes Press, 1975.

39. This highly important text has not received the attention it deserves. The most extensive treatment is still A. Kristianpoller, 'Traum und Traumdeutung im Talmud', *Monumenta Talmudica*, IV, 2/1, Vienna and Berlin: Benjamin Harz Verlag, 1923. But Kristianpoller totally ignores the literary problems of the 'dreambook' which provide the key to its interpretation. H. Lewy, 'Zu dem Traumbuche des Artemidoros', *Rheinisches Museum für Philologie*, NF 48 (1893), pp. 398-419, notes some of the detailed parallels between Artemidorus and the Talmud.

40. The version of the pericope in the Jerusalem Talmud rather more satisfactorily resolves 'Cappadocia' into Greek κάππα = 'twenty' and δοκός = 'a beam'.

41. See *Mishnat Rabbi Eliezer* I-II (ed. Enelow, pp. 10-41), where

examples are given. Further, Alexander, 'Rabbinic Hermeneutical Rules', pp. 102f.

42. There is little that is distinctively Greek about the *oneirocritica* of Artemidorus. Much of it can be paralleled in early Babylonian dream-interpretation. We are dealing here with a phenomenon common to the whole of the ancient Near East. See A.L. Oppenheim, *The Interpretation of Dreams in the Ancient Near East*, Philadelphia, 1956.

43. Lieberman, *Hellenism*, pp. 47ff.

44. Schulz, *Legal Science*, pp. 278ff., has some useful remarks on 'classicism' in later Roman jurisprudence.

45. See further L.C.A. Alexander, 'The Living Voice: Scepticism Towards the Written Word in Early Christian and in Graeco-Roman Texts', in D.J.A. Clines, S.E. Fowl, and S.E. Porter (eds.), *The Bible in Three Dimensions. Essays in Celebration of Forty Years of Biblical Studies in the University of Sheffield* (JSOT Supplements, 87), Sheffield: JSOT Press, 1990, pp. 221-47. The same author provides a new typology of schools in the Graeco-Roman world in her forthcoming article on 'Schools, Hellenistic', for the new *Anchor Bible Dictionary*.

INTRODUCING THE AKEDAH:
A COMPARISON OF TWO MIDRASHIC PRESENTATIONS

Lewis M. Barth

Hebrew Union College, Los Angeles

This *Festschrift* provides an opportunity to express appreciation for the significant contribution of Professor Geza Vermes to the historical and comparative study of Midrash and Aggadah; it is also an occasion to offer thanks for his generosity in sharing his immense knowledge, kindness and hospitality during several visits I made to Oxford. His volume *Scripture and Tradition in Judaism* remains a classic collection of scholarly studies in the Aggadah. In particular, the analysis and conclusions found in 'Redemption and Genesis xxii—The Binding of Isaac and the Sacrifice of Jesus' (pp. 193-227) stimulated the production of several books and articles;[1] it deals with the early history of the topic to be presented here.

The present study is based on a comparison of the opening passages from two midrashic presentations of the Akedah: (1) Trial Ten of the '*Homily* for the Second Day of Rosh HaShanah' found in Cambridge Add. 1497 [ff. 58r,2-60v,10] and Oxford MS Opp.Add. 4°.79 [12v-18v],[2] and (2) *Pirke deRabbi Eliezer* 31.[3] The *Homily* and *PRE* are the only compositions, as far as I know, which contain complete versions of the Ten Trials of Abraham.[4] Both compositions are 'late', probably eighth century, and stand at the end of a long development of the interpretation of the Akedah in Rabbinic texts. The comparison is designed to respond to the following questions:

1. How much and what material is shared by both the *Homily* and *PRE*, and how much and what material is unique to each collection?

2. What information can be derived from an analysis of the common and differing sources of the introductory material

in two versions for an understanding of the authors' literary treatment of the Akedah as a whole?

3. To what extent is the choice and treatment of this material influenced by: (a) formal and/or generic considerations (narrative vs. exegesis); (b) the authors' 'intention'; (c) the literary contexts in which the material is found?

It is not possible to prove which of these two presentations of the Akedah is earlier, or the extent of influence of one text upon the other. To the extent that it is meaningful or feasible to talk of authors and their intentions, these seem to be primary in the two treatments of the Akedah. Formal or generic considerations are significant, but didactic considerations—the authors' concept and message—are the controlling factor in the utilization of traditional material.

I

How much parallel Akedah material is found in the *Homily* and *PRE* in their preaching on or retelling the entire Akedah, and how much material is unique to each collection? The text of Trial Ten in the *Homily* is roughly twice the length of *PRE*; approximately one-third of the material in the *Homily* is paralleled by material in *PRE*; that material comprises approximately two-thirds of the Tenth Trial in *PRE*. I-III in the Appendix give the locations of parallels between the two compositions, and material which is distinct to each.

II

Both the *Homily* and *PRE* open with the trial number, followed by a brief identification of Trial Ten. In the *Homily* (58r.2-3) the trial is identified by the narrator's description:

> THE TENTH TRIAL: When he tested him (3) with the binding of his son.

PRE 31 identifies the trial merely by citing the biblical verse, Gen. 22.1:

> THE TENTH TRIAL: 'And it came to pass after these things, that God tested Abraham' (Gen. 22.1).

In the brief sections which follow, each work attempts to deal with the underlying issue of the trial, but the treatments reflect significantly different understandings of the Akedah. Following the identification of the trial, the anonymous preacher of the *Homily* engages his audience with the question:

> But if you ask, 'why was it necessary to test him since the Holy One Blessed Be He "probes the mind and searches the conscience" (cf. Ps. 7.10 etc.), before Him what will be in (4) Abraham's heart?' ... [58r.3-4]

Syntactically the question leaves us hanging; we expect any of the several modes of response which typically follow a sentence introduced with *w'im tômar*. What follows in lines 58r.4-20 instead is an extended composite answer, but not to this question. Although most of the material found here is known from other sources, none of it appears in *PRE*.[5]

A.1   When the Holy One Blessed Be He Created Adam, the Ministering Angels presented opposing arguments before Him saying, 'Master of the Universe, "what is man that You have been mindful of him, (mortal man that You have taken note of him?)" (Ps. 8.5)'.[6]
(5) What did the Holy One Blessed Be He do? He placed his little finger among them and burned them up!
When Adam came to sin, He saw that He gave them (6) a pretext (i.e. to the Ministering Angels to say, 'we warned You!'), and He said nothing to them. Similarly, when Cain killed Abel, He said nothing to them. So also regarding the generation of the flood, (7) and again regarding the generation of the Division (of languages at the Tower of Babel), [and again regarding the people of Sodom, until Abraham our father came along] and received all their reward. Then the Holy One Blessed Be He recounted his praise to the Ministering Angels and said to them, 'have you seen (8) how Abraham declares My unity in the world? Had I listened to you when you said in My presence, "what is man that You have been mindful of him, (mortal man that You have taken note of him?)" (Ps. 8.5), would not (9) the world already be lost?'

A.2   And, in addition, the Holy One Blessed Be He consulted with him about the people of Sodom regarding everything, as it is said, 'Now the Lord had said, "Shall I hide (10) from Abraham (what I am about to do?)"' (Gen. 18.17).
The Ministering Angels said, 'Look, we serve in His presence but He doesn't consult with us! Yet this one who is a worm and a maggot, what did He have in mind (11)

to consult with Him? If it is because He tested him with trials, yet He tested him only regarding his money, for had he tested him in his person he would not be able (12) to endure. And if it is because He tested him with circumcision, look, the Holy One Blessed Be He saved his entire body from fire. (As far as he is concerned), wouldn't he listen to Him for one limb?!'

(13) The Holy Spirit responded and said to them, 'you owe him a debt of gratitude. Because of Abraham both I and you have a place to dwell in the world.'

A.3   But (14) the Ministering Angels [continued] presenting arguments, saying, 'if so, from now on we'll forsake Your Glory and Your Kingdom and Your Cult and give praise to Abraham'.

(15) The Holy One Blessed Be He said to them, 'whoever praises Abraham and glorifies him, it is as if he glorified Me and praised Me, as it is said, "For I honor those who honor Me" (1 Sam. 2.30)'.

And therefore (16) it is written, 'After these words God put Abraham to the test' (Gen. 22.1).

A.4   Meaning: after Satan's words. [Since it was written thus], 'The child grew up and was weaned, [and Abraham held a great feast on the day that Isaac was weaned]' (Gen. 21.8).

Satan said to the Holy One Blessed Be He, (17) 'Master of the Universe, this old man, You [graciously granted] him a son when he was one hundred years old, and You gave him "issue of the womb" after his old age. But from the entire feast he gave for his son and for the kings (18) didn't he have even one turtledove or young bird or fowl to offer as sacrifice to You! Look, Scripture says, "and Abraham held (a great feast on the day that Isaac was weaned)"' (Gen. 21.8).

The Holy One Blessed Be He said to them (!), 'Did he do this only for his son? If I say to him now, "Sacrifice [your son] before Me", he would sacrifice him on the spot'.

He said, 'Test him and let's see whether this is so (20) or not'.

Immediately, 'After these words (God put Abraham to the test)' (Gen. 22.1).

A.5   And he answered, "Here I am" (Gen. 22.1). (I'm ready) for whatever you want.

Lines 58r.4–20 respond to an unstated question which has a long history in rabbinic exegesis and which, at first glance, appears to be so powerful that it controls the introduction to the Akedah in the *Homily*: the traditional interpretation of *wayyᵉhî 'aḥar haddᵉbārîm hā'ēleh*, 'after these words'.[7] What were the words and who were the speakers which the Akedah follows? A close examination of this section will help determine (1) why the anonymous preacher utilized the specific rabbinic materials he chose, (2) how he utilized them, (3) the topic he chose and (4) how he developed this topic in the *Homily*'s treatment of the Akedah.

The following represents a brief outline of this material based on identifiable individual units of interpretation. The units are described according to (1) literary form, (2) topic, theme or content and (3) primary purpose of the passage. The first large unit, 58r.4-16, numbered A.1. (58r.4-9), A.2 (58r.9-13), and A.3 (58r.13-16), although composed of discrete parts, comprises a coherent section as a whole.[8] Section A.4 (58r.16-20 beginning) is a separate unit.[9]

The literary form of A.1-3. is an aggadic narrative frame in which are contained dialogues, monologues and speeches of or between God and the Angels. Biblical verses serve as constituent elements of these forms of speech, or are used as prooftexts or provide an exegetical stimulus for the unfolding narrative. Gen. 22.1, implicitly the basis for the entire section, is cited only at the end of it, line 16, as the object toward which the narrative argument has been moving.

Regarding content, in A.1, the angels conspire to prevent the creation of Adam (humanity);[10] in A.2, the angels are jealous of God's relationship with Abraham as exemplified in the Sodom incident;[11] and in A.3, the angels conspire against Abraham by threatening to worship him instead of God.[12] In each case God verbally chastises the angels and lauds Abraham.

Two conclusions emerge from an examination of the surface use of these sections in the *Homily*. First, sections A.1-3 do not justify the Akedah. Section A.1 makes no reference to it; section A.2 does refer to trials—the angels argue that Abraham owed God at least circumcision (Trial Eight) for having been saved from the fire (Trial One/Two). Second, although sections A.1-3 do not respond to the opening question—why an omniscient God needed to test Abraham—and appear to be present only by force of tradition, they represent the conscious introduction of the central topic of the *Homily*'s treatment of the Akedah: *šibḥo šel 'Abraham*, praise of Abraham.

Several details indicate the author's attempt to exploit his material, either received or original, in relation to this topic. Abraham's life and activity take on cosmic significance, linked to creation and the continued existence of the universe. Most significant in this regard are the responses of God or the Holy Spirit to the Angels praising Abraham. Abraham is honored for having proclaimed God's unity in the world. Had God listened to the Angels, the world would have perished. Because of Abraham, there is a place for God and the Angels in the world. Whoever honors Abraham honors God.[13]

In contrast to A.1-3, section A.4 (58r.16-20), quoting *b. Sanh.* 89b, provides justification for the trial and locates it contextually in a narrative and theological frame. On the surface, then, A.4 is necessary for the unfolding 'argument', broadly conceived. After a brief narrative line which suggests that the Akedah follows on the words of Satan and links Gen. 22.1 and 21.8, we are treated to those words in the form of a dialogue between Satan and God. Satan makes the accusation that Abraham is ungrateful to God for the gift of a son. The passage ends with Gen. 22.1a, making clear the pretext for God testing Abraham.[14]

That Satan should trap God into the test also does not directly respond to the original question. The question presumes God's knowledge of Abraham's mind, gratitude and faithfulness. This is clearly borne out by the fact that section A.4 is followed in A.5 by the citation of Gen. 22.1b and the brief midrashic explanation indicating Abraham's positive response to any request which God might make: 'And he answered, "Here I am (Gen. 22.1b). (I'm ready) for whatever you want"'. It is significant that this exegetical comment is lacking both in *b. Sanh.* 89b and in the Oxford MS which follows the version of the Bavli here more closely than the Cambridge MS. Thus the words placed in Abraham's mouth appear to be a conscious insertion of the anonymous preacher. This is followed by a further citation from *b. Sanh.* 89b, an additional justification of the trial which will be discussed below. If A.4 is indeed to be considered the proximate argument which preceded and forced this last trial of Abraham, it would serve primarily to further emphasize the 'praise of Abraham' topic already introduced.

A final note regarding the traditional exegesis of Gen. 22.1: neither the *Homily* nor *PRE* cites as the referent for the 'words' the argument between Ishmael and Isaac, which is found in many sources, especially *Targum Jonathan*, a document closely related to *PRE*. Why? Because, as will be demonstrated, this argument has no significant connection to the conception of the Akedah in either composition.

The *Homily*'s original question thus far frames the narrative but does not control it. Where then does the original question come from and where is it answered? In all likelihood the source for both the question and answer surfaces later in the *Homily*'s treatment of the Akedah, in 60r.18-24, an expanded exegesis of Gen. 22.16b; this section also does not appear in *PRE*.[15] The original question appears here, but in the form of a declarative sentence placed in Abraham's mouth as he protests to God for having been tested in the first place. This section is introduced with a brief exegesis:

> (60r.18 end) 'Because you have done (this) etc.' (Gen. 22.16). What is 'this'?
> (19) For He said to him, '(and have not withheld) your son, your favored one' (Gen. 22.16, playing on v. 2).

A dialogue then follows:

> Abraham spoke in this manner to the Holy One Blessed Be He, 'Master of the Universe, if a person tests another person, he doesn't know (20) what's in his mind. But You know what is in the minds of human beings, "probing the mind and searching the conscience" (cf. Ps. 7.10; etc.). And You—God of all flesh—is (21) anything too wondrous for You (cf. Jer. 32.17)? Then why did you test me so much, and why was it not revealed to You that I would immediately slaughter him and would not hold back (22) even one moment?'
> The Holy One Blessed Be He said to him, 'It was revealed before Me that even your life, if I had asked you to sacrifice it, you would not have held (23) it back from Me even a moment. But I asked you now (in order) to make known to everyone who comes (in)to the world that not for naught did I choose you from all the nations (24) which I had made. (It was) in order to make known to them your propriety and your goodness.'

Just as we found in the introductory question, the phrase 'probing the mind and searching the conscience' (cf. Ps. 7.10; etc.) appears again. And just as we inferred the topic *šibḥo šĕl 'Abraham*, 'praise of Abraham', from the introductory Aggadot, so also is this passage designed to emphasize Abraham's qualities of loyalty and faith. The original question assumed that the reason for the trial must be other than God's desire to know Abraham's mind, since that is easily within God's grasp. God's response contains two answers: the first, 'to make know that not for naught did I choose you from all the nations',[16] and the second, 'in order to make known to them your

propriety and your goodness', a phrase unique to the *Homily* and
found only in the Cambridge manuscript.[17]

III

The narrator in *PRE* approaches the retelling of the Akedah as if he
were arguing with the *Homily* and denying the validity of its opening
question:

> He kept on testing Abraham every time (in order) to know his
> mind, whether he would be able to persevere and keep all the
> commandments of the Torah or not [Friedlander's MS adds here:
> and whilst as yet the Torah had not been given, Abraham kept all
> the precepts of the Torah], as it is said, '—inasmuch as Abraham
> obeyed My voice, and kept My charge: My commandments, My
> laws, and My Torah' (Gen. 26.5).

PRE does not assume that God, in fact, knows Abraham's mind
without testing him. Further, and this appears to me to be a separate
matter, *PRE* does not assume that God knows whether Abraham has
the ability to persevere and keep the commandments of the Torah.[18]
Finally, this passage communicates a detail of some importance in
understanding *PRE*'s general conception of Trial Ten. The narrator
appears to believe that all the tests, not merely the Akedah, were
designed so that God would discover both Abraham's mind and his
capacity to follow-through. Consequently, the narrator makes no
distinction between the Akedah and the previous tests; it is simply
last in a series.

This view of Trial Ten explains why *PRE* does not include the
following comment found in the *Homily*, 58r.20-23, from *b. Sanh.*
89a,[19] which does presume a distinction between the Akedah and the
previous tests:

> And He said, 'Take (*qaḥ-nā'*) your son' (Gen. 22.2).
> (21) Resh Lakish said, 'the expression *nā'* means "please".
> Meaning: the Holy One Blessed Be He said to Abraham, 'Look, I
> tested you many times and you endured all of them, (22) now
> please, (I ask) of you, stand fast for Me through this trial so that
> creatures might not say that as far as the first trials are concerned,
> there was no (23) reality to them'.[20]

This section is included in the *Homily* not merely because it is found
in *b. Sanh.* 89b following the section quoted above as A.4. Its
function here is to re-emphasize the importance of Trial Ten in
comparison to the previous trials.[21]

IV

From the above comparisons, it is now possible to relate the opening passages of the Akedah in the *Homily* and *PRE* to the larger conception of the Ten Trials of Abraham in these two compositions. The Akedah materials collected and shaped by the author of the *Homily* cohere nicely with the opening *peṭihtā'* of the sermon.

> (54r.5) Lection for the second day, 'Sometime afterward, God put Abraham to the test' (Gen. 22.1).
> This is what Scripture says: 'Let me sing for my beloved a song (6) of my lover about his vineyard, etc.' (Isa. 5.1)—meaning, this is the song which the Holy One Blessed Be He sang about Abraham our Father, 'a song of my lover about his vineyard'.
> And concerning Abraham it is said, (7) 'Why should My beloved be in My House' (Jer. 11.15).
> Just as it is in the nature of a vineyard, if it does not have ten properly planted vines it is not called a vineyard, so (8) from the day when the Holy One Blessed Be He created His world, the world was not worth anything to Him until Abraham our Father came and was tested (9) with ten trials. And these are as follows:

In this *peṭihtā'* it is argued that prior to Abraham's being tested with ten trials the world was worth nothing to God. The thesis of the *Homily* is that Abraham's life and the trials he endured are essential to the value of the world in God's eyes, that without Abraham the world itself would have perished and no place found in it for God and the Angels. This thesis emphasizes the strong connection between God and Abraham. It assumes that Abraham stands for Israel. It explains why the Akedah is the most important of the trials.

In contrast to the *Homily*, the basis of *PRE*'s attempt to justify the trial is an obvious divine doubt about Abraham. Presumably that is why *PRE* does not view the Akedah as unique, qualitatively different from the other trials.[22]

How does this relate to the opening of the Ten Trials in *PRE*? Not at all. *PRE* merely echoes the opening line of *m. Abot* 5.3a, 'Our father Abraham was tried with ten trials and he stood firm in them all'.[23]

The reason that *PRE* has supplied the answer we find at the beginning of Trial Ten is the quote from Gen. 26.5: '—inasmuch as Abraham obeyed My voice, and kept My charge: My commandments, My laws, and My Torah'. This verse appears in the biblical narrative considerably after the Akedah. *PRE* reads the verse back into

Abraham's life and trials, as if all the trials demonstrated this result. Scripture has provided the answer, there is no reason to question specifically why Trial Ten occurs! Several scholars have noted that the author of *PRE* is retelling a story primarily by summarizing midrashic tradition in narrative form, and linking it with the biblical text.[24] In contrast to the 'preacher' of the *Homily*, he is no longer probing the difficulties explicit or implicit in the scriptural account. Between these two activities there is all the difference in the world.[25]

APPENDIX:
COMPARISON OF TRIAL TEN IN THE *HOMILY* AND *PRE*

I. *Parallel Passages*

Homily Trial No.		PRE Trial No.
	Gen. 22.2	
58r.23-25		69b.3-10
		Friedlander 223-24
		Horowitz 105,9-17
58v.2-3		69b.10-70a.4
		Fr. 224
		Hor. 105.17-23
	Gen. 22.3	
58v.15-20		70a.4-12
		Fr. 224-25
		Hor. 105.23-34
58v.20-24		70a.13-20
		Fr. 225
		Hor. 105.36-46
	Gen. 22.5	
59r.11-22 (note both MSS!)		70a.20-70b.6
		Fr. 225-26
		Hor. 105.46-62
	Gen. 22.5, 7	
59r.24 (see: Ox.₂)-59v.4		70b.66-11
		Fr. 226
		Hor. 105.63-106.1

	Gen. 22.9	
59v.10-15		70b.11-17
		Fr. 226-227
		Hor. 106.1-8
	Gen. 22.13	
60r.3-7		71v.10-17
		Fr. 228-229
		Hor. 106.40-48
	Gen. 22.17	
60r.25-60v.1		71v.17-21
		Fr. 229
		Hor. 106.49-54

II. Sections in Homily which have no parallel in PRE (including opening question or organizing biblical verses

Opening question	Gen. 22.9
58r.2-3	59v.9-10
Gen. 22.1	Gen. 22.10-11
58r.4-20	59v.15-16
Gen. 22.2	Gen. 22.12
58r.20-23	59v.16-23
58r.25-26	Gen. 22.13
58r.26-58v,1	59v.23-60r.3
58v.3-15	60r.7-11
Gen. 22.3	Gen. 22.14
58v.24-59r.6	60r.11-12
Gen. 22.4	Gen. 22.16
59r.6-11	60r.12-24
Gen. 22.5	Gen. 22.17
59r.22-24	60r.24-25
Gen. 22.7	60v.1-3
59v.4-6	Gen. 22.16(20, 21, 1)
Gen. 22.8	60v.3-10
59v.6-9	

III. Sections in PRE 31 which have no parallel in Homily

PRE	Horowitz	Friedlander
69a.12-69b,2	105.1-7	223
69b.2-3	105.7-9	223
70a.12-14	105.34-36	225
70b.17-71b.10	106.9-40	227-28
71b.21-72a.13	106.55-70	229-30

NOTES

1. See bibliography cited in the notes to Robert Hayward, 'The Present State of Research into the Targumic Account of the Sacrifice of Isaac', *JJS* 32 (1981), pp. 127-50.

2. Lewis M. Barth, 'Lection for the Second Day of Rosh Hashanah: a Homily Containing the Legend of the Ten Trials of Abraham', *HUCA* 58 (1987), Hebrew Section, pp. 1-48; Trial Ten begins p. 30, f. 58r.2.

3. References to *Pirke deRabbi Eliezer* (*PRE*) are to (1) *Pirke Rabbi Eliezer HaGadol*, with the commentary of David Luria, photo-offset, New York, 1946, cited by folio; (2) Fr. = *Pirke De Rabbi Eliezer*, trans. Gerald Friedlander, London, 1916; (3) Hor. = *Pirke De Rabbi Eliezer: Critical Edition*, Codex C.M. Horowitz, Jerusalem, 1972.

4. For references to the tradition that Abraham endured Ten Trials, see Barth, *art. cit.*, pp. 1-4, and Chart and Sources, pp. 47-48.

5. For a more extensive listing of sources for Trial Ten in the *Homily*, see Barth, pp. 9-10 and footnotes which follow here.

6. The following signs are used within the translation: [ ] indicates a reading from the Oxford MS, ( ) indicates completion of a biblical verse or addition to text for sake of continuity or clarity.

7. Also, 'actions', 'scenes' or 'events'. The *Homily*'s unstated question is specificlly mentioned in three sources which it utilized: (1) *b. Sanh.* 89b: (*'aḥar ma'i*)? (2) *Gen. R.* 55.4 (Theodor-Albeck [T-A] p. 587,4, and note): *hirhureî debārîm hāyû šām, mî hirher*? (3) *Tan. Wayērā'* 18: *umah debārîm hāyû šām*? See also *Tan. Wayērā'* 42, and Yaakov Elbaum, 'From Sermon to Story: The Transformation of the Akedah', *Prooftexts* 6.2 (May, 1986), p. 100 and p. 111, note 9.

8. This larger passage, with some modification and a somewhat different ending, is cited in *BerRbti* = *Midrash Bereshit Rabbati*, ed. Ch. Albeck (Jerusalem, 1940), pp. 85-86.

9. This passage (as well as lines 20 end-24, a comment on Gen. 22.2), is based primarily on *b. Sanh.* 89a. As Professor Vermes noted, *Scripture*, p. 200, the motif of the angel's jealousy of Abraham as the cause of the Akedah is already attested in the first-century work, Pseudo-Philo 32.2-4.

10. The origin of this argument between God and the Ministering Angels requires analysis. Do the Ministering Angels object to the creation of the world or of Adam? When is the link made between the opposition of the Angels to the creation of the world or Adam and God's response justifying creation because of Abraham? There seems to be a confluence of several separate traditions here. *B. Sanh.* 38b refers to creation of Adam, and is the source for the statement, 58r.5, that when the Angels objected, God placed His little finger among them and burned them up. See also *Gen. R.* 8.6 (T-A, p. 61.1-5), on Gen. 1.26, linked to the interpretation of Ps. 8.5-10; also *Gen. R.* 31.12 (T-A, p. 285,7). The citation of Ps. 8.5 is found in all parallels, no

matter how they conclude the passage. For the source of the phrase *qošrîn qatigor* in the *Homily*, see *t. Sota* 6.5 (Lieberman, pp. 184-85; *Tosefta Kifshuṭa, Nashim*, p. 669). For a comparison of *Gen. R.* and *Tan.*, see Elbaum, 'Transformation', pp. 100-102, and note 14; Shalom Spiegel, *The Last Trial*, trans. Judah Goldin, New York, 1969, p. 117, note 148.

11. See *BerRbti*, p. 85; *Yalq. Bereshit*, pp. 433.18-434.21, note 18. Presumably the source of this passage may now be identified as the *Homily*, or the source from which the *Homily* took this passage.

12. *BerRbti*, p. 86.

13. The large unit, A.1-3, probably did not exist as a whole prior to its utilization and thus creation by the anonymous preacher of the *Homily*. The sub-sections represent both prior tradition and newly developed material which the preacher combined to form the larger unit.

14. The development of this passage requires fuller examination. *B. Sanh.* 89b opens with Satan's accusation against Abraham for his not offering God a sacrifice on the occasion of Isaac's birth and God's response. The exegesis continues with Gen. 22.2 and then returns to 22.1 with the argument between Ishmael and Isaac. In *Gen. R.* 55.4 (T-A, p. 587,4) the opening question is followed by (1) Abraham's thoughts on his not offering God a sacrifice on the occasion of Isaac's birth and God's response, (2) the Ministering Angels' thoughts on the same subject and God's response and (3) the argument between Ishmael and Isaac. In *Tan. Wayera* 18, the question is followed by (1) the argument between Ishmael and Isaac and (2) the Ministering Angels' opposition to creation of the world [or Adam] and God's response.

15. Note Albeck's reference to the connection of the original question with Abraham's statement, *BerRbti*, p. 85, note 16, referring to this passage which is cited there, p. 90. Albeck did not know of the existence of the *Homily*. See p. 85, note 15.

16. *Tan. Šlaḥ* 14; *TanB Šlaḥ* 27; *Num. R.* 17.2. This comment, in slightly different form, appears in these sources in the context of a *pᵉtîḥtā'* within a *pᵉtîḥtā'*. For exegetical basis, see *Gen. R.* 56.7 (T-A, p. 603).

17. Note: this passage ends on *tûbkâ*, 'your goodness'. The next verse, Gen. 22.17, is quoted immediately, *kî-bārēk ᵘbārekᵉkā*.

18. An alternate view of RADAL would suggest, against my argument here, that what I have indicated as two separate issues are in fact one. He notes that the language of *PRE* is based on Deut. 8.2b, '. . . that He might test you by hardships to learn what was in your hearts: whether you would keep His commandments or not'.

19. Attributed to Resh Lakish in the *Homily*, but to R. Simeon b. Abba in the Talmud.

20. See *b. Sanh.* 89b; *Gen. R.* 56.11 (T-A, p. 610, 1-2).

21. Note that already in section A.2 of the *Homily*, previous trials are mentioned in a context which suggest a more severe trial is about to take place.

22. In fact, the author of *PRE* may have conceived of Trial Three as the most severe. Note the phrase, *wᵉhaṭilṭûl qašeh l'ādām mikol*. See Friedlander, p. 189 and note 5. *Midrash Ha-Gadol*, along with other texts, cites Gen. 12.1 as the First Trial, and utilizes the language of *PRE*. See *MHG Bereshit*, pp. 215-16.

23. The first editions insert here: 'and it was foreseen by Him that his children would be destined to tempt the Holy One Blessed Be He with ten trials, and He anticipated the cure for their wound, and He tried him with ten trials'. See Friedlander, p. 187, notes 1 and 2.

24. On literary aspects of *PRE*, Joseph Dan, *The Hebrew Story in the Middle Ages*, Jerusalem, 1974, pp. 133-44; Elbaum, 'Transformation', p. 109. On the literary qualities of late midrashim in general and the comparison with homiletic literature, see Elbaum, 'Between Editing and Writing: On the Character of Late Midrashic Literature' [Hebrew], *Proceedings of the Ninth World Congress of Jewish Studies*, 3 (5746), pp. 57-62; Jonah Frankel, 'Major Features of the Textual History of the Aggadic Narrative' [Hebrew], *Proceedings of the Seventh World Congress of Jewish Studies* (Jerusalem, 1981), pp. 64-69; Jonah Frankel, 'Hermeneutic Questions in the Study of the Aggadic Story' [Hebrew], *Tarbiz* 47 (5738), pp. 150ff.; Ofra Meir, 'The Homiletical Narrative in Early and Late Midrash' [Hebrew], *Sinai* 86 (1980), pp. 246-66; Ofra Meir, 'The Story of the Illness of Hezekiah in Rabbinic Aggadah' [Hebrew], *Hasifrut* 30-31 (April, 1981), pp. 109-30; Ch. Milikowsky, 'Jacob's Punishment—a Study of the Editorial Techniques of Midrash Tanhuma' [Hebrew], *Bar-Ilan University Year Book* 18-19 (1981), pp. 144-49. On *PRE*, its dating and relation to Islam, see the literature cited in Barth, p. 4, note 16.

25. A form of this paper was read at the Association of Jewish Studies Conference, Boston, 1988. Appreciation for helpful comments and suggestions, especially by David Halperin and Asher Finkel, is gratefully expressed.

THE TWO WAYS AND THE PALESTINIAN TARGUM

Sebastian Brock

Oriental Institute
University of Oxford

φίλος πιστὸς σκέπη κραταιά,
ὁ δὲ εὑρὼν αὐτὸν εὗρεν θησαυρόν.

Discussion of the theme of the Two Ways has normally been focussed on the well-known passage in the *Didache* (1.1) and the *Letter of Barnabas* (18).[1] Shortly after the publication of the *Didache* (1883) C. Taylor drew attention to the parallels to the content of the teaching in the *Didache* concerning the Two Ways which were to be found in Rabbinic literature; Taylor indeed saw *Didache* 1-6 as 'possibly a reproduction of some treatise on the "two ways", of life and of death, which is much older than the *Teaching* in its entirety'.[2] A number of other scholars, writing in the first decade of this century, preferred to see an oral, rather than a written, Jewish source.[3] In the following decades, however, largely thanks to the influence of a number of articles by J.A. Robinson, the hypothesis of a Jewish source, oral or written, for the Two Ways teaching in *Didache* and *Barnabas* came to be dropped by all but a few scholars; instead, the author of the *Letter of Barnabas* was seen to be the originator of the theme, and it was from him that the author of the *Didache* took it over.[4]

It was the discovery of the Dead Sea Scrolls and the publication of the *Community Rule*, or *Manual of Discipline* (1QS), with its teaching on the two spirits, that brought about a return to the hypothesis of a Jewish source.[5] Ironically, in this document no specific mention is ever actually made of 'the two ways', the way of life and the way of death (as found in the *Didache*); instead 1QS 3.20-21 speaks of 'the ways of light' and 'the ways of darkness' (*bdrky 'wr... wbdrky ḥwšk*). Not only does this phraseology introduce a dualist element, totally absent from the *Didache*, but, by using the plural, 'ways of light/darkness', it also lacks any idea of *two* ways. Apart from this matter of the two ways, the parallels are somewhat closer with *Barnabas*, for there we have both the opposition of light with darkness, and the idea of the angels of God/Satan in charge of each way, corresponding to the roles of 'the Prince of Light' and 'the Angel of Darkness' in the *Community Rule*.[6]

In view of these closer links between 1QS and *Barnabas* it is perhaps not surprising that several scholars[7] have, at the same time as reverting to the hypothesis of a Jewish source, also taken over the view of Robinson[8] and others that the *Didache* derived its teaching on the two ways from *Barnabas*. According to this view, the concept of the two ways was a 'Spiritualisierung des mythischen Stoffes'[9] concerning the two spirits.

Other scholars, notably Audet in his monograph on the *Didache*,[10] have preferred to see the *Didache* as drawing directly upon a Jewish source, and quite independent of *Barnabas* (thus allowing the *Didache* priority in date). This source lacked the dualist overtones of 1QS, the *Doctrina Apostolorum* and *Barnabas*.

It is a matter of considerable astonishment that in all the secondary literature on the subject there appears to be no reference to the fact that 'the way of life' and 'the way of death' have actually been introduced at two places by the Palestinian Targum tradition into Deuteronomy 30, a chapter whose importance for the background of the two ways teaching had actually been adumbrated by a number of older and more recent scholars. Thus Audet himself points out in passing[11] the relevance of Deut. 30.15-20, while K. Baltzer, in his *Das Bundesformular*,[12] deals with the covenantal significance of the Two Ways, with special reference to Deut. 30.15ff.; finally, A. Orbe, in a characteristically fascinating article entitled 'El dilema entre la vida y la muerte (Exegesis prenicena de Deut. 30,15, 19)',[13] actually pinpoints the two verses where the Palestinian Targum introduces 'the way of life' and 'the way of death', without, however, being aware of the testimony of this tradition (a consequence of his sole reliance on Strack-Billerbeck for Jewish parallels).[14]

What, then, does the Palestinian Targum tradition have to offer at Deut. 30.15 and 19?

(a) Deut. 30.15. MT: See, I have provided before you (sing.) this day life and good, death and evil.

Neofiti (text): See that I have set out before you (pl.) this day the order of life and the good, and the order of pestilence[15] and their opposites.

Neofiti (margin): See that I have set out before you this day the life of the world to come and the blessing of the Garden of Eden, and the death by which the wicked will die and the evil state of Gehinnom.

Fragment Targum (V): See, I have put before you (pl.) this day the way of life, which is the good way, and the way of mortality (*mītūtā*) which is the evil way.

Pseudo-Jonathan: See that I have set out before you this day the way of life, by which the good reward for the just is fulfilled, and the way of death by which the evil reward for the wicked is fulfilled.

(b) Deut. 30.19. MT: (I call heaven and earth to witness against you this day), life and death have I provided before you (sing.), blessing and curse; and you shall choose life, in order that you may live, (you and your seed).

Neofiti: . . . the way of life and the way of mortality have I provided for you, the blessing and the curses; and you shall choose the way of life, in order that you may live. . .

Pseudo-Jonathan: Life and death have I set out before you, blessing and its opposite; and you shall take delight in the way of life, which is the Law, in order that you may live in the world to come. . .

Before considering these passages in the Palestinian Targum any further it is worth pointing to the remarkable fact that a quotation of Deut. 30.15, in a form very similar to that on the Fragment Targum,[16] is also to be found in Greek dress, in three early Christian writings:[17]

Clementine Homilies XVIII.17.2. ὁδὸς δὲ ἡ πολιτεία ἐστὶν τῷ καὶ τὸν Μωυσῆν λέγειν. Ἰδοὺ τέθεικα πρὸ προσώπου σου τὴν ὁδὸν τῆς ζωῆς καὶ τὴν ὁδὸν τοῦ θανάτου. The ensuing words, καὶ ὁ διδάσκαλος συμφώνως εἶπεν· Εἰσέλθετε διὰ τῆς στενῆς καὶ τεθλιμμένης ὁδοῦ δι᾽ ἧς εἰσελεύσεσθε εἰς τὴν ζωήν, are based on Matt. 7.14, a passage also alluded to in a sermon by Peter at Sidon, again in the context of the two ways (*Hom.* VII. 7.1-2): . . . προμηνύω ὑμῖν ὡς ὁδοὺς δύο,. . . ἡ μὲν οὖν τῶν ἀπολλυμένων ὁδὸς πλατεῖα μὲν καὶ ὁμαλωτάτη,. . . ἡ δὲ τῶν σῳζομένων στενὴ μὲν καὶ τραχεῖα, σῴζουσα δε. . .

Origen, *De Principiis* III.1.6 = *Philocalia* 21 (Origen here combines elements from both v. 15 and v. 19).[18] . . . καὶ Μωσῆς· τέθεικα πρὸ προσώπου σου τὴν ὁδὸν τῆς ζωῆς καὶ τὴν ὁδὸν τοῦ θανάτου (v. 15). ἔκλεξαι τὸ ἀγαθὸν καὶ πορεύου ἐν αὐτῷ (cf. v. 19). Elsewhere Origen quotes Deut. 30.15 in the standard Septuagint form.[19] *Apostolic Constitutions* VII.1.1. ἰδοὺ δέδωκα πρὸ προσώπου ὑμῶν τὴν ὁδὸν τῆς ζωῆς καὶ τὴν ὁδὸν τοῦ θανάτου, (καὶ ἐπιφέροντος) Ἐκλεξαι τὴν ζωὴν ἵνα ζήσῃς (vv. 15, 19). This is followed by Elijah's words at 1 Kings 18.21, 'How long will you be lame on both your hams (ἰγνύαις)?',[20] and Jesus' saying about serving two masters (Matt. 6.24); then comes an adaptation of the opening words of *Didache* 1, on the two ways.

The close similarity of these three independent Greek quotations to the common core of the *Fragment Targum* and to *Pseudo-Jonathan*, once each of these is stripped of its supplements, is remarkable, and can hardly be fortuitous; accordingly it would seem justified to suppose that we have in them three separate new witnesses to an earlier form of the Palestinian Targum tradition to Deut. 30.15 than that preserved in *FT* and *PsJ*. In effect, this earlier form has been created simply by fusing Deut. 30.15 with Jer. 21.8, 'Behold, I provide before you the way of life and the way of death'.

While τέθεικα[21] in the *Clementine Homilies* and in Origen supports the Palestinian Targum's use of 'set out' (*sdryt, N, PsJ*)[22] or 'put' (*śwyt, FT*) in place of MT's 'provide' (*ntty*), it is the *Apostolic Constitutions* which supports the Palestinian Targum's alteration of the singular 'you' to a plural (in v. 15).

If we turn to midrashic literature, it is striking that the theme of the two ways is introduced primarily in connection with the same two verses of Deut. 30: thus *Deuteronomy Rabbah* 4.3 quotes Deut. 11.26 (whose wording is very close to Deut. 30.19) and then cites R. Haggai: '(God said) And what is more, not only have I provided *two ways* for you, but I have not dealt with you according to the strict letter of the law, and I said to you, "Therefore choose life" (Deut. 30.19).'

The link with Deut. 30.15 and 19 also occurs in *Sifre* (*Pisqa* 53): 'Israel might say, Since God has provided before us *two ways, the way of life and the way of death* (v. 15), we will follow whichever one we want; therefore the verse says, Choose life' (v. 19). The two ways are also associated with Deut. 30.15 in *Pirqe deRabbi Eliezer* 15: 'Behold, these *two ways* have I given to Israel, the one which is good is of life, and the one which is evil is of death. The good way has two byways, one of righteousness, the other of love,[23] and Elijah... is placed exactly between these two ways.' In view of these close associations between the two ways theme and Deut. 30 it is likely that *T. Asher* 1.3, 5 also have Deut. 30.15 and 19 in mind,[24] even though the recipients are humanity, and not just Israel (for this extension, see further below): (3) δύο ὁδοὺς ἔδωκεν ὁ θεὸς τοῖς υἱοῖς τῶν ἀνθρώπων (καὶ δύο διαβούλια καὶ δύο πράξεις καὶ δύο τρόπους καὶ δύο τέλη...) (5) ὁδοὶ δύο καλοῦ καὶ κακοῦ, ἐν οἷς τὰ δύο διαβούλια ἐν στέρνοις ἡμῶν διακρίνοντα αὐτάς.

Although it is not my concern here to reexamine the theme of the two ways in the *Didache* and *Barnabas*, a few brief observations may be offered in the light of these recurrent links between the two ways and Deut. 30.15 and 19.

The wording of the *Didache* (1.1 ὁδοὶ δὲ δύο εἰσι, μία τῆς ζωῆς καὶ μία τοῦ θανάτου) is clearly closer to the Palestinian Targum tradition in Deut. 30 than is that of Barnabas 18 (ὁδοὶ δύο εἰσι διδαχῆς καὶ ἐξουσίας. ἥ τε τοῦ φωτὸς καὶ ἡ τοῦ σκότους). In view of this it can hardly be doubted that those scholars who have seen Deut. 30 as the background to the opening of the *Didache* are correct. The covenantal associations are in fact brought out in the *Didache* immediately afterwards, with the exhortation to love God (cf. Deut. 30.20, 'loving the Lord your God...').

In *Barnabas*, on the other hand, the substitution of light and darkness, and the reference to 'the light-bearing angels' and 'the angel of Satan' set over the two ways, moves away from the biblical basis of the imagery of the two ways and has links, though hardly close ones, with the dualistic world view of 1QS.[25] As we have them, neither 1QS nor Barnabas (nor indeed the *Doctrina Apostolorum*) has any obvious link left with Deut. 30, yet, in the light of *T. Levi* 19.1 it seems likely that this was in fact again the original starting point: *T. Levi* 19.1 reads.. ἔλεσθε οὖν ἑαυτοῖς (cf. Deut. 30.19) ἢ τὸ σκότος ἢ τὸ φῶς, ἢ νόμον Κυρίου ἢ ἔργα Βελιάρ. Here the verb 'choose', followed by the invocation of witnesses (v. 3), strongly suggests that Deut. 30.19 is in the background.[26]

Thus, whereas the *Didache* harks back more or less directly to Deut. 30.15-19, fused with Jer. 21.8 (as also witnessed in the Palestinian Targum tradition), the *Doctrina Apostolorum* and *Barnabas* do so only indirectly, by way of the intrusion of the non-biblical moral opposition of light and dark, also to be found in 1QS.

The different witnesses to the Palestinian Targum tradition at Deut. 30.15, 19 all introduce an eschatological element: the two roads lead to life or death, the Garden of Eden, or Gehinnom, in the world to come. This stands in sharp contrast to the (deliberately?) low-key interpretation given to Deut. 30.19 in *Eccl. Rabbah* 9.9, *y. Sotah* 9.15 and elsewhere, where the verse is seen as referring to the need to learn a trade (since one's life may depend on it). An eschatological interpretation attributed to Yoḥanan b. Zakkai, is, however, implied at *b. Berakhot* 28b, where R. Yoḥanan says on his deathbed, 'When there are two ways before me, one leading to Paradise and the other to Gehinnom, and I do not know by which I shall be taken (sc. at death), shall I not weep?' Here, comparison with *Neofiti* at Deut. 30.15 strongly suggests that R. Yoḥanan was understood to be alluding to that verse.

The eschatological reference to the Garden of Eden in *Neofiti* has obvious protological overtones as well, and it is not very surprising to find 'the way of life' featuring in *Pseudo-Jonathan*'s expanded version of Gen. 3.24 (in the Hebrew the cherubim with the flaming sword 'guard the way to the Tree of Life'):[27]

> He then drove Adam from the place where he had caused the glory of the *Shekhina* to dwell, since the beginning, between the two cherubim. Before creating the world he had created the Law, prepared the Garden of Eden for the just so that they might eat and enjoy the fruits of the Tree, seeing that they had laboured during their lives in the study of the Law in this world and kept the commandments. For the wicked he prepared Gehinnom which is like a sharp sword devouring on both sides; he prepared in its midst sparks of fire and burning coals whereby to judge the wicked who rebel during their lives against the teaching of the Law. Better is the Law for the person who cultivates it than the fruit of the Tree of Life, for the *Memra* of the Lord has prepared it (sc. the Law) for its keeping, so that the person who walks in the paths of the way of life may continue to the world to come.[28]

The mention of 'the way to the Tree of Life' in Gen. 3.24 probably provides the stepping-stone for the wholesale transfer of Deut. 30.15, 19 from the scenario of the Lawgiving to that of the creation of Adam, such as we find underlying the exegesis given to *mimmennû* (Gen. 3.22),[29] attributed to R. Aqiba in *Gen. Rabbah* 21.5: 'The Holy One provided *two ways* before him (sc. Adam), and he *chose* the other way'. This universalizing of the choice between the two ways of

Deut. 30.15 and 19, achieved by transferring the reference from Israel to Adam/humanity, is already found in Philo, in his *Quod Deus sit immutabilis* 50:[30] 'Hence one finds the following saying written in Deuteronomy, Behold, I have provided before you life and death, good and evil; choose life' (Deut. 30.15 and 19 fused together). Two points are made here: on the one hand, humans are born having knowledge of what is good and its opposite; and on the other, they ought to choose (αἱρεῖσθαι) the better in preference to the worse, seeing that they possess within themselves reasoning (λογισμόν), which, like an unbribable judge, agrees to what correct reason suggests, but refuses what its opposite (proposes)'. Similarly Justin Martyr,[31] writing approximately a century later, specifically states that Moses' words in Deut. 30.15 and 19 were addressed to the protoplast (τῷ πρώτῳ πλασθέντι ἀνθρώπῳ).

Failure on Adam's part to choose the way of life thus led to the closing of 'the way to the Tree of Life' (Gen. 3.24), and his choice of 'the other way' led to the state of mortality.[32] Whereas Jewish texts such as Enoch 25 and the Palestinian Targumim have an eschatological interest in Gen. 3.24, for early Christianity there were soteriological overtones as well. This was largely the result of typological considerations; the way to the Tree of Life, cut off by the sword of the cherubim[33] as a consequence of the wrong choice (or, in Christian terms, disobedience or sin) of the First Adam, was seen as being opened up again by the Second Adam (and more specifically, by the lance which opened up the side of the Second Adam on the cross, John 19.34),[34] thus enabling Adam/humanity to have full access to the Tree of Life, identified as Christ.

Jewish eschatological exegesis of Gen. 3.24 appears to have shown no interest in any idea of the removal of the sword in order to open up Paradise for the just—with one possible exception,[35] *T. Levi* 18.10, where 'the new priest' ἀνοίξει τὰς θύρας τοῦ παραδείσου καὶ στήσει τὴν ἀπειλοῦσαν ῥομφαίαν κατὰ τοῦ Ἀδάμ (whereupon he will give to the holy ones to eat of the Tree of Life, v. 11). Although v. 10 has not been singled out as one of the Christian interpolations in this chapter by Hultgård[36] or (it appears) others, the concern here with the sword sounds to my ears suspiciously Christian.

It is worth noting here, by way of parenthesis, that the theme of the opening up of the way to the Tree of Life by the Second Adam probably provided the basis for a phrase which is characteristic of early Syriac Christian traditions, 'Christ has trod out for us the way (*draš ʾurḥā*)ʾ; significantly in the earliest texts the phrase is regularly associated with the way from death to life.[37] Hesitantly one might suggest that it was as a result of such Christian usurpation of some of the phraseology of Gen. 3.24 that all mention of *the way* to the Tree of Life is absent from the Palestinian Targum tradition (apart from *Pseudo-Jonathan*), despite its presence in the Hebrew text.

Summing up thus far, it would seem that there are sufficiently strong grounds for supposing that the starting point for the theme of the two ways lay in the combining of Jer. 21.8 with Deut. 30.15, 19, such as we find in the Greek quotations of Deut. 30.15 in the *Clementine Homilies* (second century CE), Origen (first half of third century) and the *Apostolic Constitutions* (late fourth century);[38] various expanded forms of this occur in the Palestinian Targum tradition. Possibly this stage is already implied in Philo, *de Plantatione* 37.

Then, from this starting point we have the following developments:
(1) the concept of *two* ways: for this the earliest witness is probably *T. Asher* (of disputed date), followed by the *Didache* (usually dated to the late first century CE), the *Doctrina Apostolorum* and *Barnabas*; subsequently it appears in *Genesis* and *Deuteronomy Rabbah*, *Sifre* and *Pirqe deRabbi Eliezer*. In all but the midrashic texts the starting point (Deut. 30) is no longer explicit.[39]
(2) the opposing ways are described in dualistic terms of light and dark, again without explicit reference to Deut. 30. This is first attested in 1QS (late second, or first century BCE), where the idea of only two ways is abandoned (whereas in early Christianity, in the *Doctrina Apostolorum* and *Barnabas*, the original theme of two ways is preserved).
(3) The theme is given eschatological overtones (Palestinian Targum, *b. Ber.* 28b).
(4) The words of Deut. 30.15, 19 are seen as addressed to Adam (Philo; Justin; R. Aqiba *apud Gen. R.* 21.5).[40]
(5) The eschatological and protological references (i.e. (3) and (4)) may be combined and, in Christian authors, given a soteriological dimension as well (possibly already,[41] by implication, in *Odes of Solomon* 17.9, and then prominently among early Syriac writings from the *Acts of Thomas* onwards).

Given the nature of our evidence, it is not possible to attach any absolute chronology to these developments, but provided it is accepted that the ultimate source of the phraseology 'the ways of light' and 'the ways of darkness' in 1QS lies ultimately in Deut. 30, then we can assume that the linking of Jer. 21.8 with Deut. 30.15, 19 must go back to at least the second century BCE.

Before drawing this brief exploration to a close, two observations of a methodological nature are worth making.

First, it should have become apparent how motifs such as 'the two ways' tend to be linked with specific biblical passages. Thus any study of these motifs needs to keep the relevant biblical passages and their exegetical history in mind, even when the motif is no longer attached to them.

Secondly, close attention needs to be paid to the details of wording.[42] This means, in the context of the theme of the two ways, that we need to distinguish between the following (the references do not aim to be exhaustive):

(1) *Overt mention of two ways*
—'two ways': *T. Asher* 1.3, 5; *Didache* 1; *Doctrina Apostolorum* 1; *Barnabas* 18; *Clementine Homilies* 7.7.1; *Gen. R.* 21.5; *Deut. R.* 4.3; *Sifre* 53; *b. Ber.* 28b; *PRE* 15; *2 Enoch* 30.15; *Or. Sib.* 8.399.
—the two ways identified as the way of life and the way of death: *Didache*; *Doctrina Apostolorum*; *Rabbinic references*; *Or. Sib.* (as above).
—the two ways identified as the way of light and the way of darkness: *Doctrina Apostolorum*; *Barnabas*; *2 Enoch*.[43]
—the two ways identified as the way of good and the way of evil: *T. Asher*.
—the two ways identified as the broad and smooth way and the narrow and rough way: *Clementine Homilies*.

(2) *Two ways implied by inference*
—way of life and way of death: Jer. 21.8; Deut. 30.15 (*FT*, *PsJ*, *Clem. Hom.*, Origen, *Apost. Const.*); Philo, *de Plant.* 37.
—way of life and way of mortality: Deut. 30.15 (*FT*[N]); Deut. 30.19 (*N*).
—way of good and way of evil: *y. Ber.* 12(13).3.
—way of truth and way of falsehood: Ps. 119.29-30 (MT).
—way of truth and way of iniquity: Ps. 118(119).29-30 (LXX).
—way of virtue and way of wickedness: Philo, *Vit. Mos* II.138; *de Plant.* 37.
—narrow way and broad way: *T. Abraham* 11.2[44] (cf. Matt. 7.13-14).

(3) *Plurality of ways*
—ways of light and ways of darkness: 1QS.
—ways of truth and ways of iniquity: *1 Enoch* 91.18 (Aram); 94.1
(Aram.); cf. Tob. 1.3 + 4.5.
—ways of truth and ways of corruption: *Odes Sol.* 33.7-8.
—ways of righteousness and ways of iniquity: *1 Enoch* 91.18 (Eth.);
94.1 (Eth.).

By way of conclusion it is perhaps worth reflecting on why the
witness of the Palestinian Targum to 'the two ways' tradition has
been consistently neglected. The reason is not far to seek. At the
time when the *Didache* was first published (1883) the Palestinian
Targum (then represented only by the *Fragment Targum* and *Pseudo-
Jonathan*) was regarded as a late midrashic expansion of *Onkelos*,
and so was considered of little or no interest for the study of the
Jewish background to emergent Christianity. Consequently, even if
anyone had happened to notice the parallel with the *Didache* and the
Letter of Barnabas, the Palestinian Targum would not have been
considered to be of sufficient interest to quote.

It was for precisely the same reasons that Strack and Billerbeck
paid no attention to the Targum in their extensive—but too
influential!—collection *Kommentar zum Neuen Testament aus Talmud
und Midrasch* (1922-28).[45] It was not until Kahle's publication of the
comparatively early fragments of Palestinian Targum manuscripts
from the Cairo Geniza in 1930[46] that greater attention came to be
paid to the Palestinian Targum, but by that date the hypothesis of a
Jewish source for the two ways teaching in the *Didache* and *Barnabas*
was no longer in fashion. Ironically, it was only with the discovery of
the Dead Sea Scrolls and the publication in 1950 of the *Community
Rule* (1QS)—which never actually mentions the two ways, or the
way of life and the way of death—that the idea of a Jewish
background to these early Christian documents came to be taken
seriously again. By the time that the Deuteronomy volume of the
dramatic new Palestinian Targum witness in MS *Neofiti 1* came to be
published (1978), the standard modern critical editions and
commentaries for the *Didache* and *Barnabas* had already appeared
(1978 and 1971 respectively).[47] And so the Jewish background to the
two ways theme is discussed in these volumes primarily in
connection with 1QS.

How effective was the unwitting censorship imposed on the

Targumim by Strack and Billerbeck's *Kommentar* can well be seen from Orbe's reliance on that collection for Rabbinic parallels; for a discussion of the Palestinian Targum's handling of Deut. 30.15 and 19 would have been highly illuminating for his whole argument. The harmful effect that sole reliance on Strack and Billerbeck's *Kommentar* by students of the New Testament and early Christianity has had on much scholarship in this area is well known, and has been well brought out by Geza Vermes in his 'Jewish Studies and New Testament Interpretation'.[48] Our present case history simply emphasizes the points that he has already so incisively made.

Blessed with the benefit of hindsight we can, then, look back over the history of scholarship on the two ways with a wry smile as we perceive the various blind spots of the past—a warning of course that we no doubt have our own, but different, ones. Like the lame man in the allegory of the body and soul in *b. Sanhedrin* 91, we would be ill-advised to reject the help of the blind man; rather, we should climb on to his back and thus together, by our cooperative effort, we may perhaps be able to reach to pick the fruit in the orchard.

NOTES

1. The texts are cited below.
2. C. Taylor, *The Teaching of the Twelve Apostles with Illustrations from the Talmud*, Cambridge, 1886. Curiously, he cites none of the midrashic parallels to the concept of the two ways (he concentrates instead on the content of the teaching concerning the two ways).
3. Notably G. Klein, *Der älteste christliche Katechismus und die jüdische Propaganda-Literatur*, Berlin, 1909, pp. 157ff. This work contains many insights which still retain their value. A series of monographs by A. Seeberg on the content of the two ways teaching are of less interest today.
4. See the helpful survey of scholarship on the two ways by W. Rordorf, 'Un chapitre d'éthique judéo-chrétienne: les deux voies', *RSR* 60 (1972) = *Judéo-Christianisme. Recherches historiques et théologiques offertes en hommage au Cardinal Jean Daniélou*, pp. 109-28 (reprinted in his *Liturgie, foi et vie des premiers chrétiens. Etudes Patristiques* (Théologie historique, 75, 1986), pp. 155-74; cf. also M.J. Suggs, 'The Christian Two Ways tradition: its antiquity, form and function', in D.E. Aune (ed.), *Studies in New Testament and Early Christian Literature* (NTSupp., 33), 1972, pp. 60-74.
5. Initiated by J-P. Audet, 'Affinités littéraires et doctrinales du Manuel de Discipline', *RB* 59 (1952), pp. 219-38.
6. The Latin *Doctrina Apostolorum* belongs to the same general tradition,

for although it is for the most part a translation of *Didache* 1, its opening combines the *Didache*'s 'life/death' with 'light/darkness', and introduces the two angels (of right and wrong, *aequitatis*. . . *iniquitatis*).

7. Thus evidently E. Kamlah, *Die Form der katalogischen Paränese im Neuen Testament* (WUNT, 7), 1964, p. 214.

8. The view in fact goes back much earlier, to Harnack.

9. Thus Kamlah, *Die Form*, p. 173.

10. J-P. Audet, *La Didaché* (Etudes Bibliques), Paris, 1958.

11. Audet, *La Didaché*, p. 256. The importance of Deut. 30 had already been emphasized by Klein, *Der älteste christliche Katechismus*, p. 163.

12. *Das Bundesformular* (WMANT, 4), 1964, p. 133.

13. In *Gregorianum* 51 (1970), pp. 305-65, 509-36. Similarly J. Daniélou, *Études d'exégèse judéo-chrétienne* (Théologie historique, 5), 1965, p. 64, also points to the importance of Deut. 30.15, 19.

14. For this, see below.

15. The text has *mwtnh*, which is probably a corruption of either *mwth*, 'death', or *mtwth*, 'mortality'.

16. And *Pseudo-Jonathan*, if one removes the relative clauses.

17. These are usually described as free paraphrases (thus, for example, Orbe, 'El dilema', pp. 315-17).

18. He goes on to cite Isa. 1.19-20.

19. E.g. *Dialogue with Heracleides* 27.11.

20. 1 Kings 18.21 in this sense may be reflected by LXX Ben Sira 2.12 οὐαὶ. . . ἁμαρτωλῷ ἐπιβαίνοντι ἐπὶ δύο τρίβους.

21. τέθεικα is quite widely attested in quotations of the LXX form of this passage, e.g. Methodius, *de Resurrectione* 1.32.5; Clement of Alexandria, *Stromateis* 6.8.7 (but not 5.96.5); Origen, *Comm. Matt.* 15.23 (but not 12.33). τέθεικα is used a number of times in the LXX in a covenantal context. Similarly *Apoc. Bar.* 19.1 quotes Deut. 30.15 (+19) with *sāmet* (= *τέθεικα); cf. also *Or. Sib.* 8.399 προέθηκα.

22. The verb *sdr* is also found in the Syriac translation of Ben Sira 45.6(5), which probably has Deut. 30.19 in mind (LXX ἔδωκεν; Heb. *wyśm*).

23. Clement of Alexandria also has a subdivision into two ways, but these are ἔργα and γνῶσις (*Stromateis* 4.39.1, on which see J. Wytzes, 'The two-fold way: Platonic influences in the work of Clement of Alexandria', *Vigiliae Christianae* 11 [1957], pp. 226-45). At a greater remove are the 'paths' alongside the way in the Syriac *Liber Graduum*, ch. 19.

24. *Pace* H.W. Hollander and M. de Jonge, *The Testaments of the Twelve Patriarchs. A Commentary* (SVTP, 8), 1985, p. 343, who say, 'This passage does not suggest acquaintance with a "two ways catechism"'.

25. The same applies to the *Doctrina Apostolorum*; the two angels also feature in Hermas, *Mandates* VI.2.1. Outside 1QS the 'two spirits' are also found in *T. Judah* 20.1 and (by implication) in Philo, *Quaestiones in Exodum* 1.23, on which see M. Philonenko in *Hellenica et Judaica: Hommage à*

V. Nikiprowetsky, Leuven/Paris, 1986, pp. 61-68.

26. Even though LXX has ἔκλεξαι at Deut. 30.19. The choice of ἔλεσθε in *T. Levi* may be due to the influence of LXX Joshua 24.15 where that verb is used (ἐκλέξασθε in B derives from Theodotion: see L.J. Greenspoon, *Textual Studies in the Book of Joshua* [HSM, 28], 1983, p. 111). Note that Philo, *Quod Deus sit immutabilis* 50 (cited below) uses αἱρεῖσθαι in connection with Deut. 30.19.

27. The Law is identified as 'the way of life' by *Pseudo-Jonathan* at Deut. 30.19, but as the Tree of Life by *Neofiti* at Gen. 3.24 (in the latter passage neither *Neofiti* nor the *Fragment Targum* has anything corresponding to 'the way to' the Tree of Life; for a possible reason for this curious omission, see below).

28. There is some confusion in the text of Add. 27031 at the end of the verse, but the above follows the generally accepted understanding.

29. Taking the suffix to be 3rd sing., rather than 1st plur. (as in modern translations). Among the ancient versions all the Targumim (Palestinian, Babylonian and Samaritan) and Symmachus take it as 3rd sing.

30. Cf. Daniélou, *Études d'exégèse judéo-chrétienne*, p. 64.

31. Justin, *Apology* I, 44.1; compare also Tertullian, *de Castitate* 2.3, and *de Monogamia* 14.7.

32. Does *mtwth*, 'mortality', instead of *mwth*, 'death', in *FT* at Deut. 30.15 and in *N* at Deut. 30.19 deliberately imply a link with Gen. 2-3?

33. According to early Syriac exegesis it is the sword of Gen. 3.24, rather than the Law, which constitutes Paul's φραγμός (*syāgā* in Syriac) at Eph. 2.14; see, for example, Aphrahat, *Dem.* XIV.31; XXIII.3; Ephrem, *Comm. Gen.* II.7; *Liber Graduum* XV.2.

34. E.g. Ephrem, *H. de Nativitate* VIII.4, 'Blessed be the Merciful One / who saw the sword beside Paradise, / barring the way to the Tree of Life; / he came and took to himself a body / which was wounded so that / by the opening of his side / he might open up the way into Paradise'. The theme is very common, especially from the fourth century onwards; see R. Murray, 'The lance which reopened Paradise', *Orientalia Christiana Periodica* 39 (1973), pp. 224-34, 491.

35. *T. Levi* 18 is the sole reference given by P. Volz, *Jüdische Eschatologie von Daniel bis Akiba*, Tübingen/Leipzig, 1903, p. 377.

36. A. Hultgård, *L'eschatologie des Testaments des Douze Patriarches*, Stockholm, 1977, 1982, I, pp. 283-84; II, pp. 228-38. Hultgård's view is surprisingly followed by M. Alexandre in her richly documented 'L'épée de flamme (*Gen.* 3,24): textes chrétiens et traditions juives', in *Hellenica et judaica: Hommage à V. Nikiprowetzky*, Leuven/Paris, 1986, p. 422, note 95.

37. Thus *Acts of Thomas* 10 and 156 (two liturgical passages addressed to Christ), 'You trod out for the way from Sheol to the height'. Similarly Aphrahat, *Dem.* XII.8, and many passages in subsequent Syriac literature.

(Some examples are given by R. Murray, *Symbols of Church and Kingdom*, Cambridge, 1975, pp. 246-49, 299-301).

38. The same applies to the various references to the Two Ways in the Midrashim.

39. In this connection it is worth observing that *4 Ezra* 7.129 speaks of 'the way (sing.) which Moses spoke of', in connection with Deut. 30.19.

40. This development might also be implied by Ben Sira 15.17 ἔναντι ἀνθρώπων ἡ ζωὴ καὶ ὁ θάνατος.

41. So Murray, *Symbols of Church and Kingdom*, p. 299. (The Odes probably belong to the late second century, though the date is disputed.)

42. Thus, for example, P. Prigent, *Épître de Barnabé* (Sources chrétiennes, 172), 1971, p. 19, misleadingly speaks of 'voie de lumière et voie de ténèbres' in connection with 1QS; whereas the text has the plural (voies) in both cases.

43. Ephrem's reference to 'the two ways of darkness and of light' (*H. de Fide* XX.14) is intriguing, since he knew neither the *Doctrina* nor *Barnabas*.

44. *Pace* M. Delcor, *Le Testament d'Abraham* (SVTP, 2), 1973, pp. 133-34, this passage can hardly fail to be Christian (Matt. 7.13-14 is often thought to be based on the theme of the two ways).

45. For the two ways, see vol. I, pp. 461-63; cf. W. Michaelis in *TDNT*, V, pp. 58-59.

46. In his *Masoreten des Westens* II (BWANT, III.14).

47. Sources chrétiennes, 172 (*Barnabas*), 248 (*Didache*). Attention was drawn to the interest of the Palestinian Targum in this matter in the course of my review of R. Le Déaut's French translation of *N* and *PsJ* (Sources chrétiennes, 271), 1980 in *JTS* ns 34 (1983), pp. 617-18.

48. In *JJS* 31 (1980), pp. 1-17, esp. 5-6.

THE RABBINIC VIEW OF SCRIPTURE*

Arnold Goldberg

University of Frankfurt

In the context of the present topic I may be forgiven for summarily referring to the group of Jewish teachers of the first to the fifth centuries CE, who concerned themselves with interpreting the bible, as 'the Rabbis'. It is of course true that it is generally not warranted to designate them in this manner without further qualification or distinction. They approached the Bible in various ways and for a variety of purposes, be it to furnish guiding norms for the religious life, or to teach on God or the world. Yet, despite the variety of methods of interpretation, there was a broad consensus on how to arrive at interpretation and on what it means to accord to Scripture the status of revelation, and thus the treatment of the Rabbis as a collective seems permissible.

The investigation of the rabbinic view of Scripture is not identical with an examination of the ways and means of interpretation. The question is, rather: What was the object of rabbinic interpretation? What was Scripture itself in the view of the Rabbis? Here a distinction has to be made between Scripture's communication, that is, what the Rabbis understood as its contents and message on the one hand, and on the other, Scripture as a number of linguistic signs which prior to being interpreted are just signs. Our topic is the latter, namely that aspect of any piece of written communication which constitutes a basis of communication, a thing, and also an artefact.

'Holy Scripture', *Tanakh*, is, according to the Rabbis, of divine origin. It contains a communication from God to man. The sole content of this divine communication is what God has to say to man, or more precisely, to his people Israel. However, not only what the Prophets or Moses told the Israelites in their time constitutes this communication, but also what today is still said about that in Scripture.

To be sure, rabbinic exegesis does ask questions like: Who wrote down the books of the Prophets? But it asks so in a merely historical manner, in the sense of: When was the book written down, and by whom?[1] The book as it is present today is Scripture from God for man; it contains communications on something and this something (what it is about) has to be distinguished from what is being communicated. It is extremely important for the exegesis to keep Scripture as communication apart from the event which is being communicated. Exegesis can ask: What is the meaning of this word? What does the speaker mean by that expression? What perhaps may he give to understand? The second kind of question exegesis may pose concerns the norm or event conveyed in Scripture, for instance: What happened?

It is most remarkable that rabbinic exegesis does concentrate to a very large extent on the linguistic sign, not the event. It typically asks: What does this sign mean, that is, what does God or Scripture want to say by it? Only rarely do the Rabbis *comment*, for example by asking: Why did Moses do this or that? Rabbinic exegesis, viz. *Midrash*, is almost without exception meta-linguistic. It is discourse on the meaning of liguistic signs, it expresses what God wants to say with his word. Rabbinic interpretation seldom deals with the empirical world which is also contained in Scripture; rather, it makes the linguistic world of Scripture its world of experience.[2]

Scripture is therefore a communication of God to Israel, and as such divorced from the events reported in it. The reader of Scripture perceives that what is being said is that this or that event took place, but he also apprehends that he has no immediate access to that event. He has only access to a linguistic communication. This is the reason why the rabbinic exegete could never be a historian. The events naturally are important: Israel was indeed redeemed from Egypt. But there is only one reliable report on the events, and that is what God says about them in Scripture. A record by a contemporary and eye-witness, the kind of document a historian would wish to have, would be useless for the rabbinic reader of Scripture, for only God's Holy Writ is ultimately dependable. What is true with regard to the exodus is true for the world as a whole: reliable knowledge about the world can only be gained from what God says about it.

Scripture, then, is distinct from what it communicates. What is communicated are things past, while the communication as such is valid and present at any given time.

The historian, the hermeneut of our days, discriminates. He establishes that a document written in the distant past has a different meaning from a writing of today. There is no such distinction for the Rabbis. Moses spoke to his contemporaries in the situation of the desert journey, but God communicates this for the future. Scripture is present and being interpreted today. To the rabbinic exegete the idea that God would write it differently today is not acceptable.

As a consequence, Scripture loses its context. Moses spoke in the context of the exodus and the desert journey, or so it appears, according to the will of the author of the report. The reader or listener is integrated into this context of Moses' speech. God himself, however, communicates this without historical context. For in the view of the Rabbis Scripture is not a writing which was produced by God at a certain time for certain people, but a work which is true and valid without any contextual constraints. The events are historical, not the writing; despite being produced in time, it is independent of any particular time. Rabbinic interpretation of Scripture thus knows of no historical relativism. Though the event conveyed is an event in time, the communication about the event is free from all temporal limitations.

Obviously, such a view will cause considerable problems in the course of the passing of centuries or millennia. It is clear that the increase of knowledge about the world takes place without regard to the Torah. To solve this problem is the task of the exegetes. If historical relativism is not at their disposal, they have to fit the present to Scripture by way of interpretation, or we could say, re-interpretation. They have to give Scripture a meaning acceptable to their own times. This is where the concept of Scripture without context is of use. The exegete does not have to state what Scripture's meaning was at the time of its origin (and what it therefore could not mean today in the same manner anyway)—this is the historian's task. He has to say what it means today, and this is only possible if Scripture has no historical context. The exegete can say, 'This sign means today...', and proceed as if Scripture had been written just a moment ago—for God would write today as he wrote then. Scripture does not change, but its interpretation develops in the course of time. God without doubt knew this and wanted it this way. The interpretation is inherent in Scripture from the beginning, but the exegete understands Scripture's meaning in his own time. Thus, the present, at any given moment, forms the context of Scripture.

In this way Scripture is always synchronous with the exegete, and a projection of Scripture into the past cannot change its meaning. Scripture is also—and this has been observed repeatedly—synchronous with itself. The book *Bereshit* (Genesis) and the book Jeremiah share the same time dimension—just as they are given in Scripture simultaneously. Any part of Scripture can be linked with any other part, any sign related to any other sign. Since the signs are independent of any context, interpretation becomes inter-textual: Scripture is interpreted from Scripture, not from the world.

This opens the possibility to relate signs to each other after they have been isolated from their original contexts. The phenomenon of this atomistic approach of the Rabbis to Scripture has often been noticed. It allows the interpretation to concentrate on a single sign, from a grapheme upwards to the sentence or verse (but rarely beyond that) without regard to the surrounding text (co-text) and thus without taking notice of the overall sense. The rabbis do not produce commentaries which continuously interpret Scripture. Such commentaries, if one can call them that, emerge only in the process of redaction which lists the individual interpretations in the order of Scripture. The individual interpretation often pays no attention at all to the Scriptural co-text, the textual neighbourhood, in which the interpreted sign is found.

What then is the nature of Scripture, what kind of thing was it to the Rabbis? Clearly, written revelation is a sequence of linguistic signs in a written document. But what is a linguistic sign?

In order to answer this question one can collect statements from rabbinic literature dealing with essential aspects of their view of Scripture. At the same time, it is necessary to look at the practice of rabbinic exegesis to establish what the Rabbis took for a linguistic sign. Most of this is generally known and therefore rather trivial. However, it is not these facts that concern us here, but rather their consequences. The question is: What is the document which is the object of interpretation? I would like to concentrate as a first step on the five books of the Torah, for the rabbinic opinions on this topic are quite easy to make out.

The Rabbis were convinced of Moses' authorship of the five books to such a degree that it could be called a dogma. How his authorship came about in detail, whether God dictated the Torah to him and he wrote it down, whether the Holy Spirit rested on him, all may have been open to controversy. What is certain is that in the end Moses held a book, a scroll with writing, in his hand. It is to be presumed that Torah scrolls like the ones still in use today, were, in the view of the Rabbis, accurate copies of this original Scroll. If this is not accepted, it can be argued from the *halakhah*: All Scrolls are to be produced according to a common standard. The scroll, the ink, the distance between the words, the exact form of the signs, every single letter, all these things are prescribed, no doubt in fulfilment of divine command. God wants the Torah which is heard in the congregation and also interpreted by readers to have exactly this outward appearance. Torah then is, in contrast to all oral revelation (which is not our topic), a thing, an *artefact*, a product of hide or parchment and ink, and at the same time a product of certain signs and letters. This product has an exactly prescribed outward shape.

A very important first conclusion is given with this fact. Torah is not speech which happens to be written down (as one could be led to believe by the frequent 'thus spoke *'Adonai*'), but is—regardless of how the product was brought about in the beginning—essentially a written thing, a piece of writing. It would be simply speech recorded in writing only if God had dictated Moses the text, and Moses had written it down in his usual handwriting, according to the rules to which he, Moses, adhered—but this is not the case. The difference between speech written down and a piece of writing which is the result of an act of writing seems *prima facie* to be very small, the distinction even far-fetched. But it is of prime importance for our topic. In the case of a speech written down the act of speaking precedes the act of writing: a spoken word is being recorded by means of a system of graphic signs. If, however, God himself, or he by the hand of Moses, did the writing, the product is the result of an act of writing, and the corresponding act of reception is not hearing or listening to the speech of God (or to someone who reads what God has spoken), but seeing or reading. The product, Scripture, is above all perceived with the eyes.

What is at stake here is the oral or literary nature of the text. If God had said to Moses 'exactly like this speak to the children of Israel' and Moses had written this text down, then he would have had to memorize it just 'like this': with all the dynamics of voice, intonation of questions, pauses between parts of speech. The text would have remained oral and the taking it down in writing would only have produced a subservient record. Torah would have had to be transmitted orally and remain oral, for just how it was right could only have been learned from the mouth of the expert. But since

Torah is in writing, all that is required for a written work to
constitute a text must be done by the reader himself. He has to find
out how a sign is to be read and what its significance beyond the
phoneme might be.

The primacy of writing, however, gives rise to a dilemma, for the
text should also be read aloud and heard. This dilemma finds its
apparent solution in *Qerê* and *Ketîv*, the text 'as read' and the text 'as
written'. It is likely that in the times of the Rabbis there already
existed a tradition of how to read the text of the Torah and the other
writings, viz. a *Masora*—of course not necessarily the one known to
us from a later age. It follows that the text as read aloud was
prescribed. This is true in particular for the public delivery of
Scripture in the synagogue. The sound of the signs was therefore
already determined—necessarily in accordance with the divine
will.

But the *Qerê*'s force is restricted to the oral delivery or any
enunciation of Scripture. It does not cancel the force of the *Ketîv*, as
if, since this is the way it has to be pronounced, the result of a
different way to read it is excluded. If that were the case, the *Ketîv*
would only be an obsolete orthography safeguarding the text against
modification. It would mean that the *Ketîv* had no significant
function and a whole range of graphic signs would be superfluous,
just as one would have to say that a number of graphic signs was
lacking (namely the graphemes of the words spelled defectively). But
this is hardly acceptable for a text of revelation. Rabbinic exegesis
indeed assumes the *Qerê* as the received and intended text, i.e. the
Qerê is always correct.[3] But exegesis takes account of the *Ketîv* as
well. The *Ketîv*, too, has significance, and the exegetes do ask, for
example, why a word is spelled *plene* or defectively, or why once *plene*
and at other times defectively.[4] One answer to this question is of course
inadmissible, namely that the orthography is arbitrary and both
spellings are equally possible. The real answer is that God communicates
something by *Ketîv* as well as by *Qerê*. This *Ketîv* does not only give
a number of readings that differ from the *Qerê*, but they cannot even
be pronounced.

Establishing the fact that revelation is originally and primarily
writing is absolutely essential, in that this written nature implies the
correspondent performance of reading. Not only what can be heard,
but also what can be seen is significant and meaningful. The views of
the Rabbis on this will now briefly be documented by collecting some
of the statements on Scripture in rabbinic writings.

In general the following assumptions hold true: Revelation is a text in human natural language (this may have to be modified later on), its author being a perfectly competent speaker. This means that there are no linguistic defects to be found in the text—each sign is absolutely meaningful. The controversy between Ishmael and Akiva about the question whether Scripture speaks in the way of human language or not is well known. Thus Rabbi Ishmael views the doubling of verbs (in the infinitive absolute construction) as following man's usage, which is also binding for God, while R. Akiva takes it to be a doubling of meaning. R. Akiva's opinion seems to have prevailed. His position implies already what later became generally accepted, namely that there is no redundancy in Scripture, i.e. no superfluous or meaningless linguistic signs. Accordingly, signs which have probably merely syntactical function such as the accusative particle *'et* (*nota accusativi*), became the object of interpretation. It may be noted in passing that it is quite possible to find linguistic arguments in favour of some aspects of this position. The prohibition of redundancy, as this maxim could be called, has consequences for the *halakhic* mode of interpretation as well. It stipulates that two verses of Scripture which have the same or a very similar wording cannot really contain the same norm. God says many things in one word, but he never says anything twice—two sentences, even two words must therefore have two different meanings.[5] Furthermore, there are no synonyms in Scripture. This is generally true, and applies to the text as enunciated as well as to the written text. It is possible to extend the redundancy prohibition to graphic signs. While it is true that there are no explicit statements in rabbinic literature to the effect that graphic signs cannot be redundant (that God does not write anything superfluous or meaningless), one finds support for this suggestion in the actual rabbinic practice of interpreting graphic signs. First, I would like to draw attention to the interpretation of *haseroth* and *yeteroth*, *plene* or defective spelling. Phonetically it is irrelevant whether a word is spelled one way or the other; the pronunciation is safeguarded by the *Masora*. But for exegetical purposes it is assumed that *plene* spelling points to fullness or means increase, whereas defective spelling implies decrease. For example, the proper name Ephron is spelled *plene* in the whole of Genesis 32, except for verse 16. By this is expressed—according to the exegete—that God has diminished the name of Ephron, because he was envious and mean.[6]

Secondly, mention must be made of the changed readings, the *šinnuyîm*. The unvocalized text may for instance admit different readings. While the *Masora* safeguards a constant, unambiguous reading, we have already seen that, for the purposes of interpretation, the *Qerê* can be suspended. The reading may then vary and it is permissible to assume a different vocalization. For example, Isa. 40.1, *naḥᵃmû naḥᵃmû 'ammî*—'comfort, comfort my people', may also be read as *naḥᵃmû 'immî*, 'comfort with me'.[7] But in *al tiqre* interpretations not only vocalizations may be changed, but even changes of the consonantal spelling are allowed. They illustrate that even graphemes whose pronunciation is unambiguous can be modified in their reading, thus e.g. *sin* and *samekh* can be exchanged. The justification of this procedure is that in Scripture itself different graphemes can be found to represent the same phoneme, resulting in the occurrence of one and the same sign with different consonants.[8]

The original validity of the sign and its meaning are by no means cancelled by such procedures. 'Comfort, comfort my people' remains just as valid as 'comfort with me'. As a rule the newly generated readings and meanings are additional, not exclusive. 'Comfort, comfort my people' may be explained as 'comfort my people with me'.

Consequently, the question whether, historically speaking, the prophet said 'my people' or 'with me', i.e. *'ammî* or *'immî* cannot be posed this way. Rather it is to be asked: Did God write that the prophet said *'ammî*, or did he write that the prophet said *'immî*? The answer then must be: God has written in such a way as to admit both readings, therefore he intended that it should be read either way. The non-ambiguity of oral speech is not lost in writing because of any deficiency of Scripture (God could have written down the vocalization), but because he communicates different things by way of the ambiguities.

The particular rabbinic procedures are well-known. I shall only add a mention of the *notarikon* operation which alters the sign completely: each syllable or letter stands for a different word, and the new signs share with the sign as found in Scripture merely one grapheme or phoneme each. Moreover, in *gematria* signs can be related to numerical values and exchanged with other signs of identical numerical values. Even the shape of graphic signs can be taken to be invested with meaning. Torah begins with the letter *beth*, which is closed to three sides, in order to teach that it must not be asked what is before the world, what is above the heavens, and what is below the earth.[9]

Of course, the interpretation of graphic signs is not the only way to read and interpret Scripture. A reading of the text of Scripture yields in the first instance its ordinary meaning: Genesis is a creation story and a tale about the patriarchs. The exegesis of the Rabbis does not stop at this aspect of the reading performance, which in the process of oral delivery or reading produces just such a literary text. Rabbinic exegesis goes on to interpret. It does so, however, not by taking the text in its unity of contents, in which case the result could be a new, quasi-biblical book, but always by focussing exclusively on the individual signs in isolation.

The signs of Scripture continually acquire meanings in the course of interpretation. This has consequences for all areas of life, affecting everything from norms of behaviour to historical narration and statements on the divine order of the world. To be sure, some exegetical procedures are excluded from the realm of *halakhah*, but this does not impede the generation of new meanings everywhere. Even if they are not created by uniform means, their starting point is always the written text as a linguistic entity and the interpretation of signs. This important point is well worth repeating: New meanings are not created by speculation on what God or Moses might have meant, or what might follow from what God said, but always through the exploration of signs. New propositions (or insights) are arrived at (in *Midrash* at least) exclusively by way of interpretation. As a rule, exegesis says, 'This sign means . . .'; and since the sign is part of divine Scripture, its meaning must be true—if it has been correctly interpreted.

In the historical reality of the situation of the Rabbis, the truth of interpretation surely depended in the last instance on its acceptance by the community or at least part of the community. But truth, that is the correctness of any interpretation, is not something which is established by authoritarian imposition. Rabbinic exegesis is principally discursive, ever ready to justify a claim through reasoned argumentation. The truth of any interpretation therefore rests in its justifiability.

For the examination of the function of Scripture in exegesis it is quite irrelevant why Scripture was interpreted in the rabbinic literature like this. Nothing is said about the style of exegesis if one states that Scripture has to go on answering new practical questions, posed by changing circumstances of life, even after being considered complete; and that the means of arriving at these answers is interpretation. It is an empirical fact that the completion of a canonical text leads to the creation of a series of new texts on the significance of the canonical one, for after canonization the Holy Text cannot be continued according to the needs of the society for which it is in force. This, however, only explains *why* Scripture was interpreted, not why in this particular way. As a matter of course an interpretation was needed. Once prophecy and verbal revelation as well as pseudepigraphic continuation of the writings of Scripture as exemplified in the apocalyptic literature or the Temple Scroll from Qumran was rejected (there had been a decision, for whatever reasons, to regard revelation as completed and terminated), one was left with Scripture alone. As for the kind of interpretation, however, there were a number of possibilities. For reasons unknown to us rabbinic exegesis opted for this, its peculiar method: it conceives of and uses Scripture as a graphic basis of communication; this is the precise nature of Scripture in the exegetical practice of the Rabbis, even though the term was of course unknown to them. Scripture is, to start with, nothing but a series of graphic signs. These signs have to be interpreted, at least read and perceived, before a communication can be erected on this basis of communication. Only through interpretation of the graphic signs can the communication, God's message, which is found in Scripture, be construed. In contrast to other actually occurring or conceivable kinds of exegesis the graphic sign is taken to be the thing communicated by God and interpretation acts upon this graphic sign. Exegesis thus is not just merely meta-linguistic, but also meta-graphical, since it first interprets the graphic sign and then also the linguistic sign constructed from the graphic sign.

Meanwhile the numerical quantity of graphic signs apparently remains the same: not a *Yod* of Scripture must be changed: a Torah Scroll with even minor scribal flaws is unfit. Certainly the shape of the letters, their sequence and number are also immutable. But in reality the number of linguistic signs grows continuously, for new linguistic signs are found in the course of time; more and more things in Scripture become signs. This leads to a constant expansion of what Scripture says. I should stress: of what Scripture itself says.

At this junction the question concerning the nature of the canon as posed by Jacob Neusner[10] has to be asked. If the meaning of

Scripture, i.e. what Scripture says, is increasing continuously, then the term canon cannot be applied to it. Neusner does not at all question the fact that the Rabbis made a clear distinction between the text as found in the Torah Scroll and what they said about the meaning of that text. But with the Rabbis what they say about Scripture ranks as high if not higher than what is actually written in the Torah Scroll. Neusner's question or proposition may seem far-fetched: The difference between the canonical text as written in the books of the Bible and that which is said about that text in, for example, the rabbinical *Midrash* seems obvious. But I think it is quite wrong to dismiss Neusner's statement out of hand, just because it is surprising. The question concerning the canon is legitimate. But it has to be posed somewhat differently and Scripture itself has to be integrated into the framing of the question which Neusner, as far as I can see, does not do.

Let us therefore re-phrase the question in the following way: What exactly is it that the Rabis canonized? We have to leave aside the whole complicated and unsolved problem of when the canon was decided upon and what it included. It will do to assume that at a time around the beginning of the second century CE a final decision was taken: these are the books from God (whatever the precise channel of revelation) and shall from now on be the canon of Holy Scripture; more precisely, they shall be what we today call a canon, for the word was unknown to the Rabbis. They have canonized a text which consists, according to the perhaps more recent *Masora*, of a sequence of sounds, if enunciated (this being the *Qerê*), and which can be understood, e.g. in the case of the book *Bereshit*, as a creation and a tale of patriarchs in such and such a way. This 'such and such' is by no means unambiguous, but only approximate. Certainly one has to read the first two words, for example, as *bᵉrē'šît bārā'*. What this means is not at all clear. Does *bᵉrē'šît* mean 'in the beginning'? And what kind of beginning is this? What kind of creating is this? What then was canonized by the Rabbis? The answer must be that a sequence of graphic signs was canonized, and this in two respects: (a) as a maximally exact sequence of graphic scriptural signs which was assumed to be of divine origin in precisely this form; and (b) as a pronunciation directive for the conversion of graphic signs into phonemic signs. One thus knows which words, which graphic or phonemic signs, belong to this canon. One knows what kind of text is constituted by transforming the signs into language in the process of reading. The meaning of the signs, on the other hand, is always open, for otherwise there could have been no controversies among particular groups as to how to understand Scripture. It was thus a certain quantity of signs which was canonized, which corresponds to a continuously growing and at the same time changing quantity of meanings. Indeed, the meaning of the signs could never be limited by a canon. In other words: It was not the communication that was canonized, but the basis of communication. Neusner's position confuses this basis, the continuum of signs, with the store of meanings. The Rabbis made a careful distinction here; they did not tamper with the Torah Scroll. On the contrary, they saw to it that it was copied as meticulously as possible, and just this, or so it seems to me, is the 'canonized text'. They wrote the meaning of this text in separate books or in the margin of manuscripts or elsewhere, but never into the basis of communication itself. What a modified basis of communication would look like can be seen in the *Temple Scroll* or the book of *Jubilees*.

At this point note should be taken of a peculiarity of rabbinic exegesis. As a rule the attempt is made to render a canonical text unambiguous through interpretation, i.e. to create monosemy. Rabbinic exegesis takes the opposite route: while it carefully preserves the graphic signs, it steadily acquires more meanings. The word $b^e r\bar{e}'\check{s}\hat{\imath}t$ at the beginning of the Bible does not become unambiguous in the process of exegesis, but accrues continuously additional imports. Polysemy in Scripture is, as we have seen, intended. By contrast, what is said about the meaning of Scripture in exegesis is unambiguous.

We may now try to determine what Scripture is in the view of the rabbinical exegetes. It is an exactly determined quantity of graphic signs. The artefact 'Scripture' answers to a precise description and cannot be changed. To this pre-determined and finite number of graphic signs corresponds a still open quantity of linguistic signs. The quantity of linguistic signs grows in the process of interpretation, for constantly new things are discovered to be linguistic signs. This identification of new carriers of meaning may take place on the level of the mere graphic sign (it is always possible to understand something else in Scripture as meaningful), or on the other levels up to the sentence and the pericope. The number of meanings is continually increasing without any effect on Scripture as artefact.

In the process of rabbinic exegesis the quantity of scriptural signs becomes a world of signs, or so one could understand it. For the signs of Scripture are interpreted in essentially the same way as the signs of the empirical world, namely with the help of a system of rules which change in time—one only has to compare the manner of early rabbinic interpretations with that of the *Zohar*, for example. In the interpretation of these signs a world is created, just as a world is constructed in the interpretation of empirical phenomena. However, the world given by the continuum of signs of Scripture is a purely linguistic world; they are signs of language (not of nature) and interpreting them is in the first instance always exegesis of linguistic signs.

This seems to me to be the characteristic and perhaps unique trait of rabbinic Scriptural exegesis, that it constructs from the artefact, the Torah Scroll, first a world of linguistic experience and then, through this linguistic world, the world in which the exegete as well as the pious Jew are at home.

There was in the age of the Rabbis no empirical and no scientific world besides this linguistic world of experience, constructed from the signs of the artefact 'Holy Scripture', which could lay a rival claim to truth. To be sure, there was the experience of the sun's setting and rise; the signs of the empirical world did have their validity. But the sun which goes down and rises is identical with the sun of which Scripture speaks. The empirical world and the world of Scripture could be and indeed had to be one; they did not diverge. The empirical world was checked against the world of Scripture, just as we today check our everyday world against and interpret it according to the world of scientific models. This world of Scripture was the communication which emerged from the continuous exegesis of the graphic basis of communication which is 'Scripture'.

In brief, the following conclusions may de drawn from the foregoing discussion: The Scriptural canon of the rabbinic exegetes is a graphic basis of communication of divine origin consisting of a quantity of signs whose form and number cannot be changed. These graphic signs are understood as linguistic signs, with the number of linguistic signs constantly growing in the course of continuous exegesis. The linguistic signs which are established in the pronunciation of the text, viz. the *Qerê*, are only a part of the total number of the meaningful and the canonized signs. The canonized text of the Rabbis is not just the audible *Qerê*, but also the graphic *Ketîv*.

In the interpretation of these signs a linguistic communication is constructed which is without context, i.e. permanently valid, communicated by its producer God to each new reader and exegete. This communication in turn serves to interpret and order the world of experience in a rational way.

These characteristics should provide the starting point for any attempt to compare rabbinic Scriptural interpretation with other types of exegesis.

NOTES

*The original version of this paper was delivered as a presidential address at the 3rd Conference of the *EAJS*, Berlin 1987. The German text appeared in *Frankfurter Judaistische Beiträge* 15 (1987), pp. 1-15. It has been translated by Alexander Samely, John Rylands Research Institute, Manchester.

1. Cf., for example, *b. Baba Bathra* 14b.
2. Cf. A. Goldberg, 'Die funktionale Form Midrasch', *Frankfurter Judaistische Beiträge* 10 (1982), pp. 29 and 38f.
3. Cf. *b. Sanh.* יש אם למקרא but also יש אם למסורת.
4. A collection of such interpretation can be found in the Midrash *Haserot Wiyeterot (Bate Midrash*, Vol. II, pp. 202-332).
5. *B. Sanh.* 34b.
6. *Gen. R.* 58-7 (627).
7. *Pesiqta Rabbati* 29/30-11; see B.A.A. Kern, *Tröstet, tröstet mein Volk!... (Pes. R. 30 und 29/30)* [=*Frankfurter Judaistische Studien*, Vol. 7], Frankfurt a.M., 1986, p. 493.
8. S. Waldberg, *Sefer darke ha-shinuyim*, Jerusalem, 1970.
9. *Gen. R.* 1-10 (8).
10. Jacob Neusner, *Midrash in Context, Exegesis in Formative Judaism*, Philadelphia, 1983, pp. 135-37.

BEN SIRA 42.9-10 AND ITS TALMUDIC PARAPHRASE*

Jonas C. Greenfield

The Hebrew University
Jerusalem

Ben Sira's views about women are well known and have been discussed often. His words may be taken either as a reflection of his times or as his personal views expressed with vigor and vehemence.[1] His anxiety over the behavior of daughters is first stated in 7.24-27; this is taken up again in 22.3-5 and culminates in a diatribe against the daughter as a constant source of worry for her father (42.9-14).[2] A paraphrase of 42.9-10 is found in the Babylonian Talmud, *Sanhedrin* 100b.

The Talmud and other parts of rabbinic literature provide an important early source for the Ben Sira tradition. Rabbi Sa'adya Gaon (d. 942) had a pointed text of Ben Sira,[4] from which he quoted, and the medieval *Alpha Beta deBen Sira* also preserved some authentic Ben Sira material in Aramaic translation.[5] The potential value of these texts can be seen in particular in the examination of a text such as Ben Sira 3.21-22. There are two divergent Geniza Texts (A,C), the Greek and Syriac translations, and four differing rabbinic texts: *y. Ḥagigah* 2.1. 77c; *b. Ḥagigah* 13a; *Gen. R.* 88; Sa'adya Gaon. Comparison of these texts is an enlightening exercise in textual transmission.

The longest section dealing with Ben Sira in the Talmud is in the aforementioned *b. Sanhedrin* 100b, in which the question of the moral value of reading Ben Sira is raised. Some of the texts quoted there occur in Ben Sira wholly or partially, while some are not known at all. It is here that the Talmudic parallel to Ben Sira 42.9-10 is quoted.

This reads[6]

בת לאביה מטמונת שוא מפחדה לא יישן
בקטנותה שמא תתפתה
בנערותה שמא תזנה
בגרה שמא לא תנשא
נשאת שמא לא יהיו לה בנים
הזקינה שמא תעשה כשפים

and may be translated:

> A daughter is a false treasure to her father—
> for fear over her he does not sleep;
> while a child lest she be seduced,
> in her youth, lest she play the whore;
> when she matures lest she not be married,
> when she marries lest she have no children;
> when she grows old lest she practice sorcery.

A comparison of this text with almost any modern translation of Ben Sira proper will show that, in distinction to most other identifiable Ben Sira texts in rabbinic literature, this was clearly a remade text. That is, the elements of the text of Ben Sira were known but they have been rearranged following a clear pattern.

The early publication of the Ben Sira text from Masada has allowed scholars to study development and divergence.[7] For the Hebrew text we have essentially three versions—Masada (M), a *genizah* text, part of ms. B (B) and marginal notes to B (B Marg).[8] There is also the Greek translation, made by Ben Sira's grandson from a Hebrew version that diverged from these, and also a Syriac translation that also used a different, and often shorter Hebrew text. Before dealing with the Talmudic text I wish to present a rationalized version of the Masada text using the insights of various scholars who have contributed to its study.[9]

9a-b נומה יד[תפר]ראגה   שק[ר]מטמון לאב ב[ת] Yadin records a *šin* as the first letter, but this must best be taken as a scribal error for a *bet* corrected, albeit in a clumsy manner.[10] For מטמון which is found also in B Marg, both B and T have the later(?) form מטמנת.[11] B also reads שקר, which is supported by G's *agrupnia* 'sleeplessness', commonly accepted to be based on שקד, as in 34.1, which in this verse is a misreading of שקר. T. substitutes שוא for שקר.[12]

ראגה 'worry', so B, with B Marg's ראגתה making the subject more explicit. תפריד נומה: this restoration, rather than תניד נומה,[13] is based on combining יר...נומה of M and תפ... of B; it matches the widespread use of פרד with words for sleep in the various Aramaic dialects and in late Hebrew.[14]

9c-d בנעוריה פן [ת]מאם   צ[בל]ה פן ת[שנ]ה

The reading of the first hemistich is clear: a word like תמאם could stand behind G's *parakmasē*, and S's *tištaḥē*.[15] The choice of word may have been influenced by the use of מאם in Isa. 54.6. B's תגור is usually explained by Aramaic גור 'to commit adultery'; this is reflected in T's בנעוריה פן תזנה. Yet, in Jewish usage גור should properly be used of a married woman, not the unmarried girl predicated by this passage. Perhaps, גור means simply 'lest she dwell', i.e. in her father's house and not be married. M presents no such problems.

וּבְעָלָה, accepting Strugnell's reading with a slight modification.[16] As he noted, G reads here *kai sunōkēkuia* which is ובעולה. S's *wĕmen ba'lāh* points in the same direction. As has long since been noted, B's ובבתוליה is out of place here, and surely lifted from the following line. The final word of this line may best be restored תשנה for תשנא.[17]

10 a-b בבתוליה פן תחל   ועל אישה [פן] תשטה

There is no problem with the reading of this line. The verb תחל matches, and was surely influenced by, כי תחל לזנות of Lev. 21.9, with the same Greek verb *bebēlōthē* in the LXX of Lev. 21.9 and G here. S's *titparsē* 'will be disclosed, brought into ill repute' is an interpretive translation. The תפותה of B and תתפתה of B Marg and T replaces a recondite word with a familiar one. תשטה is undoubtedly the original reading and is attested to by G's *parabē* which also translates תשטה in Num. 5.12. The *tešṭe* of S means something different than Heb. תשטה but serves as a witness to the text.[18] Of B there is little more left here than ובבית. From B Marg one can restore ובבית בעלה לא תנשה but the translation of תנשה as 'will be forgotten' is difficult in context. It may be proposed that the original reading in the source of B Marg was תשנה. The meaning of B Marg would then be 'and that she does not commit adultery in her husband's house'.[19]

10 c-d [ר]צ [תע] פן ובעלה   תזריע פן אביה בית

The first hemistich is not problematic, and as has been noted it matches the Greek text.[20] The verb תזריע is a *hapax* in Biblical Hebrew (Lev. 12.2) but the verb used in the LXX is different than that used by G.[21] The B text can be restored to match M [ת]בית אביה פן זריע. The second hemistich may be restored [ובע]לה and read ובְעָלֵה with Strugnell or one may assume that the בית of the first hemistich is to serve this word too, i.e. בית בעלה. The restoration of the last word, proposed by Yadin, agrees with the remnants of B צר[תע] and B Marg תעצר. This would match G's *steirōsē*. The putative בעלה [ובבית] is matched by ובבית אישה in B and B Marg.

The following translation, avoiding literary pretense, is offered for the reconstructed Masada text:

> 9. A daughter is a false treasure for (her) father,
>   and worry over her drives away sleep—
> lest in her youth she be rejected,
>   and when married lest she be hated;
> 10. while unmarried, lest she be defiled,
>   and lest she prove unfaithful to her husband;
> lest she becomes pregnant while in her father's house,
>   and lest she be barren when married.

Before turning to the Talmudic version two pertinent remarks are in order. The first remark deals with the structure of the text and has been noted by others. After the introductory lines 9a-b the six hemistichs that make up this section can be divided into two complementary sections. Section A consists of lines 9c, 10a and 10c and Section B consists of 9d, 10b and 10d; Section A deals with the daughter's pre-marital state, and Section B with her married state.[22] The second remark is that these lines show, in the M text a great dependency on pentateuchal vocabulary: תחל, בעולה, תמאס, מטמון, נעוריה, בית אביה, תעצר, תזריע, תשטה. Many of these words had by Ben Sira's days lost their early meaning or gone out of use entirely. The writer depended on his audience's knowledge of Biblical verse, or incorporated an earlier bit of wisdom as the introduction to his own harangue (vv. 11-14).

A comparison of the lines discussed above with those of the Talmudic paraphrase shows that a different compositional principle is at work. Indeed, one may argue that a text closer to B was available to the Rabbis, but the compositional principle behind B is the same as that of M.[23] There is no longer a contrast between the two states noted above, unmarried and married, but rather a progression of ages: הזקינה, נישאת, בגרה, נערות, קטנות. This matches בוגרת, נערה, קטנה, זקנה, נשואה. Four of these are definite halakhic stages. The קטנה is a child younger than twelve, the נערה is limited to the age of twelve to twelve and a half, the בוגרת is older than twelve and a half, and has presumedly reached puberty. The נשואה is the married woman, without implication of age, while the זקנה, if the age sixty used of the male is also true for the female, is a woman who would not be normally involved in sexual activity. But if menopause is the criterion, then the age would be lower, and would be an individual matter. The term כשפים is used in the broad sense of magic and, as is well known, women, and especially older women, were frequently accused of being witches in the ancient Near East and the classical world, as well as in various modern societies. In its own right זקנה is not a halakhic category, but the death penalty was due witches (Exod. 22.17) and the father had good cause to worry.

I do not believe that the other quotations from Ben Sira extant in rabbinic literature lend themselves to this sort of analysis but there is no doubt that the student of Ben Sira must take them seriously.[24]

NOTES

* This paper has its origins in a seminar in Oxford led by Sebastian Brock and Geza Vermes during Trinity term, 1987.

1. The most recent work on the subject is W.C. Trenchard, *Ben Sira's View of Women: A Literary Analysis*, Chico, 1982, which has been critically reviewed by A.A. Di Lella in *CBQ* 46 (1984), pp. 332-34 and C. Meyers, *BSOAS* 47 (1984), pp. 339-40.

2. I agree with Smend, and most recently Di Lella, that 26.10-12 deals with a wife and not a daughter. See Patrick W. Skehan and A.A. Di Lella,*The Wisdom of Ben Sira*, New York, 1987, pp. 346-50.

3. They were first gathered by A.E. Cowley and A. Neubauer in *The Original Hebrew of a Portion of Ecclesiasticus*, Oxford, 1897. The subject has been dealt with extensively by M.H. Segal, *The Complete Book of Ben Sira* [Hebrew], 2nd edition, Jerusalem, 1958, pp. 38-44, 66-68.

4. See the detailed discussion by Segal in *Sefer Rab Sa'adya Ga'on*, Jerusalem, 1943, pp. 98-118.

5. See the excellent edition of Eli Yasif in his *The Tales of Ben Sira in the Middle Ages* [Hebrew], Jerusalem, 1984, pp. 261-83.

6. I am indebted to Dr Chaim Milikowsky who checked the manuscript

readings of this Talmudic passage for me; they were remarkably without variants.

7. Y. Yadin, *The Ben Sira Scroll from Masada*, Jerusalem, 1965, pp. 24–25.

8. B and B Marg are in Cowley-Neubauer (above, n. 3). They are also readily available in *The Book of Ben Sira, Text, Concordance and an Analysis of the Vocabulary* [Hebrew], Jerusalem, 1973, p. 48.

9. J. Strugnell, 'Notes and Queries on the Ben Sira Scroll from Masada', *EI* 9 (1969), pp. 109-19, esp. 115b; S. Lieberman, 'Forgotten Meanings', *Leshonenu* 32 (1968), p. 92 [Hebrew]; J. Baumgarten, 'Some Notes on the Ben Sira Scroll from Masada', *JQR* (ns) 57 (1966-67), pp. 323-27; M. Kister, 'In the Margin of Ben Sira', *Leshonenu* 47 (1983), pp. 125-46, esp. 145-46 [Hebrew], as well as the commentary of Skehan—Di Lella (above, n. 2) and G. Sauer, Gütersloh, 1981.

10. Yadin, p. 24, col. a. The 'possible *he*' that he detected after the putative *šin* was probably part of the *taw*.

11. In Mishnaic Hebrew, beside the מטמונה of the Ben Sira quotation, the plural מטמוניות is found. This may be the plural of מַטְמֹנֶת as well as מַטְמֹנִית.

12. In 34.1 B has שקר and B Marg שקד. G's *agrupnia* and context support שקד as the correct reading there, but there can be no doubt that שקר is the correct reading here. See too M. Kister (above, n. 9), p. 145 n. 10. It is indeed surprising that adherence to the reading of G may be found in Skehan-Di Lella: 'A daughter is a treasure that keeps her father awake' (which is virtually the same as the New American Bible). But how is one to explain such curious translations as 'keeps her father secretly wakeful' (RSV), 'is a secret anxiety' (NEB), 'Unknown to her, a daughter keeps her father awake' (Jerusalem Bible), and the like in some other modern attempts? Hebrew is not a cryptic tongue.

13. The restoration תניד נומה was proposed by J. Baumgarten, *JQR* (ns) 57 (1966-67), p. 326, and by P.W. Skehan, *JBL* 75 (1966), p. 260.

14. For this idiom see H. Yalon, *Quntresim* I, Jerusalem, 1938, p. 7, and M. Kister (above, n. 9), p. 145 n. 10.

15. The verb *parakmazein* means 'to be past the prime'; its occurrence is unique here in the Greek version of the Bible. Syriac *tištaḥē* is 'will be reviled, accused of sin' and, unless a different Hebrew text is assumed, this is an interpretive translation.

16. Strugnell, p.115b, has suggested וּבְבְעָלֶיהָ for וּבְעָלֶיהָ* and has translated this as 'when she is married', but a noun בְעוּלִים is not known in either Biblical or Mishnaic Hebrew, and is not a likely form. I am also not convinced that the letter before the last is a *yod*.

17. Strugnell doubts the reading of the final *he*, but his suggested תעצ[ר] is not satisfactory at this point. S. Lieberman, *Leshonenu* 32 (1968), p. 92, has proposed reading תשנה here with the meaning 'to be unfaithful, commit

adultery', but 'will be hated' better fills the needs of the context. Note too that מאס and שנא occur together in Amos 5.21. See also Kister (above, n. 9), p. 143 n. 90. Lieberman refers to his remarks in *Hellenism in Jewish Palestine*, New York, 1950, pp. 49f.; see also H. Yalon, *Megillot Midbar Yehudah*, Jerusalem, 1967, pp. 104-105; *Pirqē Lašon*, Jerusalem, 1971, pp. 151-54.

18. Syriac *šēṭā*, although meaning basically 'to commit folly', is used especially of conjugal infidelity, as noted by Payne-Smith.

19. Applying Lieberman's suggestion concerning תשנה (above, n. 17) to this line.

20. Note that in G 10c comes before 10b.

21. Note that B Marg reads פחזה 'she has fornicated'. I have dealt with פחז in *Studies in the Bible and the Ancient Near East presented to S.E. Loewenstamm*, Jerusalem, 1978, pp. 35-40. Could B have read תזנה? Syriac peters out here, but *wĕtezal bāṭar gabrā ḥrenā* could reflect ותזנה, the lone remnant of this line before the Syriac translator.

22. It is difficult to know why the Greek text has the order 10a-10c, 10b-10d, unless one assumes that the order was unmarried-married in this verse.

23. Kister has proposed (above, n. 9), p. 146, that the text available to the Talmudic paraphraser followed the order of the Greek, but this is not convincing.

24. This article was completed before I was able to consult Milward D. Nelson, *The Syriac Version of the Wisdom of Ben Sira Compared to the Greek and Hebrew Materials*, Atlanta, 1988.

JACOB'S SECOND VISIT TO BETHEL
IN TARGUM PSEUDO-JONATHAN

C.T.R. Hayward

University of Durham

The contribution which Geza Vermes has made to the study of the Aramaic Targumim needs no documentation. Indeed, he has been intimately associated with the revival of scholarly interest in these texts which began over forty years ago, and which shows few signs of losing its impetus. In considering the relationships of the various Pentateuchal Targumim to one another, Vermes has for long suggested the possibility that *Ps-Jon.*, either in its present or some earlier form, constitutes the basis of Targum Onqelos: *Ps-Jon.* would thus, in essence, preserve material of great antiquity, even though its final redaction took place in the Islamic period. In recent years, however, it has become fashionable amongst students of the Targumim to regard *Ps-Jon.* as a late, literary composition, produced in the Islamic period as an anti-Islamic polemic. It is seen as depending on the Palestinian Targumim and late midrashic collections like the *Pirqe deRabbi Eliezer* (*PRE*) for much of its exegetical paraphrase, its language having been modified under the influence of the 'official' and authoritative Targum Onqelos.[1]

In two articles which have been be published elsewhere, we have argued that the case for a post-Islamic date for *Ps-Jon.* rests on very shaky foundations, and that the simple dependence of *Ps-Jon.* on late works like *PRE* is open to question.[2] In this essay we shall attempt a different kind of exercise, undertaking an analysis of a chapter in which the Targum's exegesis is, in places, very much *sui generis*. *Ps-Jon.* Gen. 35.1-15 has no points of contact with *PRE*, and Islam is nowhere in view. Even though this is the case, certain features in the text might seem, superficially, to indicate a late date. Whether such a view may be sustained can only be determined by careful comparison of *Ps-Jon.* with the other Targumim of Gen. 35 and with other interpretations of the chapter. We shall attempt to relate *Ps-Jon.*'s exegesis to that found in other sources, seeking, wherever possible, to uncover its particular purpose. Only then will the character of the Targum of this chapter begin to emerge, and some possible hints as to its relative dating.

We begin with a close investigation of those verses which show significant addition to, and alterations of, the Hebrew original, which we indicate in our translations by the use of italics.

Verse 2

> And Jacob said to *the men of* his house and to all who were with him: Remove entirely the *idols of the nations* which are among you, *which you took from the idols' house of Shechem*, and purify yourselves *from the impurities of the slaughtered men whom you have touched*, and change your garments.

Following God's command that he go to Bethel and build an altar to the One who appeared to him when he fled from his brother (Gen. 35.1), Jacob orders his entourage to dispose of foreign gods and to purify themselves. The Bible clearly links Jacob's second visit to Bethel with his previous journey recorded in Gen. 28 and, as we shall see, *Ps-Jon.* of Gen. 35.7 is keen to do the same. The Bible gives as a reason for this second visit Jacob's desire to build the altar to the God who answered him when he was in distress and who was with him; the Targumim follow suit.[3] The Midrashim, however, discuss the vow which Jacob had made on his first visit to Bethel (Gen. 28.20-22), and note that he had not fulfilled it; like the pre-Christian book of *Jubilees*, they warn against delay in carrying out vows, and present Jacob's return to Bethel as necessary for the vow's completion.[4]

Such lack of interest in the matter of vows on the part of the Targumim serves to underline their evident concern with the business of foreign gods. *Ps-Jon.* renders the Hebrew expression *'lhy hnkr* as 'the idols of the nations (or: Gentiles)', as does Onqelos (*TO*); Neofiti (*TN*) speaks of idolatry, and its censored marginal gloss (*Ngl*) probably refers to images of idols. At a very early period the question of the origin of these idols arose: *Jubilees* states that they were the property of Laban which had been with Jacob's family since he had fled from his father-in-law, and some later sources agree with this.[5] But *Ps-Jon.* is quite specific in saying that they came from Shechem, in particular from the house of idols which was there. Indeed, this Targum goes out of its way to stress Shechem as their home, as may be seen in its rendering of v. 4.

Verse 4

So they gave *over into the hand of* Jacob all the *idols of the nations* which were among them, *which they had taken from the idols' house of Shechem*, and the rings which were in *the ears of the inhabitants of the city of Shechem, on which were depicted the likeness of its image*; and Jacob hid them under the oak which is *near to the city of Shechem*.

One immediate effect of *Ps-Jon's.* exegesis is to establish a firm link between Jacob's second visit to Bethel and the events of the preceding chapter, which tells of the notorious attack on Shechem by Simeon and Levi. The Targumim of Gen. 34.31 leave one in no doubt that Shechem was full of idol-worshippers; indeed, Simeon and Levi give this as a reason for their action on behalf of their sister Dinah.[6] *Ps-Jon.* appears to assume what Rashi later states openly, that the idols came into Jacob's possession as part of the spoils of the victorious war against Shechem.[7] The Targum reinforces this understanding by speaking further of the purification needed after contact with the bodies of those killed in the battle.

The idols, then, are not some family heirloom, but plunder taken from a city which has a 'house of idols', *byt ṭ'wwt*. This expression is used only here in the whole of *Ps-Jon.*, and suggests that the Targum regarded Shechem as having once been a supreme metropolis of paganism. Even the earrings of its inhabitants are idolatrous; and the abominations are there to this very day, albeit buried by Jacob under an oak tree near to the city. The meaning of this is evident, in that *Ps-Jon.* is heaping calumnies on the people who regard Shechem and nearby Mount Gerizim as a holy place. These are the Samaritans; they are not directly called idolaters, since the idols have been removed. But they are the object of contempt; and the Targum's strong language must, presumably, have been forged at a time when relations between Jews and Samaritans were more than usually strained.

Ps-Jon. is fairly precise about the kind of idols which were buried. They are the statues which had been kept in the idol-house, and ear-rings painted with the likeness of what, one may presume, were the same statues. This precision contrasts, to some extent, with the rather general terms in which the Talmud and Midrash speak of what Jacob buried. Thus Talmud Yerushalmi *Avodah Zarah* 7.5.4 has R. Ishmael tell in the name of R. Jose how he went to Neapolis and encountered the Kuthim, the Samaritans.

> He said to them: I see you, that you do not worship (at) this mountain, but rather the images which are under it, for it is written, 'And Jacob hid them (the foreign gods) under the terebinth which is with Shechem'.[8]

The text goes on to tell how the Rabbi heard the Kuthim plotting to kill him, so he fled from the city. Similarly, in *Gen. R.* 81.4 R. Ishmael, again in the name of R. Jose, takes one of the Samaritans [*ḥd šmryy*] to task as he passes by the 'Palatinos', the site of the Samaritan temple on Mount Gerizim:

> I say to you, Why are you like a dog which has a passion for carrion [*nblh*]? It is so, since you know that idolatry is hidden beneath it: 'and Jacob hid them. . . ' (Gen. 35.4). That is why you have a passion for it.

From the first century CE we have the testimony of the *Liber Antiquitatum Biblicarum*, falsely attributed to Philo, which indicates a strong tradition of idols buried in the vicinity of Shechem. The tribe of Asher, asked by Cenez to reveal their wrong-doings, announce:

> We found seven golden images which the Amorites called holy nymphs, and we carried them off with the most precious stones which had been put on them, and we hid those things. And now behold: they have been laid down under the summit of mount Sichem.[9]

Earlier in the same section of the *LAB*, the tribe of Naphtali say that they wish to make what the Amorites made, and that these things are hidden under the tent of Elas, a Latin transcription of the Hebrew Elah ['*lh*], the oak or terebinth, probably a covert reference to the terebinth of Gen. 35.4.[10] According to *LAB*, all these items were deposited later than the time of Jacob, in the period of the Judges; and they are a powerful means of bringing into disrepute the cult which was offered at Shechem. Indeed, anti-Samaritan polemic has long been recognized, at least by some authorities, as an element in the *LAB*'s general programme.[11]

While the *LAB* seems to refer only in passing to the events of Gen. 35, it is nonetheless illuminating in two respects. First, it shows that by the first century CE the idolatrous cache in and near Shechem had become part of a general anti-Samaritan polemic. Second, the idols themselves are described in some detail as nymphs; and Bogaert has suggested that this designation may have arisen from confusion of the word *byt 'l*, baetyl, sacred stone, with Hebrew *btwlh* or Aramaic *btwlt'*, virgin, nymph. In any case, statues or figurines are, it seems, presupposed, and it may be that *LAB* is in fact expounding the text of Gen. 35.4 in a discreet and indirect manner.[12]

Given the Jewish material at our disposal, it is not easy to see what light it may cast on *Ps-Jon.*'s exegesis of these two verses. The view that Shechem was the original home of the idols is found again at the earliest in Rashi's commentary on v. 2. The *LAB*, while indicating that idolatrous statues and figurines were buried at Shechem, offers no real help, since the burials are not directly associated with Jacob. We might, therefore, be tempted to conclude that *Ps-Jon.* presents us with late and largely unparalleled musings on the text of these two verses.

Such a conclusion, however, would be both hasty and intemperate. For if we extend our investigations beyond Rabbinic and pre-Rabbinic Judaism, into the writings of the early Church Fathers, we shall find three authors who offer vital evidence for the history of exegesis of these verses. First is Procopius of Gaza (c. 456–c. 538 CE), who lived and worked in the land of Israel, and who thus had access to Jewish exegetical traditions. Commenting on Gen. 35.2, he explains that the foreign gods were not only those which Rachel had taken from Laban, but also those captured from the Shechemites. Thus he demonstrates the currency in his day both of the pre-Christian tradition that the idols were Laban's and the notion that the gods were booty from the sacked city of Shechem.[13]

Second, we have the evidence of John Chrysostom (c. 347–407 CE) that the ear-rings described in Gen. 35.4 were signs of the idols.[14] More detailed, however, is the third authority, Augustine of Hippo (354–430 CE), who not only describes the ear-rings as phylacteries of idols, but also tells how the pagans of his own day wore such ornaments in the service of their gods, a practice which he castigates as a superstition and the service of demons.[15]

Ps-Jon.'s exegesis is not, therefore, quite so out of the ordinary as it may at first appear: two important elements in it are attested by

Christian writers of the fourth and fifth centuries CE. To this we may add a general observation, that Islam would soon have eradicated the use and the memory of idolatrous ear-rings; and the coincidence of *Ps-Jon.* with Christian writers on the nature of these ornaments may indeed be a pointer to the pre-Islamic date of the exegesis. The powerful anti-Shechemite, that is, anti-Samaritan stance of *Ps-Jon.* shares more, in broad and general terms, with the *LAB* than with the *Yerushalmi* and *Genesis Rabbah*. The latter sources, nonetheless, are hostile to Shechem, and, like *Ps-Jon.*, think it worthwhile to heap contempt on that place of worship. Hostility of such a kind would make good historical sense earlier than the reign of Justinian who, in the year 529 CE, inflicted a heavy defeat on the Samaritans.[16] Their recovery from that blow was very slow, and thereafter they seem not to have threatened Jewish religious sensibilities as in the preceding period. With some degree of confidence, then, we may provisionally suggest a pre-Islamic date for *Ps-Jon.*'s interpretation of Gen. 35.2, 4.

Verse 5

So they journeyed *from there, giving thanks and praying before the Lord*, and there was trembling *from before the Lord upon the nations who were in* the cities round about them; and they did not pursue the sons of Jacob.

In this verse, *Ps-Jon.* links hands with old and well-established interpretations found in Jewish texts from before the Christian period. *Jub.* 30.25 specifies that it was the Lord's terror in particular, and that it fell on the cites surrounding Shechem, a significant note given *Ps-Jon.*'s interest in that city. The terror of the Lord also features in other, later works, and came to be elaborately expounded in such a way that some sources speak of Israel's full-scale victories over the Gentiles.[17] *Ps-Jon.* does not allude to these tales, and its sober exegesis is in keeping with the restrained language of *Jubilees* as it re-writes this verse.

Verse 7

And he built there an altar, and called the place El *who caused his Shekhina to dwell in* Bethel; for there *the angels of the Lord* had been revealed to him when he had fled from before *Esau* his brother.

Ps-Jon. here directly recalls Jacob's first visit to Bethel recorded in Genesis 28. There the angels are a biblical datum (Gen. 28.12); and the *Fragment Targum* likewise recalls their presence.[18] The mention of God's *Shekhina* as dwelling in Bethel is intended to remind us that Bethel has already been identified as the place of the Temple: so much is made clear in *Ps-Jon.* Gen. 28.11, 12, 17, 19 and 22. The Targum's intention is to indicate the consistency and unity of the biblical revelation.

Neither *TN* nor its marginal gloss (*Ngl*), however, refers to the angels; nor do they allude to the dwelling of the Shekhina in Bethel. According to the latter, Jacob set up an altar

> and worshipped and prayed there in the Name of the Word of the Lord, the God who had appeared to him in Bethel; for there the Glory of the Shekhina of the Lord had been revealed to him at the time when he had fled from before Esau.

The interpretation of this verse in the Targumic tradition has been well discussed by Andrew Chester, who notes the use made of it by the *minim* and the concerns of Rabbinic authority to counteract the heresy of the 'two powers in heaven'. The *Ngl*, quoted above, firmly rules out any possible heretical use of the verse.[19] Chester, however, remains undecided whether *Ps-Jon.* here represents a further development of basic Targumic tradition, or an early tradition of an angelophany.[20] Whatever concern *Ps-Jon.* may have felt about heresy, if indeed any was felt at all, it seems that its essential purpose is to assert, above all else, that Jacob's visit was a return to the very place of his original vision. Why this should be so will, we hope, become clear when we examine the strongly cultic interpretations of vv. 11 and 14.

Verse 8

> Then died Deborah, the *tutor* of Rebekah and she was buried beneath Bethel *in the extremity of the plain. And there the news was also told to Jacob about the death of his mother Rebekah*; so he called its name '*Other* Weeping'.

That the news of his mother's death reached Jacob at this point is a well-known and widespread tradition, represented not only by the *Fragment Targums (FT)*, but also by *Gen. R.* 81.8 and other midrashic sources.[21] The Bible does not report Rebekah's death; but from the first century CE at the latest it was believed that it had happened during Jacob's second visit to Bethel: so much is plain from Josephus's statement that, on his arrival in Hebron, Jacob found that she had died.[22] Since, by this exegesis, two deaths are involved, *Ps-Jon.* joins with the Midrashim in expounding the Hebrew *'ln*, oak, as if it were Greek *allon*, other.[23]

Verse 9

> And *the Lord* was *revealed* to Jacob again when he came from Paddan *of* Aram, and *the Lord* blessed (him) *in the Name of His Word after his mother had died.*

This interpretation is remarkable for its failure to cite an extended paraphrase, found in *TN* and the *Fragment Targums*, which lists God's blessing of bride and groom in the persons of Adam and Eve; his visiting the sick in the case of Abraham; and his blessing of the mourners, exemplified by this verse, which seemingly acts as the Biblical springboard for the exegesis.[24] It has been argued that a *piyyut* of Yannai on these same themes may be dependent on the Targumim (except, of course, *Ps-Jon.*) of this verse; so those Targumim would represent a fairly early liturgical composition.[25] *Ps-Jon.* does, however, record what some regard as a similar paraphrase at Deut. 34.6 in a form more extended than that found in the Targumim of Gen. 35.9. For this reason, we may venture two brief comments.

First, Shinan has argued that *Ps-Jon.* characteristically moves haggadic material from verses to which it properly belongs, as attested by the other Pentateuchal Targumim, to other verses of its own choosing. Such behaviour is, he believes, evidence of the late, literary, and secondary artificial nature of the Targum.[26] *Ps-Jon.*'s treatment of Gen. 35.9, therefore, indicates the late date of the Targum. Against Shinan, however, it is possible to bring evidence to show that *Ps-Jon.*'s version of Deut. 34.6 is the original form and location of the paraphrase, and recently Chester has shown how this may be done. But he does not find such evidence entirely convincing, and regards the originality of *Ps-Jon.* simply as a possibility.[27]

One could, however, add to the evidence which Chester uses such that the character of *Ps-Jon.* of Deut. 34.6 becomes much more clearly defined. It is noticeable that both Shinan and Chester stop short of detailed comparison and analysis of the relevant texts. Thus they fail to note how *Ps-Jon.* is concerned to list six good deeds held in high esteem by Jews, which are nevertheless not specifically commanded by Scripture. These are the clothing of the naked, the joining of bridegroom and bride, visiting the sick, comforting mourners, provision for the poor, and the burial of the dead. From very early times all these actions were viewed as obligatory for pious Jews; indeed, one need only consider texts like Tobit 1.16-18; 4.12, 16-17. The wish to root them in Scripture, then, would be natural and compelling. *Ps-Jon.* does that very thing, showing how God taught them not by a verbal commandment, but by his actions. The thrust of the paraphrase in *TN*, *Ngl*, the Geniza Manuscripts (*GM*) and *FT* is quite different, having a strongly liturgical character not found in *Ps-Jon.*, and a tendency, beginning in *TN* and gathering force in *FT* and *GM*, to provide explicit Scriptural proof-texts for God's actions. It is thus possible to argue that the paraphrase in *Ps-Jon.* is related only superficially, or even not at all, to the paraphrases in *TN* and the other Targumim.[28] If such be the case, there is then little likelihood that *Ps-Jon.* moved a tradition from its rightful place in Gen. 35.9, and Shinan's observations based on this suggested transfer of texts have to be evaluated accordingly.

Second, a long paraphrase of the sort found in *TN* fits uneasily with the overall aims and objectives of *Ps-Jon.* in this chapter. As we shall see in the next verse, those aims are quite specific, and may have their roots in very ancient preoccupations indeed.

Verse 11

> And *the Lord* said to him: I am El Shaddai. Grow and multiply. A *holy* nation and an assembly of *prophets and priests* shall be from *your sons which you shall beget*; *and again, two* kings shall go forth from *you*.

Comparison of this verse with the interpretations of the other Targumim will, we believe, highlight the peculiar concerns and ultimate purpose of *Ps-Jon.*'s exegesis of the whole of this chapter. In the Hebrew original God's promise to Jacob's consists of two parts: a nation and a congregation of nations (*gwy wqhl gwym*) will come from him; and kings shall issue from his loins. *Ps-Jon.*'s rendering of the first promise as referring to a holy nation and an assembly of prophets and priests is unique among the Pentateuchal Targumim. *TO* speaks of a people and an assembly of tribes, echoing thereby its

own exegesis of the similar divine promise in Gen. 28.3. *Ps-Jon.* of
the latter verse also takes up the theme of the tribes, and, along with
TO, does so again at Gen. 48.4. That God's promise referred to the
future tribes is a view found also in a number of midrashim.[29] *TN* of
Gen. 35.11, however, promises that an assembly of righteous peoples
shall arise from Jacob, repeating here its exegesis of Gen. 28.3 and
paving the way for its identical rendering of Gen. 48.4. *FT* of Gen.
35.11 and 48.4, however, speaks only of assemblies of many
crowds.[30]

The second part of the promise *Ps-Jon.* understands as referring to
two kings, thus in a general way joining hands with those Midrashim
which name two particular royal individuals.[31] *TO*, *TN*, and the *FT*,
however, speak of kings who shall rule over the nations as issuing
from Jacob; thus these Targumim allude to their identical interpretation
of earlier divine promises set out clearly in their versions of Gen. 17.6
and 16, verses where *Ps-Jon.* as well speaks of kings who shall rule
over the nations destined to issue from Abraham.[32]

Leaving aside for the time being *Ps-Jon.* of Gen. 35.11 and its
peculiarities, we should note that the general Targumic tradition of
exegesis of all these verses is potentially very old, essential elements
within it being clearly represented in the book of *Jubilees*. Thus, in
re-writing Gen. 28.3, *Jub.* 25.3 promises to Jacob a righteous
progeny, as does *TN*; and the idea that his descendants will rule the
nations is asserted with some directness in *Jub.* 32.18-19 in much the
same way as in the Targumim of Gen. 17.6, 16; 35.11. In all these
texts there is the hope of Israelite political power, which finds its
most natural setting before the tragedy of the Second Revolt against
Rome.[33]

Ps-Jon. of Gen. 35.11, however, looks not to Israel's rule over the
nations, nor to righteous peoples and tribal groups. Its language
clearly recalls God's command of Exod. 19.6, that Israel shall be for
him a kingdom of priests and a holy nation, interpreted there by *Ps-
Jon.* to mean that Israel shall be kings binding on the crown and
ministering priests and a holy nation.[34] And *Ps-Jon.*'s description of
Jacob's progeny follows immediately the Scriptural verse (Gen.
35.10) which tells how God had changed the Patriarch's name to
Israel, a fact which *Ps-Jon.* reports without any exegetical elaboration.
The Targum here stands side by side with Philo, who remarks that
Jacob, prepared by the angels of reason for struggle with the passions,
is the source of the twelve tribes whom Scripture calls a royal house

and a priesthood of God (*De Sobrietate* 65-66). We should note also most particularly that Philo clearly associates the change of Jacob's name to Israel with the description of the nation in Exod. 19.6 as a royal house, a priesthood, and a holy nation (*De Abrahamo* 56). Philo's direct linking of Exod. 19.6 with the patriarch Jacob and his descendants is remarkable, and points to the antiquity of *Ps-Jon.*'s exegesis of Gen. 35.11, an exegesis not represented elsewhere in rabbinic literature.

In fact, *Ps-Jon.* of Gen. 35.11 sets out to anticipate the setting up of Israel's formal structures of lawful government and worship. The prophets belong to the very same structures, as *Ps-Jon.* of Deut. 18.14 explains, contrasting Israel with other nations:

> For these people whom you are *about to* dispossess pay attention to *deceivers of the eye* and practisers of divination; but you are *not like them. Rather, priests consulting Urim and Thummim and upright prophets* the Lord your God has given you.

Ps-Jon. of Exod. 33.16 also shows how Israel's possession of the spirit of prophecy differentiates it from the nations of the world:

> And by what means shall it be known that I have found *mercy before you, except when your Shekhina speaks with us, and miracles are done for us when you take up the spirit of prophecy from upon the nations, and when you speak in the Holy Spirit to me and to your people,* so that we are different from all the peoples who are on the face of the earth?

It should be evident that, since *Ps-Jon.* has been content elsewhere to speak of future Israelite kings ruling over the nations, its interpretation of this verse is not dictated by the possible disappearance in its day of Israel's political hopes for the future. On the contrary, its exegesis seems to be determined by an ancient tradition that circumstances surrounding Jacob's second visit to Bethel led to the choice of Levi for the high priesthood and the blessing of Judah as a royal prince. This can be properly appreciated on examination of what follows.

Verse 14

> And *he* set up there a pillar in the place where He had spoken with him, a pillar of stone; and he poured a libation upon it, *a libation of wine and a libation of water: for thus his sons are destined to do on the Feast of Tabernacles*; and he poured out upon it *olive* oil.

This verse receives very little attention in rabbinic literature.[35] The ritual of Sukkoth as required by rabbinic law, not by the written Torah, is explicitly described (cf. *m. Sukkoth* 4.9), and *Ps-Jon.* fixes the incident in relation to this Feast; *Jub.* 32.3-29 likewise places this, and a whole complex of related events, at Sukkoth.

At the end of the last century, Adolf Büchler listed numerous points of contact between *Jubilees* and *Ps-Jon.* in matters of cultic and priestly law and traditions.[36] Much more recently, Joshua Schwarz has carefully analysed *Jubilees* 31-32, and has concluded that its traditions of Jacob's cultic activity during his second visit to Bethel were possibly known to the Rabbis, although in garbled form. Thus he specifically notes that *Ps-Jon.* of Gen. 35.14 refers, like *Jubilees*, to Sukkoth.[37] Points of contact between aspects of the *Jubilees* tradition and *Ps-Jon.* should not, therefore, surprise us. It seems to us that such contact does exist; although it should be made clear at once that *Ps-Jon.* of Genesis 35 is far from being directly dependent on *Jubilees*. The relationship between the traditions recorded in the two texts is much more complex. Thus, while there are major areas of agreement between the two texts, they also diverge at various key points. We must now turn to fuller discussion of these matters.

What *Ps-Jon.* shares with *Jubilees* is substantial. The events surrounding Jacob's second visit to Bethel take place at Sukkoth; during this period, *Jubilees* relates that Levi was chosen in heaven for the high-priesthood (30.18-20) because of his right conduct in sacking Shechem (30.1-17). *Ps-Jon.*'s comment that priests would come forth from Jacob is in line with this general tradition, as is his reference to the kings; in *Jubilees*, Isaac blesses not only the future tribe of Levi as priests, judges, and rulers, but also Judah as a prince, as well as one of his sons (31.5-20).

While both *Ps-Jon.* and *Jubilees* stress the link between the attack on Shechem and Jacob's visit to Bethel, the nature of the link is by no means the same in both sources. Here *Ps-Jon.*'s insistence that the idols removed by Jacob were of Shechemite origin finds no place in *Jubilees*, which says nothing of Shechemite idolatry. In this respect, *Jubilees* tallies with other pre-Christian sources.[38] So far as I am aware, the earliest datable written source which makes polemical use of the idols hidden at Shechem is the first-century CE *Liber Antiquitatum Biblicarum*. Further, in re-writing Genesis 35 and the surrounding chapters, *Jubilees* says nothing about prophets as a major constituency in Israel along with kings and priests.[39] Neither does *Ps-Jon.* refer to Jacob's visit to his father Isaac at this time, a prominent feature of the narrative in *Jub.* 31.5-30.

Some tentative conclusions and suggestions may now be offered. Much of what we have examined may be explained if we are prepared to envisage *Ps-Jon.* as engaged in an attack on the Samaritan community based at Shechem. Taking the outlines of a very old exegesis on Genesis 35 of the kind extant in *Jubilees*, the Targum re-arranges them in order to deal with a new situation. It emphasizes the Shechemite origin of the idols still buried in the vicinity of the mountain, and goes on to assert that at Bethel, which it is careful to identify with the Jerusalem Temple on Mount Zion, God promised that kings and priests and prophets would come forth from Jacob. This happened at the Feast of Sukkoth, whose ritual is described in terms explicitly required by rabbinic law: libations of wine are accompanied by water libations, the latter not demanded by the written Torah, so that they became a notorious bone of contention among Jewish groups.[40]

The promise of a future legitimate priesthood is firmly located in Jerusalem: the localization of the promise in Bethel-Jerusalem is significant, in view of the Samaritans' claim to possess the true priesthood ministering on Mount Gerizim, and their contention that the Jewish priesthood originated improperly in Eli's unlawful migration from Shechem to Shiloh, where he set up a false sanctuary in the days of the Judges.[41] Furthermore, *Ps-Jon.* says that there will be prophets arising from Jacob's sons in the future, a telling prediction given the Samaritans' rejection both of the prophets who succeeded Moses and of the sacred books ascribed to them. About the identity of the kings to come forth from Jacob *Ps-Jon.* is discreetly vague, avoiding the names of the northerners Jeroboam and Jehu suggested by some midrashim.[42] And it may also be that the Targum's interpretation of Migdal-Eder, to which Jacob eventually repairs (Gen. 35.21), as

> the place from where the King Messiah is to be revealed at the end of days

is intended to put the Messianic hopes of Israel firmly in the tribal area of Judah and outside the sphere of the territories once occupied by Ephraim, Manasseh, and the other Northern tribes.[43]

The apparently anti-Samaritan nature of the Targum's interpretation of these verses is therefore quite strongly marked, and is directed at a number of fundamental beliefs and practices over which Jews and Samaritans were in profound disagreement. *Ps-Jon.* seems to have a very negative view of Shechem and, by implication, the mountain of Gerizim, which the Samaritans hold to be the site of the legitimate temple. As we have already hinted, a time before 529 CE would best account for *Ps-Jon.*'s exegetical furniture and attitudes: a date in the Islamic period seems to us extremely improbable, considering the weakened state of Samaritanism at that time. This last point is strengthened by the Targum's familiarity with interpretations of individual verses found in *Jubilees* and Philo, but absent from the Rabbinic commentaries.[44] We have also seen that *Ps-Jon.*'s failure to insert the long paraphrase found in *TN* and other Targumim at v. 9 does not afford solid grounds for a late dating of the text. Similarly, items which might at first blush appear post-Islamic in date, such as the identification of the idols as of Shechemite origin, turn out on examination to have good pre-Islamic credentials. Without offering a precise date for *Ps-Jon.*'s interpretation of these verses, we may nevertheless conclude that we are dealing with material deriving from pre-Islamic times. It is possible, indeed, that the sharpness of the polemic against Shechem originated in some specific event or series of events; and the major Samaritan religious revival in the fourth century CE associated with the names of Marqah and Baba Rabba would no doubt have called forth some Jewish protest, of which *Ps-Jon.* to Gen. 35.1-15 may have been a part.[45]

To determine precisely how much older than the seventh century the text here considered might be is a task for those who, like Geza Vermes, are concerned to chart the history of Jewish exegesis through its many and varied stages of development. This essay is presented to him in grateful acknowledgment of his major contribution to Jewish studies, in thanks for his friendship, and with good wishes for his happiness in the coming years: may they be many and prosperous.

NOTES

The following editions of Targumim of the Pentateuch have been used: E.G. Clarke, in collaboration with W.E. Aufrecht, J.C. Hurd, and F. Spitzer, *Targum Pseudo-Jonathan of the Pentateuch: Text and Concordance*, New York: Ktav, 1984 (*Ps-Jon.*); A. Sperber, *The Bible in Aramaic*, vol. 1, *The*

Pentateuch according to Targum Onkelos, Leiden: Brill, 1959 (*TO*); A. Díez Macho, *Ms. Neophyti I*, 5 vols. Madrid-Barcelona, 1968-1978 (*TN*); M.L. Klein, *The Fragment Targums of the Pentateuch according to their extant Sources*, 2 vols., Rome, 1980 (*FT*); *Geniza Manuscripts of Palestinian Targum*, 2 vols., Cincinnati, 1986 (*GM*).

1. See G. Vermes, 'The Targumic Versions of Genesis 4.3-16', *Annual of the Leeds University Oriental Society* 3 (1961-1962), pp. 81-114, reprinted in *Post-Biblical Jewish Studies*, Leiden: Brill, 1975, pp. 92-126. The notion that *Ps-Jon.* is an anti-Islamic polemic was argued by M. Ohana, 'La Polémique judéo-islamique et l'image d'Ismaël dans Targum Pseudo-Jonathan et dans Pirke de Rabbi Eliezer', *Augustinianum* 15 (1975), pp. 367-87. The consequent late date of the Targum is argued by A. Shinan, *The Aggadah in the Aramaic Targums to the Pentateuch*, 2 vols., Jerusalem, 1979 [in Hebrew]; 'The "Palestinian" Targums—Repetition, Internal Unity, Contradictions', *JJS* 36 (1985), pp. 72-87; D.M. Splansky, *Targum Pseudo-Jonathan: Its Relationship to Other Targumim, Use of Midrashim, and Date* (unpublished dissertation, Hebrew Union College—Jewish Institute of Religion, 1981); and A.N. Chester, *Divine Revelation and Divine Titles in the Pentateuchal Targumim*, Tübingen, 1986, pp. 252-56.

2. 'Targum Pseudo-Jonathan and Anti-Islamic Polemic', *JSS* 34 (1989), pp. 77-93; and 'The Date of Targum Pseudo-Jonathan: Some Comments', *JJS* 40 (1989), pp. 7-30.

3. See Gen. 35.1, 2. In *Ps-Jon.* of v. 3 Jacob plans to build an altar 'to God who *received my prayer* on the day of my distress, and *whose word has been for my help* on the journey which I have made', thereby referring back to his vow recorded in Gen. 28.20. In the latter verse, *Ps-Jon.* has Jacob make his vow conditional upon God's keeping him free of idolatry (*inter alia*); cf. *Gen. R.* 70.4 (ed. J. Theodor and Ch. Albeck, Berlin, 1903-1936), and *Tanḥuma Wayyišlaḥ* 8.

4. See *Jub.* 31.29; *Gen. R.* 81.1; *y. Nedarim* 1.1; *Tanḥuma Wayyišlaḥ* 8.

5. See *Jub.* 31.2; Midrash *Sekhel Ṭov* to this verse cited by M. Kasher, *Torah Shelemah*, vol. 5, Jerusalem, 1935, p. 1337.

6. See *Ps-Jon.* of Gen. 34.31, where Simeon and Levi assert that it would not be proper for Israelites to say that uncircumcised and idolaters had defiled Jacob's daughter; and cf. *TN*, its marginal gloss (*Ngl*), and *FT* of this verse.

7. See Rashi on Gen. 35.2, and cf. *Midrash Ha-Ḥephetz* cited by Kasher, *op. cit.*, p. 1337.

8. Quoted by Kasher, *op. cit.*, p. 1340.

9. *LAB* 25.10. For recent discussion of *LAB*'s date, see E. Schürer, *The History of the Jewish People in the Age of Jesus Christ*, vol. III.1, rev. and ed. G. Vermes, F. Millar, and M. Goodman, Edinburgh, 1986. We have used the text of *LAB* edited by D.J. Harrington, *Pseudo-Philon. Les Antiquités Bibliques*, vol. 1 (Sources Chrétiennes, 229), Paris, 1976.

10. *LAB* 25.8. On these passages, see the important comments of C. Perrot, P.-M. Bogaert, and D.J. Harrington in *Pseudo-Philon*. *Les Antiquités Bibliques*, vol. 2 (Sources Chrétiennes, 230), Paris, 1976, pp. 152, 154-56. M.F. Collins, 'The Hidden Vessels in Samaritan Traditions', *JSJ* 3 (1972), pp. 114-15, suggests that the material which we have quoted from the Rabbis and *LAB* may have been a direct response to Samaritan claims that sacred vessels of their cult had been buried by Moses on Mount Gerizim.

11. See especially A. Spiro, 'Samaritans, Tobiads, and Judahites in Pseudo-Philo: Use and Abuse of the Bible by Polemicists and Doctrinaires', *PAAJR* 20 (1951), pp. 279-355; A. Zeron, 'Einige Bemerkungen zu M.F. Collins, *The Hidden Vessels in Samaritan Tradition*', *JSJ* 4 (1973), pp. 165-69; and the considered views of Bogaert and Harrington, *Pseudo-Philon*, vol. 2, p. 29, who quote Vermes, 'La Figure de Moïse au tournant des deux Testaments', *Cahiers Sioniens* 8 (1954), p. 89, linking *LAB*'s polemic with that of the Targumim.

12. See *Pseudo-Philon*, vol. 2, pp. 154-55.

13. Procopius of Gaza, *Commentarii in Genesim* 35.2 in *PG* LXXXVII Part 1 (Paris, 1865), section 184. Cf. also Epiphanius, *Panarion Haer.* 9.2.4, who describes the Samaritans as unwitting idolaters, since the idols of four nations are concealed on Gerizim.

14. John Chrysostom on Gen. 35.1-6 in *Homily* LIX.4.

15. Augustine, *Quaestionum S. Augustini in Heptateuchum* I.cxi: Ergo illae inaures quaecum idolis datae sunt, ut dictum est, idolorum phylacteria fuerunt; cf. *Epistle* ccxlv.2.

16. On the revolts of the Samaritans in Justinian's reign, and earlier rebellions quelled by Rome, see M. Avi-Yonah, *The Jews of Palestine: A Political History from the Bar Kokhba War to the Arab Conquest*, Oxford, 1976, pp. 214-43.

17. See the treatment of this in *Yalquṭ Shim'oni*, *Midrash Wayyissa'u*, and other texts quoted in full by Kasher, *op. cit.*, pp. 1341-45.

18. So *FT* according to Mss. Paris 110 and Vat 440 of Gen. 28.12.

19. See A. Chester, *Divine Revelation*, pp. 23-27.

20. Chester, *op. cit.*, p. 27.

21. *TO*, *TN*, and *Ngl* make no mention of her death, which is recorded by *FT* Ms. Paris 110 of the following verse. The Targum of Geniza Ms. C to this verse is very close to *Ps-Jon.*; see Klein, *GM*, vol. 1, p. 75; and cf. *Pesiqta Rabbati* 12.4; *Pesiqta deRab Kahana* 3.1; Kasher, *op. cit.*, p. 1347.

22. See Josephus, *Antiquities* 1.345.

23. Cf. R. le Déaut, *Targum du Pentateuque*, vol. 1. *Genèse* (Sources Chrétiennes, 245), Paris, 1978, p. 325.

24. See *Gen. R.* 81-5 (R. Aha in the name of R. Jonathan).

25. See M. Zulay, *Zur Liturgie der babylonischen Juden*, Stuttgart, 1933, pp. 63-65; A. Shinan, *The Aggadah*, vol. 1, pp. 69-70, 117; vol. 2, pp. 235, 305; and Chester, *op. cit.*, pp. 39-45.

26. See Shinan, *The Aggadah*, vol. 1, pp. 155-60.

27. See Chester, *op. cit.*, p. 45.

28. Even where items listed by *Ps-Jon.* agree with those in *TN* and *FT*, there are clear differences between the paraphrases. *TN* speaks of the *blessing* of bride and groom and God's blessing of Jacob as a mourner; it uses the stock phrases 'our father Abraham', 'our father Jacob'; and it attempts to use Gen. 35.9 as a proof text, an attempt carried further by *Ngl* and *FT*. None of these things appears in *Ps-Jon.*, whose lack of liturgical interest only strengthens the halakhic value of his paraphrase. He has the angels present at the burial of Moses: with this, compare the presence of the archangel Raphael when Tobit buried the dead (Tob. 12.13).

29. The reasons for this are set out in *Pesiqta Rabbati* 3.4; *Eykhah Rabbah Petichta* 33. *Gen. R.* 82.4 refers *gwy* to Benjamin and *qhl gwym* to Ephraim and Manasseh. But *Ps-Jon.* does not allude to this, and seems unaware of the problems which prompted the exegesis.

30. See also Klein, *GM*, vol. 1, p. 75, for the same interpretation.

31. They are variously identified: in *Gen. R.* 82.4, R. Berekhiah and R. Helbo in the name of R. Samuel b. Naḥman state that they are Jeroboam and Jehu; but the Rabbis understand them to be Saul and Ish-bosheth. See further Kasher, *op. cit.*, p. 1352.

32. This departure of *Ps-Jon.* of Gen. 35.11 from the common Targumic understanding is thus all the more striking.

33. Notice how *TN*, using the root *tqp*, has God say to Abraham, 'I will make you exceedingly powerful' for the Hebrew 'I will make you fruitful' at Gen. 17.6. It uses *tqp* again at Gen. 28.3; 35.11; and 48.4; with the last two verses, cf. also Klein, *GM*, vol. 1, pp. 75, 151.

34. For further comment on this and what follows, see J. Potin, *La Fête Juive de la Pentecôte*, vol. 1, Paris, 1971, pp. 207-26.

35. See A. Hyman, *Sefer Torah Haketubah Vehamessurah*, 2nd edn rev. by A.B. Hyman, vol. 1, Tel-Aviv, 1979, p. 67; and Kasher, *op. cit.*, p. 1355.

36. See A. Büchler, *Die Priester und der Cultus im letzten Jahrzehnt des jeruschalmischen Tempels*, Vienna, 1895, pp. 151-59.

37. See J. Schwarz, 'Jubilees, Bethel, and the Temple of Jacob', *HUCA* 56 (1985), pp. 63-86, especially p. 84.

38. Idolatry does not feature in the condemnations of Shechem found in Ben Sira 50.26; *Test. Levi* 7.1-4; or Theodotus, Fragment 7 in Alexander Polyhistor *apud* Eusebius, *Praeparatio Evangelica* 9.22.9. See also R.J. Coggins, *Samaritans and Jews*, Oxford, 1975, pp. 91-93.

39. In this respect, cf. *1 Clement* 31.4–32.2, which speaks of the dignity of Jacob, noting that all the priests and Levites who serve the altar come from him, as do the Christ according to the flesh, and the kings, rulers and leaders who arise from Judah. In the preceding section (31.3), Clement has referred to the sacrifice of Isaac, and shows knowledge of Jewish exegesis of Genesis 22 by stating that Isaac went willingly and knowingly to be sacrificed. It is

thus possible that his treatment of Jacob owes something to Jewish opinion current in his day.

40. See R. Patai, *Man and Temple*, New York: Ktav, 1967, pp. 24-53.

41. See J. MacDonald, *The Theology of the Samaritans*, London, 1964, pp. 16-17, 310-13.

42. See above, n. 31.

43. See R. le Déaut, *La Nuit Pascale*, Rome, 1963, p. 277. *Ps-Jon.*'s exegesis is found in *T. Micah* 4.8; otherwise Gen. 35.21 is hardly referred to in rabbinic literature: see Hyman, *op. cit.*, p. 156, and le Déaut, *Targum du Pentateuque*, vol. 1, p. 329.

44. On this point, cf. most recently M. Niehoff, 'The Figure of Joseph in the Targums', *JJS* 39 (1988), pp. 234-50.

45. On Marqah and Baba Rabba, see MacDonald, *op. cit.*, pp. 36-40.

THE STORY OF R. PHINEHAS
BEN YAIR AND HIS DONKEY
IN *B. ḤULLIN* 7a-b

Louis Jacobs

Lancaster University

In the previous passages in *Ḥullin*, there are references to the maxim: 'If the Holy One, blessed be He, allows no mishap to result through the animals of the righteous, *a fortiori* He does not allow it to happen to the righteous themselves'.[1] In illustration of the maxim the Talmud tells the story of R. Phinehas and his donkey.

> R. Phinehas b. Yair was on the way to redeem captives. When he came to the river Ginai[2] he said: 'O Ginai, divide thy waters on my behalf that I may cross over'. Said the river: 'Thou art going to do the will of thy Maker and I am going to do the will of my Maker. For thee it is doubtful whether thou wilt carry it out whereas I certainly carry it out'.[3] Said he to the river: 'If thou wilt not divide I shall decree that no water will ever pass through thee', so it divided for him. There was another man there carrying wheat for Passover. Said he to the river: 'Divide also for that man who is engaged in the performance of a *mitzvah*!' It divided for him. There was an Arab accompanying them. He said to the river: 'Divide also for that man so that people should not protest: "Is that how one treats companions on a journey?"' The river divided for him as well. Said R. Joseph: 'How much greater was the power of this man than that of Moses and the six hundred thousand! For there was only a single division of the sea and here it happened three times'. But perhaps here, too, there was only a single parting?[4] Say, rather: 'Like Moses and the six hundred thousand'.[5] When he arrived at an inn they cast some barley before his donkey but it refused to eat. They winnowed the barley but it still refused to eat. They cleansed it but it still refused to eat. Said he to them: 'Perhaps they have not been

tithed', whereupon they gave the tithes and the donkey ate the barley. Said he: 'This poor creature is going to do the will of its Maker[6] and you dare to make it eat untithed produce'. But is there any obligation for produce to be tithed in such circumstances? Have we not learned:[7] 'If one buys produce for sowing or for an animal or flour for skins or oil for lighting or oil to polish utensils there is no obligation to give the tithes for produce of uncertain status'?[8] But there we have the observation of R. Johanan who said: 'This only applies where he bought the produce for an animal in the first instance. Where he bought it for human consumption and then changed his mind to give it to the animal he does have an obligation to tithe it.' And so we have been taught: 'If one buys produce in the market place in order to eat it himself and then changes his mind and decides to give it to his animal he must not give it to his animal or to his neighbour's animal until he has given the tithes'.

Rabbi (Judah the Prince) heard that he was coming and went out to meet him. Said he: 'Wilt thou dine with me?' 'Yes', he replied, whereupon Rabbi's face shone with delight. Said he: 'Dost thou imagine that I have given a vow never to enjoy any benefit from Israelites? Israelites are holy.[9] But there is one who desireth (to invite guests) but he hath no means and there is one who hath means but no desire, and it is written: 'Eat thou not the bread of him that hath an evil eye, neither desire thou his dainties. For as one that hath reckoned within himself, so is he: "Eat and drink", saith he to thee; but his heart is not with thee' (Proverbs 23.6-7). Thou, however, hast the means and the desire. Yet now I must make haste for I am busily occupied in carrying out a *mitzvah*. I shall come to thee on my return.' On his return he happened to enter by a door where he saw standing some white-legged mules. Said he: 'The angel of death is in this one's house and shall I dine with him?'[10] Rabbi heard of his coming and he went out to meet him, saying: 'I shall sell them'. Said he: '"Thou shalt not place a stumbling block before a blind man"' (Leviticus 19.14).[11] Said he: 'I shall abandon them'.[12] Said he: 'There will then be an increase of harm'.[13] Said he: 'I shall hamstring them'. Said he: 'That will offend against the prohibition of cruelty to animals'.[14] Said he: 'I shall kill them'. Said he: 'That would offend against the prohibition: "Thou shalt not destroy"' (Deuteronomy 20.19).[15] He was very insistent but a mountain rose between them.[16] Rabbi wept saying:[17] 'If this is how it is with them during their lifetime how much more when they are dead'. For R. Hama b. Hanina said: 'Greater are the righteous in their death than in their lifetime, as it is said: "And it came to pass, as they were burying a man, that, behold, they spied a band; and they cast the man into the sepulchre of Elisha; and as soon as the man touched the bones of Elisha, he revived and stood upon his feet"' (2 Kings 13.21).[18] Said R. Pappa to Abbaye: 'Perhaps it was in order for Elijah's blessing to be fulfilled[19] as it is written: "Let a double portion of thy spirit be upon me"?' (2 Kings 2.9). Said he: 'In that case why have we been taught, "He stood on his feet but did not return to his home"?' But then how was Elijah's blessing fulfilled?[20] As R. Johanan said, in that he healed the leprosy of Naaman, a leper being considered as one dead, as it is written: "Let her not, I pray, be as one dead" . . . (Numbers 12.12).[21] They said regarding R. Phinehas b. Yair that in all his days he never broke bread over a loaf that did not belong to him and from the day he reached independence[22] he did not enjoy a repast of his father.[23]

Thus far the story and its elaboration in the Babylonian Talmud. It is fruitful to compare this version with that in the Jerusalem Talmud,[24] appended to the Mishnah in *Demai*, quoted in *BT* as part of the discussion and evidently quoted in *JT* for the same purpose. First, however, in *JT* a series of stories about the miraculous powers of R. Phinehas b. Yair occurs. For the purpose of comparison three of these stories (there are others in the list) must be examined. In the first of these, the donkey of R. Phinehas is stolen by robbers during the night. For three days the robbers tried unsuccessfully to feed the donkey but it refused to eat. Fearful that it would die and cause a stench in their hideout the robbers decided to return the donkey to its owner, R. Phinehas. The donkey began to bray as it reached the gateway of R. Phinehas's house. R. Phinehas urged the members of his household to open the gate since, he said, this poor animal[25] has not eaten for three days.[26] They let it in and R. Phinehas ordered them to give it food. They placed barley before it but it refused to eat. 'Rabbi', they declared, 'it refuses to eat'. 'Did you separate the tithes from the *demai*[27] produce?', asked R. Phinehas. They replied: 'But our Master has taught us that if one buys Demai produce for an animal there is no need to tithe it' (quoting the Mishnah to which the story is appended, as in *BT*). R. Phinehas replied: 'What can we do if this poor beast wishes to be strict beyond the letter of the law?' They thereupon gave the tithes and the donkey ate.

The second story in *JT* relevant to our purpose tells how R. Phinehas b. Yair went to the House of Learning.[28] The river Ginai, being in full flood, was a barrier. R. Phinehas said: 'O Ginai, why dost thou prevent me from going to the House of Learning?' So the river parted for him to cross. His disciples asked him whether the river would part for them. He replied: 'Whoever knows that in all his days he had never put a fellow Israelite to shame may cross and it will not be deducted from his merits'.[29]

The third story tells of R. Phinehas b. Yair visiting Rabbi (Judah the Prince, *Nasi*) in order to express his disapproval of the latter's attempt to permit work in the fields on the Sabbatical year.[30] Rabbi asked R. Phinehas whether the produce in the fields was doing well. He asked him this twice but each time R. Phinehas replied: 'The endives are doing well', from which reply Rabbi understood that R. Phinehas was not in agreement with him regarding the Sabbatical year.[31] Rabbi then invited R. Phinehas to dine with him but when R. Phinehas came to Rabbi's house he saw the mules[32] of Rabbi standing there. R. Phinehas expressed his astonishment that Jews[33] should keep such dangerous animals and he expressed the hope that Rabbi would fail to note that he had arrived at the house. When Rabbi was told that R. Phinehas had returned home he sent messengers to apologize to R. Phinehas. R. Phinehas at first requested his townsfolk to surround him so that the messengers of Rabbi would not be able to reach him. The townsfolk, however, left R. Phinehas out of respect for Rabbi, whereupon R. Phinehas asked the members of his household to surround him and eventually fire came down from Heaven to cut R. Phinehas off from Rabbi's messengers. When this was told to Rabbi he exclaimed: 'Since I did not have the privilege of seeing the splendour of his countenance[34] in this world, perchance I will enjoy the privilege in the World to Come'.

In the *JT* version we have three stories each relating to a separate event in the life of R. Phinehas: the story of the donkey who refused to eat; the story of the river through which R. Phinehas passed; and the story of the meeting between Rabbi and R. Phinehas. In the *BT* version these three separate stories have become three episodes in the same story. It follows that the three story version must be the earlier. One can readily understand how, for the purposes of dramatic effect and in order to produce a coherent and consistent narrative, the three separate stories have been told as a single story. But it is impossible for an original single story to have been separated into three separate ones, each with circumstantial detail on its own, different from the details in the single story. Moreover, the *JT* version records the three stories together with other separate stories about R. Phinehas. It is as clear as can be that the *BT* version consists of a re-working of the earlier material. This is not, of course, to suggest that the *BT* editors had the actual text of the *JT* version before them,[35] only that in *JT* an earlier version has been preserved. Nor does it necessarily rule out the possibility that the *JT* version is also a re-working of earlier material.

We must now revert to the *BT* version to compare it with the *JT* version, noting the strong resemblances and the equally strong differences, for which latter some explanation must be sought.

In the *BT* version, as the beginning, corresponding to the second story in the *JT* version, R. Phinehas is on an errand of mercy, to redeem captives. In *JT* he is journeying to the House of Learning. In both versions he meets the resistance of the river Ginai and in both there are others who wish to cross the river; in *BT* the man with wheat for Passover and the Arab, in *JT* the disciples. In *JT* there is no lengthy dialogue with the river as in *BT*. It is possible that 'redemption of captives' is used in the *BT* version because here the river is made to argue that R. Phinehas can only be in doubt whether he will be successful in his errand; i.e. the captives may have escaped or he will fail to ransom them. Conversely, in the *JT* version the 'house of Learning' may be R. Phinehas's destination because the disciples are going on the same errand for the same purpose. That there are three persons in *BT* may be because of the general fondness of *BT* for sets of three.[36] The comparison of R. Phinehas's powers to those of Moses and the six hundred thousand is possibly due to the tendency of *BT* generally to ascribe exaggerated miraculous powers to the saints.[37] For the same reason it may well be that in *BT* R. Phinehas threatens the river that unless it parts he will decree that water will never flow through it, *BT* believing strongly in the powers of the saint to issue such decrees.[38] To be noticed, too, is the play on doing God's will in *BT*. R. Phinehas goes to do the will of his Maker, so does the river, and, in the continuation of the story, so does the donkey, which, evidently, goes to do God's will because R. Phinehas is riding on the donkey when he goes to redeem the captives.

In the story of the donkey refusing to eat, the *BT* version places the episode at an inn, whereas in the *JT* version the donkey is first stolen by the robbers and its final refusal to eat is at the home of R. Phinehas where the donkey has been returned. The difficulty from the Mishnah that animal food need not be tithed is raised in both versions (in *JT* of R. Phinehas by his servants, in *BT* by the Talmud)

but in *BT* a legalistic distinction is made, whereas in *JT* R. Phinehas
states that the animal is strict beyond the letter of the law.[39] The
difference is no doubt because in the *BT* version, since the affair
happens at an inn, the barley might well have been bought for
human consumption. In the *JT* version, on the other hand, it occurs
in R. Phinehas's own home and he orders the servants to feed the
donkey. In such circumstances they would presumably give the donkey
its usual feed of barley, and the reply in *BT* will not be applicable.

In the continuation of the story in *BT* and in the third story in *JT*,
R. Phinehas meets Rabbi but in the *JT* version R. Phinehas journeys
especially to Rabbi to express his disagreement with the latter's
attempt to abolish the Sabbatical year prohibitions. In *BT* R.
Phinehas is in any event reluctant to eat at another's table, using the
mules as a valid excuse, whereas in *JT* the sole reason for R.
Phinehas's refusal to dine with Rabbi is because of the mules.
Reflected in both stories is the suggested conflict between the House
of the *Nasi* and others who resented his authority.[40] In both stories
there is a miraculous intervention—the mountain in *BT*, the fire
from Heaven in *JT*—to prevent Rabbi inviting R. Phinehas. In both
versions the 'punch-line' has to do with this world and the next but there
is a vast difference between the two versions. In *JT* Rabbi expresses the
hope that he will meet with R. Phinehas in the next world. In *BT*
there is nothing about Rabbi meeting with R. Phinehas in the next
world but Rabbi declares that if R. Phinehas has these powers in this
world how much more in the next. Indeed, it is possible that the *BT*
version means that if Rabbi did not have the merit of inviting R.
Phinehas in this world how much less will he have the opportunity in
the next.[41] This would explain why Rabbi weeps in the *BT* version.
The *BT* story concludes with the statement about R. Phinehas's
independent spirit, a motif of the *BT* version but unknown in the *JT*
version.

The whole passage in *BT* is a carefully worked-out story, each
feature of which is made to be introduced at just the right time. The
third episode, the meeting of Rabbi and R. Phinehas, must come at
the end, after the other two, as the climax of the story, Rabbi and R.
Phinehas parting forever. The whole story is presented so as to
convey progressively the powers of the saint. First he exercises his
power over the river. Then even his donkey is seen to have been
imbued with this power. Finally, the power works not only against a
natural object, the river, and not only against the ignorant men at the

inn, but also against the *Nasi* who is obliged to admit that the power
will be even greater after the saint's death. Implied in the whole
manner in which the tale is told is the idea that because the saint is
determined to do the will of his Maker, his Maker bows, as it were, to
his will,[42] so that he can threaten the river and bring about its
parting; he can avoid unwittingly have his donkey eat untithed food;
and he can pursue without hindrance the way he has chosen of
refusing to enjoy any benefit from others. In the story, too, R.
Phinehas does not go out intentionally to exercise his powers but
does so only when he is obliged to face opposition through
unforeseen circumstances. He is no knight in shining armour going
out to do battle but a good man doing God's will and only invoking
the powers he has when he has no alternative. This explains the
verbs used in the narrative. R. Phinehas *meets*[43] the river. He
happens[44] upon an inn. The man with the wheat and the Arab just
happen to be there. Rabbi happens to *hear*[45] that R. Phinehas has
come. When R. Phinehas returns he just *happens*[46] to enter the gate
where the mules are waiting to provide him with the excuse he needs.
In the Elisha story, too, the dead man is accidentally cast into
Elisha's sepulchre.

The story of R. Phinehas and his donkey is also told in *Genesis
Rabbah*.[47] This is basically the story as told in *JT* with a few variants.
Thus in the Midrash the robbers send the donkey away and it arrives
by itself at the house of its master and R. Phinehas replies to the
question: 'What can I do if she wishes to be strict?'[48]

In *Aboth deRabbi Nathan*[49] there is yet another parallel to the *JT*
story, but here the story is in Hebrew and is not told of R. Phinehas
ben Yair but of the other renowned miracle-working saint, R. Hanina
ben Dosa. In this version, too, the donkey makes its own way home
but it is the saint's son who recognizes from the braying of the
donkey that it is their own donkey. More significantly, in this version
there is no reference to the donkey refusing to eat the barley because
it is untithed. Here the point of the story is rather that the animal
refused to eat or drink in the robbers' den.[50]

In both the *Genesis Rabbah* and the *JT* versions, the story of R.
Phinehas and the donkey that would not eat untithed produce is told
in connection with the story of R. Jeremiah who sent a basket of
untithed figs to R. Zera. R. Jeremiah relied on R. Zera not to eat until
the figs had been tithed while R. Zera relied on R. Jeremiah to have
tithed them. In connection with this it is said that R. Abba bar

Zamina said in the name of R. Lezer:[51] 'If the earlier teachers were like angels we are like human beings. But if they were like human beings then we are like donkeys.' To this R. Mana adds: 'We are not even like donkeys. The donkey of R. Phinehas b. Yair was given untithed barley and it did not eat but we have eaten figs that were untithed.'[52]

One further source must now be mentioned. This is in *b. Shabbat* 112b and reads: 'R. Zera said that Rabbah bar Zimona[53] said: If the earlier teachers were the sons of angels we are the sons of human beings. But if the earlier teachers were sons of human beings then we are like donkeys but not like the donkeys of R. Hanina b. Dosa[54] or R. Phinehas b. Yair but like other donkeys.'

In the light of the above analysis the development of the tale can plausibly be traced. Of the sources referred to above we have the following:

A. *The ARN version*
Hero of the tale: R. Hanina b. Dosa. The donkey neither eats nor drinks in the hideout of the robbers. Thus the theme is that of the animal who prevents his master benefiting from stolen property. The passage is in Hebrew.

B. *The Genesis Rabbah version*
Hero of the tale: R. Phinehas b. Yair. The donkey does not eat in the hideout of the robbers, hence the stolen property motif (and it is appended to the account of Abraham's camels who did not enjoy stolen food). But here the additional motif is found of the animal refusing to eat untithed food (appended to the story of R. Jeremiah and R. Zera).

C. *The JT version*
This is a parallel to B but is presented as one in a series of tales about R. Phinehas b. Yair and other miracle-workers (including R. Hanina b. Dosa, but excluding the story of his donkey as in *ARN*). (In both B and C the saying, 'If the earlier ones . . . ', occurs, but they both end only with the donkey of R. Phinehas b. Yair, no reference being made to R. Hanina b. Dosa).

D. *The BT version*
Hero of the story: R. Phinehas b. Yair. But here the three separate stories of the *JT* version have been put together to form three

episodes in the same story as a coherent tale. The robbery motif is not found here. Further motif found only here: 'If God prevents a mishap through the animal of the righteous. . . '

E. *The BT Shabbat passage*
'If the earlier ones . . . ' as in B and C but here in Hebrew. And in addition to the donkey of R. Phinehas b. Yair there is the donkey of R. Hanina b. Dosa.

F. *The BT passage Taanit 24a* (a similar story)
Hero of the story: R. Jose of Yokereth. Motif: the donkey who prevents his owner enjoying benefit from stolen property as in A.

It would appear that, in the stories told regarding the donkeys of the saints who refused to eat, the reason for the refusal was either to prevent their owner enjoying benefit from stolen property (R. Hanina b. Dosa in A and R. Jose of Yokereth in F) or from enjoying benefit from untithed property (R. Phinehas b. Yair in B, C and D). In B and C there are echoes of the robbery motif in the beginning of the story which makes the robbers steal the donkey which refuses to eat in their hideout. The conclusion drawn from the story is: 'If the earlier ones. . . ' In D the robbery motif is omitted, probably because it is necessary to give a coherent tale of the events that befell R. Phinehas on his travels in which the saint presumably rides on his donkey; to have the donkey stolen would interrupt the narrative for no purpose. Here in D the conclusion drawn from the story is: 'If God does not allow a mishap to the animals of the righteous . . .' E seems to know of both motifs (unless the reference to R. Hanina b. Dosa or R. Jose of Yokereth is a later gloss, in which case the saying is a paraphrase in Hebrew of that in B and C). In any event it is clear that in the D passage, our chief concern in this article, earlier material has been used and reshaped in order to provide a consistent and coherent narrative with a beginning, middle and end.

NOTES

1. *B. Ḥullin* 5b, 6a and 7a. The maxim is also found in *Yevamot* 99b; *Ketubot* 28b; *Gittin* 7a. I hope that this analysis is a not unfitting contribution to a *Festschrift* for a scholar who has done important work on Talmudic notions of saintliness and saintly powers.

2. There is no other mention in the Talmud of a River Ginai. In the parallel passage in *y. Demai* 3 (22a) R. Phinehas finds *ginai* in flood, not 'River Ginai'. See Jastrow (*s.v.*), for *ginai* as 'a dyke for irrigating gardens' (from *gan*); but it is unlikely that such a dyke is referred to since here the reference is to the *River* Ginai which could not be crossed except by a miracle. For the redemption of captives as a great *mitzvah*, see *b. Baba Bathra* 8a.

3. That the doubtful yields to the certain (*eyn safek motzi meydey vaddai*) is a legal principle, see *b. Pesahim* 9a.

4. Rashi: this means R. Phinehas kept the river 'talking' so that the other two could cross, but the river was only parted once.

5. Exodus 14.21-22.

6. I.e. on the errand of mercy; the same expression 'will of the Maker' is used in the narrative previously by R. Phinehas and by the river.

7. *M. Demai* 1.3.

8. The significance of this is that the barley had the status of food brought from an *am ha-aretz*, *demai* which is only prohibited, when untithed, by Rabbinic law and hence there are certain leniencies.

9. Rashi: 'and it is fitting to enjoy benefit from them'. The expression *yisrael kedoshim hem* is found in *b. Niddah* 17a. The expression *yisrael kedoshim* without *hem* is found in *b. Hullin* 91a, 92b and *b. Pesahim* 83b, all three, in fact, the same text.

10. See *b. Nedarim* 49a where the expression 'the angel of death is in this one's house' is used by a physician who sees in a house he visits food injurious to health.

11. Interpreted by the Rabbis to include causing another to sin. Since it is forbidden to keep these dangerous animals it is forbidden to sell them, because then the purchaser would sin and the seller would have placed a 'stumbling block before the blind'.

12. Rashi comments: 'I shall send them away into the forest', i.e. simply to abandon them would still offend against placing a stumbling block before the blind, in that those who acquired the mules after they had been abandoned would be guilty of keeping dangerous animals.

13. Rashi: since in the forest they will run wild without anyone to keep them in check.

14. Rashi: this would not offend against the prohibition of wanton destruction, mentioned after this, since the mules, no longer dangerous, could still be used for ploughing.

15. Interpreted by the Rabbis as referring to any unnecessary waste of natural resources.

16. This expression might be understood figuratively as 'they fell out' or 'they were no longer on speaking terms', and is so used in post-Talmudic literature, but here it seems to have been intended to be taken literally. In the parallel passage in *JT* it is 'fire from Heaven' that causes the separation of one from the other.

17. For Rabbi 'weeping' see *b. Ḥagigah* 15b; *b. 'Avodah Zarah* 10b, 17a, 18a—all these in connection with someone's death and his entrance into Paradise.
18. Rashi: but during Elisha's lifetime great effort was required for him to revive the son of the Shunamite (2 Kings 4.32-38).
19. Rashi: and had nothing to do with Elisha's own powers.
20. Rashi: Elisha had to revive *two* corpses for Elijah's one.
21. Here is inserted some further material by association, but this is not germane to our theme.
22. Lit. 'from the day he stood by his own mind'.
23. In *Seridey Bavli*, ed. Z. Dimitrovsky, New York, 1979, the text has 'even of his father'.
24. *Y. Demai* 1.3 (21d-22a).
25. *ha-da alivta* but here in *BT aniyah zo* in Hebrew. Although the framework of the story is in Aramaic most of the direct speech is in Hebrew.
26. That is, R. Phinehas knows that the animal would not have eaten outside its own house in the hideout of the robbers. There is consequently a double theme: a) the animal refused to eat *anything* in the den of the robbers; b) the animal refused to eat untithed food even in its own home.
27. Here in *JT* it is stated explicitly that it was *demai* produce that was given to the donkey.
28. *Bet Vaad* usual in *JT* for *Bet ha-Midrash*.
29. See *b. Shabbat* 32a for the idea that if a miracle is performed on a man's behalf there is a deduction from the reward due to him because of his merits. Possibly, the idea here is that if the disciples 'give way' to others the river will 'give way' to them; see *b. Yoma* 23a 'whoever gives way (*ma'avir al middotav*) his sins will be forgiven'.
30. Because, in Rabbi's day, the majority of Jews did not live in Palestine and hence the Sabbatical Year was no longer in operation.
31. I.e. because R. Phinehas referred to the endives and so avoided any reply to Rabbi's question about produce. For a similar evasion by referring to something other than the topic of the question, see *b. Pesaḥim* 3b.
32. Here in *JT mulvata*, in *BT kudnaita*.
33. *yehudai* see *Peney Moshe*, possibly a pun on R. Yehudah; or perhaps *yehudai* does not mean 'Jews' but 'of Yehudah', i.e. the servants of R. Judah the Prince.
34. Lit. 'to be sated by him'.
35. On this question see L. Greenwald, *Harau Mesaderey ha-Bavli et ha-Yerushalmi*, New York, 1954 and J.N. Epstein, *Mevuot le-Sifrut ha-Amoraim*, Jerusalem, 1962, pp. 290-92. On the use of Palestinian material in the Babylonian Aggadah, see the important remarks of J. Heinemann, *Aggadot ve-Toledotehen*, Jerusalem, 1974, chapter 11, pp. 163-79.
36. See my article, 'The Numbered Sequence as a Literary Device in the

204

Babylonian Talmud' in *Biblical and Other Studies in honor of Robert Gordis*, ed. Reuben Ahroni, *Hebrew Annual Review* 7 (1983), pp. 137-49. It might also be noted that in the *JT* version only two attempts are made to feed the donkey but in the *BT* version there are *three* attempts.

37. See e.g. *b. Berakhot* 20a and the miracle tales in the third chapter of *Taanit* (unless R. Joseph is being sarcastic; but this is unlikely).

38. See *b. Shabbat* 59b, where the same root *gazar* is used.

39. Lit. 'she is very strict with herself'; but obviously the meaning is on behalf of R. Phinehas, not that the donkey had to obey the law or be very strict in its observance.

40. See A. Büchler, 'The Conspiracy of R. Nathan and R. Meir against the Patriarch Simon ben Gamaliel', in *Studies in Jewish History* by A. Büchler, ed. I. Brodie and J. Rabbinowitz, Oxford, 1956, chapter 6, pp. 160-79. Rabban Simon b. Gamaliel was, of course, the father of Rabbi Judah the Prince.

41. The meaning then would be: if there was a miraculous intervention to separate the two in this world *a fortiori* they would be kept apart in the next world. Cf. *b. Baba Bathra* 75a for the righteous occupying separate 'canopies' in Paradise.

42. Cf. *m. Abot* 2.4 'Make His will as thy will so that He will make thy will His will'.

43. *paga' beh.*

44. *'ikliai.*

45. *šama'.*

46. *'itrami.*

47. *Gen. Rabbah* 60.8, ed. Theodor-Albeck, pp. 648-50.

48. In *y. Demai* R. Phinehas replies: 'What can I do if this poor beast is very strict on herself?' There is no significance to these minor variants. On the relationship between *JT* and *Genesis Rabbah*, see Epstein, *Mevuot*, pp. 287-90.

49. Ed. Schechter, New York, 1967, A, chapter 8, p. 38.

50. In the *Genesis Rabbah* passage the story of R. Phinehas is appended to the verse, 'and he freed the camels' (Gen. 24.32), upon which there is the comment: 'he undid their muzzles'. Abraham's camels were muzzled (*Gen. R.* 59.11) so that they would not eat of anything that did not belong to their owner. To this the question is asked: why did Abraham's camels require to be muzzled (see Albeck's note 3 on this), since R. Phinehas's donkey did not eat and the beasts of Abraham would surely not be inferior to R. Phinehas's donkey. This 'robbery' motif is the one in *ARN* where R. Hanina b. Dosa's donkey refuses to eat or *drink* in the robber's hideout, i.e. because their food and drink was all stolen property.

51. Thus in *Genesis Rabbah*, adding the name *Zeira* after R. Lezer—R. Lezer Zeira (see Albeck's note for variants). Eleazar Zeira is mentioned in *Baba Kamma* 59b. Is it possible that he was called Eleazar *Zeira* ('young',

'immature', 'inferior') because he was the author of this saying that the later ones were 'inferior' to the ancients? On the phenomenon of the author of a saying having a name connected with the saying, see my article, 'How much of the Babylonian Talmud is Pseudepigraphic?', *JJS* 28 (1977), p. 56 n. 30.

52. In the parallel passage in *y. Shekalim* 5.1 (48 c-d) R. Mana says, 'At that time they said', i.e. when R. Jeremiah sent the untithed figs to R. Zera, 'they' being R. Jeremiah and R. Zera. Possibly 'R. Mana' is a corruption of the name 'Zamina' or perhaps there is a confusion with R. Zera.

53. Here the order is reversed. It is certainly puzzling that 'Zamina' resembles 'R. Mana' and 'Eleazar Zeira' resembles 'R. Zera'. The texts are in any event confused.

54. Thus the reading in the current texts. But see Rashi and the marginal note in the Vilna Romm edition for the reading 'R. Jose of Yokereth' (in *Taanit* 24a), as in F.

TANNAITIC EXEGESIS OF THE GOLDEN CALF EPISODE[1]

Irving J. Mandelbaum

The University of Texas at Austin
Rutgers University

Introduction

One[2] of the questions that arise in studying early rabbinic interpretation of the Bible concerns whether exegetical traditions attributed to authorities of a specific period present a coherent account of a particular biblical episode. At issue is whether a scriptural passage has a single 'tannaitic' or 'amoraic' interpretation, a view that is shared by traditions assigned to different authorities and appearing in diverse documents. In this paper I examine this question with regard to exegeses of the golden calf episode (Exodus 32)[3] that are attributed to *tannaim*.[4] What I aim to show is that a common view of this story does inform the various interpretations that are assigned to these authorities. Specifically, virtually all of these exegetical traditions treat the incident of the calf as a classic story of sin and atonement. All assume that Aaron and Israel commit serious sins, are punished for their transgressions, and are ultimately forgiven by God. The coherence of this reading of the calf-story, moreover, becomes clear when its interpretation is contrasted with that of certain traditions attributed to *amoraim*. These latter exegeses present a strong apologetic for the main characters of this episode, defending Aaron's actions as justified or absolving Israel of any guilt. In contrast with this view, traditions assigned to *tannaim* choose to maintain that Aaron and Israel did transgress, and that their only defense is that they repented of their sin. These exegeses, therefore, view the incident of the golden calf as illustrating the process of sin and atonement: Israel sins and receives punishment for its sins, but it is also offered the possibility of atonement, even for the worst of its transgressions.

This study selects from compilations of tannaitic materials[5] those
exegeses that deal with three main themes of the golden calf episode:
(1) the seriousness of the sin of the calf, (2) the punishment for
Israel's sins, and (3) God's forgiveness of Aaron and the people.[6] In
discussing these topics I first present each pericope individually,
analyzing its literary structure and determining its main point. Then
follows a summary of the interpretations that these pericopae
present, showing how they relate to the theme in question. In this
way I demonstrate how diverse exegeses attributed to *tannaim* all
share the same understanding of the golden calf episode as a story of
sin and repentance.

Three themes in the Tannaitic exegesis of the golden calf episode

The seriousness of the sin

I begin with the theme of the seriousness of the sin of the calf. The
pericopae that deal with this theme are found at *t. Shab.* 1.16 and
Sifre Deut. 1.9 and 10. *T. Shab.* 1.16 reads as follows:[7]

> A.   These are among the laws which they stated in the upper
>   room of Hananiah b. Hezekiah b. Gurion when they went
>   up to visit him. They took a vote, and the House of Shammai
>   outnumbered the House of Hillel. Eighteen rules did they
>   decree on that very day [*m. Shab.* 1.4A-C].
>
> B.   And that day was as harsh for Israel as the day on which the
>   golden calf was made.
>
>   (ed. Lieberman, *Tosefta Moed*, p. 4, ll.36-38;
>   B: *y. Shab.* 1.4 [3c]; *b. Shab.* 17a)

Commenting on *m. Shab.* 1.4, Tosefta compares the day on which
House of Shammai attained a majority to the day of the making of
the calf. While this comparison is perhaps exaggerated,[8] of interest
here is that the making of the calf is used as an example of an evil day
throughout Israel's history. Rather then seek to minimize Israel's sin,
Tosefta here uses this event as a standard against which other evil
happenings are measured. The day of the golden calf thus remains on
Israel's calendar as a reminder of its sin.

Sifre Deut. 1.9 and 1.10 separately[9] link the sin of the calf to the
term 'Di-zahab' (Deut. 1.1). *Sifre Deut.* 1.9 reads as follows:[10]

> 1.   A.   'And Di-zahab' (Deut. 1.1)—
>   B.   He said to them, 'I would have overlooked (*wtrh*)

everything that you have done, [but] the incident of the calf is worse for me than all of them'.

2.   A.   R. Judah would say, 'A parable: To what may this be likened? To one who caused a great deal of trouble to his fellow. In the end he added one more trouble. [His fellow] said to him, 'I would have overlooked everything that you had done to me, [but] this is worse for me than all of them'.

        B.   'Thus God said to Israel, "I would have overlooked everything that you had done, but the incident of the calf is worse for me than all of them"'.

(ed. Finkelstein, p. 6, ll.1-5)

This pericope continues *Sifre Deut.* 1's exegesis of Deut. 1.1 as a list of wilderness locations at which Israel sinned. 1.A-B interprets 'Di-zahab' as *dai-zahab*, that is, 'the [sin of the] gold[en calf] is enough', or one sin too many.[11] The point of 1.A-B (as illustrated by Judah's parable in 2.A-B), therefore, is that the sin of the calf is the worst of all of the transgressions that Israel committed in the wilderness.

Sifre Deut. 1.10 supplements 1.9.1-2 with a similar exegesis of 'Di-Zahab':

1.   A.   R. Simeon says, 'A parable: To what may this be likened? To one who used to entertain sages and their disciples, and everyone praised him.

        B.   'Gentiles came and he entertained them [as well]; robbers, and he entertained them [also].

        C.   'People said, "That is so-and-so's nature—to entertain anyone at all"'.

        D.   'So did Moses say to Israel, "Enough gold" (*wdy zhb*) for the tabernacle, and "enough gold" for the calf'!

2.   A.   R. Benaiah says, 'The Israelites worshipped idols, and so are liable to extermination. Let the gold of the tabernacle come and effect atonement for the gold of the calf'.

3.   A.   R. Yose b. Haninah says, 'You shall make a cover (*kprt*) of pure gold' (Exod. 25.17)—

        B.   'let the gold of the cover come and effect atonement (*wykpr*) for the gold of the calf'.

(ed. Finkelstein, p. 6, ll.6-11;
3.A-B: *y. Sheq.* 1.1 [45d])

Like *Sifre Deut.* 1.9.1A-B, Simeon's parable also interprets 'Di-Zahab' as *dai-zahab*, though now the term is understood to imply that 'there is enough gold' for the calf as well as for the tabernacle. This parable, which stresses Israel's giving to the calf as well as to the tabernacle, is then supplemented by the exegeses of both Benaiah (2A) and Yose b. Haninah (3A-B), which view Israel's giving to the tabernacle as atoning for its making of the calf. By including these latter two traditions, it is possible that the redactor of the pericope intended to offset Simeon's negative saying about Israel with a more positive view of precisely the same actions. At the same time, however, these exegeses (and that of Benaiah in particular) do not deny that Israel was guilty of idolatry, but rather emphasize that Israel atoned for that sin. Even in portraying Israel more positively, therefore, the redactor of *Sifre Deut.* 1.9 cites traditions that accept Israel's responsibility for its sin. All of the views cited in the pericope, therefore, agree that Israel worshipped the golden calf and thereby committed a serious transgression.

The exegeses of *t. Shab.* 1.16 and *Sifre Deut.* 1.9 and 10 thus all treat the episode of the calf as a major sin. This was the worst of all of Israel's sins in the wilderness, and appears as the paradigmatic evil day on Israel's calendar. Even the traditions that stress Israel's repentance for this sin treat it as a grave transgression that almost destroys the people. All of these exegeses, therefore, stress that Israel sinned greatly in making and worshipping the golden calf.

The punishment for the sin
The seriousness with which tannaitic exegeses viewed the incident of the calf also finds expression through the punishments that are assigned to this sin. Four pericopae deal with this matter: *Sifre Deut.* 319.3, *Mekhilta Baḥodesh* 2 and 9, and *Sifre Num.* 1.10.2-3. Let us examine each of these units in turn.

Sifre Deut. 319.3 speaks of the punishment for the calf in a general way:

1. A.   Another interpretation: 'You neglected (*tšy*) the Rock that begot you' (Deut. 32.18).
    B.   'Whenever I want to do good things for you, you weaken (*mtyšym*) the power of heaven.
    C.   'You stood at the sea and said, "This is my God and I will glorify him" (Exod. 15.2).
    D.   'I wanted to do good things for you, but you backslid and said, "Let us set a head and return to Egypt" (Num. 14.4).

E.   'You stood before Mount Sinai and said, "All that the Lord has spoken we will faithfully do" (Exod. 24.7)!

F.   'I wanted to do good things for you, but you backslid and said to the calf, "These are your gods, O Israel" (Exod. 32.4).

G.   'Accordingly, whenever I want to do good things for you, you weaken the power of heaven'.

           (ed. Finkelstein, p. 365, ll.9-14; F-G: *Lam. R.* 1.33)

This pericope describes the sin of the calf, together with that of the spies, as one of reneging on one's promises. Israel is therefore punished for this sin by God's withholding of certain good things that they might otherwise have received.

This same idea, that Israel loses certain gifts because of the sin of the calf, also appears in an exegesis found at *Mekhilta Baḥodesh* 2:

A.   From here they said, 'Israel had been worthy to eat of the Holy Things before they made the calf.

B.   '[But] once they made the calf, [the Holy Things] were taken from them and given to the priests.'

           (ed. Horovitz-Rabin, p. 209, ll.4-6)

A-B appears in a series of exegesis of Exod. 19.5, 'You shall be to me a kingdom of priests and a holy nation'. A takes the phrase 'a kingdom of priests' to mean that, at Sinai, Israel had the right to eat holy things, as priests do. B then states that this right was taken away from Israel because of the sin of the calf, so that now only actual priests may eat these foods (Lev. 22.10). The making of the calf thus leads Israel to lose its priestly status and privileges.

An exegesis found in *Mekhilta Baḥodesh* 9 similarly states that Israel lost immortality because of the calf:

A.   'May they always be of such mind, [to revere Me and follow all My commandments, that it may go well with them and with their children forever!] (Deut. 5.26).

B.   'If it were possible to cause the Angel of Death to pass away [from them], I would do so, but the decree has already been decreed.'

C.   R. Yose says, 'It was on this condition that the Israelites stood on Mount Sinai, on condition that the Angel of Death not rule over them,

D.   as it is said, "I had said: You are divine beings, sons of the Most High, all of you" (Ps. 82.6).

E.   'But you have corrupted your deeds,
F.   '"Surely you shall die as men do, fall like any prince" (*ibid.*,
            v. 7)'.

                    (ed. Horovitz-Rabin, p. 237, ll.8-12; C-F: *b. A.Z.* 5a)

Yose (C-F) applies Ps. 82.6-7 to the condition of Israel before and after their sin. Israel had originally been promised immortality in return for their observance of God's commandments, but this regard was taken away from them when they 'corrupted their deeds'. Although this phrase does not mention a specific transgression, it most likely refers to the making of the calf.[12] The exegeses found in *Mekhilta Baḥodesh* 2 and 9, therefore, both portray the sin of the calf as the major transgression of Israel, a sin that causes the people to lose God's gifts.

Finally, the idea that the sin of the calf marks a turning point in Israel's history also appears in *Sifre Num.* 1.10.2-3:[13]

2.   A.   R. Yose the Galilean says, 'Come and take note of how great is the power of sin. For before the people had laid hands on transgression, people afflicted with flux and lepers were not located among them, but after they had laid hands on transgression, people afflicted with flux and lepers did find a place among them.

     B.   'Accordingly, we learn that these three events took place on one and the same day: [transgression, the presence of those afflicted with flux, the development of leprosy among the people].'

3.   A.   R. Simeon b. Yohai says, 'Come and take note of how great is the power of sin. For before the people had laid hands on transgression, what is stated in their regard?'

     B.   '"Now the appearance of the glory of the Lord was like a devouring fire on the top of the mountain in the sight of the people of Israel" (Exod. 24.17).

     C.   'Nonetheless, the people did not fear, nor were they afraid.

     D.   'But once they had laid hands on transgression, what is said in their regard?

     E.   "And when Aaron and all the people of Israel saw Moses, behold, the skin of his face shone, and they were afraid to come near him" (Exod. 34.30).'

                            (ed. Horovitz, p. 4, ll.14-20)

Sifre Num. 1.10.2 and 1.10.3 appear to have been redacted by the same hand, for both begin with the clause, 'Come and take note of how great is the power of sin' (2A, 3A), and both include the phrase, 'but once they had laid hands on transgression' (2A, 3D). Although only Simeon b. Yohai explicitly identifies this transgression with the sin of the calf, it seems likely that Yose the Galilean refers to this major sin as well, and the redactor of the pericope perhaps implies this understanding of Yose's saying in formulating and linking these two sayings together. Both of these authorities, therefore, appear to use the golden calf to illustrate the power of sin, viewing this transgression as permanently changing either Israel's state of purity or its psychological condition.

We thus see that unrelated traditions from three different documents, *Sifre* to Deuteronomy, *Mekhilta* of R. Ishmael, and *Sifre* to Numbers, all treat the punishment for the incident of the calf in a similar manner. All of these exegeses regard the sin of the calf as in some way seriously altering Israel's condition as a people, whether by losing the right to eat holy things or by becoming subject to either fear, uncleanness, or death. In this view the episode of the calf may be compared to the story of the fall of Adam and Eve in Genesis 3. Just as the first man and woman disobey a direct command by God, and so cause a worsening of their condition, so does Israel suffer a loss of status and privileges when it goes back on its promise at Sinai. The incident of the calf is thus viewed by the above exegeses as the story of Israel's fall, describing the most significant sin, accompanied by the most serious punishments, in Israel's history.

Atonement and forgiveness
I turn now to the theme of atonement. This question, already mentioned above at *Sifre Deut.* 10.1, is developed most thoroughly by *Sifra*, which attemps to show that Aaron and Israel are forgiven for their sin on the eve of Aaron's consecration as high priest. *Sifra* explores this issue at *Ṣav, Mekhilta de-Miluim* 1.1, and *Shemini* 1.3-5, 8. Let us examine each of these pericopae in turn.

Sifre Ṣav, Mekhilta de-Miluim 1.1 discusses the effect of the sin of the calf on Aaron at the time of his consecration:

A. 'And the Lord spoke to Moses, [saying], "Take Aaron along with his sons"' (Lev. 8.1).
B. Why does Scripture say this?
C. Because it says, 'And the Lord sent a plague upon the people

for what they did with the calf that Aaron made' (Exod. 32.35)—this implies that Aaron had been distanced [from God].

E. Whence do we know that Moses knew that Aaron had been distanced [from God]?

F. As it is said, 'Moreover, the Lord was angry enough with Aaron to have destroyed him; so I also interceded for Aaron at that time' (Deut. 9.20),

G. and it is not said concerning [Aaron, as it is said regarding the people], 'And that time, too, the Lord gave heed to me' (Deut. 9.19).

H. [Thus] when it says, 'Take Aaron along with his sons', Moses knew that Aaron had been brought near.

I. Whence do we know that it was in Aaron's heart that he had been distanced?

J. It is said at the end of the matter, 'Come forward to the altar' (Lev. 9.7).

K. But had not Moses already arranged before him all of the offerings, [so that this command is unnecessary]?

L. But [this was said] so that [Aaron's] heart should not stray (*šl' yhyh lbw ldbr 'ḥr*), [that is, lest Aaron be unwilling to officiate because he knew that he had been distanced from God].[14]

M. [Thus] when it says, 'Take Aaron along with his sons', Aaron knew that he had been brought near.

(ed. Weiss, 40d)

This pericope makes three points concerning the punishment of Aaron: (1) that God had distanced Aaron from himself because of the sin of the calf (A-D), (2) that Moses knew of this 'distancing' because God did not respond to his prayer on behalf of Aaron as he had to his prayer for the people (E-H), and (3) that Aaron himself sensed God's anger and was therefore reluctant to take up his duties (I-M). A-D and E-H underline the seriousness of Aaron's offense, for even Moses' prayer could not help him, and he remains unforgiven up to this point. I-M then proves that Aaron himself was conscious of his alienation from God.[15] The point of this unit, therefore, is that Aaron was not only punished for the sin of the calf, but he was aware of this punishment, and only God's explicit command at his consecration tells him that he is now forgiven.

The theme of forgiveness is developed with regard to both Aaron and Israel at *Sifra Shemini* 1.3-5. *Shemini* 1.3 reads as follows:

A. 'And he said to Aaron, "Take a calf of the herd for a sin offering [and a ram for a burnt offering, without blemish, and bring them before the Lord]"' (Lev. 9.2).

B. This teaches that Moses said to Aaron, 'Aaron, my brother, even though the divine presence is reconciled to forgive your sin, you have to place [something] in Satan's mouth. Send a gift before you enter the sanctuary, lest he accuse you[16] when you come into the sanctuary.

C. 'And lest you say, "Am I the one who required atonement? But Israel also requires atonement!"

D. '[This is so], as it is said, "And speak to the Israelites, saying, take a he-goat for a sin offering; [a calf and a lamb, yearlings without blemish, for a burnt offering; and an ox and a ram for an offering of well-being to sacrifice before the Lord; and a meal offering mingled with oil; for today the Lord will appear to you]"' (Lev. 9.3-4).

E. And why did Israel see fit to bring more than Aaron?

F. Rather, [Moses] said to them, 'You had something in your hands, [that is, you transgressed] at the beginning, and you had something in your hands at the end.

G. 'You had something in your hands in the beginning, "[Then they took Joseph's tunic], slaughtered a he-goat, [and dipped the tunic in the blood]" (Gen. 37.31).

H. 'And you had something in your hands at the end, "They have made themselves a molten calf" (Exod. 32.8).

I. 'Let the he-goat come and atone for the incident of the he-goat, and let the calf come and atone for the incident of the calf.'

(ed. Weiss, 43c)

A-D makes the point that the sin offerings of both Aaron and the people are meant to atone for the sin of the calf. B and C-D, however, appear to present different views of Aaron's atonement, for B states that Aaron's offering is intended as a bribe for Satan, and specifically not to atone for the transgression, as C-D implies. It is possible, therefore, that, for a reason now unclear, B sought to emphasize that Aaron had been forgiven even before his consecration. This point, however, was lost with the addition of C-D to B. A-D as a whole, therefore, implies that both Aaron and the people are forgiven through their respective sacrifices.

E-I supplements A-D with a discussion of Israel's sin offerings. Apparently reading Lev. 9.3 as 'Take a he-goat for a sin offering and a calf', rather than 'and a calf and a lamb... for a burnt offering', E-I explains that Israel had to bring two sin offerings instead of Aaron's one in order to atone for Joseph's kidnapping as well as for the calf. In the view of this pericope, therefore, the sin offerings of Lev. 9.2-3 correspond to the sin of the calf, and it was therefore at Aaron's consecration that both Aaron and Israel are forgiven for this sin.

Sifra Shemini 1.4 similarly takes the sacrifices of Lev. 9.2-4 to correspond to the sin of the calf:

A. '[And speak to the Israelites, saying: Take a he-goat for a sin offering; a calf and a lamb, yearlings without blemish, for a burnt offering;] and an ox and a ram for offerings of well-being' (Lev. 9.3-4).

B. [The calf and the ox are necessary] because the sin was compared to two kinds [of animals],

C. as it is said, 'They have made themselves a molten calf' (Exod. 32.8),

D. and below it says, 'They exchanged their glory for the image of a bull that feeds on grass' (Ps. 106.20).

E. Let the ox come and atone for the making of the bull, and let the calf come and atone for the making of the calf.

F. Know that the divine presence is reconciled to forgive your sins, for the [animal corresponding to the] sin that you are [most] afraid of has already been sacrificed before the divine presence,

G. as it is said, 'To sacrifice before the Lord' (Lev. 9.4).

H. Said Israel before Moses, 'But how can a province praise the king and not see the face of the king?'

I. He said to them, 'For this reason, "For today, the Lord will appear to you"' (Lev. 9.4).

(ed. Weiss, 43c-d)

This pericope consists of three comments (A-E, F-G, and H-I) to successive parts of Lev. 9.4. Of present concern are A-E and F-G. Like *Sifra Shemini* 1.3, A-E views Israel's offerings as related to the sin of the calf, with the calf and the ox of Lev. 9.3-4 corresponding respectively to the bull of Ps. 106.20 and the calf of Exod. 32.8. F-G states that the people feared that God would not forgive them for the sin of the calf, and that Moses reassured them by noting that their sacrifice of the calf atones for that sin. F-G thus develops with regard to the people two themes which we have seen raised with respect to Aaron, namely, the fear of the sin of the calf and the offering of a calf in atonement for that sin. The point of F-G, therefore, is that the people were afraid of not being forgiven, but that the offering of a calf ensured their atonement.

Sifra Shemini 1.5 similarly emphasizes God's forgiveness of the people:

A. 'They brought [to the front of the Tent of Meeting] the things that Moses had commanded' (Lev. 9.5)—with haste.

B. 'And the whole community came forward and stood before the Lord' (*ibid.*)—

C. They all approached joyfully and stood before him.

D. A parable: A king was angry with his wife and expelled her.

E. After some time he was reconciled to her. She immediately girded her loins and bound her shoulders and served him excessively.

F. Thus also Israel, once they saw that God was reconciled to forgive their sin, they came near in joy and stood before him.

G. Thus it says, 'And the whole community came forward and stood before the Lord'.

(ed. Weiss, 43d)

C interprets Lev. 9.5 to mean that Israel came forward joyfully before God, and D-G explains that this was because they were forgiven for their sin. Lev. 9.5 is thus understood here to describe the result of God's forgiveness of the people for the sin of the golden calf.

Finally, *Sifra Shemini* 1.8 returns to the subject of Aaron's state of mind at his consecration:

A. '[Then Moses said to Aaron], "Come forward to the altar"' (Lev. 9.7).

B. A parable: To what may this be likened?

C. It is similar to a human king who married a woman, and she was embarrassed [to come] before him.

D. Her sister came to her and said, 'Why are you entering into this matter if not to serve the king? Be bold and come and serve the king.'

E. Thus Moses said to Aaron, 'Aaron, my brother, why were you chosen to be high priest, if not that you should serve before the Holy One, Blessed be He? Be bold and come and perform your service.'

F. And some say that Aaron saw the altar as [being in] the image of an ox, and was afraid of it.

G. And Moses said to him, 'My brother, do not [be afraid] of that of which you are afraid. Be bold and come forward to it.'

H.   Thus it says, 'Come forward unto the altar'.

                                                  (ed. Weiss, 43d)

This unit first compares Aaron's reluctance to serve God to a new queen who hesitates to go in to her king (A-E). F-G (with G formulated to accord with C-E) then presents Aaron as so obsessed with the sin of the calf that the altar takes the shape of that animal. Like *Sifra Ṣav, Mekhilta de-Miluim* 1.1, therefore, this pericope explores the psychological effect of the sin upon Aaron. In both pericopae Aaron's consciousness of his sin makes him unwilling to take on his new duties, and in both instances Moses encourages him by implying that God has forgiven him. In the view of *Sifra*, therefore, the sin of the calf greatly troubles Aaron at his consecration, but at the same time he is forgiven for this transgression.

We have thus seen how *Sifra* emphasizes that God forgives the sin of the golden calf at Aaron's consecration. Although both Aaron and Israel are fearful of not receiving atonement, Sifra seeks to show that God does become reconciled to them at this time. Thus Aaron could serve as high priest, and Israel could offer sacrifices, without concern that the sin of the calf would render the service of the Tabernacle unacceptable. The point of these pericopae, therefore, is that Aaron and Israel are greatly concerned about their sins at the golden calf, but are forgiven with Aaron's elevation to the high priesthood.

Conclusion

The story of sin, punishment, and atonement that is told by the traditions attributed to *tannaim* stands in sharper focus when contrasted with the view of certain later, amoraic exegeses. For example, *Lev. R.* 10.3 offers a number of possible explanations as to why Aaron built the altar: (1) because he feared the people would kill him and be beyond forgiveness (10.3.1),[17] (2) in order to delay its completion until Moses could arrive, (3) to dedicate the altar to God rather than to the calf (10.3.2), or (4) to take the guilt of the people upon himself alone (10.3.3). Similarly, *Lev. R.* 27.8 relieves Israel of responsibility by explaining the building of the calf in a number of ways: (1) the people were falsely accused of idolatry (27.8.1), (2) the 'mixed multitude', and not Israel, made the calf (27.8.2), or (3) Israel sinned inadvertently (27.8.3). Such attempts to defend the actions of Aaron and Israel are conspicuous by their almost total absence among the tannaitic traditions.[18] Rather than treating Aaron as well-intentioned or the people as innocent, traditions attributed to *tannaim* affirm that both Aaron and Israel did indeed sin. The incident of the calf is not to be explained away, but instead should be seen to serve as a model for a study of sin and atonement.

The tannaitic exegeses of the golden calf episode, attributed to various authorities and drawn from different documents, thus all appear to view this bibilical incident in a similar way. Common to all of these traditions is the view that the event takes place just as Scripture describes it. Aaron makes the calf and builds the altar, and Israel commits the sin of idolatry. These actions are not defended or excused, but rather used to teach important lessons. Israel's transgression teaches about the power of sin, which can cause the fall of an entire people from a highly elevated status. Aaron's repentance in turn illustrates the power of atonement, which enables even an idolater to be accepted as high-priest. The overall message of these tannaitic exegeses, therefore, concerns the reality for Israel of both sin and atonement: Israel can and does commit serious sins, thereby meriting the severest of punishments, but it also possesses the ability to repent, and so to receive the forgiveness of God that is always at hand.

NOTES

1. Dr Geza Vermes, as my supervisor at Oxford, introduced me to the study of biblical exegesis in general and to the history of interpretation of Exodus 32 in particular ('Early Jewish Exegesis of Exodus 32: A Study of Targum Pseudo-Jonathan', M. Phil. thesis, 1979). I am very grateful to Dr Vermes for what he taught me then, and for his support, collegiality, and warm friendship throughout the years since.

2. A previous version of this paper was presented at the History and Literature of Early Rabbinic Judaism Section of the Annual Meeting of the Society of Biblical Literature, Chicago, Illinois, USA, November 22, 1988. I would like to thank in particuiar Professor Alan Avery-Peck (Tulane University), who read an earlier draft of this paper and offered numerous helpful comments and suggestions. I am grateful as well to Professors Martin Jaffee (University of Washington) and Lawrence Schiffman (New York University) for their comments and suggestions. Any errors in the paper remain my responsibility alone.

3. By 'exegeses of the golden calf episode' I refer both to traditions that comment directly on Exodus 32 and to sayings that mention the incident of the calf without verses from this chapter.

4. I do not assume that the attributions of sayings to *tannaim* can be accepted at face value, or that exegeses found in so-called 'tannaitic' compilations (namely, *Mekhilta deRabbi Ishmael, Mekhilta deRabbi Simeon b. Yohai, Sifra, Sifre* to Numbers, *Sifre Zuta, Sifre* to Deuteronomy, and *Avot deRabbi Nathan*) necessarily reflect biblical interpretation in the time of the *tannaim* (c. 70-220 CE). Rather, I agree with Gary Porton's statement on this question ('Defining Midrash', in Jacob Neusner, ed., *The Study of Ancient Judaism*, New York: Ktav, 1981, I, p. 78):

> The classification of some *midrashim* as Tannaitic should also be abandoned. If by the term one means that only *tannaim* are cited in the text, the rest of the midrashic literature should be classified as Tannaitic-Amoraic, a classification which, to my knowledge, fortunately has not been proposed by anyone. If the term is meant to indicate the period in which the texts came into being, I believe that the work has not been done which would establish this as a fact. Therefore, I suggest that we also abandon this term as a classification for midrashic documents.

'Tannaitic' compilations, therefore, refer only to documents that contain exegeses attributed solely to *tannaim*. While the redactors of these documents perhaps view them as forming the earliest stage of rabbinic exegesis, we have no evidence that this is indeed the case. Rather, we can conclude that these documents present us with the earliest traditions assigned to *tannaim*.

I note that in not accepting the tannaitic attributions at face value, and in distinguishing between exegeses attributed to *tannaim* in earlier and later documents, this paper differs from two earlier studies of the exegesis of the golden calf episode, A. Marmorstein, 'Judaism and Christianity in the Middle of the Third Century', in J. Rabbinowitz and M.S. Lew, eds., *Studies in Jewish Theology. Arthur Marmorstein Memorial Volume*, London: Oxford University Press, 1950, pp. 179-224, and L. Smolar and M. Aberbach, 'The Golden Calf Episode in Postbiblical Literature', *HUCA* 39 (1969), pp. 91-116. While there is much to be learned from both of these studies, their conclusions must be carefully reviewed in light of the methodological issues mentioned above.

5. These compilations include *Mishnah, Tosefta*, and the documents listed in note 3. I select traditions solely from tannaitic compilations in order to examine the earliest traditions attributed to *tannaim*. A separate study is necessary to examine tannaitic traditions that appear in later documents.

6. In order to focus on these themes in particular, I include only those tannaitic traditions that directly deal with them. Other traditions dealing with the golden calf and atrributed to *tannaim* (excluding those concerned with the breaking of the tablets and the role of the Levites, which require studies of their own), include *m. Meg.* 4.10C-D, *t. Meg.* 4(3).36-37, *t. Kippurim* 5(4).17L-V, *t. Sot.* 6.6, *t. A.Z.* 3(4).19, *Mekhilta Wayassa* 1 (ed. Horovitz-Rabin, p. 153, ll. 6-17), *Mekhilta Beshallah* 7 (ed. Horovitz-Rabin, p. 112, l. 16-p. 113, l. 3), and *Sifre Deuteronomy* 43.3-4. With the exception

of *t. Kippurim* 5(4).17V (cited in note 18, below), however, all of the other tannaitic traditions are consistent with the interpretation that this is a story of sin, punishment, and forgiveness.

7. The translation is that of Jacob Neusner, *The Tosefta Translated from the Hebrew. Second Division. Moed (The Order of Appointed Times)* (henceforth: *Tosefta Moed*), New York: Ktav, 1983, p. 3.

8. For a discussion of the possible reasons for this comparison, and for a similar statement in Tractate *Sofrim* that compares the translation of the Torah into Greek to the day of the calf, see Saul Lieberman, *Tosefta Kifshutah: A Comprehensive Commentary on the Tosefta*, New York: Jewish Theological Seminary, 1962, III, p. 15, on ll. 37-38.

9. So Reuven Hammer, *Sifre: A Tannaitic Commentary on the Book of Deuteronomy*, New Haven: Yale University Press, 1986, p. 391 n. 25.

10. The numbering of pericopae in *Sifre Deuteronomy* is that of Jacob Neusner, *Sifre to Deuteronomy: An Analytical Translation*, Atlanta: Scholars Press, 2 vols., 1987. The translation of this and all pericopae from *Sifre* to Deuteronomy draws upon the translations of both Neusner and Hammer (*ibid.*). The translation of biblical verses throughout this paper is generally that of *Tanakh: A New Translation of the Holy Scriptures According to the Traditional Hebrew Text*, Philadelphia: The Jewish Publication Society, 1985, except where cited as part of another translator's rendering of a rabbinic text or where modified to fit the rabbinic context in which the verse is cited.

11. See Hammer (*ibid.*, p. 391 n. 23), who explains 'the gold is enough' to mean 'the sin of the golden calf was sufficient to establish their guilt and to make it impossible for God to overlook what they have done. All else pales in comparison with this sin.' On the meaning of *wtrh* as both 'sufficient' and 'overlook', see Hammer, *ibid.*, n. 24. B's comment may also be based in part on the appearance of 'Di-Zahab' last in the list of Deut. 1.1, which might have been taken to imply that the sin of the calf was the climax of the series of transgressions that Israel committed in the wilderness.

12. See, for example, *Targum Pseudo-Jonathan* to Exod. 32.7, which cites this phrase with reference to the calf.

13. The translation of *Sifre Numbers* 1.10.2-3 is that of Jacob Neusner, *Sifre to Numbers: An American Translation and Explanation*, Atlanta: Scholars Press, 1986, I, pp. 56-57.

14. See the comment of Rabad, *ad loc.*

15. I-M's discussion of Aaron's own consciousness of his situation may have originally not concerned the sin of the calf at all, for, in contrast to C and F-G, J-L does not mention this transgression. Moreover, the phrase *šl' yhyh lbw ldbr 'hr* ('so that his heart might not stray') may refer simply to a general reluctance to assume public office, rather than a concern with this particular sin (see Rabad's explanation of *Sifra, Ṣav, Mekhilta de-Miluim* 1.2, where this phrase is used with regard to the Levites and Joshua as well as of Aaron).

In addition, we would expect M to cite Lev. 9.7 rather than Lev. 8.1. It is possible, therefore, that the redactor of the pericope reinterprets J-L, which may have originally concerned a general unwillingness to assume public office, to refer to the sin of the calf in particular. If so, the redactor sought to supplement A-D and E-H, which describe Aaron's distancing, with an account of Aaron's own inner feelings.

16. So Nahmanides (*Commentary to the Pentateuch*, cited by Weiss, *Masoret Hatalmud, ad loc.*), reading *ystynk* ('[lest] he accuse you') for *ysn'k* ('will hate you'). The former reading seems preferable, for according to it Moses and Aaron fear not Satan's hatred, but Satan's role as accuser, for Satan could bring up the sin of the calf and prevent Aaron from fulfilling his duties.

17. The numbering of pericopae in *Leviticus Rabbah* is that of Jacob Neusner, *Judaism and Scripture: The Evidence of Leviticus Rabbah* (Chicago: The University of Chicago Press, 1986).

18. As far as I can determine, the only tradition attributed to *tannaim* that apologizes for the actions of Israel is that of Akiba at *t. Kippurim* 5(4).17L-V (trans. Neusner, *Tosefta Moed*, p. 210):

L.	At what point in the service does he say the [confession on the Day of Atonement]?
M.	After the Prayer.
N.	The one who passes before the ark says it in the fourth [benediction].
O.	R. Meir says, 'He prays seven [benedictions] and concludes the confession [with a blessing]'.
P.	And sages say, 'He prays seven [benedictions] .
Q.	'And if he wanted to conclude the confession with a blessing, he does so.'
R.	'And he has to specify each individual sin', the words of R. Judah b. Patera,
S.	as it is said, 'O Lord, these people have sinned a great sin [and have made a god of gold]' (Exod. 32.31).
T.	R. Akiba says, 'It is not necessary [to list each sin].
U.	'If so, why does it say, "And made a god of gold?"'
V.	'But: Thus did the Omnipresent say, "Who made you make a god of gold? It is I, who gave you plenty of gold."'

In contrast to Judah b. Patera, who understands 'and made a god of gold' (Exod. 32.31) to be Moses' specification of Israel's sin, Akiba apparently attributes this phrase to God rather than to Moses, and understands it to imply God's acceptance of responsibility for the sin. I note, however, that Akiba's purpose is to render Exod. 32.31 compatible with his ruling at U, and not primarily to defend Israel's actions. In any event, it is noteworthy that this is the only tradition among exegeses attributed to *tannaim* that denies Israel's responsibility for the sin of the calf.

BIBLIOGRAPHY

1. *Editions of primary works*

Finkelstein, Louis (ed.), *Sifre on Deuteronomy*, 1939. Reprint, New York: The Jewish Theological Seminary of America, 1969.

Horovitz, H.S. (ed.), *Siphre d'be Rab*, 1917. Reprint, Jerusalem: Wahrmann Books, 1966.

Horovitz, H.S. and Israel Rabin (eds.), *Mechilta d'Rabbi Ishmael*, 1930. Second edition, Jerusalem: Wahrmann Books, 1970.

Lieberman, Saul (ed.), *The Tosefta According to Codex Vienna, with Variants from Codices Erfurt, London, Genizah Mss and Editio Princeps (Venice, 1521). II. The Order of Moed*, New York: The Jewish Theological Seminary of America, 1962.

Weiss, I.H. (ed.), *Sifra debe Rab*, 1862. Reprint, New York: Ohm, 1946.

2. *Translations and secondary works*

Hammer, Reuven, *Sifre: A Tannaitic Commentary on the Book of Deuteronomy*, New Haven: Yale University Press, 1986.

Lieberman, Saul, *Tosefta Kifshutah: A Comprehensive Commentary on the Tosefta. III. Shabbat-Erubin*, New York: The Jewish Theological Seminary of America, 1962.

Marmorstein, A., 'Judaism and Christianity in the Middle of the Third Century', in J. Rabbinowitz and M.S. Lew (eds.), *Studies in Jewish Theology. Arthur Marmorstein Memorial Volume*, London: Oxford University Press, 1950, pp. 179-224.

Neusner, Jacob, *Judaism and Scripture: The Evidence of Leviticus Rabbah*, Chicago: The University of Chicago Press, 1986.

—*Sifre to Deuteronomy: An Analytical Translation*, Atlanta: Scholars Press, 2 vols., 1987.

—*Sifre to Numbers: An American Translation and Explanation*, Atlanta: Scholars Press, 1986.

—*The Tosefta Translated from the Hebrew. Second Division. Moed (The Order of Appointed Times)*, New York: Ktav, 1983.

Porton, Gary, 'Defining Midrash', in Jacob Neusner (ed.), *The Study of Ancient Judaism*, I, New York: Ktav, 1981, pp. 55-92.

Smolar, L. and M. Aberbach, 'The Golden Calf Episode in Postbiblical Literature', *HUCA* 39 (1969), pp. 91-116.

Tanakh: A New Translation of the Hebrew Scriptures According to the Traditional Hebrew Text, Philadelphia: The Jewish Publication Society, 1985.

PART IV

JUDAISM AND CHRISTIANITY IN HISTORY

KOSHER OLIVE OIL IN ANTIQUITY

Martin Goodman

Oxford Centre for Postgraduate Hebrew Studies

I hope that it may be thought appropriate to offer to Geza Vermes, who has dedicated much of his scholarly life to the elucidation of the varied nature of Judaism and the attitudes of Jews towards their tradition in late antiquity, a study of a religious development which both originated and came to an end in this period.

The problem to be tackled may be stated quite succinctly. In the hellenistic period some Jews objected to using oil produced by non-Jews. Some time in the third century CE the rabbinic patriarch and his court decreed that the ban on gentile oil was no longer to be enforced, and their decision seems to have been generally followed, if not immediately then at least within a few generations. No ancient text gives an adequate explanation either of the original prohibition or of the later relaxation. My purpose is to investigate the underlying religious attitudes which might account for both developments.[1]

Olive oil was an item of considerable importance in the economy of the land of Israel. Oil was one of the three staple products of the land (Deut. 11.14; 2 Kings 18.32). Of the many varieties of oil, olive oil was among the most expensive, but it was widely used for cosmetics (Eccl. 9.7-8), for medicine (Isa. 1.6), and as a fuel for lamps (cf. R. Tarfon in *m. Shabb.* 2.2, on the Sabbath lights). It was of course a ubiquitous ingredient in food. Josephus made special mention of the productivity of olive trees in the hills of Galilee (*BJ* 2.592). The concern of the inhabitants to ensure their supply of olive oil is illustrated by finds of oil presses on Mount Hermon some way above the height at which olive trees flourish.[2] Whether olives actually grew at such a height in antiquity or were transported raw to the upland settlements for processing is unclear. In either case the importance attributed to the product is striking.[3]

In this reliance on olive oil the Jews of Palestine shared in the general culture of the Mediterranean region. By the time of the early Roman empire olive cultivation was almost universally found in lowland coastal regions, and the long-distance trade in high quality luxury oil was equalled in bulk and distribution only by the trade in wine.[4]

When Jews decided in the Hellenistic and early Roman imperial period not to use gentile olive oil, they were, then, deliberately turning their backs on some of the more widely traded goods in their society. But it may be that by the time such trade had fully evolved in the last centuries BCE, Jews could already justify the taboo to themselves by claiming reliance on ancient tradition, for the first evidence for a prohibition on the use of gentile oil may date back to before 281 BCE.

According to Josephus (*Ant.* 12.119-120), Seleucus Nicator, who ruled from 312 to 281 BCE, gave special privileges to the Jews as follows.

καὶ γὰρ Σέλευκος ὁ Νικάτωρ ἐν αἷς ἔκτισε πόλεσιν ἐν τῇ Ἀσίᾳ καὶ τῇ κάτω Συρίᾳ καὶ ἐν αὐτῇ τῇ μητροπόλει Ἀντιοχείᾳ πολιτείας αὐτοὺς ἠξίωσε καὶ τοῖς ἐνοικισθεῖσιν ἰσοτίμους ἀπέφηνε Μακεδόσιν καὶ Ἕλλησιν, ὡς τὴν πολιτείαν ταύτην ἔτι καὶ νῦν διαμένειν· τεκμήριον δὲ τοῦτο τοὺς Ἰουδαίους μὴ βουλομένους ἀλλοφύλῳ ἐλαίῳ χρῆσθαι λαμβάνειν ὡρισμένον τι παρὰ τῶν γυμνασιάρχων εἰς ἐλαίου τιμὴν ἀργύριον ἐκέλευσεν· ὃ τοῦ δήμου τῶν Ἀντιοχέων ἐν τῷ νῦν πολέμῳ λῦσαι προαιρουμένου, Μουκιανὸς ἡγεμὼν ὢν τότε τῆς Συρίας ἐτήρησεν.

Seleucus Nicator granted them citizenship in the cities which he founded in Asia and Lower Syria and in his capital, Antioch, itself, and declared them to have equal privileges with the Macedonians and Greeks who were settled in these cities, so that this citizenship of theirs remains to this day; and the proof of this is the fact that he gave orders that those Jews who were unwilling to use foreign oil should receive a fixed sum of money from the gymnasiarchs to pay for their own kind of oil; and, when in the present war the people of Antioch proposed to revoke this privilege, Mucianus, who was then governor of Syria, maintained it.

If Josephus is to be trusted, at least some Jews in Asia Minor and/or Syria were unwilling to use foreign oil before 281 BCE. How many Jews followed this line is not clear: τοὺς Ἰουδαίους μὴ βουλομένους may mean '*the* Jews who did not want' or, more probably, '*those*

Jews—i.e. only some—who did not want'. It is quite likely on general grounds that Josephus ascribed the grant of this privilege to an earlier period than was the case, and that in fact a later Seleucid monarch, such as Antiochus III, who ruled from 223 to 187 BCE, was responsible,[5] but in any case it seems certain that the custom was well established in the Hellenistic period.

Whenever the taboo started, two things about it are established from this passage. First, Jews kept up the habit in the late sixties CE during the First Revolt, when Mucianus as governor of Syria permitted them to maintain their privilege. Second, the complaint expressed about unkosher oil was that it was foreign, *allophulon*, and Josephus could take it for granted that the reasonableness of this objection was sufficiently self-evident not to need spelling out to his readers, most of whom would be gentile.

Josephus' reason for taking the taboo so much for granted was probably simply that it was part of his own lifestyle, for the only other context in which the ban on gentile oil is mentioned in his writings involved an incident in his own career. The incident was described by Josephus twice, with interesting divergences between the two accounts.

First, at *BJ* 2.591-592, Josephus included the following passage in his attack on his long-standing rival, John of Gischala.

ἔπειτα συνθεὶς σκηνὴν πανουργοτάτην, ὡς ἄρα φυλάττοιντο πάντες οἱ κατὰ τὴν Συρίαν Ἰουδαῖοι ἐλαίῳ χρῆσθαι μὴ δι' ὁμοφύλων ἐγκεχειρισμένῳ, πέμπειν αὐτοῖς ἐπὶ μεθορίαν ἐξῃτήσατο. συνωνούμενος δὲ τοῦ Τυρίου νομίσματος, ὃ τέσσαρας Ἀττικὰς δύναται, τέσσαρας ἀμφορεῖς, τῆς αὐτῆς ἐπίπρασκεν τιμῆς ἡμιαμφόριον. οὔσης δὲ τῆς Γαλιλαίας ἐλαιοφόρου μάλιστα καὶ τότε εὐφορηκυίας, εἰς σπανίζοντας εἰσπέμπων πολὺ καὶ μόνος ἄπειρόν τι πλῆθος συνῆγεν χρημάτων, οἷς εὐθέως ἐχρῆτο κατὰ τοῦ τὴν ἐργασίαν παρασχόντος.

He next contrived to play a very crafty trick: with the avowed object of protecting all the Jews of Syria from the use of oil not supplied by their own countrymen, he sought and obtained permission to deliver it to them at the frontier. He then bought up that commodity, paying Tyrian coin of the value of four Attic drachms for four amphorae and proceeded to sell half an amphora at the same price. As Galilee is a special home of the olive and the crop had been plentiful, John, enjoying a monopoly, by sending large quantities to districts in want of it, amassed an immense sum

of money, which he forthwith employed against the man who had
brought him his gains.

However tendentious and exaggerated the attack, Josephus must
have assumed that it would at least sound plausible to Jewish
readers. The oil supplied μὴ δι᾽ ὁμοφύλων in this passage is the
equivalent of the ἀλλοφύλον ἔλαιον in the passage from *Antiquities*
first quoted.

When Josephus returned to the same incident in his later account
in the *Vita* (74–6), he gave a slightly different version of the same
events.

καὶ δευτέραν Ἰωάννης ἐπεισέφερεν πανουργίαν· ἔφη γὰρ Ἰουδαίους
τοὺς τὴν Φιλίππου Καισάρειαν κατοικοῦντας, συγκεκλεισμένους
κατὰ προσταγὴν τοῦ βασιλέως ὑπὸ Μοδίου τοῦ τὴν δυναστείαν
διοικοῦντος, πεπομφέναι πρὸς αὐτὸν παρακαλοῦντας, ἐπειδὴ οὐκ
ἔχουσιν ἔλαιον ᾧ χρίσονται καθαρόν, ποιησάμενον πρόνοιαν
εὐπορίαν αὐτοῖς τούτου παρασχεῖν, μὴ δι᾽ ἀνάγκην Ἑλληνικῷ
χρώμενοι τὰ νόμιμα παραβαίνωσιν. ταῦτα δ᾽ οὐχ ὑπ᾽ εὐσεβείας
ἔλεγεν Ἰωάννης, δι᾽ αἰσχροκέρδειαν δὲ φανερωτάτην. γινώσκων
γὰρ παρὰ μὲν ἐκείνοις κατὰ τὴν Καισάρειαν τοὺς δύο ξέστας
δραχμῆς μιᾶς πωλουμένους, ἐν δὲ τοῖς Γισχάλοις τοὺς ὀγδοήκοντα
ξέστας δραχμῶν τεσσάρων, πᾶν τὸ ἔλαιον ὅσον ἦν ἐκεῖ διεπέμψατο,
λαβὼν ἐξουσίαν καὶ παρ᾽ ἐμοῦ τὸ δοκεῖν· οὐ γὰρ ἑκὼν ἐπέτρεπον,
ἀλλὰ διὰ φόβον τὸν ἀπὸ τοῦ πλήθους, μὴ κωλύων καταλευσθείην
ὑπ᾽ αὐτῶν. συγχωρήσαντος οὖν μου πλείστων χρημάτων ὁ
Ἰωάννης ἐκ τῆς κακουργίας ταύτης εὐπόρησε.

This knavish trick John followed up with a second. He stated that
the Jewish inhabitants of Caesarea Philippi, having, by the king's
order, been shut up by Modius, his viceroy, and having no pure oil
with which to anoint themselves, had sent a request to him to see
that they were supplied with this commodity, lest they should be
driven to violate their legal ordinances by resort to Grecian oil.
John's motive in making this assertion was not piety, but
profiteering of the most barefaced description; for he knew that at
Caesarea two pints were sold for one drachm, whereas at Gischala
eighty pints could be had for four drachms. So he sent off all the oil
in the place, having ostensibly obtained my authority to do so. My
permission I gave reluctantly, from fear of being stoned by the mob
if I withheld it. Thus, having gained my consent, John by this sharp
practice made an enormous profit.

The story as a whole is more plausible in this version. Only the Jews
of Caesarea Philippi are involved, and it is easier to imagine

economic interchange of this sort in the middle of a war if it took place between the rebels in Galilee and the subjects of the Jewish, if pro-Roman, king Agrippa II, than to credit the claim in *BJ* that John traded with 'all the Jews in Syria', a province firmly controlled by the Roman enemy. In this case the kosher oil, described as pure (καθαρόν), is contrasted to a specific form of gentile oil, namely Grecian oil (ἑλληνικόν). It is asserted that the concern of the Jews in Caesarea Philippi was over the use of such oil for anointing themselves (if, as I think preferable, the minority manuscript reading χρίσονται is read rather than χρήσονται). Again, it is significant that Josephus took it for granted that his readers would appreciate the issues at stake—unlike his earlier works, Josephus' *Vita* was aimed primarily at a Jewish audience. For such readers the statement that Jews using Grecian oil would transgress the laws (τὰ νόμιμα παραβαίνωσιν) would sound like a straightforward statement that such behaviour involved breaking the Torah.

If such an attitude was so standard among Jews at the end of the first century CE, some explanation needs to be found for the remarkable statement dropped into the Mishnah tractate *Abodah Zarah* (2.6), redacted a little over a century later.

אלו דברים של גוים אסורין ואין אסורן אסור הנאה: חלב
שחלבו גוי ואין ישראל רואהו והפת והשמן שלהן—רבי
ובית דינו התירו בשמן—ושלקות וכבשין שדרכן לתת
לתוכן יין וחמץ וטרית טרופה וציר שאין בה דגה כלבית
שוטטת בו והחילק וקרט שלחלתית ומלח סלקונטית
הרי אלו אסורין ואין אסורן אסור הנאה—

> These things of gentiles are forbidden, but it is not prohibited to derive any benefit from them: milk that a gentile milked but no Israelite watched him, and their bread and their oil—Rabbi and his court permitted the oil—boiled or preserved vegetables into which it is their custom to put wine or vinegar, and hashed, pickled fish, and brine in which no fish is distinguishable (with no sticklebacks floating in it), and the finless fish, and drops of asafoetida, and lumpy salt. Behold, these are forbidden, but it is not prohibited to have any benefit from them.

'Rabbi and his court permitted the oil.' The clause looks like a later insertion into a list of the forbidden food of idolaters. It does not fit its present context either in its meaning or in its grammar. In the Babylonian Talmud (*b. Abodah Zarah* 37a) it is in one place assumed that it was not R. Judah I but his grandson, R. Judah Nesiah, who took the lenient decision described. Since the Mishnah was compiled by R. Judah I, the lack of editing to incorporate the words into the surrounding texts fits well into the tradition that the reform took place two generations after his time. However, both Talmuds also referred the reform at other places to R. Judah I.[6] Perhaps in the case of a controversial decision which relied on the authority of the issuing court and which elicited opposition (as the *gemara* attests [see below]), both patriarchs felt impelled to issue decrees, just as Roman emperors sometimes reissued laws when they were not widely observed.

The Mishnah text itself gave absolutely no explanation either for the original ban or for its lifting. This is not unusual for halakhic decisions recorded in tannaitic texts, but this particular case rather puzzled the amoraim, as can be seen from an examination of the discussion of the point in the Babylonian Talmud. The most relevant part of the text, to be found at *b. Abodah Zarah* 35b-36a, reads as follows.

1

והשמן שלהן שמן רב אמר דניאל גזר עליו ושמואל אמר זליפתן של
כלים טמאים אוסרתן

אטו כולי עלמא אוכלי טהרות נינהו אלא זליפתן של כלים אסורים אוסרתן

2

א״ל שמואל לרב בשלמא לדידי דאמינא זליפתן של כלים אסורים אוסרתן
היינו דכי אתא רב יצחק בר שמואל בר מרתא ואמר דריש רבי
שמלאי בנציבין

שמן רבי יהודה ובית דינו נימנו עליה והתירוהו

קסבר נותן טעם לפגם מותר

אלא לדידך דאמרת דניאל גזר עליו

דניאל גזר ואתא רבי יהודה הנשיא ומבטל ליה

והתנן אין בית דין יכול לבטל דברי בית דין חברו

אלא אם כן גדול הימנו בחכמה ובמנין

3

א״ל שמלאי לוראה קא אמרת שאני לוראה דמזלזלו
א״ל אשלח ליה אכסיף

אמר רב אם הם לא דרשו אנן לא דרשינן

דהכתיב וישם דניאל על לבו אשר לא יתגאל בפתבג המלך וביין משתיו
בשתי משתאות הכתוב מדבר אחד משתה יין ואחד משתה שמן

רב סבר על לבו שם ולכל ישראל הורה

ושמואל סבר על לבו שם ולכל ישראל לא הורה

4

ושם דניאל גזר והאמר באלי אבימי נותאה משמיה דרב
פיתן ושמנן יינן ובנותיהן כולן משמנה עשר דבר הן
וכי תימא אתא דניאל גזר ולא קיבל ואתו תלמידי דהילל ושמאי וגזור וקיבל
א״כ מאי אסהדרותיה דרב

אלא דניאל גזר עליו בעיר ואתו אינהו וגזור אפילו בשדה
ורבי יהודה הנשיא היכי מצי למישרא תקנתא דתלמידי שמאי והילל 5
והתנן אין בית דין יכול לבטל דברי בית דין חברו
אלא אם כן גדול הימנו בחכמה ובמנין
ועוד הא אמר רבה בר בר חנה א"ר יוחנן
בכל יכול לבטל בית דין דברי בית דין חבירו חוץ משמונה עשר דבר
שאפילו יבוא אליהו ובית דינו אין שומעין לו
אמר רב משרשיא מה טעם הואיל ופשט איסורו ברוב ישראל
שמן לא פשט איסורו ברוב ישראל . . .

Section 1: And their oil. As regards oil Rab said: Daniel decreed against its use; but Samuel said: The residue from their unclean vessels renders it prohibited. Is this to say that people generally are concerned to eat their food in a state of ritual purity!—Rather the residue from their prohibited vessels renders it prohibited.

Section 2: Samuel said to Rab: According to my explanation that the residue from their prohibited vessels renders it prohibited, it is quite right that when R. Isaac b. Samuel b. Martha came he related that R. Simlai expounded in Nisibis: As regards oil R. Judah and his Court took a vote and declared it permitted, holding the opinion that [when the forbidden element] imparts a worsened flavour [the mixture] is permitted. But according to your statement that Daniel decreed against it, [can it be thought that] Daniel made a decree and R. Judah the Prince then came and annulled it? For have we not learned: A Court is unable to annul the decisions of another Court, unless it is superior to it in wisdom and numerical strength!

Section 3: Rab replied to him: You quote Simlai of Lud; but the inhabitants of Lud are different because they are neglectful. [Samuel] said to him: Shall I send for him? [Rab] thereupon grew alarmed and said: If [R. Judah and his Court] have not made proper research, shall we not do so? Surely it is written, 'But Daniel purposed in his heart that he would not defile himself with the king's meat nor with the wine of his drinking'—the verse speaks of two drinkings, the drinking of wine and the drinking of oil! Rab was of the opinion that Daniel purposed in his own heart and decided similarly for all Israel; whereas Samuel was of the opinion that he purposed in his own heart but did not decide similarly for all Israel.

Section 4: But did Daniel decree against oil? Behold Bali declared that Abimi the Nabatean said in the name of Rab: Their bread, oil, wine and daughters are all included in the eighteen things! Should you argue that Daniel came and made the decree but it was not accepted, and then the disciples of Hillel and Shammai came and made the decree and it was accepted; in that case what was the purpose of Rab's testimony?—But Daniel decreed against the use of the oil in a city, and [the disciples] came and decreed against its use even in a field.

Section 5: How, then, was it possible for R. Judah the Prince to permit [what was forbidden by] the ordinance of the disciples of Shammai and Hillel, seeing that we have learned: A court is unable to annul the decisions of another Court, unless it is superior to it in wisdom and numerical strength! Furthermore, Rabbah b. Bar Hanah has said in the name of R. Johanan: In all matters a Court can annul the decisions of another Court except the eighteen things, for even were Elijah and his Court to come we must not listen to him!—R. Mesharsheya said: The reason is because their prohibition has spread among the large majority of Israelites, but the prohibition concerning oil did not so spread.

The amoraim were concerned to establish whether the original interdiction was a precaution against contamination by vessels rendered unkosher by other ingredients or was the result of a decree issued either by Daniel (relying on the pleonastic 'wine of his drinking' in Daniel 1.8, which they took to include oil as a second forbidden beverage after wine) or by the Houses of Hillel and Shammai as one of the eighteen decisions of the disciples at the start of the great revolt against Rome. The main rabbis cited, Samuel and Rab, taught in the second quarter of the third century or later and, since they appear to respond to it, presumably after the lifting of the ban by R. Judah Nesiah. Two reasons are given in this passage for that lifting. According to R. Simlai, as quoted by R. Isaac b. Samuel b. Martha, R. Judah held that the forbidden element in the oil imparts a worse flavour, and therefore the oil is permitted. The second opinion is put forward in the name of R. Mesharsheya, that the ban was in any case not in general accepted by Jews.

Discussion of the various opinions put forward by the sages in this passage may be further complicated by noting a variant reading of line 3, which is to be found in the early commentaries.[7] These texts, which read זליפתן של גוים instead of זליפתן של כלים, imply in the light of *t. Abodah Zarah* 4(5).8 that Samuel's opinion was not that the discharge of the impure or forbidden vessels in which oil was stored that made it unfit, but that they were defiled through the gentile habit of sprinkling olives with wine or vinegar to facilitate the removal of the pits. This understanding of the Mishnah's prohibition brings the ban on oil into the same category as the vegetables which are mentioned next in the text, since they too are prohibited because sprinkled with wine or vinegar. However, no reference is made to such sprinkling in the ban on gentile milk and bread, which appear immediately before the ban on oil in the Mishnah text.

Reference to the discussion of the same Mishnah in the Yerushalmi (*y. Abodah Zarah* 2.8, 41d) produces more opinions but no greater clarity on any of these issues.

מי אסר את השמן רב יהודה אמר דניאל אסרו   1
וישם דניאל על לבו וגו'

ומי התירו רבי התירו ובית דינו בשלשה מקומו'   2
נקרא רבי יהודה הנשיא רבותינו בגיטין
ובשמן ובסנדל וקרו ליה בי דינא דשרו מישחא
כל בית דין דשרו שלשה דברים נקרא בי דינא שריא

אמר ר' יודן בית דינו חלוק עליו בגיטין מהו שתהא   3
מותרת להינשא רבי חגיי אמר מותרת להינשא
רבי יוסי אמר אסורה להינשא

רבי אחא רבי תנחום בר חייה בשם רבי חנינה   4
ואמרי לה בשם רבי יהושע בן לוי שהיו עולין
להר המלך ונהרגין עליו

יצחק בר שמואל בר מרתא נחת לנציבין אשכח שמלאי   5
הדרומי יתיב דרש רבי רבי ובית דינו התירו בשמן
אמר שמואל *אכל רב לא קביל עליה מיכול א''ל
שמואל אכול דלא כן אנא כתב עליך זקן ממרא
א''ל עד דאנא תמן אנא ידע מאן עדר עליה
שמלאי הדרומי א''ל מר בשם גרמיה לא אכל
ר' יודן נשייא אטרח עליו ואכל

רבי יוחנן בעי ולא כן תנינן שאין ב''ד יכול לבטל   6
דברי ב''ד חבירו עד שיהא גדול ממנו בחכמה ובמניין
ורבי ובית דינו מתירין מה שאסר דניאל וחביריו

רבי יוחנן כדעתיה א''ר יוחנן מקובל אני מר' לעזר   7
בי ר' צדוק שכל גזירה שו''ד גוזרין ואין רוב
ציבור מקבלין עליהן אינה גזירה בדקו ומצאו
בגזירתו של שמן ולא מצאו שקיבלו רוב הציבור עליהן

<hr>

*אבל in Krotoschin edition

1: Who forbade the oil? Rab Judah said, 'Daniel forbade it: "And Daniel resolved, etc."'

2: And who permitted it? Rabbi and his court. In three settings R. Judah the patriarch is referred to as 'our rabbi', in the context of writs of divorce, oil, and [producing an abortion in the shape of a] sandal. In consequence they referred to his court as the court that permitted anointing [with oil]. Any court that gave a lenient ruling in three matters is called a permissive court.

3: Said R. Judan, 'Rabbi's court differed from him in the matter of the writ of divorce'. What is [the issue]? That [the woman] is permitted to [re]marry. R. Haggai said, 'She is permitted to marry'. R. Yose said, 'She is forbidden to marry'.

4: R. Aha, R. Tanhum bar Hiyya in the name of R. Haninah, and some say it in the name of R. Joshua b. Levi: 'Because they were going up to the Royal Mountain and being put to death on it'.

5: Isaac bar Samuel bar Marta went down to Nisibis. He found Simlai, the southerner, sitting and expounding: 'Rabbi and his court permitted oil'. He said [the rule before] Samuel, [who thereupon] ate. Rab did not accept the rule for himself or eat. He said to him, 'Samuel ate. If you do not do the same, I shall decree concerning you that you are a "rebellious elder".' [Rab] replied to him, 'When I was still there [in the Land], I know that Simlai, the southerner, rejected'. [Samuel] said to him, 'Did [Simlai] say this in his own name? Did he not say it in the name of R. Judah Nesiah?' Samuel nagged him about the matter until he too ate.

6: R.Yohanan raised the question: 'And have we not learned in the Mishnah that a court has not got the power to nullify the opinion of another court unless it is greater than it in wisdom and in numbers? Now how is it possible that Rabbi and his court should permit what Daniel and his colleagues had prohibited?'

7: R. Yohanan is consistent with his opinion expressed elsewhere. For R. Yohanan said, 'I have received it as a tradition from R. Eleazar of the school of R. Sadoq that any decree a court should issue, and which the majority of the community should not accept upon itself, is no decree'. They looked into the matter and found in the decree against oil and they did not find that the majority of the community had accepted upon itself.

The view ascribed in the Babylonian Talmud to Rab, that the ban was initiated by Daniel, was here attributed to his pupil R. Judah bar Ezekiel (*fl.* end of third century). No mention was made of any discussion by the Houses of Hillel and Shammai. Some modern scholars have assumed that the obscure statement given by R. Aha and (?) R. Tanhum bar Hiyya in the name of R. Haninah or R. Joshua b. Levi, the last named being an amora contemporary with R. Judah Nesiah, that something happened 'because they were going up to the Mountain of the King and being killed (on this account? on the mountain?)' was given as an explanation of the acceptance of Daniel's prohibition, on the grounds that Jews thus avoided the gentiles who inhabited the mountain.[8] But this is not the only possible interpretation of the phrase, for other scholars have supposed that, on the contrary, it was intended to explain the lifting of the ban, on the grounds that the mountain was farmed by Jews and was therefore the best place to get pure oil.[9] It also seems to me possible that neither of these hypotheses is correct and that the statement may have referred not to oil at all, but to the issue raised in the immediately preceding discussion in the talmudic text, which concerned the remarriage of a widow whose husband had given her a writ of divorce to become valid if he did not return within twelve months but had died within that period.

These diverse explanations by the amoraim of the ban on gentile oil seem to me irreconcilable and the distinction proposed anonymously in the Babylonian Talmud passage (Section 4) between decrees valid in a city and those valid in a field strikes me as a counsel of desperation by an editor or editors determined to resolve discord whenever possible. Such irreconcilability is not altogether uncommon in rabbinic texts. More significant is the weakness of each of the amoraic opinions when they are examined individually. Such weakness can only be demonstrated by looking at each opinion in some detail.

Following the order in the Babylonian Talmud, I shall start with the views of Rab, who ascribed the ban both to Daniel and to the eighteen decisions of the Houses of Hillel and Shammai. Neither notion is very convincing. Rab's exegesis of Daniel 1.8 was hardly the obvious reading of the biblical text and seems to have been unknown to earlier commentators on the passage. Thus Josephus described Daniel and his friends as determined to stay vegetarian but prepared to eat any non-animal food provided to them (*AJ* 10.190-194).

As for the ascription of the decree to the eighteen decisions of the Houses in 66 CE, the link was not mentioned in the discussion of oil in the Jerusalem Talmud or in the earliest extant rabbinic lists of the components of the decrees. In the Mishnah (*m. Shabb.* 1.4) the precise contents of the decrees were not spelled out and the whole discussion in *b. Shabb.* 13b-17b presupposes great uncertainty as to what they were. In *y. Shabb.* 1.5, 3c, the list of eighteen things ascribed to R. Shimon bar Yohai (*fl.* mid second century) did not include oil, although oil was included in an anonymous baraita in the same passage.[10] But in any case it is hard to reconcile an origin of the custom in 66 CE with Josephus' assertion that the taboo was already long-standing in Antioch by that time, and it can be reckoned most unlikely that Josephus would have mentioned the custom with apparent approval if it had originated in a fit of anti-Roman zealotry. It is worth noting that the Jews of Syria and/or Caesarea Philippi who observed the taboos in 67 CE were presumably not strongly anti-Roman since they had not gone south to join their compatriots in revolt. (Josephus stated [*Vita* 74] that the Jews had been shut up in Caesarea Philippi by Modius, Agrippa II's viceroy, but if John of Gischala's kosher oil could get in, presumably Jews could get out.)

Attempts have been made in the past to circumvent this problem of an apparent conflict between the evidence in Josephus and the evidence in the Talmud by distinguishing the ban described by Josephus from that ascribed to the Houses.[11] Thus, as Hoenig pointed out, the prohibition to which Josephus referred was observed in the diaspora and is not explicitly attested in Judaea, where the Houses issued their decree. Hoenig claimed that this is best explained if the diaspora ban was observed only as a way of avoiding idolatry, and the xenophobic decree of the Houses was therefore something new and specifically Judaean. The idea is not impossible but, although oil was indeed one ingredient in pagan ritual, this fact is not given as a reason for avoiding gentile oil in any ancient text. It may be added in support of Hoenig that Josephus seems to have envisaged a taboo on the use of gentile oil as an ointment whereas the rabbinic texts include oil in the list of forbidden foods but, again, I am not sure how much can be made of this. It may be assumed that any substance considered unfit as ointment was *a fortiori* reckoned unsuitable as food. (The only reason I can find to doubt this is the testimony of Josephus [*BJ* 2.123], that Essenes, who may well have used oil of some kind in their food, refused to put any oil on their bodies, reckoning it as a defilement [κηλίδα]. But the case was not strictly parallel, for Essenes simply wished to keep their skin dry.) In any case the contrast betwen oil as food and oil as ointment may be spurious, for the word used to designate oil in one place (Section 2) in the Jerusalem Talmud passage quoted above was מישחא, i.e. 'anointing'.

Rather more convincing than Rab's ascription of the ban to a decree at one time or another is the explanation for the ban put forward according to the Babylonian Talmud by Mar Samuel, that the oil was in some way contaminated by gentiles' additives. This view fits in with Josephus' description of Jewish oil as 'pure' (*Vita* 74), and, as Samuel is made to point out in the Talmudic passage (Section 2), it did at least make sense of the reason for lifting the ban attributed to R. Judah by R. Simlai, that when the forbidden element in a mixture imparts a worsened flavour the mixture is permitted.

But that reason itself has an air of improvization. The residue or sprinkling believed to make oil forbidden consisted probably of gentile wine suspected of use in libations, although it cannot be shown that other contaminants were not also envisaged. If 'residue' is read, it is possible that an amphora or other container once used for wine and re-used for oil might impart a taste to the oil; if it was resinated wine, the taste of the oil might be rather unpleasant, so that the alleged reason for lifting the ban would also make sense. However, there is not much evidence for such re-use of amphorae or other vessels, for reasons which are clear enough: if the wine residue made the oil taste worse, gentiles will only have re-used vessels when no more appropriate container was available. Since the quantity of pottery produced throughout the Roman empire was vast, this was surely a rare occurrence, and it is hard to imagine that suspicion of such defilement was the main reason for the banning of gentile oil. Similar arguments apply to the sprinkling of olives with wine or vinegar by gentiles, if גוים is read rather than כלים (see above). The practice certainly occurred, for it is explicitly described at *t. Abodah Zarah* 4(5).8. But it can surely be assumed that, unless the gentiles concerned were very foolish, the custom was not believed to impart a worse taste to the oil.

It seems to me best to stop looking for biblical proof texts or specific occasions for the ban and to accept instead that the confusion of the amoraic sources may have reflected a genuine lack of considered reasons for the prohibition. That is to say, the widespread custom among Jews of avoiding gentile oil may have been based neither on biblical exegesis nor on a decision by an accepted authority but on a pervasive religious instinct which was all the more powerful for its lack of rationale.

The instinct to avoid gentile foodstuffs of various common kinds was a novel phenomenon among Jews of the late Persian or early Hellenistic period. It had no explicit connection with a concern for levitical purity. Since it occurred after the composition of most of the holy books eventually reckoned canonical, the phenomenon was hardly attested in biblical texts which could be used as justification for the custom. The late books in which the practice is assumed (e.g. Judith 10.5; 12.1-4; Tobit 1.10-11) were not included in sacred scripture, apart from the book of Daniel.[12] It is a plausible hypothesis (which by its very nature can neither be proved nor disproved) that this extension of food taboos to separate not just holy from profane but, more specifically, Jew from gentile, is best explained by social and cultural changes in the lives of Jews in this period rather than the development of novel religious theories.

If this is correct, it may be misleading to describe intertestamental Judaism as did the amoraim, as if it consisted essentially in a number of competing systems of halakhah which differed either because of the decrees of competing religious authorities or because of their divergent methods of interpreting the Bible. Biblical interpretation was undoubtedly one generating force in religious innovation. But in many cases where a biblical text was cited in support of particular behaviour, the impetus for that behaviour was already present in the form of custom or instinctive attitude. Whether such custom counted as part of the Torah for any set of Jews was perhaps only a matter of terminology. It might also depend on the audience addressed: some of the unexpected items in Josephus' list of the Jewish laws in *C. Ap.* 2.190-219, such as the Jewish ban on taking spoils from the corpses of their enemies (212), might be seen by some Jews as custom rather than law, but it suited Josephus' apologetic when writing for gentiles to include such philanthropic behaviour within the law.[13]

If the taboo depended on instinct rather than biblical interpretation or a religious authority, why and how was it successfully abolished? It cannot be said that the reasons given in the rabbinic sources themselves for the decision by R. Judah and his court are very convincing. The view attributed to R. Judah by R. Simlai, that mixture with a forbidden substance did not invalidate oil because it left a bad taste, has been discussed above and found not impossible but rather implausible. Little can be achieved by expatiating on the strange reference, also discussed above, to death on the King's Mountain. It is hard to know how much credence to give to the claim of R. Mesharsheya that the ban was easily lifted because it was not observed by the majority of Israel; since Mesharsheya spoke in the name R. Samuel b. Abba, who in turn quoted R. Yohanan, the younger contemporary of R. Judah Nesiah, he himself probably taught a considerable time after R. Judah and may not have preserved accurate traditions about religious attitudes which prevailed long before his birth. It is difficult to explain why Jews should have dropped the traditional aversion to gentile oil which had apparently been so keenly felt in Josephus' day. It may be worth pointing out that, according to the Jerusalem Talmud passage quoted above (Section 7), Yohanan taught not that the *nasi*'s lifting of the ban was justified but that it was unnecessary, because any decree which the majority of Jews ignore is not a decree, and this was the case with Daniel's prohibition of gentile oil.

If adoption of any one of the amoraic opinions is not satisfactory, the only way to account both for R. Judah's action and for the diversity of rabbinic opinion about it is to construct a plausible model into which the disparate evidence can be seen to fit. Various more or less fanciful pictures can be imagined. It is not impossible, for example, that R. Judah issued a deliberate challenge to his contemporaries' deep religious feelings in order to demonstrate his authority by imposing his will; some evidence survives of a power struggle between the *nasi* and the sages in his day and the issue of gentile oil might have been a trial of strength.[14] More plausible is an economic motive, although quite what it would be is hard to envisage: the Jews in Galilee for whom R. Judah Nesiah is most likely to have legislated in the mid-third century inhabited one of the more favoured olive producing regions of the Near East and, whatever other goods they may have lacked, it is implausible that Jewish olive oil was a scarce commodity. If there were other, more complex, economic reasons for lifting the ban, no evidence of their nature survives.[15]

It seems to me that a more plausible model may be constructed by trying to explain rabbinic legislation about gentile oil against the background of a general picture of the development of Jewish law in the Hellenistic and early Roman periods. There are good reasons to

suppose that much of the law enshrined in the Mishnah was not
originally enacted by rabbis but existed before 70 CE in the form of
customary law. Thus the marriage, divorce and contract law in use in
the early second century in the Dead Sea area had much in common
with the law presupposed by the Mishnah.[16] This does not require
(though it does not preclude) the origin of that law having been in
rabbinical schools but it is more likely that the Mishnah consists to a
large extent of the rationalization of an existing legal system. Such
rationalization involved deduction following a series of rules, some of
which were at some time codified as the thirteen *middoth* of R.
Ishmael (*Sifra Lev.* 1). Whenever possible a rule was to be derived
from an existing rule or directly from a biblical text.

In most cases a rationale of current behaviour could be found but
not all existing custom could pass the rabbis' logical test. The
hypothesis I wish to propose is that R. Judah could find no such valid
arguments for the ban on gentile olive oil, and that he therefore
decided that it should be abolished.

How plausible is this reconstruction of events? It cannot of course
be proved, but the curious data from Josephus and the rabbinic texts
discussed in this paper can all, I think, be accounted for more or less
satisfactorily if it is taken as correct. It may be assumed that the
tradition mooted after R. Judah's decision by Rab, that the ban was
one of the eighteen decisions of the Houses in 66 CE, was not
accepted by (or known to?) the patriarch since, as Rabbah b. Bar
Hanah stated in the name of R. Yohanan in the Babylonian Talmud
passage (Section 5), it was not permitted to overthrow such decisions
and R. Judah would therefore have been courting unnecessary
trouble by doing so. It may further be assumed that, if he was aware
of Rab's other suggestion that the prohibition derived from Daniel
1.8, he found it unreasonably far-fetched—according to Rab in the
extract quoted above from the Babylonian Talmud (Section 3), of
course, he was ignorant of the Daniel proof text because he had failed
to undertake proper research.

To sum up. What I suggest is that, since no reason for the ban
could be found by extension of existing halakhah or by biblical
exegesis, R. Judah was forced to surmise an explanation of the taboo.
All he could come up with was the supposition that contamination
from the vessels or gentile sprinkling habits must have been the issue.
But such an explanation seemed to him patently unsatisfactory. His
only possible reaction was to lift the ban.

If this hypothesis is accepted, the whole saga may bear a lesson of somewhat wider significance. Codification may sometimes have implied leniency. If so, the general picture derived both from the rabbinic tradition itself and from the hostile depiction of Judaism in some early Christian texts may usefully be adjusted. According to that picture, halakhah was a system that constantly increased the burden of the law by seeking new ramifications for its effective imposition. But in some cases at the start of rabbinic codification in the tannaitic and early amoraic period the same processes of 'legalism' may have had an opposite effect. If my suggestion is correct, it was precisely the rationalization of the halakhah that eventually abolished the concept of gentile olive oil as unkosher. At any rate, since soon after the time of R. Judah Nesiah, all Jews, it seems, have used such oil with a good conscience.[17]

NOTES

1. The only work specifically devoted to this topic is S.B. Hoenig, 'Oil and Pagan Defilement', *JQR* 61 (1970/71), pp. 63-75.

2. Cf. S. Dar, 'The History of the Hermon Settlements', *PEQ* 120 (1988), p. 37.

3. Apart from the greater ease in the transport of olives rather than oil, it may be that people preferred to process their own oil to prevent adulteration by inferior olives or other substances.

4. On the olive trade of the early Roman empire, see in general D.P.S. Peacock and D.F. Williams, *Amphorae and the Roman Economy: an Introductory Guide*, London and New York, 1986. For the economic importance of this trade, see D.J. Mattingly, 'Oil for Export? A Comparison of Libyan, Spanish and Tunisian Olive Oil Production in the Roman Empire', *JRA* 1 (1988), 33-56, but note that there has been more study of the trade in this period in the Western Mediterranean than in the Levant. For olive oil production in Roman Palestine, see the articles and bibliographies in M. Heltzer and D. Eitamn, eds., *Olive Oil in Antiquity: Israel and Neighbouring Countries from Neolith to Early Arab Period*, Haifa, 1987.

5. See R. Marcus, ed., *Josephus: Works*, vol. VII, Appendix c, 'The early Seleucid Rulers and the Jews', Cambridge, Mass., 1943, repr. 1966, pp. 737-42.

6. See *b. Abodah Zarah* 36a and *y. Abodah Zarah* 2.8, 41d, both cited below. H. Albeck, *Shisha Sidrei Mishnah, Seder Nezikin*, Jerusalem and Tel Aviv, 1953, p. 331, asserts simply that the Mishnah refers to R. Judah Nesiah.

7. For the rest of this paragraph, see Z.A. Steinfeld, 'Concerning the Prohibition against Gentile Oil', *Tarbiz* 49 (1980), pp. 264-77.

8. Cf. J. Neusner, *The Talmud of the Land of Israel: a Preliminary Translation and Explanation*, vol. 33, *Abodah Zarah*, Chicago, 1982, p. 99. In favor of this interpretation, note that in the parallel version of this passage in *y. Shabb.* 1.5, 3d section 4 is placed immediately after section 1.

9. Cf. A. Oppenheimer, *The 'Am Ha-aretz: a Study in the Social History of the Jewish People in the Hellenistic-Roman Period*, trans. I.H. Levine, Leiden, 1977, p. 65. G. Alon, *The Jews in their Land in their Talmudic Age (70-640 C.E.)*, trans. G. Levi, vol. II, Jerusalem, 1984, p. 736, also understood the text in this way and suggested that the enthusiasm of R. Simlai of Lod for the lifting of the ban was occasioned by the greater threat to safety in the south than in Galilee, since the royal mountain is to be located in the Judaean hill country.

10. On the decrees, see the recent discussion of the tradition in I. Ben-Shalom, 'The Shammai School and its Place in the Political and Social History of Eretz Israel in the First Century A.D.', Ph.D. thesis Tel Aviv, 1980, pp. 562-98 (in Heb.).

11. Hoenig, 'Oil', *passim*. G. Alon, *Jews, Judaism and the Classical World*, trans. I. Abrahams, Jerusalem, 1977, pp. 156-57, suggested that the eighteen decrees (including the ban on oil) were a reinforcement of non-biblical halakhot about gentile food which were not sufficiently observed in some circles. This is possible, but there is no first-century evidence for such failure to observe the taboo on oil.

12. Note that among the gentile foodstuffs avoided by Judith was gentile oil (Judith 10.5).

13. See G. Vermes, 'A Summary of the Law by Flavius Josephus', *NT* 24 (1982), pp. 289-303.

14. On the relationship of the *nasi* to the rabbis, see L.I. Levine, 'The Jewish Patriarch (Nasi) in Third Century Palestine', *ANRW* II (Principat) 19, part 2 (1979), pp. 678-80.

15. Cf. M. Goodman, *State and Society in Roman Galilee, A.D. 132-212*, Totowa, NJ, 1983, p. 276, with a brief discussion of other possible (but hypothetical) economic arguments, such as the possibility that high quality Galilean oil might be exported at a sufficiently high price to pay for imports of low grade foreign (gentile) oil, while leaving a surplus for other purchases. S. Applebaum, 'Judea as a Roman province: the countryside as a political and economic factor', *ANRW* II (Principat) 8 (1977), p. 373 n. 84, puts forward an ingenious argument that the ban was lifted to benefit middlemen who purchased olives for resale. The Jews who would benefit most might be those in the Diaspora, but there no evidence that a third-century *nasi* would legislate with them primarily in mind.

16. See P. Benoit, J.T. Milik and R. de Vaux, *Les Grottes de Murabba'at* (Discoveries in the Judaean Desert, vol. II), Oxford, 1960.

17. I am grateful to participants at the Symposium on Jewish Food, held in Yarnton in June 1989, and to the members of the regular Yarnton discussion group in October 1989, for their helpful comments on earlier drafts of this paper.

JUDAISM AND CHRISTIANITY IN THE FIRST CENTURY: HOW SHALL WE PERCEIVE THEIR RELATIONSHIP?*

Jacob Neusner

University of South Florida

From the Nazi period onward, the Roman Catholic Church has formulated its relationship with Judaism in language and symbols meant to identify with the Jewish People, God's first love. To signal his opposition to anti-Semitism, Pope Pius said, 'Spiritually, we are all Semites', and, in the aftermath of 'the Holocaust', successive Popes and princes of the church have claimed for Roman Catholic Christianity a rightful share in the spiritual patrimony of Abraham. The epoch-making position of Vatican II marked only a stage forward in the process of conciliation and reconciliation that has marked the Roman Catholic framing of its relationship with both the Jewish People and with Judaism. As an American I have followed with enormous pride the particularly sustained and effective redefinition of that relationship, which has had its effect upon the civil order and public policy of my own country. The sages of Judaism define the hero as one who turns an enemy into a friend, and the present century's record of the Roman Catholic church, seen whole and complete, must be called heroic.

And yet in consequence of that sustained and, I believe, holy work, a theory of the relationship between Judaism and Christianity in the first century has taken shape that I believe has exacted a price in both learning and also self-esteem. That theory stems from the correct claim of Christianity, in its embodiment here in Rome, to share in the heritage of Abraham, spiritually to be Semites. That claim in its initial formulation stands before us on the Bible, which is the

---

*The text of this paper was delivered as a lecture at the Pontifical Lateran University, Rome, in January 1989.

systemic document of Christianity, and that Bible comprises the Old Testament and the New Testament. I need hardly rehearse the simple facts of the formation, by the Church of the second and third centuries, of the Bible, the Christian Bible, the Bible that made Christian the Hebrew Scriptures of ancient Israel. When the Church Fathers took their stand against Marcion and in favor of the Gospels' view of Christianity as the natural continuation of ancient Israel's faith, the fulfillment of ancient Israel's prophecy, they rejected the alternative position. It was that Christianity was something new, plunged downward from Heaven without place, without origins, without roots. Quite to the contrary, they maintained (and so has Christianity ever since), in the line of the apostle, Paul, Christianity is the olive branch, grafted onto the tree; Christianity begins with the First Man; Christianity now fully and for the first time grasps the whole and complete meaning of the scriptures of ancient Israel. These and similar affirmations accounted for the rereading of those scriptures and enriched the faith of the church with the heritage of the Torah, the prophets, and the writings, that, by that time, Judaism knew as 'the written Torah'. That 'written Torah' for Christianity constituted 'the Old Testament'.

Now, along with Cardinal Ratzinger, I maintain that hermeneutics forms a chapter in the unfolding of theology, bearing no autonomous standing in the intellectual life of faith. And the hermeneutics that flowed from the formation of the Bible—New Testament and Old Testament—took the position that Christianity was 'wholly other', that is to say, a completely new and unprecedented intervention of God into the life of humanity—but. And the 'but' stood for the appropriation of the life of humanity from the creation of the world onward, as the Evangelists and the author of the Letter to the Hebrews would maintain before Constantine, Eusebius afterward. Christianity did not begin with Jesus whom the Church called Christ, but with humanity, in the First Man, reaching its fulfillment in Jesus Christ, risen from the dead. That position left open the question of the place, in God's plan, for the Israel 'after the flesh' that all of the Evangelists and Paul identified as the bearers of the grapecluster and the original children of Abraham, Isaac, and Jacob.

But that position left no doubts as to the autonomy of Christianity, its uniqueness, its absoluteness. Christianity did not suffice with the claim that it was part of ancient Israel, or that it had adopted the

Torah of ancient Israel. The earliest Christians were not gentiles who became Jews; they were Jews who thought that their Christianity was (a) Judaism. More to the point, Christianity did not constitute a reform movement within Israel, that is to say, a religious sect that came along to right wrongs, correct errors, end old abuses, and otherwise improve upon the givens of the ancient faith. Whatever the standing of the old Israel, the new Israel was seen to be the true Israel. And that meant it would not be represented as merely a reform movement, playing the role, in the drama of the history of Christianity, of the Protestant Reformation to Judaism's Roman Catholic Church. Christianity was born on the first Easter, with the resurrection of Jesus Christ, as the Church saw matters. And that event was unique, absolute, unprecedented. Christianity did not have to present itself as a reformation of Judaism, because it had nothing to do with any other formation within Israel, God's first love. Christianity was not a Judaism: it was Judaism, because it was Christianity, from Easter onward; so, I think, the Church understood. And, as part of that understanding, in later times, the Church gave birth, within its tradition, to the Bible.

But in representing Christianity as a reform movement within an antecedent and an on-going Judaism, this received self-understanding of the Church was set aside. And, I am inclined to think, our century has witnessed a fundamental theological error, which has, as a matter of fact, also yielded an erroneous hermeneutics, in that order. It is, moreover, to speak plainly, a Protestant error. The theological error was to represent Christianity as a natural, this-wordly reform, a continuation of Judaism in the terms of Judaism. The New Testament would then be read in light of the Old, rather than the Old in light of the New. And that forms the hermeneutics that has predominated. We go to the Judaic writings of the age, or of the age thereafter, to discover the context in which Christianity was born; and Christianity then is understood to be represented by the Bible, or the New Testament in particular: a problem of reading writing, not of sifting through the heritage of tradition that the Church conveyed. The theological error of seeing Christianity as continuous and this-wordly, rather than as a divine intervention into history and as supernatural, affected not only the Christian understanding of Christianity. It also carried in its wake a theory of who is Israel, Israel after the flesh, that contradicted the position of the Church before our time.

The Church, in the tradition of the apostle Paul in Romans, affirmed the salvation of Israel through the heritage of Abraham and Sarah. But now, that 'Judaism' that had become Christianity was given an autonomous standing, on the one side, and also assigned negative traits, on the other. Christianity became necessary in this-wordly terms to reform Judaism, and that reformed Judaism defined the theological verities for Christianity. It was a Christian theology of Judaism as an 'if-only. . . '-theology of Judaism: if only Judaism were done rightly, it would have been (and would be) all right with God. That theology yielded a hermeneutic in which the faults of 'the Jews' or of 'Judaism' were contrasted with the virtues of Jesus and of Christianity. Judaism then required reformation; Judaism now is a relic. Judaism then bore deep flaws, ethical flaws for example, so that the principal value of Jesus was not as Christ risen from the dead but as a teacher of ethics, as though the Sermon on the Mount contained much that would have surprised informed hearers on one's duty to the other or on the social responsibility of the society. And Christians, for their part, found themselves in a subordinate position in the salvific story of humanity, becoming not the true Israel by faith in Christ Jesus (as Paul would want us to maintain) but merely Israel by default, that is, by default of the old Israel.

The appeal of the Reformation Churches, their theology, and, consequently, their hermeneutics, to a theory of Christianity as a (mere) reform of Judaism, and of Judaism as hopelessly requiring a reformation, framed on the state of the first century the world-historical drama of the sixteenth century. In their picture of the founding of Christianity, the Reformation theologians imputed their own situation to that time of perfection that formed the authority and the model. *Sola Scriptura* carried with it not only an apologetic for the new, but also a reconstruction of the old; only by reference to Scripture shall we know what Christ really had in mind, and Scripture, read independently of the heritage of the tradition that the Church sustained, meant the New Testament in light of the Old. And that brings us back to our own century, its theology, and its hermeneutics.

The theology that saw Christianity as a reformation of Judaism, so identifying the Reformation as the new, and sole, Christianity, yielded a hermeneutic that would read the life of Jesus as continuous with the Judaism of his day, and the salvation of Christ as an event within the Judaism of the first century. What that meant is that scholars would turn to the Judaic writings of the time not merely for information about how things were and were done, at that time, but for insight into the meaning and message—the religious message, the theological truth—of the New Testament. It was kind of a reverse-Marcionism. Instead of rejecting the Old Testament in favor of the New, the hermeneutics that has guided thought on the relationship of Judaism and Christianity in the first century has appealed to 'the Talmud', that is to say, to the literature of the ancient rabbis broadly construed, as the keystone and guide in the reading of the New. The Old Testament then would be set aside as merely interesting; salvation would come of, not the Jews, but the rabbis.

And that observation about the current state of New Testament hermeneutics draws us back to the point at which I began, namely, the affirmation of the Church as 'Semitic', the declaration, in the very teeth of Nazism, that 'spiritually, we are all Semites', the insistence upon the Judaic heritage of the Church and of Christianity. Given the tragedy of Christianity in the civilization of Christian Europe, perverted by Nazism and corrupted by Communism, given the natural humanity that for the first time accorded to suffering Israel after the flesh an honorable place within the faith, we must admire the intent. Everyone meant well, and today means well. But the result is an unChristian reading of the New Testament, and, as a matter of fact, a misunderstanding, from the viewpoint of the history of religion, of the New Testament and the whole of the Bible as well.

I have already made clear what I mean by an unChristian reading of the New Testament. It is the hermeneutic that appeals for the solution of exegetical problems to Judaic sources, in the manner of Strack-Billerbeck, for instance. That hermeneutic, I have argued, flows from the theology of Christianity as a continuation of, and mere improvement upon, Judaism. But if, as I have pointed out, Christianity understands itself as autonomous, unique, absolute, then Christianity cannot be a mere reformation. And not only so, but if, as we Jews maintain, the Torah of our Rabbi Moses, encompassing both the written Torah and the Oral Torah, bears no relationship whatsoever to any other revelation that God may have had in mind—if, as we hold, what God wants of all humanity rests in the commandments to the children of Noah, then we cannot find a compliment in this same notion. We are no relic; ours is not the unreformed sediment, nor are we the stubborn and incorrigible heirs of a mere denial. We bear the living faith, the Torah, of the one true God, creator of heaven and earth, who gave us the Torah and who implanted within us eternal life: so is the faith of Israel, God's first love. But in the context of this tragic century, we too have found reasons to affirm the picture of the first century as an age of reform, of Christianity as profoundly interrelated with Judaism in the way in which Protestant theology maintained.

The theological error does not dwarf the one that has characterized the historical account of the religions, Judaism and Christianity. The error as to history of religion is distinct. It is in two parts, one theological, the other religious. The theological error concerns history, not belief but (mere) description. As Cardinal Raztzinger warned as to theology and hermeneutics, it too represents a hermeneutical error, concerning the reading now of history, flowing from a theological position. The theological error, in this case, comes not from Christianity but from Judaism. It is the position that there was, is, and can forever be, only one Judaism, the Orthodox one. Speaking from the perspective of Sinai, one surely affirms that view. But translating theological truth into historical fact reduces theology to a matter of description, and that is an error. And it consequently imposes upon history the burden of faith. And that is as grave an offense against religion as asking science to conform in its results to Scripture in its crudest interpretation. In the case of the first century, we have been asked to see one Judaism, the Orthodox one, and to see that Judaism in the first century as an exact representation of what would emerge, in the Talmud of Babylonia seven hundred years later. It would follow that if we want to know what Judaism, the one, Orthodox, Judaism was in the first century, we have simply to consult the later writings in which that Judaism came to full and complete expression. That Orthodox theology of Judaism stands behind the possibility, represented by Strack-Billerbeck, of interpreting the New Testament as an essentially Judaic book, the life of Jesus as the story of a great rabbi, the formation of the Church as an aberration, and the work of the apostle Paul as a betrayal, an invention of Christianity Rabbi Jesus never contemplated—and on and on.

The theological error on the Christian side is to read Christianity as a continuation and reform of Judaism. That makes possible the hermeneutic, supplied by Orthodox Judaism, by Jewish apologists, by Christian friends of the Jewish People, by pretty much everybody of good will in our own awful century, that reads Christianity as contingent upon Judaism, secondary to Judaism, not absolute, not unique, not autonomous. The theological error on the Judaic side is to seek in the social facts of the history of the here and now the replication of God's Torah's picture of holy Israel. It was (and is) a positivist conception that the facts of history settle the affirmation of faith, that the sanctity of holy Israel living by the Torah is to be affirmed because in the first century (first only for the Christians, after all), there was that one true, orthodox, Orthodox Judaism that pretty much everybody affirmed (even Jesus), and that, as a matter of mere fact, Christianity distorted—so runs the apologetic.

I spoke of an error as to history of religion, and, in correcting that error, I propose to set forth a constructive program, one that accords with the theological self-understanding of absolute Christianity and unique Judaism alike. Out of the history of religion I want to form the possibility of a new classicism in theology of Judaism and theology of Christianity—no mean ambition. This program aims at allowing Christianity to be absolute, Judaism to be unique, and the two to define, for the twenty-first century, a shared range of genuinely religious discourse, one to which the facts of history are not critical, but the confrontation with God, central. I wish, in a word, for Judaism to be Torah, the one whole Torah God revealed to Moses at Sinai, not subject to the uncertainties of time or the varieties of circumstance; and I want, for Christianity, that autonomous standing, that confidence, that permits the end to the question, addressed here, there, and everywhere: why not? (that is, why not become like us?), and permits the asking of the question: how? (that is, how shall we all find, in Christian language, each his or her cross; in Judaic language, each in the face of the other the image and likeness of God?).

No small task, no mean ambition. Where to begin? Just as theology comes prior to hermeneutics, so religion comes prior to hermeneutics. We have therefore, in the realm of history of religion, to undertake first to define what we mean by religion, then to carry that definition onward to the reading of the holy books that concern us. A shift in language is required, however, from 'religion' to 'religious system'. When I speak of 'religious system', I refer to the cogent statement, framed in supernatural terms, of a social entity concerning its way of life, its world view, and its definition of itself. When a group of people, whether numerous, whether few, share a conception of themselves as a social entity, when they explain by appeal to transcendent considerations the very everyday pattern that defines what they do together, then the conception they set forth to account for themselves comprises their religious system. In simple terms, a religious system is made up of a cogent theory of ethics, that is, way of life; ethos, that is, world-view; and ethnos, that is, social entity.

Religions seen in this way form social worlds and do so through the power of their rational thought, that is, their capacity to explain data in a (to an authorship) self-evidently valid way. As to hermeneutics flowing from this theory of religion, the framers of religious documents answer urgent questions, framed in society and politics, to be sure, in a manner deemed self-evidently valid by those addressed by the authorship at hand. Religious writings present striking examples of how people in writing explain to themselves who they are as a social entity. Religion as a powerful force in human society and culture is realized in society, not only or mainly theology; religion works through the social entity that embodies that religion. Religions form social entities—'churches' or 'peoples' or 'holy nations' or monasteries or communities—which, in the concrete, constitute the 'us', as against 'the nations' or merely 'them'. And religions carefully explain, in deeds and in words, who that 'us' is— and they do it every day. To see religion in this way is to take religion seriously as a way of realizing, in classic documents, a large conception of the world.

That brings us to the systemic hermeneutics in the reading of the formative documents of Judaism or of Christianity. Writings such as those we read have been selected by the framers of a religious system, and, read all together, those writings are deemed to make a cogent and important statement of that system, hence the category, 'canonical writings'. I call that encompassing, canonical picture a 'system', when it is composed of three necessary components: an account of a world-view, a prescription of a corresponding way of life, and a definition of the social entity that finds definition in the one and description in the other. When those three fundamental components fit together, they sustain one another in explaining the whole of a social order, hence constituting the theoretical account of a system. Systems defined in this way work out a cogent picture, for those who make them up, of *how* things are correctly to be sorted out and fitted together, and *why* things are done in one way, rather than in some other, and of *who* they are that do and understand matters in this particular way. When, as is commonly the case, people invoke God as the foundation for their world-view, maintaining that their way of life corresponds to what God wants of them, projecting their social entity in a particular relationship to God, then we have a religious system. When, finally, a religious system appeals as an important part of its authoritative literature or canon to the Hebrew Scriptures of ancient Israel or 'Old Testament', we have a Judaism.

We describe systems from their end products, the writings. But we have then to work our way back from canon to system, not to imagine either that the canon is the system, or that the canon creates the system. The canonical writings speak, in particular, to those who can hear, that is, to the members of the community, who, on account of that perspicacity of hearing, constitute the social entity or systemic community. The community then comprises that social group the system of which is recapitulated by the selected canon. The group's exegesis of the canon in terms of the everyday imparts to the system the power to sustain the community in a reciprocal and self-nourishing process. The community through its exegesis then imposes continuity and unity on whatever is in its canon. The power of a system to persist expresses or attests to a symbolic transaction. That symbolic transaction, specifically, takes place in its exegesis of the systemic canon, which, in literary terms, constitutes the social entity's statement of itself. So the texts recapitulate the system. (In the language of Roman Catholic Christianity, the Bible is the Bible of the Church, which is to say, Scripture and tradition form the authority and criterion of Christian truth, not Scripture alone.) The system does not recapitulate the texts. The system comes before the texts and defines the canon. The exegesis of the canon then forms that on-going social action that sustains the whole. A system does not recapitulate its texts, it selects and orders them. A religious system imputes to them as a whole cogency, one to the next, that their original authorships have not expressed in and through the parts, and through them a religious system expresses its deepest logic, *and it also frames that just fit that joins system to circumstance.*

The whole works its way out through exegesis, and the history of any religious system—that is to say, the history of religion writ small—is the exegesis of its exegesis. And the first rule of the exegesis of systems is the simplest, and the one with which I conclude: *the system does not recapitulate the canon. The canon recapitulates the system.* The system forms a statement of a social entity, specifying its world view and way of life in such a way that, to the participants in the system, the whole makes sound sense, beyond argument. So in the beginning are not words of inner and intrinsic affinity, but (as Philo would want us to say) the Word: the transitive logic, the system, all together, all at once, complete, whole, finished—the word awaiting only that labor of exposition and articulation that the faithful, for centuries to come, will lavish at the altar of the faith. A religious system therefore presents a fact not of history but of immediacy, of the social present.

By the definitions just now given, can we identify one Judaism in the first centuries BCE and CE? Only if we can treat as a single cogent statement everything all Jews wrote. That requires us to harmonize the Essene writings of the Dead Sea, Philo, the Mishnah, the variety of scriptures collected in our century as the Apocrypha and Pseudepigrapha of the Old Testament, not to mention the Gospels! That is to say, viewed as statements of systems, the writings attest to diverse religious systems, and, in the setting of which we speak, to diverse Judaisms. There was no one orthodoxy, no Orthodox Judaism. There were various Judaisms. In that context, the formative writings of what we call Christianity form statements of systems, and whether we call the Judaisms or Christianities really does not affect how we shall read them—*in that context*. For reading a text in its (systemic) context and as a statement of a larger matrix of meaning requires us to accord to each system, to each Judaism, that autonomy, that uniqueness, that absoluteness, that every Judaism has claimed for itself, and, it goes without saying, that all Christianities likewise have insisted upon.

How does the approach to the study of religion define an answer to the question with which we began, the relationship of Judaism to Christianity in the first century? And what hermeneutic flows from the theory of religion I have outlined? Each document is to be read in its own terms, as a statement—if it constituted such a statement—*of* a Judaism, or, at least, *to* and so in behalf of, a Judaism. Each theological and legal fact is to be interpreted, to begin with, in relationship to the other theological and legal facts among which it found its original location. A specific hermeneutics emerges.

Let me speak of both Judaism and Christianity. The inherited descriptions of Judaism of the dual Torah (or merely 'Judaism') have treated as uniform the whole corpus of writing called 'the Oral Torah'. They have further treated Christianity as unitary and harmonious; so it may have become, but, in the first century, I think both the founder of this party and his protagonist, Peter and Paul, will have found that description surprising. When we define religion in the way that I have, we have a different task from the one of harmonization. It is the task of describing the Judaisms and the Christianities of the age, allowing each its proper context and according to each its correct autonomy. What of the relationship between (a) Judaism and (b) Christianity? There we have to appeal to Judaic writings where they bear facts that illuminate Christian ones, but we must not then reduce Christian writings to the status of dependence and accord to them a merely recapitulative intent: reform, for instance.

Some facts are systemically active: Jesus Christ rose from the dead. Some are systemically inert: they wrote writs of divorce in the first century; some people observed cultic purity even at home; they kept the Sabbath. We cannot assign to systemically inert facts an active position that they did not, and as a matter of fact, could not, have had, and we cannot therefore frame our hermeneutics around the intersections of facts deriving from one piece of writing and occurring in another, later piece of writing. In New Testament hermeneutics, salvation is not of the Jews, because the New Testament is a component of the Bible, and the scriptures of ancient Israel form the other component of that same Bible: all read as the Church has been taught to read them whole and complete, the story of salvation.

Among the religious systems of the people, Israel, in the Land of Israel, one of which we call 'Christianity', another of which we call 'Judaism'—and both names are utterly *post factum*—we find distinct social groups, each with its ethos and its ethics, each forming its distinctive ethnos, all of them constituting different people talking about different things to different people. As bearers, all of us, of the heritage of Israel and the fundament of truth of Sinai, we have therefore to affirm that God works in mysterious ways. We Jews can live with that mystery. That is why the seven commandments to which all humanity everywhere is subject make so much difference to Judaism: it is the theory of the other. God asks that much, and, if you do it, you are what God wants you to be, no less, but also no more. Why is so much asked of us and so much less of others? That is the mystery of eternal Israel. We not only live with that mystery. We are that mystery. Can Christianity live that mystery? I think that, with the Christian theology of Judaism that has taken shape in Vatican II and since that time, in the American Bishops' framing of matters in particular, Christianity too says its amen to God's work.

In that context, we now look back at the first century from a new perspective. We understand that Christianity is Christianity not because it improved upon Judaism, or because it was a Judaism, or because Christians are 'spiritual Semites', or (to complete the catalogue) because Christianity drew upon Judaism or concurred in things that Judaism taught. Christianity is Christianity because it forms an autonomous, absolute, unique, and free-standing religious system within the framework of the scriptures and religious world of Israel. It suffices therefore to say that the earliest Christians were Jews and saw their religion as normative and authoritative: Judaism. That affirmation of self then solves the problem that troubles Christians, when they (wrongly) see themselves as newcomers to the world of religion: why Judaism as a whole remains a religion that believes *other* things, or, as Christians commonly ask, 'Why did (and do) the Jews not "accept"?' or 'Why, after the resurrection of Jesus Christ, is there Judaism at all?' Often asked negatively, the question turns on *why* the Jews do *not* believe, rather than on 'what' they do believe.

Christians want to know *why not*. To me as a rabbi, the answer to that question is simple: Judaism and Christianity are completely different religions, not different versions of one religion (that of the 'Old Testament', or, 'the written Torah', as Jews call it). The two faiths stand for different people talking about different things to different people. And that explains why not: Judaism answers its questions in its way, and it does not find itself required to answer Christianity's (or Islam's, or Buddhism's) questions in the way that these are phrased. Judaism sees Christianity as aggressive in its perpetual nagging of others to accept salvation through Jesus Christ. The asking of the question—why not? rather than why so?—reflects the long-term difficulty that the one group has had in making sense of the other. And my explanation of the difference between Christianity and Judaism rests on that simple fact. Each religious tradition talks to its adherents about its points of urgent concern; that is Judaism and Christianity, respectively, stand for different people talking about different things to different people.

If we go back to the beginnings of Christianity in the early centuries of the Christian Era, we see this picture very clearly. Each addressed its own agenda, spoke to its own issues, and employed language distinctive to its adherents. Neither exhibited understanding of what was important to the other. Recognizing that fundamental inner-directedness may enable us to interpret the issues and the language used in framing them. For if each party perceived the other through a thick veil of incomprehension, the heat and abuse that characterized much of their writing about one another testify to a truth different from that which conventional intepretations have yielded. If the enemy is within, if I see only the mote in the other's eye, it matters little whether there is a beam in my own. But if we see the first century from the perspective of the twenty-first, that is not how matters are at all. Now we can affirm what has taken twenty centuries for us to understand, which is that we all believe in one God, who is the same God, and him alone we serve in reverence. And that shared life in God and for God defines the relationship of Judaisms and Christianities, then as it does now. But now, through the suffering of us Jews, eternal Israel, and through the response to our suffering of you Christians, Israel with us, we can see that truth, as before we did not and could not. So our awful century has left some good for the age that is coming.

THE HASMONEANS AND THE USES OF HELLENISM[1]

Tessa Rajak

University of Reading

I. *Concepts*

The meeting between Judaism and Hellenism is one of the most discussed relationships in cultural history. From the later nineteenth century on this has been a polarity which has assumed a special importance for scholars, both Jewish and non-Jewish, and for obvious reasons.[2] It has served both as a heuristic tool and as a target of enquiry in itself. On the one hand, certain Jewish interpreters applauded Jewish responsiveness to the forces of supposed Hellenic enlightenment, order and rationality, and perhaps even chose to emphasize areas of integration, if not assimilation, between the two cultures. On the other hand, for any historian whose education was influenced by the European classical tradition, there was an inclination to see the spread of Greek culture as the central historical phenomenon of the era of Alexander and his successors and to give it, in the recent words of Kuhrt and Sherwin-White,[3] 'overriding significance'. A Christian perspective could lend its own concern with the kinds of Judaism which were penetrated with Hellenism: Christianity, after, all *was* in some sense a cross between the two cultures. Furthermore, the dichotomy was transferred at an early stage to analyses of Christianity itself, with a contrast between a 'primitive' Palestinian Christianity and a 'Hellenistic' variety serving, at times, as a favourite tool of research for critics of the stature of Bultmann.

For all that, the Judaism-Hellenism distinction is not a modern invention. It is important to appreciate that there were moments when it loomed large in the consciousness of the actors in the ancient period itself. The very concept of Hellenism, and the related one of

Hellenization are, in fact, first and best attested in the eastern Mediterranean precisely in the context of Jewish thought; and it may even be the case that the Jews of the time were responsible for forming and transmitting the perception that the Greek culture with which they met was a force capable of encroaching upon their own values, that there was a major influence there, to be either embraced or rejected. Historically, this seems probable; and it is also what the surviving verbal evidence suggests.

For the very word *hellēnismos* first appears in the second book of Maccabees (4.13). There, in the expression *akmē tou hellēnismou*, 'a climax of Hellenism', it refers to the 'package' of Greek customs allegedly introduced into Jerusalem by the high priest Jason after he had bribed his way into the high priesthood. A Greek political entity, if not an actual *polis*, had been set up within Jerusalem. The symbols of the Greek life style that belong with it are, in this highly rhetorical chapter, made to centre upon athletic pursuits: the gymnasium with its associated institution for young men, the sports stadium, the wrestling school and the athlete's hat are all singled out for mention. Nudity as such is not alluded to here. We may wonder, in fact, whether any more than one single despised institution need lie behind the entire tirade, rather than a truly comprehensive Hellenization of Jerusalem life on the part of Jason.[4] We may also point out that the Maccabaean cultural crisis developed out of *political* quarrels concerning, in effect, conflicting relationships with the ruling power. These are points worth pondering. But the fact remains, that whatever exactly it was that was brought to Jerusalem, this was immediately seen as standing for a whole culture, and one whose pursuit contravened Jewish Law (2 Macc. 4.12). The expressions *ton Hellēnikon charaktēra* (which might be rendered 'the Greek way of life') and *tas Hellēnikas doxas* ('the Greek scale of values', perhaps) also figure. 2 Maccabees is a summary, composed before 124 BCE, of a history written close in time to the Maccabaean crisis itself.[5] Its author will be reflecting an ideology not entirely remote from those who participated or from those who observed; and there must therefore have been some who interpreted the events not just as the defence of the Temple, but as a struggle against Jewish Hellenism and against Antiochus IV or his successors as agents of Hellenization. The original history had been written in Greek, by a man known as Jason of Cyrene. Perhaps Jason's origins in the Greek-speaking Diaspora had sharpened his awareness of the boundaries between Jews and Greeks.

At the same time, the rest of Jason's history as reflected in the 2 Maccabees summary, and certainly the first book of Maccabees, with its consciously Biblical idiom, operate with quite other categories. The wars of Judas are against pollution or against the Gentiles. The pro-Seleucid Jews, to be identified with the former Hellenizers, are the 'lawless', *anomoi* (1 Macc. 9.23, etc.); when they occupy the Akra fortress, they are 'the men in the citadel'. Elsewhere, we do not hear of Greeks or Greek sympathizers. We may guess that the issue of Hellenism as such ceased for the time being to be in the forefront, overshadowed by the military struggle between the Maccabees and their opponents. In later Jewish writings, it surfaces again, as we shall see.

The key text in 2 Maccabees indicates two separate kinds of development. The one which is the most visible on the surface is that upper-class Jews in the period leading up to 165, including (or perhaps especially) members of the high-priestly circles, were attracted by practices typical of Greek cities: they were becoming *Hellenized*. The other, which is probably at the heart of the matter, is that the deliberate adoption of certain such practices were a highly contentious public issue, linked with politics as much as with religion, and able itself to divide society. The latter, conscious process, in which certain features of Greek culture possessed a kind of symbolic significance and carried political implications, will here be called *Hellenism*. This is a narrowing of the familiar usage, originated by J.G. Droysen, where 'Hellenism' refers generally to Greek civilization after Alexander the Great, as a distinctive culture, in all its aspects.[6]

II. *Hellenization*

The coming together of ancient statement with modern prejudice has highlighted Hellenization, so that it has loomed large in interpretations of post-Biblical Judaism. One major debate has focussed, on the one hand, on the assertion that Palestinian Judaism was heavily penetrated with Greek culture from an early date (as in Martin Hengel's great work), on the other, on the denial that the totality of apparent influence has any deep significance, given the continuing separation and distinctiveness of Judaism. In this debate, and equally in analyses of other periods, situations or authors, the Jewish-Greek polarity has been taken for granted.[7]

It is hard to see how such debates can ever be concluded. No one would wish to deny the steady Hellenization of the material culture of Palestine, both Jewish and non-Jewish, during the whole of the period. Most would agree that even a sealed-off environment like Qumran was not immune. Such Hellenization is visible in architecture and art, in everyday uses of the Greek language and in some aspects of political behaviour. When it comes to the higher realms of thought and belief, we have to face far greater uncertainty about the meaning of apparently parallel developments. But I think that putting the question itelf in perspective may be of some assistance. There are immense logical and empirical difficulties in seeking to measure Jewish Hellenization. They can be summed up, perhaps, by saying that there is a task which is logically prior, one whose complications historians are only just beginning to grasp. We need to get some picture of the Greek culture with which we are dealing, that is to say, of the kind of Hellenization that was embraced, or in other cases avoided, by the peoples who lived around and among the Jews. We ought not to rely on rather general and long-unexamined notions about the norms and forms of Greek city life, and to doctrines about the way in which that specially Greek institution, the *polis*, was carried to the far corners of the backward east. Only this enquiry can give any real historical sense to the specific problem of the Hellenization of the Jews, and to the possibility of Jewish impermeability.

The need for a new logic becomes clear when we remember that what we are thinking about, in thinking about Hellenization, was, after all, a two-way process, not just a matter of native cultures being imbued with the Greek one. Admittedly, a leading dynamic in the Mediterranean world (and even beyond), if we are to concentrate on major trends, was the politico-cultural imperialism, first of Alexander and of the Ptolemies and Seleucids, and then of the Romans—for the Romans were also major (probably indeed *the* major) carriers of Greek culture in the east. It is true, too, that the net effect of several centuries of change would eventually be to create, during the high Roman empire, an amazingly uniform elite culture based upon Greek rhetorical and philosophical education and on a revival of the Attic past. It would be foolish to ignore this force for movement towards ever greater Hellenization. It would also be foolish to deny that the high Greek culture had patent charms and attractions (without of course ignoring those of the late oriental civilizations, Judaism included). Nonetheless, in spite of all its pretensions, Greek culture too was constantly changing under the impact of those peoples towards whom it came. Where small groups of true Greek colonists lived in a small unit in an alien world, as they often did in the years after Alexander, there was possibly some chance of their preserving their way of life intact for several generations. But when the *ephebes* in a gymnasium or the citizens of a *polis* were native born, it would be absurd to expect them simply to conform to standard patterns, without modifying those patterns and causing something new to be transmitted.

Therefore, Hellenization can mean several different things: in its full sense, it would be the suppression of a native culture and language and its replacement with a fully or mainly Greek style— something which, I suspect, is rather rare, except over a long period; or it might be the creation of a truly mixed, hybrid form, the much-discussed *Verschmelzung*; or, again, we might see the addition of Greek elements to a persisting culture whose leading features remained visible and relatively constant. The distinctions are most easily grasped in the sphere of architecture. Thus, the well-known tombs in Jerusalem's Kedron Valley, known as the tomb of Zechariah and the tomb of Absalom but in fact belonging probably to priestly families of the first century BCE, are excellent examples of a hybrid style, with their Greek columned porticoes, their prominent pointed roofs, their separate outbuildings or *nefashim*.[8] Their mixed style is related to that of some of the Petra rock-cut tombs, which in itself is a suggestive fact about the evolution of a regional idiom embracing Nabateans as well as Jews. But, of course, the adoption of a hybrid architecture need not be associated with a comparable fusion in other departments of life. To judge whether a society at a particular time should overall be deemed Hellenized in the first, the second or the third sense will rarely be a simple matter. There is room for argument as to whether the Jews were closest to the second or the third class, but most scholars would probably hold that their Hellenization was a relatively superficial matter and that a hybrid culture was not created, thus putting them in category three.

III. *Hasmonean Hellenism*

My purpose has been to expose the complex conceptual problems that underlie any discussion of processes of Hellenization, whether Jewish or otherwise. In various departments of life, a steady influx of

Greek modes and manners will have occurred without much notice
being given to the matter: it need not have been apparent to the
agents that what they were doing or making was, or had once been,
characteristically Greek. By the time customs are taken over, they
may well be emptied of their associations, or even have acquired new
ones. Archaeological material alone can tell us nothing about such
overtones. For these reasons, it may well be more advantageous for
historians, whose concern will, after all, be with the *mechanism* of
cultural interaction, not just with labelling, to fix their attention less
on Hellenization, than on Hellenism, in the sense which I gave to
that term; that is to say, on the *conscious* adoption of Greek ways, or
else its reverse, where there is at least some indication that the agents
see a real significance (one that might be, say, political or religious) in
the Greekness of those customs. The questions that the historian will
then want to ask will be about the factors which promoted Hellenism
or anti-Hellenism in particular circumstances, involving explicit
pressure from above, commercial requirements, international contact,
intellectual links, or other matters; and about the consequences of
different choices.

The study of ancient history rarely provides us with convenient
answers even to such more narrowly delimited questions. The
sources tend to be lacking just where we most want them. Nonetheless, for the Hasmonean period, we do have the unusual advantage of
Josephus's detailed narrative, following on from the books of the
Maccabees, or rather, to be precise, overlapping with them. We are
doubly fortunate where we can combine this with archaeological,
numismatic or other types of evidence, as we can do to some extent
for the later Hasmonean period, covering the years after the
revolutionary wars of Judas, and extending from 161 to 63 BCE. They
are important years for the expression of Hellenism in Palestine and
also of antagonism to Hellenism. It will be helpful first to give some
impression of the period.

The central fact is the rise and fall in Palestine of an independent
state, comparable in Jewish history only with the kingdom of David.
This national experience marked the people, through the classical
period and far beyond. From the military leadership of Judas
Maccabaeus had emerged, in due course, permanent authority, a
dynastic succession and, eventually, a monarchy. Defensive wars led
to territorial expansion: to the west to occupy most of the cities of the
coast, to the east to the Jordan and even beyond, south into the whole

of Idumaea and north into Samaria and the Galilee. However, neither internal nor external stability of an enduring kind were achieved. Geographical factors alone would tend, of course, to make Palestine vulnerable. And elements from within declared the domination of the Hasmoneans to be unacceptable. The ruling family fell prey to a war of succession at the time of Pompey the Great's annexation of Syria, and the door was open to Roman intervention. One of the rival Hasmoneans then remained in control of a reduced Jewish entity, but one that was not as small as it had been before this period; and he was made subject to Roman taxation and Roman administrative arrangements: this was what remained, together with a divided population and substantial discontents. It would be left to the Idumaean Herod, in an inventive exploitation of the roles of eastern client king and Hellenic patron under Augustus, to reconstruct what the Hasmoneans had built, in the spirit of his own day and age.

These developments did not occur in isolation. Internal forces combined with external circumstances to make the growth of the Jewish state possible. The decline in Seleucid power, and then the collapse of that extended kingdom into continuous dynastic wars, presented the Hasmoneans first with overlords who were increasingly distracted and afterwards with opportunities for profitable meddling. Alliances with Rome, which at this stage may have helped, and certainly did not hinder the Hasmonean expansion were another part of the external contribution. Judaea was by no means the only small state in the east to achieve freedom under her own rulers in the late Hellenistic period, though her growth, with all its consequences, was particularly spectacular. What needs to be underlined was that the new state was one whose destiny depended upon the complex and sometimes chaotic interplay of eastern power-politics, and her rulers had to be able to deal confidently with a variety of other rulers or aspirants. In other words, she had become a Hellenistic kingdom. I need hardly say that no assumptions may be made as to the degree and type of Hellenization in such a kingdom.[9]

But we can at any rate see that some Greek trappings were appropriate. And the Hasmoneans did not hang back, when it came to adopting these. They appear to have stepped readily into their parts. Indeed, one may wonder whether Judas himself had been as stoutly opposed to all things Hellenized as he is painted. Since he had nailed his flag to the mast of anti-Hellenism and allied himself with the rigorous *hasidim*, the other elements in the picture could hardly be allowed to emerge in the tradition. It is noteworthy that, of our two accounts of the Maccabaean crisis (not counting Josephus's version of 1 Maccabees), the one which makes the most of Judas, to the exclusion not only of his brothers but even of his father Mattathias, is 2 Maccabees. Unlike 1 Maccabees, the epitome of Jason of Cyrene which makes up the bulk of the second book (to that epitome are added two letters), was originally written in Greek, and exploits various dramatic devices characteristic of the so-called 'pathetic' Greek historiography fashionable at the time. The more 'Hellenized' writer, therefore, is the one whose hero is Judas.[10] To this perhaps rather indirect argument might be added the general observation that the Maccabaean revolt, quite contrary to its image in later popular mythology, was never a peasant uprising, although it may well, as Josephus claims, have attracted many ordinary people at an early stage. Mattathias was addressed by the Syrian representative Apelles as an important man in his region, and a number of pointers in our narratives suggest that the family was propertied from the beginning.

Almost twenty years after the death of Judas, in 143/2 BCE, his brother Jonathan was killed by the treachery of Tryphon, a claimant to the Seleucid throne. The death seems in a sad way an appropriate one, for Jonathan's leadership of his people had moved away from the military patterns which he had inherited from Judas, to the paths of diplomacy. Jonathan had been accepted the high priesthood from one of the Seleucid rivals, Alexander Balas. Later, in a desperate attempt to outbid another claimant, Demetrius I, that same Alexander had made Jonathan *meridarch* (governor) and one of his First Friends; the latter title had given Jonathan official status at court. Jonathan's body was released and taken by his younger brother Simon for burial in the ancestral town of Modi'in. There Simon built a new family tomb, which served also for his father and mother. That 1 Maccabees stops to describe this monument in detail shows what significance was attributed to it. The grandeur, the power symbolism and the hybrid Greco-Oriental style of the tomb, so reminiscent of those in the Kedron valley mentioned earlier, shows something of the distance the family had already travelled: 'Simon had the body of his brother Jonathan brought to Modi'in, and buried in the town of their fathers [note that 1 Maccabees describes Modi'in as a *polis!*]; and all Israel made a great lamentation and mourned him for many days. Simon built a high monument over the tomb of his father and his brothers, visible at a great distance, faced back and front with polished stone. He erected seven pyramids, those for his father and mother and four brothers arranged in pairs. For the pyramids he contrived an elaborate setting: he surrounded them with great columns surmounted with trophies of armour for a perpetual memorial, and between the trophies carved ships, plainly visible to all at sea [Modi'in is at least ten miles from the sea]. This tomb which he made at Modi'in stands to this day' (1 Macc. 13.25-30).

Simon began as he meant to go on. There are several features of public life under his regime which must be described as overtly Greek. And they are acts of political importance surrounded by ceremony and display, such that they can only be seen as consciously chosen and contrived. To bring out these features of Hasmonean conduct is not to say anything new. They were emphasized, and occasionally overemphasized, by Bickerman, and well understood even by Tcherikover.[11] Schürer, I suppose, approved them, since he could not find it in himself to accept the Maccabees' earlier exploits: his words still ring out from the pages of the revised version of his first volume: 'the earliest incidents reported represent Jonathan's companions more as bandits than as members of a religious party'.[12] It is not wholly clear whether the later course of Jonathan's career make him and his followers look more, or less, like members of a religious party. What is necessary is to pursue their implications, especially because the picture as usually painted contains a large and puzzling contradiction.

Our sources give us a fair impression of some aspects of the later Maccabees' Hellenism. In the year 142 BCE, and soon, no doubt, after Jonathan's burial (the great tomb may not yet even have been completed), 'the yoke of the Gentiles was taken away from Israel', as 1 Maccabees has it (13.41-42). The autonomy here referred to, and arising in fact in the form of a grant of freedom from tribute and taxes by Demetrius II, was expressed in classic form, by the establishment of a new chronological era: 'and the people began writing on their records and their contracts, "in the first year of Simon, great high priest, commander and leader of the Jews"'. (So far as we know, this era did not endure as a lasting base of reckoning.) Simon was granted the right to issue a coinage, but he did not do so. Of course, the powers granted to Simon were defined in the manner established at Jerusalem during the Persian period, with the high priesthood as the principal political position. Traditionally Jewish, too, was the ceremonial of 141, when the liberation of the Akra from his Jewish opponents, the so-called Hellenists, was celebrated with the waving of palm branches, and with psalms and instruments. Yet in 140, when the assembled people declared Simon high priest, commander and ethnarch for ever, 'until a trustworthy prophet shall arise', the decree was inscribed in bronze and set up in the Temple precinct and in its treasury, just as was supposed to happen in a Greek city (1 Macc. 14.41ff.).

The first Hasmonean to mint his own coins was in all probability John Hyrcanus, the son and successor of Simon. That both John and all his successors confined their output to bronze *perutot*, and never produced silver, the regular sign of autonomy, is probably to be explained in purely economic terms. The familiar and very handsome Tyrian silver shekels continued to be the common large currency in the whole area, and were even acceptable for payments of the Temple tax; Judaea did not, of course, have its own source of silver. What is more telling in terms of ideology is that Hasmonean coins remained, to the end, aniconic, replacing the customary ruler's portrait with a second symbol. This might suggest that constraints were placed on the ruler by the susceptibilities of the pious, or of certain religious leaders. We have a clear indication that the symbolism of the coins was thought to matter—and can therefore be taken by the modern interpreter as a genuine reflection of the dynasty's self-image—in that it displays a manifest respect for the people's will. Hyrcanus's coins carry two types of formula, reading either 'Yehoḥanan the high priest and the council (or community, ḥever) of the Jews', or else, 'Yehoḥanan, the high priest, head of the ḥever of the Jews'. Alexander Jannaeus, more than a generation later, was unambiguously titled king; none the less, at a certain point in his reign, and perhaps in response to a major crisis with the Pharisees about which we read in Josephus, some of his coins were overstruck on the obverse with 'Jonathan, the high priest and the ḥever of the Jews'.[13]

Coinage is thus an area in which we can observe how a political exploitation of Hellenism can well be juxtaposed with a resonant assertion of native values. It is not, at all times, a matter of incompatibilities or even necessarily of oppositions. From Hyrcanus's coins, which in Jewish terms would be described as extremely conservative, we conclude that Judaea did not care to see itself as *just* another Hellenistic state and that religious tradition still had an important place. The script is a deliberately archaic palaeo-Hebrew evoking the days of the first Temple; it was used also in some Qumran texts. Yet a generation later, Alexander Jannaeus was issuing coins inscribed in Hebrew, Aramaic and Greek with his Greek name, 'Alexandros' replacing 'Jonathan' in the Greek versions. As far as the symbols went, to the small repertoire depicted on Hyrcanus's coins, which was neutral or vaguely Jewish—a wreath around the name, ears of corn and double cornucopias with a pomegranate between them—Jannaeus added a more 'international' set of symbols—a star and diadem (overtly announcing his kingship), the anchor known in the region from the coins of Antiochus VII and Antiochus VIII (though, also, of course evoking his family's tomb), and lilies also associated with coins of the same Seleucids. The development is a striking one.[14]

IV. *The Hasmonean Conquests and the Greek Cities of Palestine*

Yet, if the style of the rulers was increasingly involved with Hellenism (in the active sense which I have given to that term), their military policies, as commonly understood, reflect a very different image. The motive force is held to be an implacable enmity with the Greek cities in and around Palestine; not merely with their inhabitants, as neighbours with whom one might not agree, but with the settlements themselves and what they stood for, as representatives of a pagan, and especially (given the Hellenocentric tendencies present even in the Jewish scholarship) of a *Greek* culture which was, on this account, anathema to Judaism.[15] The picture derives from the way in which successive Hasmoneans treated alien peoples in the course of their conquering careers. From Judas Maccabaeus onwards, we find several patterns which it is possible to connect: imposed segregation of Jews from others, possibly accompanied by an act of purification; brutal reprisals against enemies, in the course of which their cities were destroyed and their citizens expelled, if not eliminated; or forced Judaization, such as was carried out in specific cases by Aristobulus in his short reign and by John Hyrcanus. Alexander Jannaeus, the most expansionist of all the rulers, emerges as the climax of these manifestations. No reconciliation has been sought between this stark picture of their actions and the other types of evidence, which indicate a fair degree of Hellenism among the Hasmoneans.

The facts that we have are these. In the books of the Maccabees, the wars of Judas Maccabaeus are conceived of as directed in an overall way against 'the Gentiles'. The origins of this hostility cannot be traced, but it evidently has some connection with the Jewish civil conflicts, for we hear how the aged Mattathias had renegade Jews chased up and circumcised and that he found them (not surprisingly) sheltering among the Gentiles (1 Macc. 2.45-48). The war between Jew and heathen is visualized in total terms: we are told that the non-Jewish inhabitants of the region flocked to the Syrian general Nicanor to escape Judas, 'thinking that defeat and misfortune for the Jews would mean prosperity for them' (2 Macc. 14.14). After Jonathan was kidnapped, the surrounding peoples are said to have been enchanted with the possibility of destroying Judaism root and branch (1 Macc. 12.53). In fact, however, we can be sure that not all the local peoples were unfriendly during this period, for the Nabataean Arabs across the Jordan gave the Maccabees useful information more than once, and, at Scythopolis, the native Gentile populace (no doubt a mixed one) offered expressions of friendship and goodwill to their own Jewish inhabitants and to Judas when he passed (2 Macc. 12.29-31). There is no reason to think that a distinction between 'Greeks' and 'Orientals' was made by the Jewish fighters: Gentiles seem to be all as one. But the basic problem is that the Biblical archaism of our narratives does not allow us to discern the real ideology of the war against the heathen: we cannot tell how far the spirit reflects the agents' own attitudes and how far it is a literary overlay.[16]

Both the separation of Jew from Gentile and the destruction of Gentile settlements seem to have been justified by Judas on the grounds either of security or of revenge; and, at the same time, the aura of a holy and cleansing war was never far away. Already in 164 BCE, the Jews were rescued from parts of the Galilee and from Gilead after fierce fighting, and transported to Jerusalem in a triumphal procession. The harbour at Joppa, where the people led their Jewish neighbours into a trap and drowned them, was burned together with its ships, but Judas left when he found the city gates closed. Very similar action is said to have been taken at Jamnia, to forestall violence against the Jews there (2 Macc. 12.3-9). In a different situation, operating among the 'Philistines', Judas burned the cult images of the deities of Azotus and pulled down their altars (1 Macc. 5.67-68). The venerable city of Hebron, in the hands of the Idumaean 'sons of Esau', appears to have been treated more leniently, with just the destruction of its fortifications and of the strongholds in the villages around it (1 Macc. 15.65).

Judas was succeeded as leader by his more politically-minded brother, Jonathan (161–143/2 BCE), who played a major role in shaping a new order. He is not, in fact, associated in 1 Maccabees with a religious militancy of the intensity of that of Judas. However, as part of an intensive consolidation of his power through Judaea, Jonathan did evict the population of Beth-Zur in southern Judaea, after besieging the town; and he put a garrison inside it. Another brother, Simon, followed Jonathan to power (143/2–135/4 BCE), and he returned to the port of Joppa, an outlet to the sea for his nascent state (1 Macc. 13.11; 14.34). There too he installed a garrison, and his expulsion of the natives was perhaps a reprisal for the atrocity they were said to have committed on Judas's day. How total the expulsion was we cannot tell, though we should observe that Philo, nearly two centuries later, could describe Joppa as a Jewish town— whatever that meant (*Leg.* 200). Simon's other major conquest, after a siege which seems to have been a highly professional affair, was Gezer (Gazara), an important defensive position lying on the west side of Judaea. In this case, there are interesting details of a cleansing operation: 'he threw them out of the town and he purified the houses in which the idols were, and so he made his entry with singing and praise, and he expelled all impurity from the town and settled in it men who practised the Law' (1 Macc. 13.47-48).[17]

From such roots came the actions of the later leaders. But, again, there are hazards in ascribing policy to action, and it is all too easy to foist an ideology onto a scattering of recorded incidents. What has happened is that the militant Judaism depicted in the Maccabees has been attached by extension to the entire history of the dynasty. The removal of Gentile pollution in conquered territory is understood as a prime aim of expansion. Judaization of the inhabitants was one possible route; their removal or even their elimination, another. The policy would thus have been expressed in a stark choice put before a defeated people, either to convert, or to face dispossession or worse. This reconstruction takes account of a distinction between, on the one hand, a small minority of peoples that did accept circumcision and all that followed—a part of the Ituraeans of upper Galilee and the Hermon area during the short reign of Aristobulus, styled 'Philhellene' (104–103 BCE; *Ant.* 13.318-319), together with the Idumaeans of southern Judaea under the expansionist John Hyrcanus (*Ant.* 13.252; 15.255)—and, on the other, the so-called Greek cities, where such a course would be out of the question. The Greek cities then emerge as the victims of the greatest hostility and the worst brutality. A view of Palestine as deeply polarized between Greek and Jew need be only a step away.

There is no doubt that, from the outside, the Jewish kingdom (as it became) was, in its own day, seen as aggressively expansionist. A valuable sentence in Strabo's *Geography* calls the Hasmoneans 'tyrants', which is a technically correct application of Greek political terminology, since their power was acquired and not inherited, and it describes them, with only a little exaggeration, as subduing much of Syria and Phoenicia. Yet we should notice that, in Strabo, there is no imputation of noteworthy enmity towards defeated aliens on the part of these rulers. Another Augustan writer, Timagenes (a man known for his obstreperousness) is cited by Josephus in a tantalizing fragment as expressing admiration for the way Aristobulus had served his country when he added the Ituraeans to it by their circumcision (*Ant.* 13.319). It is, of course, just possible that Timagenes had gone on to draw an *unfavourable* contrast with the harsher way in which Greeks had been treated by the Jews, but the apparent tone of the remark (if it be correctly quoted) does not suggest that. There are no other statements made by, or attributed to, outsiders.[18]

We depend for the most part, then, upon material found in Jewish writing, and, after the death of Simon, that means Josephus alone. However, his story is not to be taken at face value, least of all where it concerns Alexander Jannaeus. The existence of two separate Josephus versions, an early one in the introduction to his *Jewish War* and the main one in the *Antiquities*, does make it somewhat easier to stand back critically from what he says. We see that it is with Jannaeus that the image of an implacable Jewish hatred for Greek cities gets crystallized, on the basis of rhetoric incorporated in Josephus's text. The focal point lies in the connection made between Jannaeus's acts and the subsequent reversal of his dispensation brought about by Pompeius in 63 BCE, when he swept through Palestine. The Roman general, who divested Judaea of most of its Hasmonean acquisitions, came as the liberator of established Greek cities and the founder of new ones. He was presented as a latter-day Alexander and was a proponent of Hellenism in the active, political sense.[19] It would evidently have been to his purpose to have the Jewish monarchy, which he effectively terminated, depicted as an arch-enemy of Hellenism, the barbarous destroyer of the *polis*.

Moreover, for Pompeius, it was better to be able to say that he had
rebuilt a city from its foundations than that he had merely given one
a new name. We know that extensive propaganda in both Latin and
Greek accompanied and followed Pompeius's conquests and that
historians especially were (not untypically) harnessed to the cause.
Both of Josephus's known principal sources, Strabo's *Histories* (not
the *Geography*) and Nicolaus of Damascus's *Universal History*, will
unavoidably have drawn on material tainted by this propaganda, and
we can see that the Jewish writer did not escape its influence, even
though in so doing he came into conflict with the loyalties that
sprang from his own Hasmonean descent and from his Jewish
patriotism. Such a passive approach to his task as historian is also to
be found elsewhere in his work.

The link between Jannaeus's depredations and Pompeius's
restorations stands out particularly sharply in the *Jewish War*
version, where we are told that the Roman conqueror liberated and
returned to their rightful citizens all those cities of the interior which
the Jews had not earlier 'razed to the ground'—Hippos, Scythopolis,
Pella, Samaria, Jamnia, Marisa, Azotus and Arethusa (*War* 1.156).
There is also talk of the reduction of the coastal cities of Gaza,
Raphia and Anthedon to servitude. The *Antiquities* make no such
claim in connection with the seizure of Raphia and Anthedon. Nor is
any unusual devastation associated here with the siege of Gadara (in
Transjordan), by contrast with the claim in the *War* that Gadara lay
in ruins until its instant rebuilding was ordered by Pompeius to
gratify a favourite freedman, Demetrius. At Gaza, brutalities are, in
fact, acknowledged by the *Antiquities*, and there is a vivid description of
Jannaeus's army, admitted into the city by treachery, running riot
and massacring the council, while the king turned a blind eye (*Ant.*
13.262). But such uncontrolled behaviour is far from unknown in
ancient warfare, and it reflects nothing more than the savagery and
greed of the soldiery. The reputation of his antagonist, Ptolemy
Lathyrus, easily outdid that of Jannaeus, for, according to Josephus,
Strabo reported Lathyrus as ordering his troops to chop up women
and children in the villages of Judaea, boil them in cauldrons and
then taste the flesh (*Ant.* 12.345-347). It is also worth remembering
in this context that both John Hyrcanus and Alexander Jannaeus
employed mercenaries, and especially that Jannaeus, unable to rely on
local people because of their intense hostility, had drawn on Pisidians
and Cilicians, who are labelled 'Greeks' by Josephus (*Ant.* 13.374;

378). Another case of destruction in the *Antiquities* is that of Amathus, dealt with during a campaign against the Arabs and Moabites, and scarcely, therefore, a Greek centre. Its demolition is put down to the simple reason that its ruler, Theodorus, flatly refused to come out and fight.[20]

In the *Antiquities* (13.395-397), we are also given a list, avowedly partial but none the less interesting, of towns and cities 'of Idumaea, Syria and Phoenicia' which were 'held by the Jews' at the end of Jannaeus's life. Eight of these figure in the *War* among the places ruined by the Jews, but the later version bears no comment about their treatment, except in one case alone, that of Transjordanian Pella, where it is announced that the demolition was due to the particular reason that 'the inhabitants would not agree to adopt the customs of the Jews'. In spite of the marked absence of any indication that such a procedure had been applied anywhere else, the explanation would perhaps seem to imply a general practice, and to invite the conjecture that the other places listed in the *War* had suffered for a similar refusal, even if it is, to say the least, peculiar that such dramatic events should have been passed over in silence. Equally, successful conversions anywhere at all are not likely have passed unnoticed and should have remained in the record. If we are, then, disposed to envisage a widespread phenomenon behind the events at Pella, it is necessary to be clear about what that phenomenon can possibly have been. What Jannaeus may realistically have sought, and in some places achieved, was not so much the creation of thousands of new Jews, but rather a new structure that recognized the supremacy of a Jewish element in the towns and of the norms of that element. This would be an entirely intelligible move, when, in many cases, Hasmonean campaigns had been justified precisely by the ostensible need to protect Jewish communities. Such a reading of the words used by Josephus, *ta patria ethē*, 'the ancestral customs', would undoubtedly be valid, since, after all, Hellenized Jews perceived the Mosaic Law as a national constitution, at any rate when they were expressing themselves in Greek. That control of the political organs of a city could be a matter of desperate contention between Greek and Jewish co-residents, we learn from Caesarea's appeal to Nero on that very matter in the years immediately before the revolt of 66 CE (*War* 2.266). This is what Pella will have scorned, to its cost, and this is the constitutional arrangement which Pompeius will have undone on arrival in a town, the cornerstone of his much-vaunted reconstruction.

That the feature of Jewish barbarism in the stories has been played up in the historical record, and that it is simply not credible that numerous major conurbations were reduced to rubble at this time (as claimed, especially, in the *Jewish War*), when we know them to have been flourishing a generation later, are contentions recently made in an exhaustive and vigorous fashion by Aryeh Kasher. He also correctly concludes that the distortion should be traced back to Josephus's Greek sources.[21] But it is less easy to follow him in ascribing the trouble to the antisemitic impulses of those sources; not so much hostility to Judaism as enthusiasm for Hellenism would appear to be the issue, and our knowledge of the specific concerns of Pompeius offers us a precise context. Apart from that, we must remember the rhetoric which time and again led Greek historians to exaggerate the catastrophes of war; A.H.M. Jones noted comparable treatment of Alexander's operations at Gaza and at Tyre (interestingly enough, in the same part of the world).[22]

Hellenism, then, was Pompeius's instrument. It had also been Jannaeus's. Neither man could afford to go too far, because the home market would only buy so much 'Greek wisdom' (in the case of Rome, we have only to remember what Octavian was to be able to make of the Alexandrian interests of Marcus Antonius). But, in his conflict with Hasmonean Judaea, Pompeius was able to win the war of words as easily as he was able to hold the field of battle. Indeed, he was able to divest the Hasmoneans of all the credit they had laboriously built up as masters of a Hellenistic state. And, by his powerful impact on a historical record controlled by Greeks, he even brought the Hasmonean-born historian, Josephus, unwittingly into his camp.

It will be clear enough from our review that, during a century of Hasmonean activity, the leaders' relation to Hellenism did not remain constant; nor, of course, did the forms of Greek culture around them. But for our purposes, the development matters less than the pattern, and that is present already in the careers of the early leaders. Already, an understanding of the uses of Hellenism is visible. This could become a contentious matter and be seen as an assault on the Law, but often enough it was acceptable: there was no automatic contradiction between what was Jewish and what was Greek. Such a policy naturally brought in its wake an undercurrent of diffused cultural change, of Hellenization, in my sense of that term. In this, the Jews developed along lines similar to the peoples around them, in spite of the modifications wrought by the complexity of their inherited religious culture. Hellenization passed for the most part unnoticed, though it would be wrong to deny that there were moments of revulsion. Generally, it is the conscious reactions, with all their political resonances, which are most amenable to purposeful study.

NOTES

1. These ideas were first developed in a paper presented to the British Association for Jewish Studies when Geza Vermes was honoured with a second term as President. Now, what is, I hope, a better paper on the same theme is offered as part of this *Tribute*. The debt owed to his interest and prompting is thus obvious, here as elsewhere. By way of example, this analysis is much indebted to Geza's demonstration, in so much of his work, that an unclouded view of the texts can overturn many a conventional view in Jewish history. A very recent treatment of a number of the issues discussed here is to be found in Martin Hengel's *The Hellenization of Judaea in the First Century after Christ*, London and Philadelphia, 1989, esp. chs. 1 and 3.

2. For some significant works centering on this dichotomy, see I. Heinemann, *Philons griechische und jüdische Bildung*, Breslau, 1932; S. Lieberman, *Hellenism in Jewish Palestine* (Texts and Studies of the Jewish Theological Seminary, 18), New York, 1962; Martin Hengel, *Judentum und Hellenismus*, Tübingen, 1969; ET *Judaism and Hellenism*, London, 1974; Edouard Will and Claude Orrieux, *Ioudaïsmos-Hellenismos*, 1986; and the many studies by Louis Feldman of Biblical figures in Josephus's *Antiquities*.

3. Amelie Kuhrt and Susan Sherwin-White (eds.), *Hellenism in the East*, London, 1988.

4. On the 'Hellenistic reform' in Jerusalem, see E. Bickerman, *Der Gott der Makkabäer*, Berlin, 1937; idem, *From Ezra to the Last of the Maccabees*, New York, 1962, pp. 93-111; Victor Tcherikover, *Hellenistic Civilization and the Jews*, Philadelphia, 1966, pp. 152-74; Fergus Millar, 'The Background to the Maccabean Revolution: Reflections on Martin Hengel's *Judaism and Hellenism*', *JJS* 29 (1978), pp. 1-21; Klaus Bringmann, *Hellenistische Reform und Religionsverfolgung in Judäa*, Göttingen, 1983.

5. For a convenient discussion, see John J. Collins, *Between Athens and Jerusalem: Jewish Identity in the Hellenistic Diaspora*, New York, 1983, pp. 76ff. and the literature there referred to.

6. J.G. Droysen, *Geschichte des Hellenismus*, vol. 1, Hamburg, 1836; vols.

1-3, ed. Bayer, Tübingen, 1952-53. See A.D. Momigliano, 'J.G. Droysen between Greeks and Jews', *History and Theory* 9 (1970), pp. 139-53 = *Quinto contributo alla storia degli studi classici e del mondo antico*, I, Rome, 1975, pp. 187-201; also in *Essays in Ancient and Modern Historiography*, Oxford, 1977, pp. 307-24.

7. The deep penetration of Greek culture into Judaism was also stressed by Bickerman. Its imperviousness was stressed, among others, by H.A. Wolfson, in his great work on Philo (*Philo: Foundations of Religious Philosophy in Judaism, Christianity and Islam*, 1947), by Millar, by Feldman (see especially 'Hengel's *Judaism and Hellenisn* in Retrospect', *JBL* 96 [1977], pp. 371-82), and, for a later period, by M. Goodman and M. Stone. By questioning the dichotomy itself, we alter the terms of at least some of questions involved.

8. For a brief study, see N. Avigad in *Jerusalem Revealed: Archaeology in the Holy City 1968-1974*, Jerusalem: IES, 1975, pp. 17-20.

9. For types of conscious Hellenism, and also of Hellenization, in differing contexts, see Fergus Millar, 'The Phoenician Cities: a Case-Study of Hellenization', *Proc. Camb. Phil. Soc.* 1983, pp. 55-68; Simon Hornblower, *Mausolus*, Oxford, 1982; and, for reflections on Rome, Andrew Wallace-Hadrill, 'Greek Knowledge, Roman Power', *Class.Phil.* 83 (1988), pp. 224-33.

10. On the thrust of 1 and 2 Maccabees, see D. Arenhoevel, *Die Theokratie nach dem I und II Makkabäerbuch*, Mainz, 1967; Robert Doran, *Temple Propaganda: the Purpose and Character of II Maccabees* (CBQMS, 12), Washington, D.C., 1981.

11. See n. 4.

12. Emil Schürer, *The History of the Jewish People in the Age of Jesus Christ*, vol. 1, ed. G. Vermes, F. Millar, M. Black, Edinburgh, 1973, p. 174.

13. Ya'akov Meshorer, *Ancient Jewish Coinage*, vol. 2, New York, 1982, p. 77.

14. Meshorer, *op. cit.*, pp. 60-68.

15. See, notably, Schurer, vol. 1 (revised edn), esp. p. 228; and Tcherikover, whose assessment is just as extreme: *op. cit.* (n. 4), pp. 243ff.

16. Cf. Uriel Rappaport, 'The Hellenistic Cities and the Jews of Eretz Israel in the Hasmonean Period', in *The Seleucid Period in Eretz Israel*, ed. B. Bar-Kochva (1980; Hebrew), pp. 263-75.

17. For possible archaeological traces of the operation, see R. Reich and H. Geva, 'Archaeological Evidence of the Jewish Population of Hasmonean Gezer', *IEJ* 31 (1981), pp. 48-52.

18. For the Timagenes fragment, see Menahem Stern, *Greek and Latin Authors on Jews and Judaism*, vol. 1, Jerusalem, 1974, no. 81; Josephus says he has it from Strabo's *Histories*. On the Idumaeans and the Ituraeans, cf. Aryeh Kasher, *Jews, Idumaeans and Ancient Arabs* (Texte und Studien zum

Antiken Judentum, 18), Tübingen, 1988, pp. 44-86.

19. On this imitation of Alexander, see A.B. Bosworth, *Conquest and Empire: the Reign of Alexander the Great*, Cambridge, 1988, p. 181.

20. On all these episodes, see Menahem Stern, 'Judaea and her Neighbours in the Days of Alexander Jannaeus', *The Jerusalem Cathedra*, 1981, pp. 22-46.

21. See A. Kasher, *Canaan, Philistia, Greece and Israel: Relations of the Jews in Eretz-Israel with the Hellenistic Cities (332 BCE-70 CE)*, Jerusalem, 1988; Hebrew, pp. 113ff.

22. A.H.M. Jones, *The Cities of the Eastern Roman Provinces*, 2nd edn, Oxford, 1971, p. 237.

HADRIAN'S POLICY IN JUDAEA AND THE BAR KOKHBA REVOLT: A REASSESSMENT

Peter Schäfer

Freie Universität
Berlin

The search for the causes behind the violent outbreak of the Bar Kokhba revolt, whose relentlessness surpasses and whose aftermath outweighs that of even the first Jewish War, continues to occupy scholars with unmitigated intensity.[1] The three reasons afforded by the sources, namely the retraction of permission to rebuild the Temple, the foundation of Jerusalem as the Roman colony Aelia Capitolina and Hadrian's prohibition of circumcision, have been discussed at length and do not require further interpretation.[2] The first reason, the planned or initiated construction of the Temple is the least likely. As concerns the foundation of Aelia Capitolina, contemporary research is for the most part in consensus that the decision was made during Hadrian's visit to the province of Judaea in the spring of 130. To what extent this decision was responsible for the outbreak of the revolt is a moot point. The majority of the more recent scholars see the impulse to revolt less in the foundation of Aelia than in the prohibition of circumcision. Of necessity, this implies that the foundation had to have taken place before the beginning of the war (i.e. between Hadrian's visit in 130 and the outbreak of the revolt in 132).[3]

An isolated discussion of possible causes for the Bar Kokhba revolt is unproductive and is furthermore methodologically questionable. Through the critical examination of the available evidence of Hadrian's policy in Judaea and through the questioning of the sources pertaining to Jewish reaction to this policy, the following contribution attempts to define more closely the political and intellectual climate which existed before the revolt.

Judaea between 117 and 132 CE

Information regarding the state of affairs in Judaea between the suppression of the Diaspora revolt and the outbreak of the Bar Kokhba War is limited, but nonetheless the general contours of the situation are discernible. Hadrian belonged to Trajan's general staff at the start of the Parthian War in 114 and was Governor (*legatus Augusti pro praetore*) of Syria from the summer of 117. During the Parthian War, in 115, the revolt within the Diaspora broke out, beginning in Egypt and Cyrene and then extending to Cyprus and the Mesopotamian theatre of war. The revolt in North Africa was suppressed by Marcius Turbo, *praefectus Aegypti* and friend of Hadrian, while the suppression of the revolt in Mesopotamia was undertaken by the Moorish General Lusius Quietus on the command of Trajan. Lusius Quietus achieved success quickly through the use of extreme brutality and was subsequently appointed *legatus Augusti pro praetore* in Judaea in 117. Trajan, who had in the meantime become seriously ill, discontinued the Parthian campaign and died while returning to Rome in August of 117 in the city of Selinus on the Black Sea. Hadrian had himself declared Emperor by the Syrian troops as the adoptive son of Trajan and concluded the retreat initiated by him. (This adoption had probably been feigned by Trajan's wife Plotina and the *praefectus praetorio*, Attianus.) He abandoned Assyria, Mesopotamia and Armenia and subverted the power of the most prominent representatives of the warring faction. Lusius Quietus, the main advocate of the hard-liners, was deposed as Governor of Judaea and in the early summer of 118 was executed together with three of Trajan's close war companions following the accusation of having instigated a conspiracy. Hadrian's declared goal was to be remembered as an Emperor of peace and as *restitutor orbis*.[4]

1. Judaea had since 74 been an autonomous Roman province under the authority of a governor of praetorian rank. In the space of time between 117 and 132 the status of the province was changed and Judaea was raised to the rank of a consular province (i.e. with a former consul as governor). The exact date of this change is unknown although there are a number of points of reference. First of all, it is generally accepted that the dispatching of Lusius Quietus to Judaea in the rank of consul in 117 does not necessarily entail Judaea's status as having been that of a consular province, but was rather the result of the particular situation following the suppression

of the revolt in the Diaspora.[5] On the other hand, the Governor of Judaea during the Bar Kokhba revolt, Tineius Rufus, is referred to as *consul suffectus*[6] in 127, which would imply that the change in Judaea's status had to have taken place before 127. Finally, it has been pointed out that the *procurator* of the province of Judaea in 123 received the salary of a *ducenarius*.[7] This presupposes a governor of consular rank, which of necessity then places the change in the status of the province in the period prior to 123.

2. The status of Judaea as a consular province implies the stationing of a second legion in the territory. Following the first Jewish War the *legio X Fretensis* had been stationed in Judaea, with its headquarters in the destroyed Jerusalem. The Governor, however, resided with parts of the tenth legion in *Colonia Prima Flavia Augusta Caesarensis*, the Roman colony into which Caesarea had been transformed. We do not know which legion was stationed in Judaea after 117 nor when this occurred; however, since the discovery of the milestone 13 km southeast of Akko, it appears most likely that it was the *legio II Traiana*.[8] The inscription on the milestone is, by the evidence of Hadrian's fourth *tribunicia potestas*, clearly dated in the year 120. Hence it follows that the year 120 was the *terminus ante quem* for the transformation of Judaea into a consular province and the obligatory stationing of a second legion.

3. Hadrian continued the active road-construction policy of his predecessors. In Syria and Arabia this construction had been completed either under Vespasian or Trajan, and Hadrian clearly directed his attention to the province of Judaea. The milestones identified recently[9] have evidenced Caparcotna (Legio) in the Jezreel Valley as having been an important military base which was then connected with Sepphoris and further with Akko (Ptolemais) in 120. Hence, it follows that Caparcotna was the headquarters of the new legion which controlled movement between Judaea and Galilee[10] and furthermore secured the 'lebenswichtige Verbindung zwischen Ägypten und Syrien'.[11] Further construction and restoration efforts appear to have been concentrated in 129/30 and to have included Jerusalem.[12] These may be connected with Hadrian's visit to Judaea, but there can be no doubt that the Roman road construction in the provinces was primarily concerned with the improvement of military infrastructure.

4. Several changes in important cities also attest to the political activity of the Romans in the years 119/20 (following the Diaspora

revolt) and 129/30 (in connection with Hadrian's visit to the province). Tiberias had always been a city with a predominantly Jewish population, but nevertheless had a hellenistic constitution.[13] During the first Jewish War the city belonged to the territory of Agrippa II. Although the rebellious faction was dominant, parts of the population acted loyally towards Agrippa and the Romans. Thus, when Vespasian approached, the city surrendered without a fight and was for the most part spared. Coins from Hadrian's time show Zeus sitting in a temple, which is believed to represent the *Hadrianeion*[14] as attested by Epiphanius,[15] in other words the sanctuary dedicated to the Emperor cult.

Similar coins from Neapolis[16] and Sepphoris are well known.[17] Sepphoris, the capital of Galilee, likewise had a predominantly Jewish population and was decidedly against the revolt during the first Jewish War, the clear majority of its inhabitants having supported the Romans (Josephus, the Jewish commander of Galilee had to subdue the city by force). Sepphoris was in all likelihood renamed Diocaesarea in 129/30[18] and received the official title Διοκαισάρεια ἱερὰ ἄσυλος καὶ αὐτόνομος.[19] It has already been assumed by Hill[20] that the renaming of the city may have been connected with Hadrian's visit to Judaea and with his identification with Zeus Olympios.

Another *Hadrianeion* has been attested in Caesarea, which Vespasian had transformed into a Roman colony.[21] Perhaps the Hadrian statues and the portrait of Antinoos,[22] which supposedly stems from Caesarea, should also be seen in this light. Certainly the Jewish population of Caesarea was, in contrast to Tiberias and Sepphoris, not a significant factor.[23]

5. The decision to reestablish Jerusalem as the Roman colony Aelia Capitolina coheres with Hadrian's political and religious activities outlined above, namely the stationing of a second legion, the intensive road construction and the Emperor cult. Hadrian was the most active founder and builder of cities since Augustus.[24] B. Isaac and I. Roll have pointed out that the connection between road construction and the founding of colonies was 'a familiar pattern in Roman history'[25] and that the stationing of a legion generally followed the founding of a colony: 'In Judaea we have seen the foundation of Caesarea as a Roman colony at the time when X Fret. was first established at Jerusalem. Similarly there may be a connection between the two decisions taken by Hadrian: to assign a

second legion to the province and to found another colony'.[26] Although the assignment of the second legion (which Isaac and Roll date prior to 120) and the foundation of Aelia are not to be placed in an immediate temporal context, a factual connection does seem to be apparent. Today most scholars agree that Hadrian's decision to found Aelia Capitolina was made during his visit to the province of Judaea in the spring of 130. Of the evidence presented to support this claim, I do not believe, however, that the one Aelia coin which was found in a *single* hoard together with revolt coins and *denarii* between the time of Trajan and Hadrian and 130, is sufficient proof, for there is no indication that this hoard was necessarily hidden during the Bar Kokhba revolt.[27] On the other hand, there is much which supports Mildenberg's argument that the various strikings of the Hadrianic Aelia coins took place over a longer period of time than merely between the end of the war and Hadrian's death (i.e. the end of 135/beginning of 136 and July of 138).[28]

Jewish Reaction to Hadrian's Policy

The description of the political situation in the province of Judaea during Hadrian's reign is not basically controversial. What is controversial, however, is the interpretation of the evidence in relation to the question of the Bar Kokhba revolt. Does Roman action taken after 117 reflect a tense relationship between Rome and its notoriously restless province? Was the interval between 117 and 132 a period of intensified local unrest met by Roman measures of suppression which then inevitably led to the explosive outbreak of the revolt? Was this situation similar to that which existed in the years prior to the first Jewish War? These questions have been answered affirmatively by B. Isaac and A. Oppenheimer, who have characterized the transformation of the province after 117 under the rubric 'prior unrest' and summarize as follows: 'In sum, it may be concluded that there is evidence of increased Roman military activity in the area, both in the years following Trajan's death and in 129/30, which may reflect a response to local unrest, or preparations for the suppression of anticipated hostilities, or both'.[29]

1. The transformation of Judaea into a consular province and the subsequent assignment of a second legion very probably occurred, as we have seen, during the first years of Hadrian's reign. The reasons behind this action are sufficiently explained by Hadrian's desire to

secure peace on the eastern border of the Empire following his renunciation of claims to the provinces of Mesopotamia, Assyria and Armenia. At best it could be assumed that the transformation was connected with the revolt in the Diaspora, although to date no positive evidence has been presented which would suggest Judaean involvement in the uprising. (On the contrary, the reorganization of the province is one of the main arguments for an alleged involvement, or rather for the theory that the Romans, through the stationing of a second legion, prevented the outbreak of a revolt in Judaea.[30]) One must also ask why the transformation occurred so late—not until Hadrian's reign—and *following* the suppression of the revolts. Furthermore, why would Hadrian have deposed the governor of Judaea, who had been so successful in suppressing the revolt in Mesopotamia, at a time when Judaea remained a hotbed of unrest? The recalling and execution of Lusius Quietus naturally had inner political motivations, but they would have come at a very inopportune time had Judaea indeed found itself on the brink of open revolt.

2. The forced road construction is also doubtless to be seen in relation to the efforts to ensure peace and secure the borders in the Near East. The undisputedly military character of this construction does not, however, necessarily imply that it was undertaken solely in order to serve the suppression or hindrance of actual unrest in Judaea. It is much more plausible to view the extension of the network of roads under the larger aspect of improving connections between the provinces of Egypt, Arabia and Syria. Equally important is the establishment of a passageway and military corridor for the defence of the Empire's eastern borders which this construction enabled: 'His (= Hadrian's) activity was devoted chiefly to the lands which by their position were destined to be the bases on which the most important military frontiers rested'.[31] It is not, of course, possible to separate clearly the Romans' overall political aims and the local political effects. However, it is a question of the point one wants to stress. To argue that Hadrian's military road construction policy had been 'part of plans for taking drastic measures'[32] (sc. against the Jewish population of Judaea) is a rash and exaggerated conclusion.

3. Similar conclusions can be applied to the erection of the *Hadrianeia* as the centre of the Emperor cult in Caesarea and Tiberias, to the renaming of Sepphoris as Diocaesarea and to the pagan character of the coinage of Sepphoris/Diocaesarea, Tiberias

and Neapolis from 119/20. Pursuing a reference made by A.H.M. Jones,[33] Isaac-Roll[34] and Isaac-Oppenheimer[35] have interpreted the pagan coinage as evidence 'that Hadrian disenfranchised the Jewish and Samaritan aristocracies which had hitherto ruled these three cities and entrusted their government to pagans'.[36] The transference of the civic administrations to 'non-Jewish elements' is, according to Isaac-Oppenheimer, best understood as having been a deliberate anti-Jewish measure, namely the Roman response to local unrest during the years 117-118.[37]

This interpretation of an unequivocal finding is also questionable. We possess no concrete evidence that the erection of the *Hadrianeia* in Caesarea and Tiberias and the striking of pagan coins were carried out against the will of the Jewish population and despite their resistance. The passages from rabbinic literature[38] which Isaac-Roll, following the example of G. Alon,[39] provide as proof of 'political brigandage' in the years before the Bar Kokhba revolt and as the reason 'for the removal of Jewish leaders from the local administration'[40] are altogether dubious. There is absolutely no evidence which can justify classifying the 'bandits' mentioned in these passages as having been 'political terrorists'. On the contrary, there is every reason to believe that quite ordinary bandits are here being referred to.[41] Moreover, at least Tiberias, as we have pointed out above,[42] had since its foundation been a city with a Hellenistic constitution and Hadrian had therefore no need to exclude the Jewish population from the city council. Scholars do at times change trains. The same A. Oppenheimer, who, in 1985, together with B. Isaac speaks of the provocative transfer of the civic administration in Tiberias to 'non-Jewish elements' had, in 1980, argued in a very different manner: 'The Jews residing in Tiberias and Sepphoris apparently accepted Hadrian's measures in silence, and it is possible that the influential among them, some of whom were leading members of the municipal institutions, were even pleased with them'.[43]

4. What were the implications of Hadrian's decision to found the Roman colony Aelia Capitolina upon the ruins of Jerusalem? Was this the decisive catalyst which led to the revolt, following years of suppression and increased military activity? Here as well, there is a lack of direct information regarding the reaction of the Jewish population, and we can therefore only speculate as to the consequences which the foundation of Aelia had for the native population.

As has been illustrated by B. Isaac,[44] the founding of a colony was accompanied by two advantages in addition to the increase in status (for a colony ranked higher than a *polis*). First, there was the land and poll-tax exemption and, secondly, the acquisition of Roman citizenship. These privileges were granted to all inhabitants of the colony, both to Roman veterans and to the native population. In consequence, there is nothing which suggests that the foundation of a colony would have met with such bitter resistance, and this applies to Jerusalem as well. Isaac concludes that 'Jewish resistance against the foundation of Aelia may not have been directed against the establishment of a colony as such. Jews were willing to live as citizens in *poleis* and there may be evidence that the status of a colony was, in their eyes, desirable.'[45] As proof of this, he cites the desire of Agrippa I to solicit Roman citizenship, or at least tax exemption, for Jerusalem,[46] which can only be referring to the status of a colony:[47] 'We can be reasonably sure that Agrippa I would not have considered involving Jerusalem in anything abhorrent to the Jews'.[48] Although not being a historically reliable bit of information, the reported offer made by the Emperor 'Antoninus' to the Patriarch R. Jehudah ha-Nasi' to raise Tiberias's status to that of a colony[49] also displays the Jews' positive assessment of colonial status. Oppenheimer had originally argued along similar lines, and saw a direct connection between the transformation of the civic administration of Tiberias and Sepphoris and the foundation of Aelia Capitolina: 'Probably the absence of opposition in Tiberias and Sepphoris and the satisfaction revealed by the notables encouraged Hadrian in his endeavor to turn Jerusalem into a pagan city with a temple of Jupiter'.[50]

If the foundation of the Roman colony Aelia Capitolina as such had not been offensive, but perhaps even welcomed, then the provocation must have had its roots elsewhere. Oppenheimer argues that Hadrian must have known what the foundation of precisely this colony implied for the Jews (which also differed from all others, in that a legion was assigned to it): 'It is unthinkable that Hadrian, who travelled widely and was naturally curious, did not understand that he was taking action against Judaism'.[51] On the other hand, B. Isaac states: 'It is therefore quite possible that not the organization of Jerusalem as a colony provoked Jewish resistance, but the decision to make it a pagan city and the plans for the site of the temple'.[52] However, here again we find ourselves in uncertain waters. Until now, neither archaeological nor literary evidence has been furnished which clearly indicates that Hadrian had a temple to Jupiter built upon the site of the Jewish Temple. As G.W. Bowersock has shown, the often quoted statement in Xiphilinus' *epitome* of Dio Cassius, ἐς τὸν τοῦ ναοῦ τοῦ θεοῦ τόπον ναὸν τῷ Διὶ ἕτερον ἀντιγείραντος,[53] cannot be translated as 'when he, *on the place* of the Temple of God, built a different temple (dedicated) to Jupiter', but must rather be translated as 'when he, *in place (instead) of* the Temple of God built a different temple. . .'[54] It is very likely that Hadrian had two statues erected upon the ruins of the Temple[55] and built the Capitol further to the west with a temple for the Capitoline triad Jupiter, Juno and Minerva.[56] This was surely provocative enough, but not necessarily more so than the erection of a *Hadrianeion* in Tiberias. M. Hengel has, furthermore, recalled that 'die Juden auf den Trümmern Jerusalems schon seit 60 Jahren das Legionslager der 10. Legion, deren Symbol ein Eber war, und den dazugehörigen heidnischen Kultbetrieb dulden mußten'.[57] As such, neither the erection of a statue of Hadrian upon the site of the Temple, nor the construction of a temple to Jupiter upon the Capitol in the new colony Aelia Capitolina had been a dramatic new step which by itself would suffice to explain the explosive outbreak of the revolt.

The attempt to interpret Hadrian's political and military activities in the province of Judaea as anti-Jewish measures which were understood as such by the Jewish population, who then responded to them appropriately, has shown itself to be rather weak. We must ask, therefore, whether there are any other direct references to Jewish reaction, either positive or negative, towards the political situation under Hadrian. The findings here are indeed even less fertile.

1. As has been mentioned above, the few passages in rabbinic literature which refer to 'bandits' probably active during Trajan's or Hadrian's reign cannot be interpreted as referring to political terrorists fighting against Roman rule. Isaac–Oppenheimer furthermore wish to show the Rabbis of Yavneh as having been the spiritual initiators of the revolt. Their unbroken will to rebuild the Temple and aspirations towards a unified Jewish nation created the spiritual climate which then led to the outbreak of the revolt: 'In any event, it is intrinsically likely that a connection existed between the activities of the Jewish authorities at Yavneh and the revolt of Bar Kokhba'.[58] Jewry as guided by the Rabbis of Yavneh wholeheartedly and unanimously supported the revolt, and there are even clear indications that the family of the patriarch moved to Bethar near Jerusalem before

the war, thereby documenting the political desire 'that after its liberation the centre of Jewish authority would again be established there'.[59] According to Isaac-Oppenheimer, the Rabbis' policy of unification and the 'undivided resistance to Rome under the leadership of Bar Kokhba' are inseparable: 'This unity certainly contributed to the impact of the rebellion, as did the fact that there was no Jewish party at that time opposed to the revolt'.[60]

We know very little about the attitudes of the rabbinic leaders of Jewry towards Roman supremacy during the Yavneh period. Certainly it was hoped that the Temple would be rebuilt; there is, however, little indication that it was specifically the Rabbis who had been the main advocates of this goal. The thesis that there existed an unbroken political and ideological continuity from Zealot and Pharisaic circles through the Shammaites and the Rabbis of Yavneh to Bar Kokhba and his followers[61] is not very convincing. The Rabbis of Yavneh and Usha were much more concerned with the transference of the priestly halakhah to all Israel than with the rebuilding of the Temple. The only Rabbi of whom we hear *expressis verbis* that he supported Bar Kokhba was R. Akiva,[62] and it is well known that he met with the fierce opposition of the otherwise unfamiliar R. Yoḥanan ben Torta. To conclude, by basing one's argument upon this one dictum alone, that R. Akiva was the spiritual leader of the revolt and that his behaviour reflected 'the prevailing attitude of the sages to the revolt and to the man who headed it',[63] is more than hasty.

The same is true as regards the claim that Bethar was the seat 'in waiting' of the patriarch until the reconquest of Jerusalem. This assumption is based above all upon the statement made by Rabban Shimon b. Gamliel that he had been one of the many schoolchildren in Bethar's 500 schools:[64] 'We cannot assume that he was a student during the war, for he was appointed patriarch shortly afterwards. He will therefore have studied in this place before the revolt and it follows that the family of the patriarch was settled there at the time'.[65] This is a pseudo-historical explanation of an aggadic midrash, which surely is not intended to inform us that Shimon b. Gamliel was a schoolchild at Bethar and therefore not able to become the immediate successor of his father Gamliel II, who died about 120, but first became *Naśi'* following the Bar Kokhba revolt, as Oppenheimer has argued.[66] If one takes the midrash literally, then one must conclude that Shimon b. Gamliel was, on the contrary, still a schoolchild during the revolt and thus was unable to assume the office of patriarch shortly thereafter. Typical for such a pseudo-historical interpretation is the arbitrary choice of elements which fit into the historical analysis. We learn that the stated numbers of schools and pupils are, of course, exaggerated,[67] but nevertheless Shimon b. Gamliel was a student in one of the schools. Surely though, this had to have been the case some time prior to the revolt, for we know that he became *Naśi'* following the rebellion. That he claimed to be the only valiant Torah student to have survived the revolt must then be attributed to aggadic embellishment.

All in all, there is no reason whatsoever to believe that it was precisely the Rabbis, with R. Akiva at the helm, who spiritually paved the way toward the revolt and that all of the factions among the people became united under their leadership. Neither were the Rabbis of a unified opinion, as is illustrated by the controversy between Akiva and Yoḥanan b. Torta, nor do we have concrete evidence that particular Rabbis supported the revolt. Much more probable is the thesis put forward by D. Goodblatt, that it was the priestly faction who provided the ideological background for the revolt.[68] This can be implied, among other things, from Bar Kokhba's use of the title of *Naśi'*, which apparently continues the priestly traditions of Ezekiel and the Qumran community, and above all through the legend 'Elazar the Priest' which appears on numerous rebellion coins.[69] M. Hengel has further pointed out that the palaeo-Hebrew letters found on coins of both the first and second revolts are the '"nationales Schibbolet" priesterlicher Kreise' and refer to the theocratic-priestly background of both uprisings.[70] Bar Kokhba's ritual observance and devotion to the Torah, which, among other things, place great importance upon the sabbatical year and the tithe, can also be seen in this context.[71]

2. The thesis that the Jewish population, unified under the leadership of the Rabbis, fully supported the revolt must be viewed as belonging more to the realm of fantasy than to reality. This can further be illustrated by the often quoted text from the fifth book of the Sibylline Oracles:

> After him (*sc.* Trajan) another will reign,
> a silver-headed man. He will have the name of a sea.[72]
> He will also be a most excellent man and he will consider
>   everything.
> And in your time, most excellent, outstanding, dark-haired one,
> and in the days of your descendants,[73] all these days will come to
>   pass.[74]

Scholars are for the most part in agreement that the fifth book of the Sibylline Oracles originated between 80 and 132 and that it was the work of an Egyptian Jew.[75] The list of the Roman Emperors from the beginning up until Hadrian (vv. 1-50), to which the above quoted text belongs, must be considered an addition made by a second Jewish author who was active during Hadrian's reign and before the outbreak of the Bar Kokhba revolt.[76] Otherwise there is no way of explaining the extremely positive portrayal of Hadrian found here.[77] The controversial question is what conclusions can be drawn from this text. Some scholars see it as echoing the transition of power from Trajan to Hadrian and the hopes of the Jewish populace in the latter's rule, which so soon became bitterly disappointed.[78] Others place the text at the end of the period from 117 to 132 and see a connection with Hadrian's visit to Judaea in 130.[79] The interpretation of this text evidently depends upon the evaluation one makes of Hadrian's policy prior to 130. Those who view this policy as having been one of increasing suppression must play down the enthusiastic praise of Hadrian (which follows the sharp criticism of Vespasian and Trajan!) and attribute it solely to the beginning of his reign.[80] Those, however, who view the period up until Hadrian's visit to Judaea as having been a 'Zeit der Ruhe, wirtschaftlicher Erholung und des vom Kaiser geförderten Aufbaus',[81] will probably interpret the text as a reflection of the peaceful situation and will place the erosion of relations between Hadrian and the Jewish population in the period after 130.

Following upon this, it appears to me that the second possibility is the more probable one. The praise of Hadrian in the fifth book of the Sibylline Oracles seems to express a broader mentality among the Jews, as is illustrated also by the coin legends and the building of the *Hadrianeia*, one which welcomed and even actively supported Hadrian's policy of peace. It would be extremely naive to assume that all the Jews of Judaea celebrated Hadrian as *restitutor* and *sōtēr*, but equally unrealistic is the assumption that his policy was rejected by the Jews of Judaea as a whole. The praise of Hadrian in *Or. Sib.* 5 must be seen in the context of the entire evidence pertaining to the period between 117 and 130 and is by no means the single proof for support of Roman policy by hellenized or assimilated Jews in Judaea.[82]

3. In connection with his discussion of the *colonia*-status of Caesarea (following the first Jewish War) and Jerusalem (under

Hadrian's reign), which included the granting of Roman citizenship to all inhabitants of the new colony, B. Isaac has referred to two military documents which cast an illuminating light upon the situation between 70 and 135. The first (*CIL* XVI.15), from the year 71, mentions a Jew from Caesarea by the name of L. Cornelius Simon, who apparently fought as a Roman soldier during the first Jewish War. This raises no problems, since the mixed reaction of the Jewish population of Judaea during this war is undisputed. It is different with the second document (*CIL* XVI.106). Here, one Barsimso Callisthenis is named as recipient of a diploma in 157, again a Jewish soldier from Caesarea serving in the Roman army, who was apparently recruited at the start of the second Jewish War. This is, of course, much more exciting, for a Jewish legionary from Judaea, who fought against his fellow countrymen side by side with the Romans, does not at all fit into the picture of a unified national revolt which incorporated all classes of the population in the struggle against the hated Roman rule. Isaac nevertheless concludes that 'he must have been one of the few Jews who helped to suppress the revolt'.[83] However, how do we know that he was 'one of the few'? Neither this nor the opposite conclusion can be drawn from the source with any measure of certainty. The fact that such a case was mentioned at all is significant enough and proves, at any rate, that Jews had fought against Jews. This had been the case in almost all Jewish wars, and as such, it would be quite astonishing if the Bar Kokhba revolt was an exception.

4. The most important evidence for assimilatory tendencies within Judaism in Judaea before the Bar Kokhba revolt remains the text from *t. Shab.* 15 (16),9,[84] which I have discussed at length in my book on the Bar Kokhba revolt:[85]

> The *mašukh* must be (re)circumcised.
> R. Yehudah says: He does not need to be (re)circumcised if he has performed the *epispasmos*, because it is dangerous (*mipne še-hu' mesukkan*).
> They said: Many *mešukhim* had themselves (re)circumcised in the days of Ben Koziba, they had children and did not die. For it says: Circumcising, he shall be circumcised (*himmol yimmol*) (Gen. 17.13)—even a hundred times! And it is also said: My covenant has he destroyed (Gen. 17.14)—to include the *mašukh*!

Isaac-Oppenheimer have paid no attention to this text, although it makes up the main argument of my thesis on the hellenized and assimilated Jews in Judaea, who, like the hellenized Jews under Antiochus IV, conformed to Graeco-Roman culture.[86] This is even more surprising, in that Oppenheimer had, in 1980 (before the publication of my Bar Kokhba book; the passage eluded me at the time), established along these lines a connection between the Jewish city councils of Tiberias and Sepphoris, who had supported Hadrian's policy, and the *mešukhim*: 'Those were Jews with assimilationist inclinations including the "stretched", that is, men who stretched their foreskins so that they should appear to be uncircumcised'.[87]

A.M. Rabello has critically and at length analysed the text in *t. Shab.* and my interpretation of it.[88] He grants the possibility that the text may be referring to Jewish assimilationists, but believes that I had too hastily seized upon this explanation and that I took for granted, that the one who had been circumcised (an adult) either performed the operation of *epispasmos* himself, or had it performed upon him. Against this, he claims that the text is referring to fathers who performed the *epispasmos* upon their circumcised sons, fearing Hadrian's prohibition of circumcision. (The consequence of this would be that *t. Shab.* could be understood, against my argument, as stating that the prohibition was declared before the start of the revolt.) The Romans would have had little opportunity, under the tense situation before the outbreak of the revolt, to pay close attention to which children had been circumcised before the declaration of the prohibition and which had been circumcised shortly thereafter. In this case there would have existed the danger that 'innocent' children or their parents would have been killed, and therefore some parents might, out of fear, have performed the *epispasmos* upon their children. The danger, of which the Tosefta speaks, does not refer, according to Rabello, to the physical danger of two circumcisions performed within a short space of time, but to the danger which would result from the transgression of the prohibition.

This is an extremely forced (and cunning) interpretation of the text. To begin with, it overlooks the fact that the phrase, 'because it is dangerous', is not referring to the original circumcision (which would be reverted by the *epispasmos*), but to the renewed circumcision performed after the *epispasmos*. Pursuing the logic of Rabello, one would have to arrive at the following, rather senseless procedure: Fathers had their children circumcised, either shortly before or shortly after the declaration of prohibition, but then changed their minds because of Hadrian's decree and concealed the circumcision by performing the *epispasmos*. During the Bar Kokhba revolt they then wanted to reacknowledge their Jewishness, and because of the 'danger' posed by the continued prohibition, did not have to recircumcise their children.

Apart from this, Rabello's interpretation is unsupportable on the basis of other arguments. The Tosefta text, in referring to the danger connected with the repeated circumcision, uses the phrase *mipne še-hu' mesukkan* ('because it is dangerous'). In connection with the anti-Jewish decrees from the time of the Bar Kokhba revolt, however, the Mishnah and Tosefta always use the noun *sakkanah (ba-sakkanah, biš'at ha-sakkanah, min ha-sakkanah we-'elakh)*.[89] The interpretation of the 'danger' as referring to Hadrian's prohibition of circumcision therefore ignores the language of the Mishnah and Tosefta. Further-more, with regard to the contents, such an interpretation is much too limited and heedless of the context. The anonymous dictum, which contradicts R. Yehudah, and insists that a *mašukh* must be circumcised again, is clearly aimed at illustrating that no physical harm befell the many *mešukhim* as a result of a renewed circumcision: if one had performed the *epispasmos* 100 times, then he would have to be recircumcised 100 times, and no harm would befall him! That the *mešukhim* who were recircumcised did 'not die' refers to the procedure of circumcision and not to their having survived Hadrian's persecution. Finally, Rabello overlooks the fact that R. Yehudah's remark, as such, has nothing to do with the Bar Kokhba revolt, but rather deals with the problem of the *mašukh* in general without referring to the actual historical situation of the uprising. Only through the anonymous reply can a relation be drawn to the revolt, and there can be no doubt that this revolt belonged to the past.

Hadrian's Policy and the Bar Kokhba Revolt

The transformation of Judaea into a consular province together with the obligatory assignment of a second legion and the intensified road construction undertaken in Judaea cannot be seen as having been the reply to Jewish unrest, nor should it be viewed as a military intervention intended to prevent unrest. This action was not directed towards the repression of the Jewish population, but towards the establishment of peace and of secure borders in the east of the Empire. Pagan coin legends and the erection of *Hadrianeia* in cities with both pagan and Jewish inhabitants do not provide evidence for the alleged provocative paganizing of the city councils (in the sense of anti-Jewish acts). They are, rather, indications of an increasing adoption of the hellenization, as propagated by Hadrian, by assimilated Jewish circles. The foundation of Aelia Capitolina was the most logical result of this policy and was probably welcomed by hellenistic and pro-Roman elements within the Jewish population. Positive evidence, such as the enthusiastic praise of Hadrian in the fifth book of the Sibylline Oracles, the participation of Jewish soldiers on the side of the Romans during wartime and, above all, the numerous *mešukhim* prior to the outbreak of the war, illustrate that a rather considerable part of the Jewish population in Judaea had indeed imbibed the 'Zeitgeist'.

It is therefore almost certain that a group of assimilated and hellenized Jews existed in Judaea[90] who welcomed, and perhaps even actively supported, Hadrian's policy of hellenization,[91] and it appears likely that these were for the greater part city dwellers.[92] The comparison with Antiochus IV and the Hellenists in Jerusalem remains, in my opinion, not a misguided one.[93] It is, however, a different issue whether this justifies drawing a further analogy and interpreting the Bar Kokhba revolt as the result of an inner Jewish conflict between the 'assimilated' and the rest of the law-abiding population (in the terminology of the Maccabean period: between 'Hellenists' and 'ḥasidim'). It is on this point that I have received the strongest opposition.[94] M. Hengel, who has most stressed the parallel between Hadrian and Antiochus,[95] is cautious when referring to a possible inner Jewish conflict: 'Wie E. Bickerman in seinem klassischen Werk, *Der Gott der Makkabäer*, 1937... nachweisen konnte, wurde Antiochos IV. im Grunde in einen innerjüdischen, allmählich eskalierenden Streit hineingezogen. Das kann man so bei Hadrian gewiß nicht sagen, doch läßt sich eine vorausgehende innerjüdische Auseinandersetzung nicht ausschließen'.[96]

The starting point for any realistic evaluation of the situation in Judaea at the beginning of the revolt must be the realization that obviously the entire population of the province did not join unitedly in the revolt (not to mention the Diaspora). An analysis of the literary[97] and numismatic evidence[98] limits the extent of the revolt to the region south of Jerusalem to the coastal plain in the west and to the Dead Sea in the east. In particular, there is no evidence which speaks in favour of a participation on the part of Galilee. The Rabbis cannot be considered to have been the spiritual pioneers of the revolt, but rather it was the priests who supported the uprising. Furthermore, the Bar Kokhba letters also indicate that Bar Kokhba did not enjoy full support even within the region of the revolt and had trouble keeping his own men in line.[99]

Against this background, it is very probable that Hadrian's policy in Judaea was judged differently by the various Jewish groups and that the revolt was *also*[100] an expression of these diverging interests. The more rural population of Judaea in the narrower sense,[101] who were loyal to the Law and inspired by the Priests, surely viewed the development in a much different manner than did the urban population in the larger cities in Galilee and on the coastal plain, which was influenced by Hellenism. This certainly does not imply that the rural population of Judaea stumbled 'into a war against the Roman Empire because of a rivalry between the hellenized and "law-abiding" Jews in the cities'.[102] Nevertheless, the political 'cooperation' between hellenized Jews and Hadrian undoubtedly intensified the situation and perhaps led to a state of affairs in which the revolt was the only way left to stop what the 'pious' saw as a fatal development. Hadrian was, in Judaea, by no means a player unaware of the rules of the game; however, through his enforced policy of Romanization, viz. Hellenization and urbanization, and hence, through the aggressive dissemination of an intellectual climate which increasingly found followers among the Jewish population of Judaea, he may have become, like Antiochus IV, the 'catalyst' in a process over which he eventually lost control.

NOTES

1. Cf. e.g. P. Schäfer, *Der Bar Kokhba-Aufstand. Studien zum zweiten jüdischen Krieg gegen Rom* (TSAJ, 1), Tübingen, 1981; Sh. Applebaum, 'The Second Jewish Revolt (AD 131–135)', *PEQ* 116 (1984), pp. 35-41; L. Mildenberg, *The Coinage of the Bar Kokhba War* (Typos, 6), Aarau, Frankfurt a.M. & Salzburg, 1984; A. Oppenheimer & U. Rappaport (eds.), *The Bar-Kokhva Revolt. A New Approach*, Jerusalem, 1984 (Hebr.); N. Bickhoff-Böttcher, *Das Judentum in der griechisch-römischen Welt. Gesellschaftliche und politische Beziehungen und Konflikte von der Mitte des 1. Jh. v. Chr. bis zum Ende des 2. Jh. n. Chr.* (Diss. phil. Osnabrück, 1984); M. Hengel, 'Hadrians Politik gegenüber Juden und Christen', *JANES* 16-17 (1984-85), pp. 153-82 (*Ancient Studies in Memory of Elias Bickerman*); B.

Isaac-A. Oppenheimer, 'The Revolt of Bar Kokhba: Ideology and Modern Scholarship', *JJS* 36 (1985), pp. 33-60; D. Golan, 'Hadrian's Decision to Supplant "Jerusalem" by "Aelia Capitolina"', *Historia* 35 (1986), pp. 226-39. I am grateful to my student Aubrey Pomerance for the English translation of this article.

2. Cf. the summary in Isaac-Oppenheimer, *JJS* 36 (1985), pp. 44ff.

3. Cf. Isaac-Oppenheimer, *JJS* 36 (1985), pp. 45f.; further Mildenberg, *Coinage*, pp. 102ff.; Hengel, *JANES* 16-17 (1984), pp. 174ff. Mildenberg, who has critically evaluated my thesis concerning hellenized, pro-Roman Jews, has not considered my analysis of the Roman sources dealing with the prohibition of circumcision. He refers (p. 105 n. 295) to Rabello's 'full account', which is, for the most part, a repetition of Juster's arguments (A.M. Rabello, 'The Legal Condition of the Jews in the Roman Empire', in *ANRW* II.13 [Berlin & New York, 1980], pp. 699-703); cf. on the other hand, T. Fischer, Review of Mildenberg, *Coinage*, *WdO* 17 (1986), p. 183 n. 15: 'Hadrians erneutes und verschärftes Verbot der Kastration betraf m.E. die Beschneidung *nicht*'; R. Wenning, Review of Mildenberg, *Coinage*, *ThR* 84 (1988), col. 110: 'eine Datierung des Verbotes [sc. der Beschneidung] vor dem Bar Kokhba-Aufstand ist nicht gesichert und die Argumentation von Schäfer für eine spätere Ansetzung erscheint dem Rez. überzeugender'.

4. Hengel, *JANES* 16-17 (1984-85), p. 158.

5. B. Isaac & I. Roll, 'Judaea in the Early Years of Hadrian's Reign', *Latomus* 38 (1979), p. 55; E. Schürer, G. Vermes & F. Millar, *The History of the Jewish People in the Age of Jesus Christ (175 B.C.-A.D. 135)*, vol. I, Edinburgh, 1973, p. 518.

6. *Fasti Ostienses*, *Inscriptiones Italiae* XIII.1, p. 205; Schürer, Vermes & Millar, I, p. 518.

7. H.-G. Pflaum, 'Remarques sur le changement de statut administratif de la province de Judée: à propos d'une inscription récemment découverte à Sidé de Pamphylie', *IEJ* 19 (1969), pp. 232f.

8. B. Isaac & I. Roll, 'Legio II Traiana in Judaea', *ZPE* 33 (1979), pp. 149-156; J.R. Rea, 'The Legio II Traiana in Judaea?', *ZPE* 38 (1980), pp. 220-22; B. Isaac & I. Roll, 'Legio II Traiana in Judaea—A Reply', *ZPE* 47 (1982), pp. 131-32; Isaac-Roll, *Latomus* 38 (1979), pp. 56ff.

9. Isaac-Roll, *Latomus* 38 (1979), pp. 56ff.

10. Sh. Applebaum, *Prolegomena to the Study of the Second Jewish Revolt (A.D. 132-135)* (BAR Supplementary Series, 7), Oxford, 1976, p. 23; Isaac & Roll, *Latomus* 38 (1979), p. 62.

11. Hengel, *JANES* 16-17 (1984-85), p. 159 n. 33.

12. B. Isaac, 'Roman Colonies in Judaea: The Foundation of Aelia Capitolina', *Talanta* 12-13 (1980-81), p. 46; Isaac & Roll, *Latomus* 38 (1979), p. 57 n. 17.

13. E. Schürer, G. Vermes, F. Millar & M. Black, vol. II (1979), p. 179.

14. Hill, *BMC Palestine*, p. xv; A. Kindler, *The Coins of Tiberias*, Tiberias, 1961, No. 7b and pp. 21f.

15. *Adv. haer.* 30,12, *PG* XLI, col. 426; F.M. Abel, 'Chronique: II.—Les fouilles juives d'el Hammam, à Tibériade', *RB* 30 (1921), pp. 440f.

16. Hill, p. xxviii.

17. Hill, p. xii: reign of Antoninus Pius.

18. The evidence is a milestone from the year 130 with the new name; cf. B. Lipshitz, 'Sur la date du transfer de la legio VI Ferrata en Palestine', *Latomus* 19 (1960), pp. 110f.; E.M. Smallwood, *The Jews under Roman Rule. From Pompey to Diocletian* (SJLA, 20), Leiden, 1976, p. 432.

19. Hill, pp. xi-xiii.

20. Hill, p. xi. In Athens, Hadrian completed the construction of the temple of Zeus Olympios in 128/29 (Pausanias 1.18.6ff.); cf. Hengel, *JANES* 16-17 (1984-85), p. 180. Upon Garizim he probably constructed a temple of Zeus Hypsistos; see Hengel, p. 171 with n. 89.

21. Only from an inscription from the Christian era; cf. Germer-Durand, 'Mélanges III: Inscriptions romaines et byzantines de Palestine', *RB* 4 (1895), pp. 75ff.; F.T. Ellis & A.S. Murray, 'Inscription Found at Caesarea', *PEFQS* (1896), pp. 87f.

22. R. Wenning, *ThR* 84 (1988), col. 110; *idem*, correspondence from Nov. 25, 1988: 'Die beiden überlebensgroßen Sitzstatuen in Marmor und Porphyr... verstehe ich als Darstellungen des Hadrian. Bei der Marmorstatue könnte man u.U. an den Divus Traianus denken. Die Porphyrstatue könnte das Kultbild des Hadrianeums von 130 gewesen sein.' As to the bust of Antinoos, cf. R. Savignac, 'Chronique', *RB* 13 (1904), p. 84, No. 2 (plate).

23. Cf. L.J. Levine, *Caesarea under Roman Rule* (SJLA, 7), Leiden, 1975, pp. 32f., 34, 44ff.

24. Hengel, *JANES* 16-17 (1984-85), p. 171 and p. 180 with n. 123.

25. *Talanta* 12-13 (1980-81), p. 46.

26. Isaac-Roll, *Latomus* 38 (1979), p. 66.

27. Y. Meshorer, *Jewish Coins of the Second Temple Period*, Tel Aviv, 1967, pp. 92f.; cf. Schäfer, *Der Bar Kokhba-Aufstand*, p. 37 n. 32. In the meantime, B. Lipshitz ('Jérusalem sous la domination romaine. Histoire de la ville depuis la conquête de Pompée jusqu'à Constantin [63 a.C.—325 p.C.]', *ANRW* II.8, Berlin & New York, 1977, p. 481) has drawn attention to further Aelia coins which have been found near Hebron together with Hadrian coins from the time *before* the Bar Kokhba revolt: 'Ces monnaies ont fourni une preuve irréfutable que la nouvelle colonie a été fondée pendant la visite de l'empereur dans la province de Judée en 130'.

28. Mildenberg, *Coinage*, p. 100; *idem*, 'Bar Kokhba Coins and Documents', *HSCP* 84 (1980), p. 333; cf. also Hengel, *JANES* 16-17 (1984-85), p. 172.

29. *JJS* 36 (1985), p. 51.

30. G.W. Bowersock, 'A Roman Perspective on the Bar Kokhba War', W.S. Green (ed.), *Approaches to Ancient Judaism*, II, Ann Arbor, 1980, p. 133.

31. M. Rostovtzeff, *The Social and Economic History of the Roman Empire*, Oxford, 1926, p. 318.

32. Isaac–Oppenheimer, *JJS* 36 (1985), p. 51.

33. *The Cities of the Eastern Roman Provinces*, Oxford, 1937; 2nd edn, 1971, p. 279; *idem*, 'The Urbanization of Palestine', *JRS* 21 (1931), p. 82.

34. *Latomus* 38 (1979), p. 64.

35. *JJS* 36 (1985), p. 51.

36. Isaac–Roll, *Latomus* 38 (1979), p. 64; Isaac–Oppenheimer, *JJS* 36 (1985), p. 51: 'an indication perhaps that the local administration had been transferred to non-Jewish elements'.

37. Isaac–Oppenheimer, *JJS* 36 (1985), p. 51.

38. *B. A.Z.* 25b; *Lam. R.* 3.6 = *Lam. R.*, Buber, p. 128; *b. Nid.* 61a; *t. Kel. B.B.* 2.2.

39. *Toledot ha-yehudim be-'ereṣ yiśra'el bitequfat ha-mishnah we-ha-talmud*, vol. II, Tel Aviv, 1961, pp. 1-2.

40. *Latomus* 38 (1979), p. 64 n. 56.

41. Schäfer, *Der Bar Kokhba-Aufstand*, pp. 106ff.

42. See n. 13.

43. A. Oppenheimer (ed.), *The Bar-Kokhva Revolt* (Issues in Jewish History, 10), Jerusalem, 1980, p. 11; English translation under the title 'The Bar Kokhba Revolt', *Immanuel* 14 (1982), pp. 61f.

44. *Talanta* 12-13 (1980-81), pp. 31-54.

45. *Ibid.*, p. 48 n. 78.

46. Philo, *Spec. Leg.* 36, 287.

47. Following F. Millar, *The Emperor and the Roman World*, London, 1977, p. 407.

48. Isaac, *ibid.*

49. *B. A.Z.* 10a.

50. *The Bar-Kokhva Revolt*, p. 11 = *Immanuel* 14 (1982), p. 62. Compare this with my conclusion in *Der Bar Kokhba-Aufstand*, p. 49: 'Mit seinem Vorschlag, auch Jerusalem als römische Kolonie erstehen zu lassen, wollte Hadrian daher nicht gezielt-provokativ den jüdischen Nationalismus ausrotten und rannte er auch nicht unbefangen-naiv in bereits gezückte Messer, sondern setzte er eine Politik fort, die er bereits auch in *Palästina* mit einigem Erfolg begonnen hatte und von der er annehmen konnte, daß die von zahlreichen assimilierten Juden nicht nur geduldet, sondern gewünscht wurde'. I am delighted by this additional confirmation which escaped me at that time.

51. *Ibid.*

52. *Talanta* 12-13 (1980-81), p. 48 n. 78.

53. Dio, *Hist. Romana* 69.12.1.

54. *Approaches to Ancient Judaism*, II, p. 137.

55. An equestrian statue of himself and one of Jupiter (Jerome, *CCL* 73, p. 33), Gaius or Titus (Origen, *GCS* Orig. 12, pp. 193f.); the pilgrim of

Bordeaux (*CCL* 175, p. 16; cf. H. Donner, *Pilgerfahrt ins Heilige Land*, Stuttgart, 1979, p. 56) speaks of two statues of Hadrian and is probably referring to Hadrian and Antoninus Pius.

56. Bowersock, *Approaches to Ancient Judaism*, II, p. 137; J. Wilkinson, *Jerusalem as Jesus Knew It*, London, 1978, pp. 178f.

57. *JANES* 16-17 (1984-85), p. 172.

58. *JJS* 36 (1985), p. 49.

59. *Ibid.*, p. 52.

60. *Ibid.*, p. 49.

61. I. Ben-Shalom, 'Events and Ideology of the Yavneh Period as Indirect Causes of the Bar-Kokhva Revolt', Oppenheimer–Rappaport (eds.), *The Bar-Kokhva Revolt. A New Approach*, pp. 1-12 (Hebr.).

62. *Y. Taan.* 4.8, 68d.

63. Oppenheimer, *The Bar-Kokhva Revolt*, p. 15 = *Immanuel* 14 (1982), p. 67.

64. *Y. Taan.* 4.8, 69a: 'Rabban Shimon b. Gamliel said: There were 500 schools in Bethar and in the smallest of them there were no less than 500 children. They used to say: When the enemies are upon us, we will march out against them with these styluses and will pierce their eyes. When, however, the sins caused it, they (= the Romans) rolled each one of them in a scroll and had them burned, and from all of them I alone have remained'; *Lam. R.*, 2.4 = *Lam. R.*, Buber, p. 104; *b. Git.* 58a; on this see Schäfer, *Der Bar Kokhba-Aufstand*, pp. 136ff.

65. Isaac–Oppenheimer, *JJS* 36 (1985), p. 52.

66. Oppenheimer, in Z. Baras *et al.* (eds.), *Eretz Israel from the Destruction of the Second Temple to the Muslim Conquest* (Hebr.), Jerusalem, 1982, pp. 49f.

67. *Ibid.*

68. D. Goodblatt, 'The Title *Nasi*' and the Ideological Background of the Second Revolt', Oppenheimer–Rappaport (eds.), *The Bar-Kokhva Revolt. A New Approach*, pp. 113-32 (Hebr.).

69. Mildenberg, 'The Elazar Coins of the Bar Kokhba Rebellion', *Historia Judaica* 11 (1949), pp. 77-108; *idem*, *The Coinage of the Bar Kokhba War*, pp. 29f.

70. Review of Mildenberg, *Coinage*, *Gnomon* 58 (1986), p. 327; the symbolism of the coins is also a reference to the Temple (Hengel, *ibid.*, p. 330).

71. Cf. Schäfer, *Der Bar Kokhba-Aufstand*, pp. 75f., on the pertinent passages.

72. Adriatic Sea; cf. also in the rabbinic literature *M. Teh.* 93.6, ed. Buber, pp. 415f.

73. Reference to Dan. 4.21.

74. *Or. Sib.* 5.46-50; translated by J.J. Collins, in J.H. Charlesworth (ed.), *The Old Testament Pseudepigrapha*, vol. I, Garden City, NY/London, 1983, p. 394.

75. Collins, *ibid.*, pp. 390f.

76. A. Rzach, 'Sibyllinische Orakel', *PW* II.2.4 (1923), cols. 2134-36; Hengel, *JANES* 16-17 (1984-85), p. 154 with n. 7; Bowersock, *Approaches to Ancient Judaism*, II, p. 134 with n. 20.

77. Problematic then is v. 51, which includes Marcus Aurelius; this can be best understood to be a later addition: Rzach, *ibid.*, cols. 2134f.

78. Alon, *Toledot ha-yehudim*, vol. I, Tel Aviv, 1967, p. 283; Isaac-Oppenheimer, *JJS* 36 (1985), p. 47 n. 61.

79. Bowersock, *Approaches to Ancient Judaism*, II, p. 134.

80. Although they only criticize other authors, without themselves directly addressing the text, this seems to be the opinion of Isaac-Oppenheimer, *JJS* 36 (1985), p. 47.

81. Hengel, *JANES* 16-17 (1984-85), p. 158.

82. As Isaac-Oppenheimer, *JJS* 36 (1985), p. 47, have accused me of arguing. I quoted the Sibylline Oracles at the conclusion of my extensive discussion of the *mešukim*, which they have fully ignored. An altogether different question is whether tension between pro- and anti-Roman groups was also responsible for the outbreak of the war; see below.

83. *Talanta* 12-13 (1980-81), p. 50.

84. *Y. Shab.* 19.2, 17a; *y. Yeb.* 8.1, 9a; *b. Yeb.* 72a; *Gen. R.* 46.13.

85. *Der Bar Kokhba-Aufstand*, pp. 45ff.

86. M. Hengel has also recently argued along the lines of this thesis (*JANES* 16-17 [1984-85], p. 160 n. 37); 'Dies weist darauf hin, daß nicht wenige Juden im jüdischen Palästina vor dem Aufstand Apostaten geworden waren und wie einst unter dem Hohepriester Jason in der Zeit des Antiochos IV. den Epispasmos vollzogen hatten. . .'.

87. *The Bar-Kokhva Revolt*, p. 11 = *Immanuel* 14 (1982), p. 62.

88. 'Il problema della "circumcisio" in diritto Romano fino ad Antonino Pio', *Studi in onore di Arnaldo Biscardi*, II, Milan, 1982, pp. 206ff. = 'The Edicts on Circumcision as a Factor in the Bar-Kokhva Revolt', Oppenheimer-Rappaport (eds.), *The Bar-Kokhva Revolt. A New Approach*, pp. 41ff.

89. *Der Bar Kokhba-Aufstand*, p. 198 and p. 205.

90. Naturally, I meant by 'in Jerusalem' (*Der Bar Kokhba-Aufstand*, p. 48) Jerusalem as *pars pro toto* for Judaea. This misleading formulation was first brought to my attention by Mildenberg (*Coinage*, p. 103 n. 286), who ascertains a change of mind between the statements in *Der Bar Kokhba-Aufstand* and those in *Geschichte der Juden in der Antike* (Stuttgart, 1983, pp. 161f.): 'Schäfer has recently modified this point of view considerably. . .: the limitation of the pro-Roman/anti-Roman rivalry to Jerusalem is dropped in favour of a broad-based rivalry throughout Judaea. . .'

91. Cf. also R. Wenning, *ThR* 81 (1985), col. 369: 'Daß weite Teile der Bevölkerung Palästinas Hadrians "Hellenisierungspolitik" begrüßten und weiterführten, ein Vorgang, der sich nach dem BKA enorm potenzierte, ist dabei nicht in Abrede zu stellen'; Hengel, *JANES* 16-17 (1984-85), p. 160

n. 37: 'Daß diese Kreise das Beschneidungsverbot Hadrians... begrüßten, ist wahrscheinlich, ob sie die Politik des Kaisers in Richtung auf ein solches—wie einst Menachem und seine Freunde gegenüber Antiochos IV.— direkt beeinflußten, entzieht sich unserer Kenntnis und erscheint als schwer vorstellbar'.

92. Mildenberg, *Coinage*, p. 103 n. 286.

93. *Der Bar Kokhba-Aufstand*, pp. 48f.; explicitly also Hengel, *JANES* 16-17 (1984-85), pp. 180f.

94. For example, Oppenheimer, *JSJ* 14 (1983), p. 220; S.J.D. Cohen, *The Second Century* 2 (1984), p. 119; R. Wenning, *ThR* 81 (1985), p. 369; Mildenberg, *Coinage*, p. 103 n. 286 and p. 105 n. 297; Isaac-Oppenheimer, *JJS* 36 (1985), p. 47: 'This is an artificial transfer of the situation in the second century BC to that three centuries later, and the Sibylline Oracle is no sufficient basis for such a theory'; T. Fischer, *WdO* 17 (1986), p. 183 n. 15.

95. *JANES* 16-17 (1984-85), p. 180: 'In eigenartiger Analogie zu Antiochos verstand er (sc. Hadrian) sich als Repräsentant des Zeus-Jupiter auf Erden und wurde als "Olympios" im griechischen Osten mit dem Gott "identifiziert". Antiochos und Hadrian wollten durch eine panhellenische Politik die Einheit ihres Vielvölkerstaates stärken'.

96. *JANES* 16-17 (1984-85), p. 181 n. 125.

97. Schäfer, *Der Bar Kokhba-Aufstand*, pp. 102ff.

98. Mildenberg, *Coinage*, pp. 81ff.; cf. both maps on pages 83 and 86.

99. Schäfer, *Der Bar Kokhba-Aufstand*, pp. 74f.

100. Certainly not exclusively, but *also*; this 'also' (cf. *Der Bar Kokhba-Aufstand*, p. 49, at the bottom of the page) has been mostly overlooked by my critics.

101. Concerning the Jewish rural population between 70 and 132, cf. Mildenberg's apt remarks in: *Coinage*, pp. 84f.

102. This is Mildenberg's rather ironic citing of my argument, *Coinage*, p. 103 n. 286. His remark that 'Schäfer fails to explain why and how such a divided Jewry was able to wage a war of this length, extent and persistence' (p. 105 n. 297) fails to directly address my argument. The Jewry of the Maccabean revolt and of the first Jewish War was anything but united, and nonetheless was able to wage long and sustained wars—why should the Bar Kokhba revolt have been different?

PART V

NEW TESTAMENT

THE HEBREW/ARAMAIC BACKGROUND OF 'HYPOCRISY' IN THE GOSPELS

James Barr

Vanderbilt University
Nashville, Tennessee

The terms 'hypocrite' and 'hypocrisy' are frequent and highly characteristic features of the teaching of Jesus in the three Synoptic Gospels (interestingly, no case occurs in John). They occur also in a few scattered places in other New Testament writings (Gal. 2.13; 1 Tim. 4.2; 1 Pet. 2.1; and see below for the adjective ἀνυπόκριτος);[1] but apart from these all cases are in Jesus' teaching. The usage is particularly characteristic of Matthew. Moreover, the terms are commonly associated with the scribes and Pharisees, and with Jewish religious behaviour in general (e.g. 'hypocrites' are characteristically to be found praying in the synagogues, Matt. 6.2, 5). The prominence of this handling of Jewish religion in Matthew, the first of the four Gospels and in some ways perhaps the most widely read, cannot have failed to have an effect on Christian estimates of Judaism down the centuries. And a consideration of this concept cannot fail to be significant for our estimate of the originality of Jesus and of the degree to which the Gospel tradition is accurate in its portrayal of him.

What is hypocrisy anyway? Well, we all know, but as usual it is not easy to say. It is related to deceit and to pretence, but is a more specialized thing than either of these. Rightly realizing this, the Shorter *OED* finds itself forced to offer a quite long extended description, thus:

> *Hypocrisy*: The assuming of a false appearance of virtue or goodness, with dissimulation of real character or inclinations, esp. in respect of religious life or belief; hence, dissimulation, pretence, sham.

> *Hypocrite*: One who falsely professes to be virtuously or religiously inclined; one who pretends to be other and better than he is; hence, a dissembler, pretender.

Even these descriptions are perhaps not sufficient to include all the necessary features: one might add, for instance, the tendency to see faults in others and not in oneself, the tendency to draw attention to one's own virtue, and the tendency to attach higher importance to minor matters than to essential matters. Hypocrisy, as normal speech characterizes it, is thus a quite complicated, but peculiar and recognizable, bunch of features which, taken as a whole, cannot be easily replaced by any other expression.

It is possible, we may add, that in the modern world some features of the traditional meanings have begun to change. I once heard Professor John Macquarrie, in a sermon in Christ Church, Oxford, remark that hypocrisy in the modern world was no longer so much attached to religion, and seemed to find its natural home and finest exemplification in other areas, of which politics was the most obvious. And indeed it is so. With the advance of civilization, the *Sitz im Leben* of hypocrisy has moved from the synagogue worshipper with his trumpet (Matt. 6.2) to the trade union official, the public relations consultant, the media spokesman and the political leader. But in the happier, older world its central locus lay in religion.

When we turn to the judgment of biblical scholarship, however, we find some surprising uncertainty. According to one substantial trend of opinion, the ὑποκριταί of the Gospels were not hypocrites at all, not at least in the generally accepted sense as described above. They were general sinners and evildoers; they might be well described as crafty, godless, and the like, but the specific sense of hypocrisy, as usually understood, a sense that has its historical foundation more within the Gospels than any other place, is said to be largely absent from them.

And this opinion is not one expressed only by small or isolated groups among scholars. It is represented, though with some variations and hesitations, in standard reference works, as seen in the relevant articles in *The Interpreter's Dictionary of the Bible* (F.W. Young, vol. II [1962], pp. 668f.) or *Harper's Bible Dictionary* (J.M. Efird [1985], p. 414).[2] In favour of this view four different reasons appear to be put forward:

1. The Greek meaning, with its association with the theatre and the actor who 'plays a part', has no comparable suggestion in Hebrew.

2. The main Hebrew term that appears to lie behind the biblical use of 'hypocrite' is חָנֵף, which however means something more like

'godless' and is found in parallelism with expressions like 'sinners', 'wicked', 'evildoers'.[3]

3. In the LXX ὑποκριτής is used to render Hebrew חָנֵף and this appears to be a standard equivalence in the later Greek translators (Aquila, Theodotion, Symmachus) at those points where evidence exists.

4. In the Synoptic Gospels, where one book has ὑποκριταί or ὑπόκρισις, a parallel text in another book sometimes has a word that means 'wickedness' or 'faithlessness'.

We shall look again at these four arguments:

1. *The Greek Meaning.* We quote the first paragraph of Young's article:

> Originally, in the context of Greek drama, the act of playing a part and the one who plays a part. The terms were also used metaphorically to signify the action of feigning to be what one is not. In English only the metaphorical meaning remained, with the prevailing signification of the simulation of goodness. This context of meaning which originated from the Greek drama has no place in OT thought and hence no comparable Hebrew terms. The RSV reflects this fact by eliminating the words 'hypocrisy' and 'hypocrite' from their translations of the OT, whereas the KJV used them[4]...
> This background in the OT and Hebrew is very significant for interpreting the words ὑπόκρισις and ὑποκριτής in the NT, especially in the words of Jesus. The Greek meaning was as alien to Aramaic as to Hebrew. It is unlikely that Jesus in the many passages where he is reported to have attacked the Pharisees as 'hypocrites' was attacking them for simulating goodness...

In itself this view may be all very well. As a guide to the NT usage, however, it is simply not regulative, unless one is to suppose that *no* meanings whatever, other than those present in the vocabulary of the Hebrew OT, can be significant for the New Testament. Whatever was the case in the Hebrew books, there is substantial evidence of the entry of the Greek terms into Jewish use, both in the books of Maccabees and in Josephus and Philo. We shall return to this evidence later.

2. *The Hebrew (and Aramaic?) words.* It is widely accepted that, if there is a particular Hebrew term that 'lies behind' the Greek terms of the NT, that term is חָנֵף (see below). The case for this was well argued by the distinguished French Hebraist Joüon in his article of 1930.[5] But, even if we do accept it, the spread and structure of its

semantics, in Hebrew and in the other Semitic languages, are far from easy to unravel. The word is a difficult one. In the Bible, after all, there are altogether only a handful of cases. Verb forms are eleven in number; the adjective חָנֵף provides perhaps thirteen, of which eight are in Job; and the noun forms חֹנֶף and חֲנֻפָּה have one each. For the verb forms it is usual to give the sense 'be polluted': thus the earth is polluted (Isa. 24.5; Jer. 3.1, 9; Ps. 106.38); prophet and priest are polluted (Jer. 23.11). The few cases of the *hiphil* all fit with 'to pollute' (Num. 35.33, 34; Jer. 3.2) plus the one of the late Dan. 11.32, 'seduce to apostasy'. The main meaning in the verb forms is 'pollute', that in the adjective form חָנֵף is something like 'godless' or 'impious' (this may apply also to the verb in Jer. 23.11). How these two senses are connected is far from clear. The noun forms חֹנֶף and חֲנֻפָּה (both once only, Isa. 32.6 and Jer. 23.15 respectively!) might be either, but perhaps preferably 'wickedness' in the former and 'pollution' in the latter (here applying to the land, as commonly with the verb). On the connection between the two senses, 'pollute' and 'godless', Joüon, and others before and after him,[6] claim to find a link in the Arabic *ḥanafa* 'turn or bend sideways' (Wehr) and *'aḥnaf* 'afflicted with a distortion of the foot'; but this seems to the writer quixotically remote from probability, and we would do better to accept (a) that we do not know the mode of connection between the two departments of sense in Hebrew, and (b) that, if these Arabic forms have any connection at all, it is too distant to throw any light on the meanings in Hebrew.[7] Etymology, in this case, misleads rather than helps. The actual meanings in usage in the Hebrew Bible are sufficiently well known.

It seems true, then, that the biblical cases do not point particularly towards ideas of pretence, simulation or deceit. As Young rightly points out, the cases of חָנֵף are often in parallel or in collocation with 'evildoers', 'sinners' and the like (so Isa. 9.16; 33.14; Job 27.8), with bribery (Job 15.34), with 'forgetfulness' of God (Job 8.13), and often in contrast with 'righteous', 'upright' and so on (Job 17.8; 20.5); and, among all the instances, there seems not to be a single collocation with 'deceit', 'pretence', 'lies' and the like. Thus Young's observations in this regard may well be right for biblical times.

And the same seems to be true for the three known cases in Ben Sira (16.6; 40.15; 41.10). From Qumran I would range also with these the one case of חנופה in 4Q175.28, where the sense seems to be 'pollution' (in the land) and simply continues the biblical usage. But the usage in *biblical* Hebrew should not necessarily be decisive, for by later times new usages may have been introduced.[8] We shall see that this is in fact probable. Joüon had already made clear that a historical shift of meaning was involved, and this can now perhaps be further confirmed from Qumran.

The Dead Sea Scrolls have an important instance at 1QS 4.10. Here it is noticeable that חנף (surely חָנֵף) is ranged in a series with terms that are markedly terms of deceit and pretence: רמיה, כחש, שקר, all precede immediately.[9] This is much closer to the traditional 'hypocrisy' of the New Testament. *KB*³, p. 322, rightly glosses the term as 'Heuchelei'. The sense thus found comes closer to senses known from cognates in Aramaic and Syriac; the meaning in Rabbinic usage is 'flatter, be hypocritical' (Dalman: *schmeicheln, heuchelen*). חניפות has remained the central term in the area of 'flattery' and 'hypocrisy'. This Rabbinic sense is likely to be very important for the Gospels. Whether we explain it through influence of Aramaic, or through the effect of the Greek usage, or by some other means, and even if there is no more than this one case at Qumran, a semantic change from biblical Hebrew seems probable.

It is worth noticing that the vocabulary of deceit seems to have been increasingly prominent in the religious language of the later period. Deceit, indeed, is not the same as hypocrisy, but an increasing sensitivity to deceit, within religion, could be a factor that would in due course induce a perception and verbalization of hypocrisy. In biblical Hebrew, and apart from חנף already discussed, the root that might be supposed to come nearest to the meaning of hypocrisy is כחש, a semantically complex term with a variety of senses. In the Bible it is rare in relevant senses, while the Qumran texts show it twice in Kuhn's concordance. From the root רמה, clearly 'deceive', מרמה is recorded for three occurrences, and רמיה, noted just above, is recorded by Kuhn for seventeen, more than the fifteen cases known for it in the entire Hebrew Bible. Even more relevant, perhaps, is the prominent term חלקות, חלקלקות, 'slippery things' (so understood by LXX, with ὀλίσθρημα, at several points: Jer. 23.12; Dan. 11.21, 32, 34) or 'flatteries', which again comes close to the suggestion of hypocrisy. The use of language therefore may well suggest that the sense for deceit and falsity in religion had increased by the second century BCE, and this on other grounds would not be surprising.

This being so, it means that we do not *necessarily* have to find a *single* Hebrew term that formed the 'original' or background term to the ὑποκριτής, ὑπόκρισις of the Gospels. We cannot really be certain that חנף is the sole Hebrew/Aramaic term that it reflects. Although, as we have seen, Qumran evidence supports a change of meaning in this word in later times, it does not, from texts known so far, give evidence that this word had become particularly frequent or prominent. It is quite possible to say that the sense for the deceit, flattery, self-exaltation and contrast between ideal and actuality in religion had reached a high point, and was further developed by Jesus in his teaching, and that for the expression of this the Greek terms ὑποκριτής etc. were adopted by the Greek Gospels, whether there was a Hebrew/Aramaic term or not. This is quite possible, and, if it is the case, then it follows that the contrast between 'Hebrew meaning' and 'Greek meaning' is no longer relevant. This possibility has to be taken seriously. Nevertheless the likelihood of a Hebrew/Aramaic word in the background remains considerable. It is still primarily the evidence of the later Greek translators that points towards חנף as the central term.

But some other possibilities remain. Another word in the field, and one that, it seems, has been little taken into account in modern scholarly discussion, is צָבוּעַ. Originally this appears to mean 'variegated', 'painted in a variety of colours', and one can understand how from this sense it could become a term for the hypocrite. It has continued in Hebrew usage, and the expression of Jer. 12.9, עַיִט צָבוּעַ, RSV 'a speckled bird of prey', became in Jewish culture a proverbial expression for the hypocrite, familiar from the work of the early Modern Hebrew writer Mapu with that title. Now this form of speech, though doubtless mainly used in later times, has what seems to be its point of origin, so far as is known to the writer, in *b. Sota* 22b:

> Yannai before his death said to his wife: Don't be afraid of the Pharisees, nor of those who are non-Pharisees, but of the צבועין, the variegated ones (Levy: 'die Scheinheiligen [wörtl. die Gefärbten]'), who imitate the Pharisees...[10]

The recording, or the creation, of this saying is of course long after the New Testament. But it is hard to say that it is entirely irrelevant to the latter. Once again it indicates a response to the situation of the existence of something like hypocrisy as a religious problem. Whether the saying is historically genuine as a remark that Yannaeus might have made, one cannot say; it may well be only a vague later reminiscence of his reign. But the connection with the Pharisees and their opponents gives the impression of at least some connection, however distant, with the picture drawn in the Gospels. Our purpose here is not to determine the historicity of such traditions; it is rather to note that, whatever the degree of historicity, the tradition, recorded in the Talmud, appears to validate for Talmudic times the term צבוע with the sense of 'apparently, outwardly, holy', coming close therefore to 'hypocrite', a fact which makes it hard to deny at least the possibility of its existence in the first century CE. 'Die Scheinheiligen' comes remarkably close to the conceptuality of the Gospels.

Yet other suggestions have been made. Matthew Black in his *An Aramaic Approach to the Gospels and Acts* does not mention the possibilities discussed above, nor Joüon's authoritative article.[11] But he makes yet another proposal. On his pp. 177f., Black, writing of Matt. 6.2, 5, states that for the Greek ὑποκριταί the Aramaic word was *šaqqārîn* or *šaqqārê*. The point of this is that it creates a word-play in the sentence, and Black is interested, in this section of his book, in suggesting word-plays which can be detected if the original Aramaic behind the Greek is reconstructed. Thus *šaqqārîn* provides a word-play with *šûqîn* 'the streets' in v. 2 and with *šeqāqê* 'the open places' in v. 5. But this, while an interesting suggestion, carries little conviction. For *šaqqārîn* would mean 'liars', 'faithless ones', and would naturally generate in Greek ψευσταί or ἄπιστοι rather than ὑποκριταί.[12] Moreover, this meaning would not fit the contexts: blowing a trumpet to attract attention when giving alms, or loving to stand and pray in the streets, to be seen by men, may be hypocrisy, but it is hardly *lying*. Black, surprisingly, does not even consider the widely accepted idea that the underlying Semitic word was חנף or the like. Nevertheless his proposal, in itself highly unlikely, does call attention to the fact that no completely certain identification of any such Semitic word can be made. Possibly, indeed, there never was any one Hebrew/Aramaic word that formed the background to New Testament usage concerning hypocrisy: if this is so, it has considerable repercussions on our view of the relation of Jesus (or of the Gospels) to Greek or to Jewish culture respectively. Yet a connection with חנף remains probable. Even if our interest in it depends on scarce evidence from Qumran, plus the usage of the LXX and other Greek versions of the Old Testament, that usage, to which we now turn, is probably enough to demonstrate the importance of this term.

314   *A Tribute to Geza Vermes*

3. *The Greek Old Testament, and other Jewish Greek usage.* It is commonly thought that the use of ὑποκριτής to render חָנֵף in the LXX forms a starting-point for our theme. In fact, however, as Young, following Hatch, correctly notes, there are no real cases of this in the LXX proper. The two registered by Hatch and Redpath, Job 34.30 and 36.13, are both in passages which were absent from the original LXX and were later restored from Theodotion (rightly so marked in Rahlfs' edition).[13] Job 40.2, registered under ὑποκριθήσεται by Hatch and Redpath, is also a post-LXX rendering; moreover, it should doubtless (a) be read as ἀποκριθήσεται with Rahlfs' edition, in which case it is no longer relevant to our theme; and (b) in any case, rendering Hebrew ענה 'answer', even if the reading with ὑπο- should be right, it is simply a case of the older Greek sense of that form as 'answer'; it thus has nothing to do with the matter of hypocrisy.

The original LXX, then, had no cases at all of the Greek words ὑποκριτής etc. The adjective חָנֵף, which we have seen to be perhaps the most relevant of biblical Hebrew words, was mainly translated by common terms like ἄνομος (Isa. 9.16, 10.6; some MSS at Prov. 11.9; also ἄνομα for חָנֵף at Isa. 32.6); παράνομος (Job 17.8) and ἀσεβής (Job 8.13; 15.34; 20.5; 27.8). The three cases in Ben Sira are in Greek ἀπειθής (16.6), ἀκάθαρτος (40.15), and ἀσεβής (41.10). The only sharply different case is δόλος at Job 13.16, a case which may mark the first movement of a shift towards the NT sense of 'hypocrisy'; cf. the linkage of δόλος and ὑπόκρισις in Philo, *Spec. Leg.* 4.183.

The usage of the original LXX thus comes close to what we have seen of the semantics of חָנֵף in biblical Hebrew: it was a general term for impiety, disobedience to the law. The only case that suggests the nuance of dissimulation, pretence and the like, is the δόλος of Job 13.16.

Equally striking, however, is the unanimity of the later strata of Greek translation in using ὑποκριτής, ὑπόκρισις etc. in the rendering of this word. At Isa. 9.16 and 33.14 Aquila, Symmachus and Theodotion all have ὑποκριτής; at Prov. 11.9 all three have it; in Job we have already noted that Theodotion had it at 34.30 and 36.13; at 15.34 Aquila and Theodotion have it (Symmachus ἔνοχος); and Aquila has it at 20.5. At Isa. 32.6 all three have ὑπόκρισις for Hebrew חֹנֶף, and one at least of the versions has it also at Ps. 35(34).16 (Symmachus in Hatch and Redpath, Aquila in Reider-Turner). In other words, where the readings are available, the later Greek translators seem to show an almost exact correspondence between

Hebrew חָנֵף and Greek ὑποκριτής, ὑπόκρισις. The only somewhat
peculiar case is Symmachus's ὑποκριτής for Hebrew איש גרודים at
Hos. 6.9. There can be no doubt that by the time of origin of these
translations ὑποκριτής and ὑπόκρισις have become a rather standard
rendering of Hebrew חָנֵף and a rather standard element in the
vocabulary of Jewish biblical expression. This being so, it is an easy
conclusion that it fits in with the movement of the noun חֹנֶף into the
field of 'deceit, falsehood', which we have seen probably to exist, even
if rarely, in the Dead Sea Scrolls. Thus, even if the RSV was right, in
its translation of Job and other OT books, in rendering with 'godless'
or the like for the meaning in these books, the KJV with its 'hypocrite,
hypocrisy' was correctly rendering the later Jewish tradition, a
tradition which, as we now see, may well go back to Qumran times
themselves, and may well be significant for the New Testament.[14]

In this connection the usage of the Books of Maccabees is very
important. The verb occurs at 2 Macc. 5.25; 6.21, 24 and 4 Macc.
6.15, 17, and the noun ὑπόκρισις at 2 Macc. 6.25. 2 Macc. 5.25 refers
to the villainous deceit of Apollonius who, τὸν εἰρηνικὸν ὑποκριθείς
'pretending to be peaceably disposed' (RSV), was actually planning to
massacre the populace of Jerusalem. This is a villainous simulation
of goodness. The other cases are the reverse: Jews, threatened with
death for refusing to sacrifice or eat heathen meats, are offered a way
out through *pretence*: one can *pretend* to conform while not really
meaning it. This is 'hypocrisy' of a special or converse type: one is
tempted to seem *worse* than one really is, in order to save one's life.
Such a pretence, however, shatters one's inner integrity, and is
indignantly rejected by the Maccabaean heroes.[15] Pretence is here a
serious fault, for it opens a deep chasm between one's outward
behaviour and one's inner conviction and devotion. In this respect it
comes closer to the New Testament usage; but what is rejected is not
the pretence or hypocrisy of the 'right' religion, if one may so call it,
but the pretence that one is willing to conform to demands that
contravene that right religion.

Ben Sira is also important. Although, as we have seen, the three
places at which חנף is known in the Hebrew text are all translated by
other terms than the ὑποκριτής group, there are two places where we
have ὁ ὑποκρινόμενος. The first is at 35(LXX 32).15, translating
מתלהלה, and probably understood by the translator in this way:

> He who seeks the law will be filled with it,
> and he who *pretends* will find it a stumbling block.

316   *A Tribute to Geza Vermes*

Dictionaries give 'be a madman' as the sense of להלל (Prov. 26.18), but that can hardly be the sense perceived here by the translator; more likely, if we may assume that he had the same text, he took it, rightly or wrongly, to be a word for 'hesitate', 'be divided in mind', etc. The second is at 36(LXX 33).2, where we have the same rendering for מתמוטט, giving the Greek as:

> A wise man will not have the law
> but one who makes pretence of it (ὁ ὑποκρινόμενος ἐν αὐτῷ; RSV
> he who is hypocritical about it) is like a boat in a storm.

Here again we see a probable association with division of the mind, contradiction between profession and actuality.

To this finally we should add the very substantial use of the ὑποκριτής group by Josephus and also by Philo. According to the Josephus concordance, for example, this writer had ὑποκριτής once, ὑπόκρισις eight times, and ὑποκρίνομαι 26 times. The phenomenon of human simulation and pretence was highly familiar to this man of first-century Palestine. John of Gischala, his inveterate enemy, was a ὑποκριτὴς φιλανθρωπίας, one who simulated love for humanity when in fact being full of base knaveries and malicious designs (*BJ* 2. 587). Anyone who lived in Herodian Palestine was familiar with this sort of thing. Herod himself, accusing his son Antipater before Varus, professed himself astonished by his son's knavery and hypocrisy, τὸ πανοῦργον ἐν ἑκάστῳ καὶ τὴν ὑπόκρισιν (*BJ* 1.628; cf. 630). We may add that Josephus used other Greek terms for the virtues simulated by such persons; this, even if not from the same word group, corroborates the perception of what we call hypocrisy. The existence of the Josephus material has indeed been noted before, e.g. in Wilckens' *TDNT* article, but the extent of it is evidence of the familiarity that people had with hypocrisy, and their perception and verbalization of it. It was not mere evil-doing, but the simulation of goodness and the pretension of high-minded ideals on the part of evil-doers, that was the point. In Philo, the importance of our words has already been adequately registered by Wilckens, p. 565.

To sum up, therefore, up to this point: even if the older Hebrew had no widely used term in the semantic field of hypocrisy, and even if this was still so in the earlier strata of the LXX, the usage of Maccabees and of Josephus shows the entry of such terms, which the later translations of the Bible then use repeatedly. It cannot be definitely proved, but is very likely, that the old but infrequent terms חָנֵף and חֹנֶף shifted in meaning within Hebrew/Aramaic in order to adjust to the consciousness of this meaning. The change may stem in part from the impact of Greek usage, and the increasing awareness of the difference between profession and actuality that Greek culture implied, and in part also from the issue of pretence in religion which was brought to the fore in Maccabaean times. In either case it meant that Hebrew/Aramaic terms understood in the sense 'hypocrite, hypocrisy' may well have existed. The evidence of the later translators of the Hebrew Bible makes it clear that חָנֵף was understood as such a term. This in itself, however, does not prove that חָנֵף was the term, or the sole or exclusive term, used by Jesus or lying behind the gospel tradition.

4. *The Differences of Terms within the Gospels.* In arguing that the 'Greek meaning' of simulation of goodness is absent from the Gospels and is 'as alien to Aramaic as to Hebrew', F.W. Young (*IDB*, vol. II, p. 669) goes on:

> This is substantiated by the several instances in the Synoptic gospels where in the same saying we have alternate readings. E.g., the reading 'their hypocrisy' in Mk. 12.15 becomes 'their malice' (πονηρίαν) in Matt. 22.18 and 'their craftiness' (πανουργίαν) in Lk. 20.23. The words 'the hypocrites' in Matt. 24.51 alternate with 'the unfaithful' (ἄπιστοι) in Lk. 12.46.

Such argumentation, perhaps unintentionally, creates the impression that, since the quality that is 'hypocrisy' in one gospel is 'malice', 'craftiness' or 'faithlessness' in another, hypocrisy therefore is more or less the same thing as these other bad qualities and not sharply distinct from them. This, however, is surely a mistaken conclusion. A person who is a hypocrite may well be also malicious, crafty and faithless, but this does not mean that these terms are identical in scope. Each account or narrative may pick out one or another as the aspect that it wishes to identify or emphasize. There is no reason therefore, from the fact that a hypocrisy term may be replaced in another account by a different term for a fault or vice, to suppose that the texts, even when taken together, lump hypocrisy together with these other faults as just more or less the same thing.

If it is right that there is a Hebrew/Aramaic underlying term, such as חָנֵף, this could confirm the above argument even further. For we have seen that this term, though understood in later texts very markedly as hypocrisy or the like, had in its older, biblical, usage been employed in much more general senses such as 'ungodly' or 'impious', senses that were still doubtless known in Qumran times and co-existed with the later meanings. Some variations in wording as between different Gospels could thus perhaps be explained as different reflections in Greek of a word that had had a very varied semantic history. Thus, to take the most obvious case, the ἀπίστων of Lk. 12.46, at a point where the parallel Matt. 24.51 has ὑποκριτῶν, is practically identical with the ἀπειθής of Sir. 16.6, which renders חנף.

The same point may be relevant for the fact, emphasized by Hatch, that some references to 'hypocrites' in the NT may seem to be unfitting for the context. As he says, if a master finds the overseer beating his fellow-slaves (Matt. 24.51), it is not strange that the master scourges him, but it is strange that he 'appoints his portion with the hypocrites'; in what way had he been 'hypocritical'? It would be mere bathos, Hatch says, to understand this as appointing his portion 'with the false pretenders'. And so also with some other passages. Some such passages could reflect the older, biblical, sense of חנף; this fact however would not alter the reality of the designation of actual 'hypocrisy' through the same terms elsewhere. Another explanation would be that the NT condemnation of 'hypocrisy' became so influential and so noticeable that it began to be applied unthinkingly as a criticism of persons to whom it did not strictly apply.

I do not wish to place too much emphasis on this part of the argument, but it is a reasonable possibility. The Hebrew/Aramaic original would then provide a good reason for variations in the Greek terms. It would not mean, however, that the peculiar sense of 'hypocrisy' had not been meant exactly so by some Greek texts which used that word. It would mean only that an underlying Hebrew/Aramaic term was itself somewhat ambiguous and could be taken in another way.

In addition we should note the widespread distribution of the 'hypocrisy' terms in the Synoptic Gospels. That Matthew has the largest number is obvious: some of them are in material peculiar to Matthew (e.g. 6.2, 5, 16; 22.18), others are in material found in rough parallel in Luke but without the precise term 'hypocrite' (so for example Matt. 23.23, 25, 27, 29). Matthew's repeated use of the 'hypocrite' terms, as in chs. 6 and 23, makes them very obvious as a central element in his presentation. But it cannot be thought that Matthew simply maximized the incidence of these terms. At Matt. 22.18 he wrote πονηρίαν where Mark had ὑπόκρισιν and Luke πανουργίαν. And there are two places at which Luke has 'hypocrites', Lk. 12.56 and 13.15, where Matthew has no such term. The element of attention to 'hypocrisy' in the Synoptic Gospels is not confined to Matthew but appears to be common to all strands.

Conclusions

Some, at least, of the past discussion has been misled by its insistence on the distinction between the 'Greek meaning' and the direction in which the Hebrew evidence pointed. Because the Greek meaning was supposed to derive from the theatre and its actors, something quite marginal to Jewish life, it was suggested that the elements of pretence, simulation, and self-advertisement, which are characteristic of the traditional sense of 'hypocrisy', were actually muted in, or absent from, the biblical texts that handled the matter. The biblical 'hypocrite' was therefore a sinner, a breaker of the law, a godless person, rather than what has actually been understood as a hypocrite. This, it was thought, was supported by the fact that the biblical Hebrew חָנֵף, the most likely Semitic term to have been involved, was used in that way in the OT and so understood in the earlier strata of the LXX.

But this argument was mistaken. The sense of pretended and self-assumed virtue, simulation and deceit, 'hypocrisy' in the traditional sense, clearly became present in Palestinian Jewish life in the later centuries before Christ. Qumran evidence, though slight in amount, and the solid evidence of the later translators of the Old Testament, makes it probable that Hebrew/Aramaic terms, including חָנֵף, were thus understood. Whether we call it a 'Greek meaning' or not does not matter much.[16] It was a meaning present in the texts, and most obviously of course in the Gospels. Quite possibly people had no thought, in using it, of actors and the theatre: certainly a חָנֵף was not an actor in the Greek sense of an actual stage performer.[17]

The customary argument depends too much on *derivation*. The metaphorical connections of the Greek sense, even if people knew of them, were not important. In fact, it must be doubted whether the biblical ὑποκριτής should really be understood as founded upon metaphoricization from the Greek sense 'actor'. A ὑποκριτής was a person who ὑποκρίνεται. In the Attic theatre that meant 'speak in dialogue, hence play a part on the stage' (Liddell and Scott), i.e. an actor. But a ὑποκριτής could be anyone who ὑποκρίνεται in other senses of that verb, thus for example an 'interpreter' of riddles or dreams, a 'reciter'. By late Hellenistic times ὑποκρίνεσθαι was in wide usage as 'to feign, pretend'. A ὑποκριτής was one who did this. The form had indeed been used, earlier and elsewhere, of an actor on the stage, but no reference back to this sense was necessary in order that the word should be used in this newer sense. It is thus not surprising that the biblical use of ὑποκριτής is nowhere accompanied by associations of the stage, drama, tragedy, dialogue, the watching public and so on. 'It is still a puzzle however', says Wilckens tellingly, 'why it should be described as "acting"' (*TDNT*, p. 566). Not at all, because it wasn't described as 'acting'. The words meant, directly and not metaphorically, hypocrite and hypocrisy. Even if the sensitivity to this sense came out of contact with Greek culture, by New Testament times this sense had, in all probability, been taken up into Hebrew/Aramaic vocabulary.

The matter of metaphor is thus, in this case, highly paradoxical. I have suggested that ὑποκριτής of the Gospels was not really 'derived' out of the Greek sense as an 'actor', a sense that had little or no foothold in Jewish culture. But, on the other hand, it turned out coincidentally that a hypocrite *was* very like an actor. He was one who played a role, acted a part, a role that the prevailing religion required people, or some people, to play. It is not surprising therefore that the similarity to the ὑποκριτής of the Greek stage has interested readers of all kinds, even if there is no direct historical or derivational connection. The 'Greek meaning' and the biblical meaning turned out to have a lot in common.[18]

Hypocrisy was something quite different from impiety, godlessness and the like. The same people might show both, but the terms did not designate the same features. Wilckens in his important article seems, if one understands him, to want above all to show that hypocrisy is *sinful*. Well, of course it is, but that is not the main point. The point is not that hypocrisy is wrong, but that hypocrites are what the people in question are. The identification and conceptualization of a group of attitudes as 'hypocrisy' was central. It is quite wrong of Wilckens (p. 565) to say that 'the translation "hypocrisy" is hardly apt'. It is very apt. Hypocrisy was not at all 'general wickedness or evil' (Efird, *loc. cit.*), though we have admitted that there might have been some cases where inexact rendering of the ambiguous חנף could have caused this impression. It was a quite particular designation that picked out special features. To blow a trumpet when giving alms, or to discern the speck in another's eye while ignoring the large piece of wood in one's own, or to try to trap someone in argument—these things are not law-breaking or general wickedness or evil. They are a quite specific constellation of features for which 'hypocrisy' is much the best expression we have, such terms as 'pretence' or 'simulation' being only part of it.

The Synoptic Gospels brought hypocrisy into the centre of the evaluation of religion. Hypocrisy itself was nothing new, and had been widely noted. For the Maccabees it was a problem of people who were actually good but pretending to be wicked in order to sε ve their lives. In Josephus's world, there were plenty of dissembling villains, extolling virtue while pursuing vice. In Jesus' teaching, by contrast, criticism for 'hypocrisy' is directed against respectable religious figures, and this to a degree that seems unprecedented, although there may have been more of it in the Qumran community than is evidenced by the one case of חנף at 1QS 4.10. John the Baptist, greeting the Pharisees and Sadducees as 'You brood of vipers!' was doubtless also a forerunner in this as in other aspects. But the teaching of Jesus seems to have emphasized it even more.

Another factor that supports the position taken in this article is this: those who represent the modern tendency and interpret 'hypocrisy' less as pretence and more as general evildoing seem not to succeed in producing a clear or adequate account of their own position. Thus, to quote Young again:

> Jesus does not attack the Pharisees for insincerity in feigning goodness, though they knew they were evil. On the contrary, it is because they are so self-righteously convinced of their goodness that he castigates them. Their blindness sets them in opposition to God... They make [people] children of Gehenna. They are compared to unmarked graves... which contaminate those who walk upon them... This is consistently the field of meaning in the many sayings where Jesus uses the terms 'hypocrisy' and 'hypocrite'...[19]

I cannot see what difference this makes. Hypocrisy isn't pretending to be good, it is self-righteousness. But what is self-righteousness other than a more complex expression for pretending to be good, or at least a lot better than one actually is? Self-righteousness is a central ingredient in the traditional understanding of what hypocrisy is. It seems that those who wish to understand it as a more general impiety or godlessness are driven back in the end to reaffirming what they had begun by seeking to limit or eliminate.

The two great historical questions have been left to the end, and will not be answered here: (a) was the New Testament fair to the scribes and Pharisees, and to Judaism in general? Is that tradition rightly evaluated as involving 'hypocrisy' to the extent that these writings seem to imply?, and (b) did Jesus in his actual teaching lay such stress upon this judgment, or is the stress upon it a product of later church tradition, as represented, especially, by Matthew? For the first question, it may be that the wish to avoid attributing 'hypocrisy' to major traditions within Judaism has led readers to favour the re-analysis of 'hypocrisy' as basically evil-doing, godlessness and the like.[20] But even if we do not *like* the analysis of such traditions as 'hypocrisy', we have the duty of finding out as exactly as we can what was *meant* by the terms. That the analysis was *meant* as one detecting 'hypocrisy' seems to me unavoidable. Whether this was a just judgment is another matter.

Geza Vermes would be far more able than the present writer to determine whether the historical Jesus used the categorization of hypocrisy as much as the gospel traditions on their surface suggest. I would make only this point: though the general idea of hypocrisy was familiar enough, and the radicality of the contrast between high professions and low actual motivations was commonplace in first-century Palestine, the degree of its application to religious figures well respected in the culture seems highly original and idiosyncratic. As has been pointed out, the stress on it in Matthew in particular does not conceal the fact of its presence in other strands of the Synoptic material, and its complete absence from John is also significant. The form and precision of the attribution of 'hypocrisy' may well point to the creative perception of one single mind.

Even if Jesus did analyse contemporary religion as involving 'hypocrisy', this does not necessarily mean that this applied to Judaism more than to any other religion or stage of religion. The Jesus of the Synoptic Gospels addressed the dominant religious leadership of his own time and situation; the question of *Christian* hypocrisy is one that he could hardly have been expected to take up. Christian hypocrisy, however, has not been absent from the scene of history. In the earliest times it was already there. Peter himself, and his associates, were according to St Paul implicated in ὑπόκρισις (Gal. 2.13; RSV 'insincerity', KJV 'dissimulation').[21] 1 Tim. 4.2 and 1 Pet. 2.1 both warn against ὑποκρίσεις that could arise within the Christian community. The adjective ἀνυπόκριτος, 'unfeigned', is used no less than six times, of love, faith and wisdom. The story of Ananias and Sapphira does not contain the actual word 'hypocrisy', but his 'lying to the Holy Spirit' in pretending that he had given all the proceeds of his property to the apostles, while concealing that he had kept some for himself, looks like the same sort of thing. Christianity, then, had to be on the watch for hypocrisy within its own constituency.

And no wonder: for hypocrisy is not easy to be rid of. 'It is the law of goodness to produce hypocrisy', says Mozley, in a saying justly thought worthy of citation by the *OED*. Any serious religious, ethical or political system is likely to be hypocritical. People demand it. High moral standards must be professed and upheld. It is the business of religions, moral codes and political organizations to do so. A politician who openly says that he is in politics for the sake of its excellent opportunities for peculation and corruption will not be elected. A party that professes that its sole policy is to slant the economic system in favour of those who have voted on its side will be looked at askance. A newspaper that proclaims on the front page that its selection and presentation of news is motivated solely by the desire to increase its own circulation and thereby the pay packets of its staff will not be read, it is feared, as much as one that professes the highest ideals of objectivity and public service. All along, even if our actions fall short of our ideals, we want our ideals to be maintained. The higher the ideals, the greater the resultant contradictions. The teaching of 'Jesus', whether the historical Jesus or the Jesus of Matthew or of the gospel traditions, understood the existence of these problems, and its attention to them formulated and delineated the idea of hypocrisy in a classic mode, which has remained basic to human self-understanding ever since. The achievement of this insight should not be allowed to be obscured by inadequate or confused exegesis.

It is a pleasure to dedicate these thoughts to Geza Vermes, a powerful scholar and thinker in all such matters, and long a colleague and friend, especially in our years at Oxford together.

NOTES

1. Incidentally, we admit from the start that there may be cases where the Greek ὑπόκρισις does not mean as much as 'hypocrisy': so for instance at Gal. 2.13, AV already 'dissimulation', RSV 'insincerity', NEB 'played false like

the rest'; on this example see again below, n. 31. The semantic contours of 'hypocrisy' are not altered by the fact that some instances of the Greek ὑπόκρισις are not exact equivalents to the full sense of the term.

2. Possibly an even more central position belongs to the article of U. Wilckens in *TWNT*, VIII, English *TDNT*, VIII (Grand Rapids: Eerdmans, 1972, pp. 559-71), though he does not make exactly all the same points in the same way. An important older article is that of P. Joüon, ῾ΥΠΟΚΡΙΤΗΣ dans l'Evangile et hébreu HÂNÉF', *RSR* 20, 1930, pp. 312-17. Cf. even earlier E. Hatch, *Essays in Biblical Greek*, Oxford: Clarendon Press, 1889, pp. 91-93, and later G. Bornkamm, 'Heuchelei', *RGG*[3], pp. 305ff.; most recently the fuller treatment on the classical side by B. Zucchelli, ῾ΥΠΟΚΡΙΤΗΣ (Pubblicazioni dell' Istituto di Filologia Classica dell' Università di Genova, 15), 1962, which, however, is less detailed on the biblical and Jewish side, and excessively dependent, as it appears, on the work of W. Beilner, *Christus und die Pharisäer*, Vienna: Herder, 1959.

3. These two points, taken together, have sometimes had the effect of rendering Jesus' references to hypocrites and hypocrisy something of a puzzle. I have heard of a scholar who argued that, since there was no real Hebrew/Aramaic term for this concept, Jesus' frequent use of it was a proof that his actual language was Greek: not an entirely illogical conclusion!

4. KJV had used 'hypocrite' or 'hypocritical' for חָנֵף in thirteen OT passages, thus making it into a standard rendering for each one of the occurrences of this word—J.B.

5. It is also taken for granted by Strack-Billerbeck, I, p. 388.

6. In one of the few recent systematic studies of the word, R. Knierim in *THAT*, I, pp. 597-99, maintains that the basic sense is 'be twisted, perverted; pervert', apparently on the grounds that Arabic cognates meaning 'have a twisted foot' and 'turn to the side' display a 'concrete basic meaning', and he thinks that this sense 'be perverted' can be seen to continue more or less throughout the usage in biblical Hebrew. This centrality of a concrete meaning, even where it is well evidenced, seems to the writer a doubtful principle. I cannot see that these Arabic cognates, even if genuine, make any meaningful contact with the known Hebrew usage.

7. The important *ḥanīf*, on the other hand, may very probably be connected with the Aramaic form of our term, and may derive from it. But the guidance given by this fact, if it is a fact, is also ambiguous. Wilckens' statement on his p. 564, n. 25, that 'In Arab. *ḥanīf* denotes the heathen, esp. the follower of the religion of Abraham', gives a very misleading impression. This word 'appears repeatedly in the Qur'an as the name of those who possess the real and true religion. . . It is used particularly of Abraham as the representative of the pure worship of God'; so H.A.R. Gibb and J.H. Kramers, *Shorter Encyclopaedia of Islam*, Leiden: Brill, 1953, pp. 132-33. For a discussion of the difficult problems of this word, see there. If it was 'somehow' (the term used by that article) derived from an Aramaic form

meaning 'godless, heretic, heathen', its actual usage in such a good sense indicates the complexity of semantic changes possible in such a term.

8. R. Knierim's article (n. 4 above) discusses the situation in biblical Hebrew but scarcely touches on the question of relations to the 'hypocrisy' of the New Testament texts, nor does it make anything of the usage of LXX.

9. Even so it remains *possible* to render as 'evil', 'ungodliness', etc., even here: thus G. Vermes 'abundant evil', *The Dead Sea Scrolls in English*, Harmondsworth: Penguin, 1962, p. 77; nevertheless the context with terms of deceit remains significant and I prefer to understand as 'hypocrisy' with P. Wernberg-Møller, *The Manual of Discipline*, Leiden: Brill, 1957, p. 26 and p. 80 n. 33.

10. Cited in J. Levy, *Chaldäisches Wörterbuch*, Leipzig, 1866, p. 303.

11. I quote from the third edition (Oxford: Clarendon Press, 1967).

12. Cf. biblical cases as cited by Brockelmann, *Lexicon Syriacum*, p. 801b, especially those rendering Hebrew בגדה in Jer. 3.8, 10, 11. Though *šaqqār* exists in Syriac, there appears to be no case of its use to render the ὑποκριτής of the Greek New Testament.

13. Failure to take account of this important point is a serious fault in the LXX section of Wilckens' *TDNT* article, pp. 563f.

14. Wilckens, p. 564, seems to me to offer a quite distorted interpretation of these facts. 'In rendering חָנֵף by ὑποκριτής the translator undoubtedly did not have in view a hypocrite who seems to be righteous without actually being so. Rather ὑπόκρισις has for him the character of sin. . . Nowhere do words of the stem חנף have the sense of dissembling or hypocrisy, and the LXX keeps faithfully to the meaning. . . The ὑποκριτής is the ungodly man, the ungodly man is the ὑποκριτής.' All this seems to me to be plainly wrong. Because in biblical Hebrew חָנֵף meant not 'hypocrite' but 'ungodly', therefore the translators when they used ὑποκριτής meant 'ungodly'. But obviously they did not understand the word in this sense: for them it *did* mean 'hypocrite'. Like other elements in the theological dictionaries, the reflections quoted seem to be of a theological-sermonic nature rather than correct semantic analysis. For another example, cf. the dictum of G. Bornkamm, *loc. cit.*: 'Sie [i.e. hypocrisy] ist als Usurpation des göttlichen Heils ihrem Wesen nach satanisch'—a profound theological synthesis, and doubtless valid, but remote from the meaning of words in their closer contexts.

15. On this see Wilckens, *ibid.*, p. 563.

16. Wilckens' presentation of the material concentrates on the situation of *classical* Greek, where, he says, the words never had a negative ethical ring, and Jewish and biblical usage, where they were always negative—not an untypical strategy in the Kittel dictionary. A more historical approach would have shown that the Jewish/biblical usage has deep continuities with developments in Hellenistic Greek: on this cf. Zucchelli, *op. cit.* It goes beyond the scope of the present article, however, to enter into questions of the Greek development in itself.

17. Wilckens, p. 566 n. 38, does consider the possibility that a Jewish dislike of the theatre and of actors is implied by the negative usage of 'hypocrite'. This is not impossible, but what follows will show why it is both unnecessary and improbable.

18. Thus Joüon in his concluding sentence, p. 316, expressed the opinion that both Greek and Hebrew had come to the precise expression of a new notion, but by quite different paths.

19. Young, *IDB*; so likewise G. Bornkamm, *loc. cit.* Hypocrisy arises from an attitude 'that through outward action conceals the inner reality of the heart'. Yet the criticism of the Pharisees is not on the ground of their dishonesty. It is rather 'an objective self-contradiction' (Schniewind). Bornkamm goes on to explain: 'Sie "ver-messen" sich selbst im Vertrauen auf ihre eigene Gerechtigkeit (Lk 18.9), und haben vergessen, dass Gott in das Verborgene schaut'. But what difference does all this make? Does it mean, really, that the 'hypocrisy' of the Gospels is not a personal moral failure but a theological error, sincerely maintained? I can't make sense of it otherwise.

So also, on a simpler level, Efird, *loc. cit.*: 'hypocrisy' in the NT does not have the 'limited' meaning of pretending to be something that one is not. It can denote 'general wickedness or evil, self-righteousness, pretence, or breach of "contract"'. It isn't pretence, but it is pretence.

20. Thus Joüon explains the 'hypocrisy' language of the New Testament through 'the legalist and formalist spirit of the religion of Israel, insufficiently counterbalanced by the inner spirit which is needed in order to give life to rites and observances'. This way of talking was typical enough of 1930 when he was writing, but is now unfashionable; and this fact may have contributed to some of the uncertainties we have been discussing. To interpret 'hypocrisy' as general evildoing or godlessness is to escape from the unpleasantness of implying criticism of any one religion more than any other.

21. Why did KJV render as 'dissimulation' here? Did it wish to avoid the nastiness of attributing to St. Peter and his associates the more unpleasant characteristic of 'hypocrisy'? For the actual behaviour of Peter and the others is, in fact, very similar in its general characteristics to the behaviour patterns of scribes and Pharisees who were roundly described as 'hypocrites' in the Gospels. Since the Galatian letter, and the incident described in it, are earlier than the writing of the Gospels, one faces the intriguing possibility that 'hypocrisy' came to the fore as a problem *within Christianity*, and the consciousness of it was later passed over on to the Christian perception of Judaism. But this question goes beyond the bounds of what can be further considered in this article.

THE DOXOLOGY TO THE *PATER NOSTER* WITH A NOTE ON MATTHEW 6.13B

Matthew Black

St Mary's College
St Andrews

The Matthean doxology to the *Pater Noster*, as it appears in the Authorised Version (AV), 'For thine is the kingdom, and the power, and the glory, for ever. Amen' (Mt. 6.13c), has never been seriously regarded, by the learned doctors of the Christian Church, as having ever constituted an integral part of the *Pater Noster*. It is omitted altogether by the early Fathers, Tertullian, Cyprian, Origen, even in treatises on prayer, or else it is distinguished carefully, first it would seem by Irenaeus, as a liturgical appendix (*precatio ecclesiae*) from the dominical prayer (*verba scripturae*); and this early patristic view came to be shared by the Reformers.[1] Modern scholars take the same view, pointing out further that the doxology is also omitted in the oldest Greek manuscripts (א B D etc.), as it is in Luke's version of the prayer, and attested only in the late Byzantine ecclesiastical 'Received Text' (TR). Moreover, there are variant forms of the text, with individual variant readings, a longer form (as in the AV = TR) and a shorter form, as in the Curetonian Syriac, 'For thine is the kingdom and the glory, for ever and ever, Amen', or in the Old Latin (k), 'For thine is the power, for ever and ever'.

An important qualification of this traditional view has been made by the late Professor Joachim Jeremias in his book *Abba, Studien zur neutestamentlichen Theologie und Zeitgeschichte*.[2] Jeremias revives the claim of Adolf Schlatter that the *Pater Noster* must originally have had a closing doxology, since all prayers in Palestinian Judaism of that period always concluded with a doxology, known as the 'seal' (*ḥôṭāmâ*).[3] Thus Jeremias writes: '. . . it is in the Palestinian area quite unthinkable that a prayer should end [as it does in Luke] with the word "temptation" . . . in Judaism it was customary that many prayers ended with a "seal", a doxology freely formulated . . . Thus it was, without question, the intention of Jesus and the usage of the oldest congregation that the *Pater Noster* should conclude with a "seal", i.e. a doxology freely formulated by the one offering the prayer' (*op. cit.*, p. 170).

There is no suggestion by Jeremias (or Schlatter) that some form of the original *ḥôṭāmâ*, presumably used by Jesus, has survived in any of the later doxologies. Jeremias himself shares the widely held view that it is the shorter prayer in Luke which has preserved the oldest format and form of text; the longer and fuller form in Matthew is a liturgical expansion, although Matthew does offer a more faithful version of the Semitic original in the petitions he has in common with Luke (the Q tradition) (p. 160). While the Greek Gentile Church has preserved the oldest text, 'the Jewish-Christian Church, coming from a world of rich liturgical treasures and a fuller liturgical observance of prayer, has elaborated and embellished the Lord's Prayer' (p. 158). At the same time, 'the possibility that Jesus himself could have given the Lord's Prayer to his disciples, on different occasions, in different format—a shorter and a longer—cannot from the start be ruled out' (p. 159).

While the prayer is discussed in *Abba*, petition by petition (with an introduction on the prayer in the early Church), Jeremias confines his remarks on the doxology to his one point on the *ḥôṭāmâ*. Ernst Lohmeyer, in his study *The Lord's Prayer*, devotes a whole chapter to the doxology, noting parallels from the Old Testament and Aramaic targum (see further below), and drawing prominent attention (as do all commentators) to the indebtedness of the doxology to 1 Chron. 19.10f., the prayer of David as he virtually inaugurates the Temple his son Solomon is to build, especially the words 'Thine, O Lord, is the greatness, the power and the glory. . .'; he writes '1 Chron 29:10f. has often been taken as the model of our doxology' (p. 234; cf. T.W. Manson, in *The Sayings of Jesus*,[4] p. 171: 'The current form of the doxology in the AV NT. . . has some points in common with 1 Chron. 29.11f.'). C.G. Montefiore is less vague and non-committal in his estimate of the indebtedness of the doxology to the Chronicler, 'The doxology is based on I Chron. xxix 11';[5] and a similar view was taken by R.H. Charles, 'I Chron. xxix 11 . . . appears to be the original source of most of the doxologies of later times'.[6]

For this and other questions, especially as relating to the doxology in the early Church, the basic study is still the magisterial monograph of F.H. Chase, *The Lord's Prayer in the Early Church*,[7] where the doxology is studied in the light of New Testament, patristic, Old Testament and Jewish parallels, but first with reference to the foundation text, 1 Chron. 29.10-11: 'In 1 Chron xxix. 10f. we have a point where liturgical streams which afterwards flowed widely apart are united. The passage runs thus in the LXX.: [10] εὐλογητὸς εἶ, κύριε ὁ θεὸς Ἰσραήλ, ὁ πατὴρ ἡμῶν ἀπὸ τοῦ αἰῶνος καὶ ἕως τοῦ αἰῶνος [11] σύ (so Cod. B; Cod. A σοί: Hebr. לְךָ), κύριε, ἡ μεγαλωσύνη καὶ ἡ δύναμις καὶ τὸ καύχημα καὶ ἡ νίκη καὶ ἡ ἰσχύς. Chase then goes on to distinguish two different types of doxologies, the *first* hebraistic, after the pattern of 1 Chron. 29.10b, beginning with the word 'Blessed', a form frequent in the Old Testament, especially in the Psalms, but also found in the New Testament at Lk. 1.68; 2 Cor. 1.3; 11.31; Rom. 1.25; 9.5; Eph. 1.3; 1 Pet. 1.3, in the worship of the Temple (reference is made to examples cited in Johannes Lightfoot's *Horae Hebraicae* on Matt. 6.13), and very common in Jewish Prayer Books.

The *second* type of doxology, modelled on 1 Chron. 29.11 (but also to be compared with Pss. 28.1; 95.7; 103.31; 1 Chron. 16.27), beginning with σοί κύριε, ἡ μεγαλωσύνη . . ., is 'of the kind familiar to us in connexion with the Lord's Prayer'. This type of doxology is 'very common in the New Testament', and Chase draws attention to the list of such passages collected (and commented on) by Westcott (*Hebrews*, pp. 464f.): Gal. 1.5; Rom. 11.36; 16.27; Phil. 4.20; Eph. 3.21; 1 Tim. 1.17; 6.16; 2 Tim. 4.18; Heb. 13.21; 1 Pet. 4.11; 5.11; 2 Pet. 3.18; Jude 25; Rev. 1.6; 5.13; 7.12. 'Outside the Apostolic writings, it is very frequently found, its exact form varying, in the liturgical portions of the *Didache*, of Clement's *Epistle*, of the *Martyrdom of Polycarp*. The phenomena are all explained if we suppose that the liturgical usage passed over from the Synagogues of the Hellenistic Jews into those of the Christian "Brethren"' (Chase, p. 169).

In an analysis of the New Testament instances, together with those in the *Didache* and in what Westcott called 'the remarkable series' in the *Epistle of Clement*, Chase notes that the simplest form is σοί (ᾧ/ αὐτῷ) ἐστίν ἡ δόξα εἰς τοὺς αἰῶνας (τῶν αἰώνων) (Ἀμήν). While each of the elements in this form admits of variations, the bracketed variations 'are of no great importance' (p. 170). This simplest form occurs at Gal. 1.5; Rom. 11.36; 2 Tim. 4.18; Heb. 13.21; *Did.* 9.2, 3; 10.2, 4; *1 Clem.* 32, 38, 43, 45, 50, 58.

It is in the elaboration of the attribute of deity, ἡ δόξα, by additional attributes that significant variations occur, and analysis of Chase's list, supplemented by Westcott's, reveals other forms, one with no more than two attributes, but all, with one exception, with (ἡ) δόξα as a constant element. Nouns underlined come from LXX 1 Chron. 29.11.

1 Pet. 4.11; 5.11;[8] Rev. 1.6: ἡ δόξα καὶ τὸ κράτος

1 Tim. 1.17: τιμὴ καὶ δόξα

      6.16: Τιμὴ καὶ κράτος (without δόξα)

Did. 8.2; 10.5: ἡ δύναμις καὶ ἡ δόξα

      9.4: ἡ δόξα καὶ ἡ δύναμις

1 Clem. 20, 61: ἡ δόξα καὶ ἡ μεγαλωσύνη. In the three cases in the *Didache*, ἡ δύναμις is clearly a translation variant with τὸ κράτος, e.g. at Rev. 1.6; 1 Tim. 6.16, both rendering MT הגבורה at 1 Chron. 29.11.

The *third* form is a much longer type of doxology, and in the New Testament is confined to

Jude 25: δόξα, μεγαλωσύνη, κράτος καὶ ἐξουσία

Rev. 5.13: ἡ εὐλογία καὶ ἡ τιμὴ καὶ ἡ δόξα καὶ τὸ κράτος

      7.12: ἡ εὐλογία καὶ ἡ δόξα καὶ ἡ σοφία καὶ ἡ εὐχαριστία καὶ ἡ τιμὴ καὶ ἡ δύναμις καὶ ἡ ἰσχύς

The longer doxology does not appear in the *Didache* at all, and there are two cases only in *1 Clement*.

1 Clem. 64: δόξα καὶ μεγαλωσύνη, κράτος, τιμή

      65 (last chapter): δόξα, τιμή, κράτος καὶ μεγαλωσύνη θρόνος αἰώνιος. In the longer as in the shorter forms δόξα is a constituent element.

From this analysis it can be seen that (a) the simplest form of the doxology, with a single attribute of deity, σοι (ᾧ, αὐτῷ) ἡ δόξα. . . is by far the most common type, clearly a popular form, in the New Testament, the *Didache* and *1 Clement*. In composite forms, with two or more attributes, (ἡ) δόξα has become virtually, with one exception (1 Tim. 6.16), a permanent constitutive element, and in most cases given priority of place. (b) Attributes of deity in the longer forms not listed in 1 Chron. 29.11 are generally drawn from other parts of the Greek Old Testament, e.g. ἐξουσία at Jude 25 recalls Dan. 4.31 (Theod. = MT), σοφία at Rev. 7.12 is reminiscent of Job 12.13, etc.

The freedom and flexibility of these variations (their order at times seems purely arbitrary) enable changes to be rung according to context and occasion (e.g. Jude 25 and *1 Clem.* 65 in concluding verses of Epistles call for such a rhetorical climax).

How are we to explain the source of ἡ δόξα, the prime and central attribute in the Christian doxologies? The noun δόξα does appear at 1 Chron. 29.12, rendering Hebrew הכבוד in the sense of 'honour' (so NEB) but, along with 'wealth', as a gift of God not an attribute of deity. The Vulgate and the Peshitta render Hebrew התפארת (LXX τὸ καύχημα), by *gloria*, תשבחתא (so also AV 'glory'), so that, if these versions read a Greek term δόξα this could be the source of the term in the Christian doxology. Or (ἡ) δόξα could have been imported from LXX Ps. 28.1 ἐνέγκατε τῷ κυρίῳ δόξαν καὶ τιμήν.

A third possibility, however, which gives full weight to the primary position of (ἡ) δόξα in almost all variant forms of the doxology, is that this Greek noun comes from a translation, not of the Hebrew original of 1 Chron. 29.11, but from the Aramaic Targum of the verse:

> Of thee, O Lord, is the greatness/glory (דלך יהוה רבותא) who hast created the world by great might (בגבורתא רבתא)...

Aram. רבותא translates Heb. הגדלה (LXX μεγαλωσύνη), which is variously rendered into Greek by μεγαλωσύνη, μεγαλειότης or δόξα.[9]

If the Aramaic Targum is the source of (ἡ) δόξα in the *Pater Noster* doxologies, then δόξα, μεγαλωσύνη at Jude 25 would represent two translation equivalents of רבותא, and the short form ἡ δόξα καὶ ἡ δύναμις/τὸ κράτος would correspond to Pesh (cf. Targum) רבותא...גבורתא. The main conclusion, however, which I would draw from these observations is that ἡ δόξα as divine attribute, in particular in the short form of the doxology with no more than this one attribute, is to be traced back to an Aramaic Targum, written or orally transmitted, of 1 Chron. 29.11a. The liturgical streams which flow from 1 Chron. 29.10-11 are then, first, a Hebraistic/Aramaic Judaic tradition, and second, an Aramaic/Greek Christian tradition.

Lohmeyer, in his study of the doxology, detected a similar linguistic feature, which he attributed to Aramaic liturgical influence as attested in the Targum. Aramaic doxologies put the address to God in the genitive, whereas all later and even contemporaneous primitive Church doxologies follow the σοί of 1 Chron. 29.11 and

332 *A Tribute to Geza Vermes*

place it in the dative (as does also the MT); as noted above, the Targum here reads 'of thee (דלך) is the glory' for the LXX σοί, κύριε, ἡ μεγαλωσύνη. . . It is this Aramaic form we find in all doxologies of the *Pater Noster*, e.g. σοῦ ἐστιν ἡ βασιλεία. . . ; '. . . so we may assume', Lohmeyer concludes, 'that this derives from an Aramaic-speaking environment' (*op. cit.*, p. 235).

Lohmeyer takes a further step by arguing that Gal. 1.4f. and 2 Tim. 4.18 support the association of the doxology with the last petition of the prayer, Matt. 6.13a 'lead us not into temptation, but deliver us from evil/the Evil One'.[10] Thus Gal. 1.4 '(Jesus Christ) who gave himself for our sins to deliver us (ὅπως ἐξέληται ἡμᾶς) from the present evil age, according to the will of our God and Father', which immediately continues 'to whom be the glory for ever and ever. Amen' (RSV). 2 Tim. 4.18 has the same sequence: 'The Lord will rescue me (ῥύσεταί με; cf. Matt. 6.13 ῥῦσαι ἡμᾶς) from every evil (ἀπὸ παντὸς ἔργου πονηροῦ), and save me for his heavenly kingdom. To him be the glory for ever and ever. Amen.' In addition to this observation of Lohmeyer, the Galatians verse may even contain an implicit allusion to the *Pater Noster* and its second petition in the clause 'according to the will of our God and Father'; and the verbs ἐξέληται (ἐξαιρεῖν) and ῥύεσθαι, may be translation variants of the original Semitic term behind 'deliver', viz., נצל (Heb. *hiphil*, Aram. *haphel*). Was the prayer with doxology known to St Paul, perhaps in the shorter form familiar in his Epistles (see above), (ᾧ) ἐστιν ἡ δόξα εἰς τοὺς αἰῶνας (τῶν αἰῶνων) (Ἀμήν)?

If there was an original Aramaic doxology to close the *Pater Noster*, with this shorter form of the *ḥôtāmâ*, it would have read דדילך רבותא לעלם עלמין אמן; and such a short ascription would conform to the two-stress line which seems to set the pattern for at least some of the petitions of the prayer when the Greek version is turned back into Aramaic, e.g.

אבא
יתקרש שמך
תתי מלכותך
תתעבר רעותך
. . . .
דדילך רבותא
לעלם עלמין אמן

Additional Note on Matthew 6.13b

The century-old exegetical debate, whether to read at Matt. 6.13b a neuter abstract noun, 'evil', or a masculine noun 'the Evil One' (Satan), is still reflected in modern exegesis and translation (e.g. RSV 'from evil', mg. 'the evil one', NEB 'from the evil one', mg. 'from evil'); and exegetes and translators now, as in the patristic period, are just about as evenly divided as these two modern versions. If Lohmeyer is right about Gal. 1.4f.; 2 Tim. 4.18, then Paul seems to favour the neuter noun, or at least, to interpret ἀπὸ τοῦ πονηροῦ in these letters of 'the evil age', 'evil work(s)', not 'the Evil One'.

One reason given for rejecting the masculine, 'the Evil One', is that this term or designation for Satan is, outside the New Testament and dependent patristic writings, nowhere attested in classical, Hellenistic, or Jewish Greek sources. In the monumental and invaluable *Concordance Grecque des Pseudépigraphes d'Ancien Testament* of Père Albert-Marie Denis (Louvain, 1987), no single instance of ὁ πονηρός in this sense is cited; an apparent exception occurs in inferior manuscripts of the *Testament of Job* 7.1, but this is almost certainly a correction of Σατανᾶς, the usual term in the Testament, introduced by a Christian redactor.[12]

The situation is no different when we turn to Hebrew or Aramaic sources, which have their own distinctive terms for the devil, 'Belial', 'Beelzebul', 'Mastema', etc., not to mention 'Satan' itself (Greek ὁ διάβολος, 'the slanderer', a noun based on one of Satan's classic roles). Dalman rendered ὁ πονηρός in the *Pater Noster* back into Heb. הרע, Aram. בישא, but stated that 'The designation "the Evil One" (*der Böse*) for Satan never appears in Jewish literature (Heb. *hā-rā'*)'. He went on to note, however, that, in rabbinical sources, Sammael, the Tempter, Accuser and angel of death, is described as 'the most evil' (רשע) of the satans, and that R. Joshua ben Hananiah can apply the same adjective to the Serpent. He also noted the gloss on Aram. רשיעא in the Targum of Isa. 11.4 where 'the Evil/Ungodly One' is identified with Armilos (Romulus?), a kind of Antichrist.[13] The position has not, to the best of my knowledge, changed since Dalman; Harder writes of ὁ πονηρός as 'the Evil One': 'This is a distinctive NT usage for which no model has been found in the world into which Christianity came'.[14]

Some fresh evidence has come to light in the so-called Melchizedeq and Melchireša' fragments from Cave 4 at Qumran, edited by J.T. Milik and, more recently, by Paul J. Kobelski, and dated by Milik in the

second and first centuries BCE.[15] The relevant batch of fragments
consists of (1) an Aramaic text, 4Q Amram, so designated by Milik
from its scroll title 'The Visions of Amram'.[16] The fragmentary text
contains a number of dream-visions, comparable to the Daniel or
Enoch dream-visions, given to Amram, grandson of Levi and father of
Moses and Aaron, and recounted by him, on his deathbed, to his
sons. (2) Hebrew liturgical comminations for recital at 'Assemblies of
the Community' and similar to those at 1QS 2.4bf., designated
4Q280.2 and 4Q286 10 ii 1-13 (with an overlap in certain verses with
4Q287). It is at 4Q286 5 that we find the Hebrew הרשע used as a
proper name to describe Satan or Belial, in a text that is closely
related to the 4Q Melchireša' texts at 4Q Amram, and 4Q280 2.
These texts not only supply an exact Hebrew equivalent of the Greek
for the devil, but they also illustrate and fill out the Aramaic and
Hebrew background of this classic New Testament term.

(1) 4Q Amram[b] frg. 1.9-15 is an account of one of Amram's dreams in
which he has a vision of extra-terrestrial beings, almost certainly
correctly identified by Milik, in his reconstructed text, with Watchers
(עירים), also as in Daniel's and Enoch's dream-visions.[17] Two such
Watchers are represented as contending for Amram's allegiance, 'for
possession of him, body and soul' (Milik). In response to Amram's
question, who these two are who are seeking such authority over
him, they reply that 'their authority is over all mankind', and they
then ask Amram, 'By which of us do you choose to be ruled?' At this
point Amram, looking up, sees one of the two, 'of terrifying aspect,
like a serpent (Kobelski 'asp', Milik 'dragon'), his garments of
deepest, darkest hue . . . and his features those of a viper' (lines 13-
14). In frg. 2.4-6 this picture is further filled out by a statement
attributed to the second Watcher, revealing finally the identity of
both Amram's visitors, that while he himself 'rules over all light' (line
6), his antitype 'rules over all darkness' (line 5), and 'all his works are
darkness' (line 4). We have undoubtedly to do with Satan (Milik) or
Belial (Kobelski), the 'Angel of Darkness', and Michael, the 'Angel of
Light'.[18]

It is in the very broken text of 4Q Amram[b] frg. 2.3 that the name
Melchireša', 'Prince of Evil', occurs. All that is intelligibly decipherable,
however, in 2.2 are words which Milik has suggested should be read,
with bracketed supplements, as '. . . this [Watcher] who is he? And he
says to me, "This [Watcher] is . . . [and his three names are] . . . and
Melchireša'".' The speaker is the Angel of Light, and Melchireša' is

5. *Rabbinic Literature and Gospel Teachings*, New York, 1970, p. 134. He quotes the full verse, 'Thine, O Lord, is the greatness and the power and the glory and the victory and the majesty; ... thine is the kingdom, O Lord, and thou art exalted as head above all', adding, with a reference to the Authorised Daily Prayer Book [e.g. Singer's *Prayer Book*, 14th edn, London, 1929, pp. 33, 44] that these words occur in the daily liturgy of all rites, and noting further that 'S[track-]B[illerbeck] observe that the doxological application of the divine kingship was already customary during the existence of the second temple. At present, at the recital of the Shema, after the invocation, "Hear, O Israel, the Lord our God, the Lord is One", the same words as used then are still repeated today, "Blessed be the name of the glory of his Kingdom for ever and ever"'.

6. *The Revelation of St. John* (ICC), Edinburgh, 1920, p. 17.

7. Cambridge *Texts and Studies*, vol. 1, 1891, pp. 168f.

8. Reading ἡ δόξα καὶ τὸ κράτος as at 4.11 with ℵ and the Majority Text. If, with editors, we omit ἡ δόξα καί we are left with a short doxology with the one noun only τὸ κράτος, for which there is no parallel elsewhere, but cf. *Ps. Sol.* 17.3. Has ἡ δόξα καί been omitted by the author for stylistic reasons because of the previous δόξαν?

9. Cf. Ps. 145(144).3 LXX τῆς μεγαλωσύνης, Targ. (cf. Pesh.) רבותיה; Dan. 7.27 (cf. Pesh.) רבותיא, LXX τὴν μεγαλειότητα, Theod. ἡ μεγαλωσύνη, the usual Theod. rendering also at 4.22 (MT 19); 5.18 (no exact LXX equivalent in either verse). At 4.33 (LXX 36) LXX renders רבו by ἡ δόξα μου, Theod. μεγαλωσύνη, Pesh. רבותא. Cf. also *1 Enoch* 22.14, En^d 1 xi 2 frg. b רבותא standing for מרא רבותא, where the Greek gives the equivalent κύριος τῆς δόξης; see further J.T. Milik, *The Books of Enoch*, Oxford, 1976, p. 218; M. Black, *The Book of Enoch or I Enoch*, Leiden, 1985, pp. 168, 341. As noted, the Targum reading is shared by the Peshitta, where the word has the same ambiguity, but it seems remotely unlikely that a Syriac Old Testament could have influenced the New Testament doxology; all that the Syriac version of 1 Chron. 29.11 does is to confirm the Semitic origin of the Christian doxology.

10. See Additional Note at the end of this paper.

11. Cf. Lohmeyer, *The Lord's Prayer*, pp. 27f.; Burney, *The Poetry of Our Lord*, p. 115; Jeremias, *Abba*, p. 160.

12. The nearest equivalent to ὁ πονηρός for Satan noted in the Lexica is πονηρὸς δαίμων in *Pap. Lips.* 34.8.

13. *Die Worte Jesu*, Leipzig, 1930, pp. 350f., especially p. 351 foot. (The long Appendix on *Das Vaterunser* has not been translated and included in the English edition of *The Words of Jesus*, Edinburgh, 1902.)

14. TDNT, pp. 558f. Cf. further pp. 549.15f.; 550.30 and 552.13f. where Harder adds to Dalman's rabbinical usage of רשע the opinion of R. Joshua that at Job 9.24 רשע refers to Satan. See also now Bauer-Aland, *Wörterbuch zum Neuen Testament*, 6th edn, p. 1386.

15. 'Milki-ṣedeq et Milki-reša' dans les anciens écrits juifs et chrétiens', *JJS* 24 (1972), pp. 95-144. See also Emil Schürer, *The History of the Jewish People in the Age of Jesus Christ*, II, revised and edited by Geza Vermes, Fergus Millar and Matthew Black, Edinburgh, 1979, p. 526; cf. pp. 553, 4; P.J. Kobelski, *Melchizedek and Melchireša'* (CBQMS, 10), Washington, 1981. See also F. García Martínez, '4 Amram B 1.14, Melki-reša' o Melchisedeq?', *RQ* 12 (1985), pp. 111-14.

16. J. Milik, '4Q Visions de 'Amram et une citation d'Origène', *RB* 79 (1972), pp. 77f.

17. Milik, '4Q Vision de 'Amram', pp. 79f.; 'Milki-ṣedeq et Milki-reša'', pp. 126f.; Kobelski, pp. 26f.

18. Cf. 1QS 3.20f.; Y. Yadin, *The War of the Sons of Light with the Sons of Darkness*, Oxford, 1962, pp. 235f.; Milik, '4Q Visions de 'Amram', pp. 85f.; Kobelski, pp. 28, 83.

19. '4Q Visions de 'Amram', p. 85.

20. *Op. cit.*, pp. 27f., 33 (top).

21. Cf., especially, Origen's notices (reported by Eusebius), undoubtedly of the Amram apocalypse and of Melchiṣedeq; see Milik, '4Q Visions de 'Amram', pp. 85f., 93; Kobelski, pp. 75f.

22. For an up-to-date discussion of Melchiṣedeq in the Qumran texts, consult Kobelski.

23. Texts etc. in Kobelski, pp. 37f.; Milik, 'Melki-ṣedeq et Melki-reša'', pp. 126f.

24. 'Melki-ṣedeq et Melki-reša'', p. 132.

25. Schürer, *op. cit.*, II, p. 526.

THE TESTAMENT OF SIMEON PETER

A.E. Harvey

Westminster Abbey
London

I

Not the least of the influences that St Paul exercised on the development of early Christianity was in the matter of literary form. Paul's letters were real letters, in the sense that they were for the most part written at a particular moment to particular recipients. But they were also very remarkable letters, in that, quite apart from their religious content, they showed a literary quality and stylistic elaboration that (with the possible exception of Philemon and doubtless other short pieces that have not survived) put them in a different class from the products of routine letter-writing and caused them to take their place alongside the work of literary men—those who either wrote genuine letters to their friends with an eye to publication (Cicero, Seneca) or else used the letter form as a vehicle for teaching or as a means of elaborating the doctrine of a revered master (Plato, Epicurus, the authors of the 'Cynic Epistles'). The effect was to ensure that virtually all subsequent Christian attempts at religious exhortation and instruction in the New Testament and sub-apostolic periods followed Paul's example and adopted the epistolary form.

But the degree to which early Christian writers were guided or constrained by this model varied considerably. The authors of the deutero-Paulines had little choice; for their work to pass plausibly under the name of their master it had necessarily to follow the same form—roughly: greeting, prayer, argumentation, moral exhortation, valediction. Ignatius also, finding himself in a situation not unlike that of Paul, adopted a similar form for what he had to impart. But, for the rest, only 1 Peter, *1 Clement* and *Barnabas* have all the elements of a Pauline letter. The others (apart from 2 and 3 John, which have few literary pretensions in any case) are missing either the opening greeting (Hebrews) or the closing valediction (James, *Diognetus*) or both (1 John, the seven 'letters' of Revelation, 2 Peter, Jude and *2 Clement*). Moreover the content of these vestigially epistolary writings is formally different. Hebrews, *Barnabas, 1 Clement* (and to a much lesser extent James) all include substantial passages of biblical exposition and argumentation; but 1 John, 2 Peter, Jude and *Diognetus* virtually never quote the Old Testament; instead they use stock *examples* from the biblical narrative (or from apocryphal tradition) to drive home their teaching.

Clearly then these writers found in Paul's letters (which at least two of them—the author of 2 Peter and *1 Clement*—certainly knew) only limited guidance and inspiration.[1] So we may ask: what other models were available to them to follow? Their task, it appears, was to strengthen Christian congregations in their faith against the insidious influence of backsliders, deviationists and compromisers, and to exhort them to high standards of moral conduct and perseverance. What precedents were there for them to follow? It is perhaps because this question is so seldom asked[2] that the obvious answer is generally overlooked. There were indeed models ready to hand. The models were in the language (Greek) used by the Christians themselves; they were produced for a purpose very similar—to strengthen faith and morals; and their characteristic ideas and arguments were of a cultural and religious generality that made them highly suitable for Christian purposes. I refer of course to the Jewish literature written in Greek between (roughly) 100 BCE and 100 CE.

This considerable body of literature took a number of forms. Some texts (such as the work of Josephus) deliberately followed a pagan model so as to compete in the book trade of the Greek-speaking world. Some (such as *Pseudo-Phocylides*) were self-consciously learned, essays in the style of some classical author intended to show that Jewish wisdom had always been the inspiration of even the greatest of Greek poets and philosophers. But some worked within a distinctively Jewish form, through which they gave expression to characteristic monotheistic principles and moral attitudes, referring when appropriate to certain well-known episodes from the Jewish scriptures, but avoiding reference to specific observances such as circumcision and dietary laws, and with a general cultural assimilation to the moral and philosophical currency of a cosmopolitan society which must have made them easily readable by non-Jews. A popular example of this literature was the 'Testament'. The attraction of this form (apart from the divine sanction which it appeared to receive from Gen. 18.19) was the device it offered for claiming authority for moral and religious teaching. Such a form adopted the virtually universal perception that the 'last words' of a great man are particularly important to attend to. It is on his death-bed that a leader or teacher is likely to gather the fruits of a life-time's reflection and (having now nothing to lose) pass on his wisdom with the greatest candour and directness to his family, his followers or his pupils. Such 'last words' have of course inspired innumerable great passages of literature from Homer to Shakespeare. Both Socrates and Jesus very soon had 'final discourses' attributed to them. But it seems to have been only in the Jewish world that they developed into an independent literary form and became, indeed, exceedingly popular. Apart from the *Testaments of the XII Patriarchs* themselves, fragmentary Hebrew and Aramaic texts of similar 'testaments' survive in the Cairo Genizah and at Qumran;[3] a learned Jew composed one in archaic hexameters in order to show that Orpheus could be credited with an advanced type of monotheism;[4] and the strength of Christian interest is evident from the history of the text of the *Testaments*. The form was revived in the twelfth century as a vehicle for Jewish instruction[5] and remains popular to the present day.[6] And not only among Jews. It will not be necessary for our purposes to take a position in the debate about the extent of Jewish or Christian editing or interpolation in *Test. XII.*[7] The important point is generally agreed: a Christian writer had at least some part in the recension at quite an early stage. This unknown editor or interpolator must have been a Christian who saw the possibilities of this literary form for use in similar circumstances in the church. Should we not expect to find traces of the same interest already in the New Testament?

II

Jude and 2 Peter are two ostensibly independent New Testament writings that are related to each other in a singular way. They have a number of themes in common:

fallen angels (Jude 6; 2 Pet. 2.4)

stock biblical examples: Sodom and Gomorrah (Jude 7; 2 Pet. 2.6); Balaam (Jude 11; 2 Pet. 2.15); 2 Peter adds Noah (2.5); Jude adds Cain and Korah (11) angels do not blaspheme (Jude 9; 2 Pet. 2.11; Jude names the archangel Michael)

similar analogies from nature (waterless clouds, Jude 12; waterless springs, 2 Pet. 2.17)

reference to apostles as authorities (Jude 17; 2 Pet. 3.15, naming Paul)

Moreover they share a fair quantity of unusual words or phraseology and express a number of ideas in a verbally similar way. Students of the New Testament are of course used to such 'literary' relationships. It is a fundamental presupposition of most synoptic research that the authors of Matthew and Luke had some version of Mark actually on their writing desks. The author of Ephesians is usually assumed to have 'known' Colossians. Some form of literary dependence seems the most likely explanation of the strange 'doublets' in 1 and 2 Thessalonians. But this very familiarity with instances of alleged literary dependence has not helped the study of Jude and 2 Peter. Assuming that one must be 'dependent' on the other, scholars have concentrated on such questions as which was written first and which is a re-working of the other; and most are agreed that 2 Peter is more likely to be an expansion of Jude than Jude an abridgment of 2 Peter. But in fact the premise on which these arguments are based is not so obvious as it seems. The similarity between the two epistles is of a quite different character from that between other New Testament writings. It is not the case (as it is in the synoptics or certain Pauline epistles) that complete phrases re-appear verbatim in such a way that the author of one must have had the other before his eyes. What we have here is a pair of writings that are addressed to similar situations, discuss similar topics, use almost the same standard illustrations and employ similar vocabulary and phraseology. But in no case is there a verbatim repetition of a whole phrase or sentence, such as would be required to prove 'literary dependence'. Rather, in each case where the same thing is being said in similar words one of the two passages invariably uses a *variation* of the vocabulary, grammatical structure or phraseology used by the other. Of course this *could* be a case of literary dependence: one author may have had the work of the other before him and deliberately introduced these changes wherever he wished to say the same thing. But this is not the only possible explanation. The two authors may have been in close association, using (as we shall see) the same models and expressing themselves in similar ways; or the two 'letters' could be the work of a single author who was moved to compose two essays on much the same theme using similar literary resources. There is no need to decide between these possibilities. The important point gained is that we are not compelled to assume that one is a re-working of the other. It is open to us to regard them as two separate examples of a style of writing and composition not found elsewhere in the New Testament.

What is this style? All the commentators have noticed that the Greek is (for the New Testament) unusually sophisticated. It abounds in abstract nouns and relatively rare words. A former generation of scholars compared it with classical Greek and found it (despite its evident literary pretensions) seriously wanting. They would have done better to compare it with hellenistic Jewish literature, which has many of the same characteristics. In particular, there is a number of points of contact with *Test. XII*:

the content and purpose are similar: moral exhortation and prophetic warning

biblical examples are used in the same way, seldom with a direct quotation, but rather by referring to a well-known person or episode: Sodom (2 Pet. 2.6; Jude 7) is a favourite in *Test. XII*, Cain (Jude 11) is also mentioned

references to the 'rebellious angels' occur in Jude 6-7, 2 Pet. 2.4 and *T. Napht.* 3[8]

a key term in Jude and 2 Peter, 'impiety' (ἀσέβεια, ἀσέβης, ἀσεβεῖν) occurs infrequently elsewhere in the N.T. but is a favourite in *Test. XII*[9]

certain words in Jude and 2 Peter that are rare or hapax legomena in the N.T. occur also in *Test. XII*[10]

Test. XII, for prophecies about the future, rely frequently on 'the writings of Enoch'. This is also the one non-biblical and pre-Christian authority referred to in Jude (14) and alluded to in 2 Peter (2.4; 3.6)

Again, none of this need imply any direct literary relationship. The similarities are not such that the author or authors of Jude and 2 Peter must have had a copy of *Test. XII* on their writing table. But equally there can be little doubt that *Test. XII* are evidence for a literary milieu that provided these Christian authors with the style, the examples, and much of the vocabulary with which to address a similar situation in the church. The author and the readers of *Test. XII* have been well described as 'middle-class Jews in hellenistic areas, convinced of the central tenets of the Jewish faith and with an intense concern to lead a good life'; they constitute a witness to 'an early Jewish lay piety'.[11] *Mutatis mutandis*, the same description serves well for Jude and 2 Peter. Apart from a few specifically ecclesiastical matters, their main concern is the threat to faith and morals presented by certain factions within the church. Like all other NT letters (except Paul's) they have a tantalizing vagueness and generality in their description of these deviant co-religionists: we are quite unable to discern exactly what they believed or what they were doing in the church at all. Unlike Paul, these writers made no attempt to answer their opponents' arguments or to deepen Christian understanding by learning from their supposed perversions of it. Instead they concentrated on pillorying the moral and religious depravity of the deviants (allowing themselves, we may suppose, some liberty to exaggerate) and warning the faithful of the dangers of yielding to any such temptation and of the severe judgement that God would inevitably pass on the deviants. For this purpose *Test. XII* offered them precisely the resources they needed. These Jewish writings, with their general moral appeal, their widely-shared Stoic ethic,[12] their straightforward and vivid illustrations from scripture and their concern for the basic principles of monotheism rather than specifically Jewish observances, had many passages that would have served as literary models for the task our Christian author or authors had in hand. These resources would have absolved them from making more than vestigial use of the epistolary form that had been established by Paul.

III

But may not *Test. XII* have contributed more than this? May not the convention of 'last words', giving special authenticity to moral and religious teaching, have been attractive to a Christian writer? We know that *Test. XII* themselves were soon to become popular in Christian circles. May they not have seemed to offer just the model that was needed by an early Christian writer seeking to exhort his fellow-Christians to purity of faith and morals?

A number of commentators on 2 Peter appear to have recognized has seen any significance in this simple observation or used it to throw light on the composition of the epistle.[13] They have noticed the fictitious author's statement that he is shortly to die, and that this gives the letter a 'testament' character; but there are other equally striking borrowings from the convention that seem to have been generally passed over:

(a) The fictitious author is called 'Simeon Peter' (1.1). This is the only time in the New Testament that he is given the Jewish form of the name (instead of 'Simon'), apart from one reference by James in Acts (15.14). What lies behind this unusual departure from the Greek form of the name in a writing that otherwise uses such a sophisticated Greek vocabulary? This is not merely a matter of linguistic variation. 'Simeon' was not a particularly propitious name. In Genesis 49.5-7 Simeon, along with Levi, is described as one who resorts to weapons of violence and is prone to anger; and he was a chief instigator of a shameful act of deception which resulted in a massacre in Shechem (Gen. 34). It has not been sufficiently noticed[14] that a number of prominent Jews who bore the name in hellenistic and Roman times preferred to be called by their patronymics (e.g. Bar Kochba) and indeed were often known by some other more or less programmatic name in place of Simeon or Simon; and similarly sinister connotations of the name persisted into Christian times, when Simeon came to be regarded as the ancestor of the scribes who persecuted Jesus.[15] Nevertheless, Luke may have been deliberately seeking to rehabilitate the name when he made a certain 'just and devout' Simeon appear on the scene straight after Jesus' circumcision.[16] The patriarch Simeon (again with Levi) had deceitfully insisted on all the men of Shechem being circumcised before putting them to the sword to avenge the abduction of his sister Dinah (Gen. 34); Luke's Simeon reversed this deplorable precedent, and made Jesus' circumcision the occasion to proclaim 'a light to lighten the Gentiles' (Lk. 2.32). So the next Simeon, though normally called Simon, was perhaps deliberately placed in the same succession when, in a discussion whether Gentiles who became Christians should also be circumcised, he was given credit by James for relating how 'God first visited the Gentiles to take out of them a people for his name' (Acts 15.14). This at least makes it plausible to think that the author of 2 Peter intended some inference to be drawn from his introducing Peter as 'Simeon'.

Let us suppose that our author, being familiar with *Test. XII*, had resolved to use this 'model' for his message to his fellow-Christians. Simeon/Simon would have presented an attractive pairing of names. Like the patriarch, the apostle had used a weapon (Jn 18.10), shown anger (Mk 14.71) and repented with tears (cf. *T. Sim.* 2.13); there also seems to have been a tradition that he was martyred out of 'envy' (*1 Clem.* 54)—the theme of *T. Simeon*. How better, then, to alert the reader to the precedent for his 'Testament of Peter' than by calling him by his Jewish name 'Simeon'?

(b) The 'testament' form required, of course, some kind of death-bed scene: the speaker had to know he was about to die. In the case of Peter this could have presented difficulties: was he not martyred suddenly in Rome? But the 'model' provided an answer. Levi was in good health; but 'it had been revealed to him that he was about to die' (*T. Levi* 1.2). So with Peter: the Lord Jesus Christ had revealed[17] his imminent death to him (1.14).

(c) The Jewish Testaments followed a regular form, in which a recollection of some significant episode in the patriarch's own life provided the cue for teaching and exhortation. 2 Peter followed the same pattern, and provides us with the only example in the New Testament of a gospel episode being recalled by one who witnessed it. The choice of the Transfiguration, out of all the episodes in which Peter played some part, doubtless commended itself for several reasons.[18] But again, the 'model' would have made it seem particularly appropriate; both Levi (*T. Levi* 2.5) and Naphtali (*T. Napht.* 5.1) had a vision 'on a mountain', and intimations by heavenly voices (2 Pet. 1.18) had a particular authority.[19]

Once again, it is not necessary here to assume slavish imitation or direct literary dependence. But if we return to our original question and ask what model was available to an author who wished to address authoritative warnings and exhortations to his readers, it is evident that familiarity with hellenistic Jewish literature, and particularly with that form of it of which we have an extended example in *Test. XII* (and which we know to have become extremely popular among Christians and to have inspired a number of imitations) would have provided him with a number of motifs and a readily intelligible form.

2 Peter is a Christian writing. Some of the problems it addresses were similar to those faced by a Jewish community in the diaspora, and the repertory of hellenistic Jewish exhortation and warning could be adapted without much difficulty. Others were specific to the

church, and 2 Peter differs from Jude in devoting attention to some of these—the need for guidance in the interpretation of prophecy (1.20-21), the sin of apostasy after conversion (2.21), the difficulty of understanding some of the letters of Paul (3.16). Are there any matters in the overlap between these areas of concern that are illuminated when the 'model' is brought into view?

(a) It is often observed that in Jude the troubles of the church are referred to in the present tense, but in 2 Peter, though they are described in similar language, their appearance is expected only in the future. According to the current consensus (which assumes that one is a re-working of the other), 2 Peter presupposes Jude and was therefore written later. How does it happen, then, that the deviants described in Jude are still awaited in 2 Peter?

To this our model surely provides the answer. The future tense is a conventional fiction, necessitated by the scenario of a 'testament'. All of the *Test. XII* contain predictions. Of course, what are predicted are precisely instances of the kind of immorality and faithlessness which threatens the readers. It belongs to the *form* that the dying man would 'prophesy'; it was of no consequence that the content of the prophecy contained nothing the readers did not know already.

(b) One of the passages in 2 Peter most frequently referred to by Christians is that which concerns the 'scoffers' who will say, 'Where is the promise of his *parousia*?' (3.4). The almost universal assumption is that this passage reflects Christian anxieties about the apparent delay of the *parousia* of Christ—a matter on which a hellenistic Jewish 'model' could hardly have provided any material. Certainly the reference to these 'scoffers' seems to accord well with the assumed crisis that fell upon the church when the expected *parousia* of Christ failed to materialize. But there are also problems in this interpretation. One is the relatively late date that is ascribed to 2 Peter by most commentators: was the 'crisis' really a live issue at the end of the first century? (And is it not usually supposed that it had been 'solved' by Luke?) Moreover the author, though he calls on the witness of the prophets and apostles (and, standing behind them, Jesus himself) to show that such scoffers were certainly to be expected, in his answer makes no reference to any Christian teaching or authority, and simply restates a widely held view that the world, after its near-destruction through the waters of the Flood, was moving inexorably towards its final dissolution in fire on the day of judgment (3.5-7).[20]

The key to the matter is in 3.8:

> One day with the Lord is as a thousand years and a thousand years as one day.

This is usually taken to mean that God works on an altogether different time-scale from human beings. For God, a thousand years pass as quickly as a single day does for us. This is a natural way of thinking for those brought up in the western philosophical tradition, according to which God, being eternal, can have little relation to the days, months and years of human reckoning. But it would have been a strange thought to everyone in antiquity apart from the most sophisticated philosophers. Few people expected the world to last for more than a few thousand years at most.[21] Psalm 90.4 appears to be alluded to here: in the Hebrew it reads, 'a thousand years in thy sight are but as yesterday'. In the LXX it was taken to mean that for God a thousand years are equal to one day;[22] and no one doubted that the 'day' in question was one of the days of creation.[23] Of these there were six. Six thousand years therefore was the total lifespan of the world. But they were well on in the fifth thousand already, by the usual reckoning;[24] the sixth thousand could well be the time of the 'new heaven and new earth' (3.13); and who could be sure that God might not have his reasons for 'shortening the time'? Further delay could only mean that God, in his long-suffering, was allowing more time for repentance (3.9), though the piety of his elect could perhaps 'hasten the time' (3.12).[25]

If we now look carefully at v. 8, we are bound to notice that modern interpreters have jumped rather incautiously to the conclusion they expected. The first clause, 'one day with the Lord is as a thousand years', has nothing to do with Psalm 90; nor should we have expected that it would be a philosophical reflection on the timelessness of God. It is simply a reference to the standard reading of Genesis 1, according to which each day represented a thousand years of subsequent world history. The following clause, with its apparent allusion to Psalm 90, is evidently added by way of support. Some manuscripts even omit it,[26] recognizing that it is very much in the manner of a gloss. It is certainly not the clause that bears the emphasis. The reference, in fact, is in line with the whole paragraph: it appeals to the Old Testament, not to extract a proof from a particular text (which, as we have seen, is not in the style of this type of literature), but to recall well-known facts and events recorded in it: the creation 'from water through water' (3.5; cf. Gen. 1.2; etc), the Flood (Gen. 7) and the six days of creation along with their usual interpretation of one day for each thousand years of world history. It supplements this (again in the style of *Test. XII*) with allusion to standard apocalyptic notions of a final conflagration ushering in the day of judgement, followed by the destruction of the impious (3.7) and a new world of justice for the elect (3.13). At least one of these notions appears to be taken from the non-biblical authority conventionally referred to by *Test. XII*, viz. *1 Enoch* (3.6).

All of this is exactly what we should expect from a writing that draws much of its inspiration and most of its stylistic resources from the literary milieu represented by *Test. XII*. Admittedly it throws the Christian reader off the scent by using the phrase 'the promise of his (or its) appearing' (*parousia*); but a few lines further on the 'promise' is defined as that of the day of judgment (3.9) and the *parousia* as that of the day of God when the final conflagration will take place (3.12).[27] It is instructive to compare the passage with Paul's argument in 1 Cor. 15.35ff.[28] In both cases the threat is presented by people who have a broadly 'philosophical' objection to the very idea of either resurrection or a sudden end to the world. In both, the objection is supported by a common-sense argument: how could our 'flesh', with all its variety and imperfections, be raised after death (1 Cor. 15.35)? Why should there be an 'end' at all when things have gone on just the same from the beginning of history (2 Pet. 3.4)? In both, the answer is derived, not from any distinctive Christian belief, but from general notions that will have been shared by the readers: the mysterious continuity between seed and plant and the logical possibility of different kinds of 'flesh' and 'body'; and the assumption, shared by Jews with the prevailing Stoic philosophy,[29] that the present world will come to an end in fire. In both, the argument is strengthened by a reference to a well-known factor in Scripture: Adam, and the six days of creation. Characteristically, Paul quotes the actual text in order to prove his point by precise exegesis (Adam was made a 'living soul'; this shows that the 'psychic' precedes the 'spiritual', 1 Cor. 15.45). Equally characteristically, the author of 2 Peter relies simply on a reference to 'one day' to make his point, adding (unless it is a later gloss) an allusion to Psalm 90 by way of confirmation. Both, that is to say, in only slightly different idioms, were meeting the kind of objection to which fundamental Jewish beliefs were exposed from sceptical pagans;[30] and both used arguments with which their hellenistic Jewish culture furnished them.

It follows that to introduce into the interpretation of 2 Peter the assumption that it is a specifically Christian problem that is being addressed—the delay of the *parousia*—is not only to misunderstand the argument but also to do violence to the convention which the author has chosen to follow and the literary style he has adopted; a work modelled on a Jewish 'testament' would naturally concentrate on general matters of faith and morals, not on the correct interpretation of an article of specifically Christian belief. But of course there is one important difference between the Christian writing and its Jewish model. The author of *Test. XII* was unable to quote Scripture: it had not yet been written in the time of the patriarchs! But there was one set of writings—the Enoch literature—to which he could appeal with some semblance of plausibility.[31] Jude and 2 Peter, as we have seen, adopted the same supplementary source. But 2 Peter could go further. There were now Christian scriptures to appeal to. As *Test. XII* invoked the authority of Enoch, so 2 Peter invoked Paul, referring to his 'writing' (cf. the 'writing' of Enoch), and actually quoting a saying that Paul may have derived ultimately from Jesus, 'the day comes like a thief' (3.10).[32] But there is no discontinuity here. Just as Enoch, whether or not he was regarded as 'scriptural', was perceived to be speaking with the authority of one who had a special revelation of generally accepted truth, so Paul is quoted as giving his authority to a widely held Jewish view of the present age, namely that its continuance was due to the 'long-suffering' of God (3.15).[33] Even the analogy of the thief (whether or not it goes back to Jesus) does no more than emphasize the generally perceived character of the 'day of the Lord', that it will be sudden. Paul is brought in not to add any new Christian doctrine but to lend the authority of his 'writings' to general axioms shared by Jews and Christians alike.

IV

If it is accepted that this famous passage is not after all concerned with a supposed 'crisis' in the church caused by the delay of the *parousia*, but is an answer to those who were sceptical of any

ultimate dénouement in world history (such as was fundamental to
the faith of Jews and Christians alike) and whose moral alertness was
thereby reduced, we may take a fresh look at 2 Peter as a whole and
seek to place it more accurately in the milieu of early Christian and
hellenistic Jewish literature. We have been concerned mainly with
form and style. What about content? We have observed that 2 Peter
shares with its Jewish model a general concern to strengthen faith
and morals, a language for moral attitudes that was common
currency at the time, a total lack of interest in specific religious
observances and a use of Scripture and certain 'writings' that was
broadly illustrative rather than detailed and exegetical. What is there
besides? What is the distinctively Christian content? We have already
listed the small number of references to Christian or ecclesiastical
matters. In addition, we may note a Christian formula in the opening
greeting and the closing salutation; two further references to Jesus
Christ in the first chapter; the alleged 'revelation' of the supposed
author's imminent death by Christ; and his recollection of the
Transfiguration. None of these carries any doctrinal significance.
The opening and closing verses are conventional in the church; 'the
epignōsis of our Lord Jesus Christ' is simply a label for describing the
Christian community;[34] 'entry into the eternal kingdom' would pass
as a Jewish phrase, adopted by the author with the addition of 'our
Lord and Saviour Jesus Christ' (1.11); the 'revelation' of Peter's
sudden death is necessary for the fiction of the 'testament', and the
recollection of the Transfiguration is required to give authenticity to
the 'prophetic word'. That is to say: the 'Testament of Simeon Peter'
is only more 'Christian' than its Jewish model in that it is ascribed to
a Christian apostle of whom the patriarch Simeon was a suggestive
prototype. Shorn of a few adventitious Christian trimmings, it could
pass as a fair specimen of hellenistic Jewish literature.

What does this say about the relationship of the two religions in
the first century or so of Christianity? Geza Vermes, whom both
Christian and Jewish scholars are gladly honouring in this volume,
has helped us to see the common ground shared by Jesus with his
Jewish contemporaries. A comparable extent of common ground
continued to exist between the church and the hellenistic synagogue
in matters of morals and in the general eschatological expectation
which was part of the motivation to moral purity and endeavour.
The fact that a Christian author, late in the New Testament period,
could appropriate the form, the style and even the phraseology of

hellenistic Jewish literature, and needed to add only a few cosmetic touches to adapt it for use within the church, is evidence for the early acknowledgement of agreements in faith and morals that could still be a fruitful factor in the dialogue between the two faiths today.

NOTES

1. This appears to be the view of J. White in D. Aune (ed.), *Greco-Roman Literature and the New Testament*, Atlanta, 1988, p. 101.

2. C. Bigg (*A Critical and Exegetical Commentary on the Epistles of St Peter and St. Jude* [ICC], Edinburgh, 1902, p. 243), having satisfied himself that 2 Peter is pseudonymous, did go on to ask what model the author might have been following, but was unable to suggest an answer.

3. H.F.D. Sparks (ed.), *The Apocryphal Old Testament*, Oxford: Clarendon Press, 1984, pp. 510f.; M. Küchler, *Frühjüdische Weisheitstraditionen*, Freibourg, 1979, pp. 422f. and n. 33: none of these fragments is *called* a 'testament', but they clearly have this form, and are independent of *Test. XII*. For a discussion of the relationship between these and the Greek Testaments, see M. de Jonge *ANRW* 2.20.1, pp. 370-87.

4. A.M. Denis, *Fragmenta Pseudepigraphorum*, Leiden, 1970, pp. 163-67 (fr. 16 d).

5. Cf. the collection edited by I. Abrahams, *Hebrew Ethical Wills*, Philadelphia, 1926.

6. J. Riemer and N. Stampfer (eds.), *Ethical Wills: A Modern Jewish Treasury*, New York, 1983.

7. For the state of the question, see E. Schürer, *The History of the Jewish People in the Age of Jesus Christ* (ed. Vermes-Millar-Goodman), vol III/2, Edinburgh, 1982, pp. 770-72.

8. J.B. Mayor called this 'more than a casual coincidence' (*Jude & 2 Peter*, London 1907, p. clv).

9. Nine out of the seventeen instances of this word-group in the NT occur in 2 Peter and Jude (cf. W. Grundmann, *Der Brief des Judas und der zweite Brief des Petrus*, THKNT, Berlin, 1974, p. 6). It occurs 17 times in *Test. XII*.

10. ὑπέρογκα (2 Pet. 2.18; Jude 16; *T. Asher* 2.8); μιασμός (2 Pet. 2.10; *T. Levi* 17.8; *T. Benj.* 8.23); στηριγμός (2 Pet. 3.17; *T. Jud.* 15.3, ὁ στήριγμα). The use of πίστις in 1.1, which is rightly seen to be unusual in Christian writing by E. Käsemann (see n. 26 below) is similar to that in *T. Asher* 7.7.

11. M. Küchler, *op. cit.*, pp. 533f.

12. H. Kee, 'Ethical Dimensions in Test XII', *NTS* 24 (1978), pp. 259-70.

13. A number of writers recognize that 2 Peter is a kind of 'Testament': J.

Munck, *Aux sources de la tradition chrétienne*, *FS M. Goguel*, Paris, 1950, pp. 161f.; C. Spicq, *Les Epîtres de St Pierre*, Paris, 1965, p. 194 n. 2; T. Fornberg, *An Early Church in a Pluralistic Society*, Lund, 1977; but I have seen no study which justifies R. Bauckham's judgment that the implications of this 'are beginning to be explored' (*ANRW* 2.25.5, p. 3715).

14. C. Roth, 'Simon-Peter', *HTR* 54 (1961), pp. 91-7, drew attention to this, but the point has not been followed up. It was noticed by A.P. Stanley (*Lectures on the History of the Jewish Church*, London, 1883, vol 3, p. 378), quoted by W. Farmer, *Maccabees, Zealots and Josephus*, New York, 1956, p. 28, that 'the famous apostolic names . . . [John, Judas, Matthias or Mattathias] were inherited from the enduring interest in the Maccabean family'. Yet for some reason the name Simon (or Simeon) was frequently omitted in favour of the patronymic.

15. Hippolytus, *Ben. Jac.* 14 (*TU* 38, 1912, p. 29); fr. 9 *in Gen.*; Tertullian, *Adv. Marc.* 3.18; *Adv. Jud.* 10.

16. 2.25ff. Cf. J.D.M. Derrett, *Downside Review* 106 (1988), p. 276.

17. Scholars who refer this 'revelation' to John 21.18f.; *Acta Petri* 35; *Acta Petri et Pauli* 81f., seem to ignore ταχινή.

18. J. Neyrey, 'The Apologetic Use of the Transfiguration in 2 Peter 1.16-21', *CBQ* 42 (1980), pp. 504-19, argues that the Transfiguration was cited (as in certain second-century writings) as prophetic of the Parousia, but admits that the text of 2 Peter itself offers no clear evidence of this.

19. A number of smaller details could also suggest some recollection of *Test. XII*. False prophets (2.1) appear in *T. Jud.* 21.9. πλεονεξία (2.3, 14) is a favourite topic in *Test. XII*, where the word occurs seven times. The catena in 1.5-7, though a hellenistic rhetorical form, is made up of terms all but one of which occur in *Test. XII*. R.H. Charles, *The Testaments of the Twelve Patriarchs*, Oxford, 1908, Intr. para. 26, notes 2 Pet. 2.3 πλαστοῖς λόγοῖς /*T. Reub.* 3.5 πλάττειν λόγους; 2 Pet. 2.4 εἰς κρίσιν τηρουμένους/ *T. Reub.* 5.5 εἰς κόλασιν αἰώνιον τετήρηται. Further debts to the genre may be detected in 1.13 (cf. Josephus, *Ant.* 4.178) and 2.13 (cf. Ass. *Mos.* 7.4).

20. Josephus *Ant.* 1.70f.; *Vita Adam.* 49.3; *Or. Sib.* 3.54-96; etc.

21. Cf. A.E. Harvey, *Jesus and the Constraints of History*, London, 1982, pp. 68f.

22. Cf. *Barn.* 15.4.

23. *Jub.* 4.30; *2 Enoch* 33.2.

24. Josephus, *C. Ap.* 1.1.

25. *Barn.* 4.3, etc.

26. Thus 𝔭⁷² ℵ.

27. E. Käsemann, in his article published in 1952 (E.T. 'An apologia for Primitive Christian Eschatology', in *Essays on New Testament Themes*, London, 1964) well observed that the author brought other terms, such as ἐντολή, ἀλήθεια and πίστις, back from their new Christian to a more general Hellenistic sense (pp. 174-75).

28. The comparison is made by D. von Allmen, 'L'apocalyptique juive et le retard de la parousie en II Pierre', *RTP* 16 (1966), pp. 255-74, but by including the earlier part of 1 Cor. 15 he finds only differences!

29. *SVF* 1.107; 2.596-632. Cf. J. Chaine, 'Cosmogonie aquatique et conflagration finale dans la 2ᵉ Petri', *RB* 46 (1937), 207-16, who notes Justin Martyr's observation that the Stoics had the same scheme but drew different conclusions from it (1 *Apol.* 1.20; 2 *Apol.* 7). C.P. Thiede, 'A Pagan Reader of 2 Peter', *JSNT* 26 (1986), pp. 179-96, draws attention to OT antecedents of this and to a parallel in the NT: Heb. 6.8.

30. J. Neyrey, 'Polemic in 2 Peter', *JBL* 99 (1980), pp. 407-31, places this argument in the wider context of Epicurean attacks on conventional notions of providence and theodicy.

31. The appeal was conventional: no actual quotations from any known 'Book of Enoch' are given. Cf. M. de Jonge, *The Testaments of the Twelve Patriarchs*, Assen, 1953, pp. 84, 120-21.

32. 1 Thess. 5.4, derived from 'a thief in the night' (5.2). For a recent study of this saying, with full bibliography, see J. Derrett, *New Resolutions of Old Conundrums*, Shipston-on-Stour, 1986, pp. 50-60.

33. Rom. 2.4; *m. Aboth* 5.2; *2 Baruch* 12.4; *Wisd.* 12.10; cf. Philo, *Leg. All.* 3.106.

34. E. Käsemann, *art. cit.*, p. 193.

REFLECTIONS ON THE TRIALS OF JESUS

Fergus Millar

Brasenose College
University of Oxford

Introduction

If anything at all is certain about the earthly life of Jesus, it is that he was a Jew who expressed original and disturbing conceptions of what Judaism ought to mean, and was executed on the orders of a Roman *praefectus* who had little or no conception of what Judaism meant. The varied and contradictory accounts which the Gospels provide of how Jesus came to suffer crucifixion may thus be a suitable topic for me, as a Roman historian, to offer in honour of Geza Vermes, just over two decades since our joint work on the new Schürer began.

It could hardly be disputed that if we *could* recover exactly what was said and done, around the time of Passover in an indeterminate year,[1] to bring about the crucifixion, the results would be of almost limitless importance. But no such claim will be made here. Nor will the discussion take detailed account of the endless 'bibliography of the subject'.[2] Instead, the emphasis will be, first, on examining the general characteristics of the Gospels, viewed as biographical narratives (which is what they are, however 'kerygmatic' their intentions). This discussion will suggest some reasons why, if any one of the Gospels can bring us closer to the historical context and overall pattern of Jesus' activities than the others, it is John rather than any of the Synoptics;[3] while, of the Synoptics, it is Luke who has the weakest grasp on the realities of Palestine under Roman domination. It is essential to stress that it is those realities which provide the only touchstone for what *may* be veridical in any of the trial narratives, as in the Gospel narratives as a whole. These realities are genuinely accessible, to a significant degree, because— and only because—of the works of Josephus. In the case of Josephus we know who he was, what his place was in the Jewish history of his time, what he wrote, when, where and to a large degree why. Not one of those questions can be answered with any confidence for any one of the Evangelists. None the less it is highly relevant to note that Josephus' *Jewish War*, *Antiquities* and *Life* were themselves written in Rome in the 70s, 80s and 90s; a work can truly spring from the Judaea of before 70 CE without having been written either there or then.

It is the evidence of Josephus which enables us to say *not* which of the Gospel accounts is 'true', but, first, what is significant about the differences between them; and secondly, which of the things narrated by them could have been true, and conversely which could not. To take one example: the two birth narratives, of Matthew and Luke, are wholly different, and mutually incompatible; but Matthew's account fits with historical reality and *could* be true in its broad outlines, while Luke's does not, and cannot be true. This distinction does not lose its significance even if we conclude, as I believe we must, that in fact neither is true.

If we then turn to the trial narratives themselves, we may be able to find reasons why some are likely to be false, because they do not fit with what we know from more secure evidence. And we may also be able to show that one is plausible, that it does 'fit'. But that is not the same thing as proving it to be true. For it lies in the nature of arguments from coherence that we can never confidently distinguish between an essentially veridical narrative, based on first-hand reports, and a convincing reconstruction—or fiction—whose author respected historical realities. We cannot know 'what happened'; but we can certainly gain a clearer idea of the significance of the differences between the several accounts we are given.

That we are given quite different accounts is of course well known. For a start, in the Synoptics the Last Supper is a Passover meal at which the Paschal lamb is eaten, and in John it is merely a meal on the evening before Passover. We may not be able to prove which, if either, of these versions is true, though some reasons will be advanced below for preferring John's version. But what is logically beyond dispute is that they cannot both be historically true; and therefore that at least one of them is false. I make no apology for placing so much weight on the question of literal, non-metaphorical, non-theological, mundane truth or falsehood; for that after all is what historians are for.

The Gospels as Biography and History

Before offering a view on the fundamental question of historical truth, it is essential, however briefly, to look at the Gospels overall when considered as biographical narratives. I assume in the following discussion that the conventional view that Mark's Gospel is the earliest of the Synoptics is correct; but also that Matthew represents a development of Mark, and that Luke has probably used both; and that John is independent. The trial-narratives themselves, which represent so prominent a part of the structure of each of the Gospels, lend strong support to these views.

I take up no position on the sources of the Gospels, nor on the question of the absolute date when any one of them was written, nor even on whether they were written before or after the siege of Jerusalem and the destruction of the Temple in 70 CE. All that seems to me to be certain of all four is that they could not have come to be as they are without their deriving in some sense, direct or indirect, from an environment in which the geography and social structure of pre-70 CE Palestine was familiar; and, more important, an environment in which the *concerns* of pre-70 Jewish society were still significant, whether we think of the High Priests and 'the Sanhedrin', of Pharisees and Sadducees, of the relations between Galilee, Samaria and Judaea, or of the centrality of the Temple and of pilgrimage to it, and of the major festivals celebrated there, Passover above all. In a profound sense, the world of the Gospels *is* that of Josephus. But there remains one major puzzle, to which too little attention has been directed: in the Synoptic Gospels two groups called οἱ γραμματεῖς and οἱ πρεσβύτεροι play a major role. But these terms, in the plural, as designations of apparently definable groups, are unknown to Josephus' accounts of the period, in the *War* and the *Antiquities*; it may therefore be significant that they are also unknown to John. With that exception, and allowing for very considerable variations between them, the Gospels all 'belong' in pre-70 CE Palestine, and must in some sense derive from it. Within that wider framework it must be firmly asserted that the Gospels *are* biographical narratives; Matthew and Luke follow the life of Jesus from birth to death; Mark and John do so from his recognition by John the Baptist until death. The two pillars on which the structure of all four narratives rest are therefore, first, John the Baptist and his proclamation of Jesus, and secondly the Passion narratives. Only Matthew and Luke take the story back to the birth of Jesus, and do so in wholly different and incompatible ways. But we cannot understand the *significance* of this comparison unless we hold fast to the historical framework of the later years of Herodian rule and the early stages of Roman rule in Judaea, as provided by Josephus.[4] If we use this framework, we find that Matthew presents an entirely feasible succession of events. Jesus was born in Bethlehem of Judaea in the days of Herod the King (2.1), therefore not later than spring of 4 BCE. In fear of Herod, Joseph took the family to Egypt (2.14), which since 30 BCE had been a Roman province. When Herod died (4 BCE), an angel prompted Joseph to return to the land of Israel; but hearing that Herod's son Archelaus was ruling in Judaea, as he did from 4 BCE to 6 CE, Joseph was afraid. So he went instead to Galilee, and settled in Nazareth (2.23). The implication is that Archelaus was not ruling there, which is correct. It is not, however, explicitly stated at this point that the ruler there was Archelaus' brother, Herodes Antipas, who was in fact in power there from 4 BCE to 37 CE. Indeed it is not until 14.1-12 that 'Herodes the tetrarch' (his correct title) makes his first and only entrance, with a reference back to his execution of John the Baptist. So the historical framework is only partially reflected; all the same the underlying presumption that there was more to fear in Judaea under Archelaus than in Galilee under Herodes Antipas is borne out by Josephus' accounts of the two reigns.

The purpose of the story is to explain how Jesus, later to emerge from obscurity as a man from Nazareth, both belonged to the line of David (hence the genealogy in 1.1-17) and had in fact duly been born in Bethlehem (2.1-6).

Luke's birth narrative has the same purpose, but sets about fulfilling it quite differently. Even his genealogy, which he does not introduce until ch. 3, disagrees with Matthew's, beginning in the generation before Joseph; but it too includes King David (3.23-38). More important, having begun by locating the story 'in the days of Herod the king of Judaea' (1.5), he continues with the episode of Zechariah and Elizabeth, coming only in 1.26 to Mary and her fiancé Joseph, 'from the house of David', but settled in Nazareth in Galilee. The birth of Jesus in Bethlehem is brought about by the proclamation of the census, requiring all to go to be registered, each to his own city (2.1). So Joseph and Mary go to Bethlehem 'since he belonged to the house and kindred of David'.

Unfortunately the story is a historically impossible construct, which makes use of the long-remembered and traumatic moment when in 6 CE, 10 years after Herod's death, and following the deposition of Archelaus, Judaea became a Roman province, and the Roman census, a complete novelty, was imposed. A resistance movement flared up, and was repressed with difficulty. Luke is quite unaware of this precise context. But he has also forgotten something much more significant. Neither in 6 CE nor at any other time in the lifetime of Jesus was Galilee under Roman rule, or subject to the census. Furthermore, as we know from a much-quoted papyrus of 104 CE, the Roman census in fact required people to return, not to their ancestral home, but to their normal place of work and residence, which in the case of Joseph would have been Nazareth.[5]

We need not pursue the argument further. Both birth-narratives are constructs, one historically plausible, the other wholly impossible, and both are designed to reach back to the infancy of Jesus, and to assert his connection with the house of David (as it happens, almost the only characteristic of the earthly Jesus alluded to by Paul, Rom. 1.2) and his birth in Bethlehem. For if it could be known at all from where the *Christos* would come (for some doubts on this see Jn 7.27) then it ought surely to have been Bethlehem; the expectation is underlined most clearly of all in John (7.41-43): 'And they said, "Surely the *Christos* does not come from Galilee? Has not Scripture said that it is from the seed of David, and from Bethlehem, the village where David was, that the *Christos* comes?"' John does not claim that in this respect prophecy had been fulfilled; and it is he alone of the Evangelists who confronts this failed expectation.

This is not the place to attempt to examine in detail the different accounts in the Gospels of the various episodes of Jesus' ministry between his recognition by John and his journey to Jerusalem, arrest, 'trial' and crucifixion. Such a detailed discussion would serve no purpose, for, as mentioned above, all four Gospels show every sign of deriving, directly or indirectly, from the real historical environment of Jesus' preaching, in Galilee, Peraea, in the territory of Caesarea Philippi, and of Tyre and Sidon, and en route between Galilee and Jerusalem. But it is essential to state firmly that we cannot amalgamate the four accounts to construct a 'life of Jesus'. We could attempt to do so with the three Synoptics, but not with John, because the structure of his narrative is fundamentally different. For the Synoptics, there is only one journey to Jerusalem, that for the final Passover, the occasion of the crucifixion. Their narratives thus lead

from Galilee and its environs to a single climax, namely the one
pilgrimage to Jerusalem for Passover. As such, this is entirely
convincing. Josephus' two narratives of the period give ample
evidence that Passover was indeed the main national pilgrim festival,
when vast crowds assembled, from Galilee not least, and when
disturbances could be anticipated.[6]

This concentration on a single climactic visit has its effect also on
the details of the Synoptic narratives. So, for instance, in Jesus'
lifetime the Roman census was imposed, and Roman taxation was
payable, in Judaea but not in Galilee, a fact which, as we have seen,
Luke's birth-narrative overlooks. The question of payment remained
a burning issue. So all three Synoptics represent the trick question
about whether to pay 'the census' as having been posed in Jerusalem,
necessarily in the period before the last Passover (Mk 12.13-17; Mt.
22.17-22; Lk. 20.21-26). It is also in this context that they must place
the cleansing of the Temple (Mk 11.15-17; Mt. 21.12-13; Lk. 19.45-
46). But in John this episode belongs in a quite different context. For
just as his trial-narrative is structured round Pilate's movements
between Jesus, inside the *praetorium*, and his Jewish accusers
outside, as we shall see, so his narrative of Jesus' preaching is
structured round a whole series of Jewish festivals, proceeding in
what looks like an appropriate sequence through at least something
more than one year, and each necessitating an ascent from Galilee to
Jerusalem. The sequence begins with a first Passover, almost the
earliest episode in Jesus' activity as a preacher, being preceded only
by the marriage at Cana (2.1-11), an item unique to John (Cana was
a real village in Galilee, where Josephus once stayed on campaign in
67 CE [*Vita* 86]; unfortunately he does not report having heard there
any interesting local tales). It is thus very early in the narrative that
John represents Jesus as then going up to Jerusalem for 'the *pascha* of
the *Ioudaioi*', cleansing the Temple, meeting 'a man of the Pharisees,
Nicodemus by name, an *archōn* of the *Ioudaioi*', who is to reappear
later after the crucifixion (19.39), and then going out into the
countryside of Judaea (2.13-3.21). On his way back he has to pass, as
Galilean pilgrims often did,[7] through the territory of Samaria. The
picture then offered of Samaritan beliefs and attachment to their
sacred mountain (Mt Gerizim) is the most detailed in any of the
Gospels (4.1-42), and is vividly matched by Josephus' description
(*Ant.* 18.4.1 [85-87]) of an episode which belongs very soon after the
time of Jesus' preaching: a local man persuaded a large group to

ascend Mt Gerizim in the hope of finding there sacred vessels buried by Moses; but the movement was suppressed by a force sent by Pilate. The episode is followed by the dismissal of Pilate, apparently in the winter of 36/7 CE.

In John's narrative Jesus now returns to Galilee, but his work is interrupted by a 'festival of the *Ioudaioi*' (ἑορτὴ τῶν Ἰουδαίων, 5.1), perhaps Pentecost (though the words could refer to the Passover of the next year), and Jesus goes up again to Jerusalem, where he heals a lame man lying at the pool called Bethesda, and is blamed for doing so on a Sabbath (5.2-47). After his reply, and with no transition, he is found going away across 'the sea of Galilee to Tiberias' (6.1, the only reference to this new city in the Gospels). He then ascends a mountain; but here the chronological sequence may be in some way distorted, for John says that 'the *pascha*, the festival of the Jews' was near. There is no further reference to Passover in the long section which follows (6.1-71). This must be either a displacement, or a scribal or authorial error, or we have shifted forward a whole year (or even two years altogether, if the two allusions to a ἑορτὴ τῶν Ἰουδαίων should be taken as referring to two successive Passovers). But to solve the problem in that way would be to indulge in an inappropriate literalism. It is perhaps more likely that there is some mistake here, and that John is intending to portray Jesus' preaching, and his movements from Galilee up to Jerusalem and back within the framework of a cycle of festivals covering just over one year. If that is so, then it is appropriate that we come in 7.1-2 to Sukkot/ Tabernacles. Jesus is preaching in Galilee, for he fears to go to Judaea. But his followers urge him to go nonetheless, for Sukkot (ἡ ἑορτὴ τῶν Ἰουδαίων, ἡ σκηνοπηγία) is approaching. Jesus then does go, first clandestinely, then teaching openly in the Temple during the festival. No features of this festival are explicitly reflected in this section (7.1-52), except for an allusion to the last day, as being the climax (ἐν δὲ τῇ ἐσχάτῃ ἡμέρᾳ τῇ μεγάλῃ τῆς ἑορτῆς, 7.37); but the atmosphere of a popular festival centred on the Temple is felt throughout. It is worth recalling that, in a year which is probably 24 CE, almost contemporary with Jesus' preaching, the Jews of Berenice in Cyrenaica held an assembly at which they voted honours to a Roman official ἐπὶ συλλόγου τῆς σκηνοπηγίας (*IGR*, I, 1024).

As was mentioned above, we cannot regard the fact that the Synoptics represent Jesus as going up to Jerusalem only for one Passover as itself a strong argument for preferring John; for it is indisputable that Passover was indeed the major national pilgrim festival. Nonetheless John's representation of Tabernacles as being a strong reason for going up to Jerusalem clearly accords with our other evidence. Josephus emphasizes the special importance of the festival (*Ant.* 15.3.3 [50-52]) and the requirement to go up to Jerusalem to celebrate it for eight days (*Ant.* 3.10.4 [244-47]); but, apart from the rules for the festival given by Philo,[8] perhaps the most striking of all testimony to its significance in this period is Josephus' casual reference to the fact that in 66 CE Cestius Gallus was able to capture Lydda with ease, because the entire population had gone up to Jerusalem for the feast of Tabernacles (διὰ τὴν τῆς σκηνοπηγίας ἑορτήν, *BJ* 2.19.1 [5.5]).

It is also in the context of this celebration of Tabernacles that John represents differences breaking out over the inappropriateness of a *Christos* coming from Galilee, and not from Bethlehem; and it is also here that the arrest and examination of Jesus is first concretely foreshadowed, for their attendants report about him to the *archiereis* and *Pharisaioi*, who reproach them for not bringing Jesus with them. We may recall a profoundly relevant episode which, as Josephus records (*BJ* 6.5.3 [300-309]), took place at Tabernacles in 62 CE, when a peasant, also named Jesus, began to prophesy in public against Jerusalem and the Temple, was arrested by the *archontes*, brought before the then Roman governor, Albinus, flogged, cross-questioned and finally released as a lunatic.

In John's narrative there follows a long section representing Jesus' preaching and healing, with no explicit indication of his either staying in Jerusalem or leaving it ([18.1-11]; 8.12-10.21). But then there comes a festival described as τὰ ἐγκαίνια, in Jerusalem. It can only be Hanukkah, for the meaning, 'renewal', is the same, and we are in winter (χειμὼν ἦν, 8.22); Jesus spends his time at the Temple, in the 'Stoa of Solomon'. We know from Josephus that this festival was celebrated for eight days but not how it was celebrated, except (in general terms) with hymns, sacrifices and popular rejoicing (*Ant.* 12.7.7 [323-25]). Jesus again runs into danger, this time the threat of stoning by the mob, and escapes. He then leaves Jerusalem to cross the Jordan to the spot where John had first baptized him, and is called back to raise Lazarus from his tomb at Bethany near Jerusalem (10.40-11.46). It is this miracle which provokes an initial συνέδριον of the *archiereis* and *Pharisaioi*, at which they resolve to put Jesus to death for fear of the Roman reaction if all the people were to follow him. Caiaphas makes his first appearance, described as '*archiereus* of that year', and utter the proposition that one man should die for the sake of the people. This thought, John says, was in reality an inspired prophecy; for Jesus would die not only on behalf of the people, but so that he might gather together the scattered children of God (11.47-52). The last Passover is approaching, and large numbers are going up to Jerusalem in advance of it in order to purify themselves (11.55). Meanwhile Jesus goes off to the desert, then to Bethany again, and then makes his formal entry to the city (11.54–12.12).

What is beyond question is, first, that John presents to the reader an incomparably more detailed and circumstantial picture of Jewish life in Palestine, punctuated by the annual rhythm of the festivals, than do the Synoptics. He also represents the earthly activity of Jesus as reaching a series of preliminary climaxes in Jerusalem, in close association with these festivals. As indicated above, there is no way, logically speaking, in which we can distinguish between a 'true' narrative and one which is plausible and evidently related to a historical and social framework known from other evidence. On the one hand, *either* we must abandon altogether even the attempt to decide questions of literal truth; *or* we must conclude that nothing in any Gospel has any claim to truth; *or* we must choose. Either Jesus went only once to Jerusalem, for the fatal Passover, or he went several times, for a succession of festivals. Either we have no evidence at all which offers us any access to the earthly life of Jesus, or we must choose between John and the Synoptics. The only criterion of truth in the Gospels which a historian can offer is conformity with the world as portrayed by Josephus, and what we have in John may be no more than a convincing fiction. But, as we must choose, I suggest that the narrative of Jesus' ministry which brings us closest to the real world of first-century Palestine is that of John.

This suggestion can be no more than that. It is not only that we cannot prove, or disprove, the literal truth of any statements in the Gospels, or demonstrate the validity of one narrative structure as against another. Nor can we ever escape from our inability to distinguish a true story from a convincing literary construction. But since we can hardly fail to *wish* to know more about these events, whether we see them as embodying a divine revelation, or merely the most important single turning-point in world history, we both may and should form hypotheses about where we should begin in thinking about the life of Jesus. All of the available accounts give a very large place to the story of how he came to be crucified. I will therefore suggest that if we wish to consider these narratives, we should be open to the hypothesis that the one to which we should give preference is that of John.

The Trial-Narratives

As already suggested, the trial narratives occupy a central place in the structure of all four Gospels. Both in scale and in coherence they have to be taken as representing a significant aspect of what the Gospels, conceived of as narratives, are. It is also quite possible, though it cannot be proved, that they represent the earliest narrative sections to come into existence; on this hypothesis the Gospels, as biographical narratives, will have grown backwards. It is noticeable, as we have seen, that only two of them stretch back to Jesus' birth, both in unconvincing ways, though Luke much more unconvincingly than Matthew.

As is well known, the trial-narratives also present profound and irreconcilable differences, Mark/Matthew from Luke and, much more profoundly, all three Synoptics from John. The differences centre both on the timing of the Last Supper and the crucifixion, and, in ways which need more emphasis than they have received, on the *significance* of Passover as a factor which determines how the events unfold. In the Synoptics the Last Supper is a Paschal meal eaten on the first night of Passover, the examinations of Jesus take place during that night and in the following morning, and the crucifixion follows on the first day of the festival. In John all this happens one day earlier, and the beginning of Passover, on the evening of the day of the crucifixion, is still expected.

Not all the features of the celebration of Passover as it was in the first century CE, while the Temple still stood, need to be considered here; and many aspects in any case remain somewhat obscure.[9] But certain points are crucial. First, Josephus makes clear that the people would begin to assemble some six days before the festival, on the 8th of Nisan (*BJ* 6.5.3 [209]); we have already seen this reflected in John's narrative when 'many went up to Jerusalem from the country before the *pascha*, so that they might purify themselves' (11.55). Just after this a precise date is given: six days before the *pascha* Jesus goes to Bethany (12.1).

Passover proper began on the evening of 14th Nisan, though it seems clear that to accommodate the enormous number of private sacrifices now offered by the people in groups, the long sequence of sacrifices had in fact moved back into the afternoon of that day, long before sunset.[10] Indeed the festival cast its shadow even further back, for all of 14th Nisan counted as a day of preparation;[11] as we will see, John twice described this day as παρασκευή, preparation (19.14 and 31). He may also single out the first day of the festival, when the *pascha* was eaten, from the (originally separate) days of unleavened bread which followed. That depends on how we read a crucial phrase in 19.31 (see below). But in any case the later phase of Passover need not concern us. What is however crucial is the question of purification, stressed (see below) both by Ezra and by Philo, and apparently affecting all participants, and not just priests. In the same passage in which Josephus gives the total of participants at Passover of (probably) 66 CE, he too stresses the exclusion of anyone suffering from any form of impurity.[12]

These broad principles, which clearly ignore many finer points, may provide a sufficient framework for understanding the highly significant differences between the various Gospel narratives.

A. *Mark*

Mark's account begins with a Last Supper which takes place on the first night of Passover and has as its purpose the eating of the *pascha* (14.12-25), and continues with the arrival of Judas at Gethsemane, accompanied by an armed mob 'from the *archiereis* and the *grammateis* and the *presbyteroi*' (14.43). Jesus is then led to the *archiereus*, and all the *archiereis*, *presbyteroi* and *grammateis* assemble. The scene is the house of the *archiereus*, in whose courtyard Peter is warming himself. Inside, the *archiereus* and 'all the *synedrion*' hear testimonies against Jesus in order to kill him (14.55). Two questions are specifically addressed to Jesus, about his proclamation that he would destroy the Temple, and about his claim to be the *Christos*, which Jesus admits, emphasizing his claim with a quotation from Daniel (7.13).

This scene takes place at night, and at dawn Peter makes his denial, and a cock crows (14.66-72). Immediately in the morning (εὐθέως πρωΐ), having taken council (συμβούλιον ποιήσαντες), the *archiereus* with the *presbyteroi* and *grammateis* and the whole *synedrion* bring Jesus bound before Pilate, who asks him a different question, 'Are you the king of the Jews?' The *archiereis* make further accusations, receiving no reply (15.1-5). There follows an episode involving the custom of releasing a prisoner on the occasion of Pesach (κατὰ τὴν ἑορτήν), the crowd's demand for the release of Barabbas, 'imprisoned with his *stasiastai*, who had committed murder in the *stasis*', Pilate's dialogue with the crowd, its demands for the crucifixion of Jesus, the release of Barabbas and the delivery of Jesus for crucifixion. Jesus, now apparently outside, is taken within the *aulē*, or *praitōrion*, abused by the soldiers, and led off (15.16-20). Simon the Cyrenaican is commandeered en route, the procession reaches Golgotha, and the crucifixion takes place at the third hour, the cross being inscribed ὁ βασιλεὺς τῶν ᾽Ιουδαίων, in what language is not stated (15.21-32).

The whole account, from the arrest to the inscription on the cross, occupies 56 verses, or a little over one chapter. It involves two examinations of Jesus, one at night in the house of the *archiereus* and one in the early morning in the residence, or *praitōrion*, of Pilate; but it represents no formal trial or verdict. The phrase which Mark uses of deliberations in the morning, συμβούλιον ποιήσαντες (15.1) might indeed be read as meaning 'having held a council meeting'; but where he uses it elsewhere it means no more than 'took counsel' or even 'conspired' against Jesus (3.6). Pilate's order for crucifixion is prompted by the demands of the crowd.

B. *Matthew*

Matthew's account has an almost exactly similar structure, beginning with a Last Supper for the eating of the *pascha* (26.17-29). The mob which arrests Jesus, however, comes from the *archiereis* and *presbyteroi* of the *laos*. The *archiereus* to whose house Jesus is brought is identified as Caiaphas, and this time the *archiereis* are omitted from the list of those who assemble there (who are described as 'the *grammateis* and the *presbyteroi*', 26.57). Nonetheless those reported as seeking false testimony against Jesus are then described as 'the *archiereis* and the whole *synedrion*' (26.59). The reported dialogue is closely similar, and it is followed, again at dawn (πρωΐας δὲ γενομένης), by the taking of counsel (συμβούλιον ἔλαβον, 27.1) by the *archiereis* and the *presbyteroi* of the *laos*, who bring Jesus bound before Pilate (27.1-2). After a complete inserted episode relating to Judas and the thirty pieces of silver (27.3-10), Jesus appears before Pilate, and is again asked, 'Are you the king of the Jews?' The episode of Barabbas follows, with the extra detail of Pilate's being seated on his tribunal (καθημένου δὲ αὐτοῦ ἐπὶ τοῦ βήματος, 27.19) and the anecdote of his wife's dream, and the detail of his washing his hands (derived from Deut. 21.6-7). The rest follows as in Mark, except that the reported inscription on the cross is longer: οὗτός ἐστιν Ἰησοῦς ὁ βασιλεὺς τῶν Ἰουδαίων (27.37).

The narration is thus a little fuller, with extra details, and occupies 64 verses, or a matter of a chapter and a half. The structure is identical: two examinations, neither in the form of a trial concluded by a verdict, and an order for crucifixion prompted by the demands of the crowd.

C. *Luke*

Luke's account similarly follows a Last Supper which involves the eating of the paschal lamb (22.14-38), and begins with the arrival on the Mt of Olives of Judas with a 'crowd' (ὄχλος), not otherwise identified (22.47). When Jesus addresses them, however, they turn out to be (or to include) *archiereis*, *stratēgoi* of the temple and *presbyteroi*. They take Jesus to the house (*oikos*) of the *archiereus*, who is not named. Peter's denial follows (22.55-62), but the structure of the narrative then becomes crucially different. For when dawn breaks a formal council is convened: καὶ ὡς ἐγένετο ἡμέρα, συνήχθη τὸ πρεσβυτέριον τοῦ λαοῦ, ἀρχιερεῖς τε καὶ γραμματεῖς, καὶ ἀπήγαγον αὐτὸν εἰς τὸ συνέδριον (22.66). The shift is crucial in two different ways. First, Luke transfers to here Jesus' reply to the question as to whether he is the *Christos*, and his answer quoting Daniel. Secondly, this passage is the only one in the four Gospels which seems to represent a formal meeting of the body normally known in modern literature as 'the Sanhedrin'. This concept has its problems, as we will see below; and the term πρεσβυτέριον is used of 'the Sanhedrin' only by Luke himself (otherwise in Acts 22.5). However, Luke clearly intends to differentiate between an examination at night in the house of the *archiereus* and some sort of formal meeting of a council in the morning. None the less, even here, no concluding verdict of the meeting is represented.

Luke continues by specifying, as neither Mark nor Matthew does, exactly what accusations were put forward when Jesus was brought before Pilate: 'We have found this man disturbing our people, preventing them from giving tribute to Caesar and calling himself *Christos Basileus*' (23.2). However, Pilate asks the same question, 'Are you the king of the Jews?' Luke then gives a unique twist to the story by having the *archiereis* (and the crowd?) say that Jesus has been upsetting the people, teaching throughout Judaea, beginning from Galilee. This prompts Pilate to ask if Jesus is a Galilean, and, on discovering that he is, to send him for examination to Herod (i.e. Herodes Antipas, the tetrarch of Galilee and Peraea), who happens to be Jerusalem. Herodes examines him, and sends him back to Pilate (23.5-12). There is no inherent improbability in Herodes' presence; Agrippa II, when ruling part of Galilee, and other areas, but not Judaea, was to maintain a palace in Jerusalem, and came there frequently (Josephus, *Ant.* 20.5.11 [189-94]). Nonetheless Acts provides a very clear indication of how this episode came to be added by Luke, and by him alone: for in Acts 4.24-28 the early Christian community is found quoting Psalm 2.1-2, παρέστησαν οἱ βασιλεῖς τῆς γῆς, καὶ οἱ ἄρχοντες συνήχθησαν ἐπὶ τὸ αὐτό, κατὰ τοῦ Κυρίου, καὶ κατὰ τοῦ Χριστοῦ αὐτοῦ, and applying this to the double examination of Jesus before Herodes and Pilate. As is notorious, the fact that an episode in the Gospels is explained or justified in terms of a Biblical quotation does not necessarily prove that the episode concerned is invented. But the presence of this episode and its re-emphasis in Acts serves at any rate to underline the freedom of Luke's use of whatever material he had before him.

In the Gospel Luke returns to Pilate's dialogue with the *archiereis* and *archontes* of the *laos*, whom he summons for a second meeting, and duly refers to Herodes' inability to find Jesus guilty. With that variation, the exchange leads on to another narrative of the dialogue involving the release of Barabbas, brought in without any explanation of the custom or its relation to Passover, and ending with the delivery of Jesus for crucifixion. The taunting of Jesus by the soldiers is omitted, but Luke chooses to explain that Simon the Cyrenaican was 'coming from the field' (23.26), a bit of narrative colour which however sits unconvincingly with the idea that this is the first morning of Passover. The action moves to 'the place called Kranion'; the inscription on the cross is given almost as in Mark, ὁ βασιλεὺς τῶν Ἰουδαίων οὗτος, again with no indication of the language used (23.38).

The scene before Herodes, unique to Luke, remains a puzzle, and its inauthenticity certainly cannot be demonstrated. But the crucial variation is the representation of a formal council-meeting in the morning, reinforced by a very concrete later reference to Joseph of Arimathea: βουλευτὴς ὑπάρχων, ἀνὴρ ἀγαθὸς καὶ δίκαιος (οὗτος οὐκ ἦν συγκατατεθειμένος τῇ βουλῇ καὶ τῇ πράξει αὐτῶν) (23.50). Mark had indeed referred to him as a βουλευτής (15.43)—though Matthew only as an ἄνθρωπος πλούσιος (27.57)—but had necessarily not deployed any allusion to his non-participation in the relevant deliberations.

All the endlessly debated questions as to whether 'the Sanhedrin' had the formal right to pass a sentence of death, and if so whether it was compelled to have that sentence carried out by the Roman governor, can thus be relevant to the Gospels only in relation to Luke's Gospel; for it is only here that something which is clearly a meeting of 'the Sanhedrin' is represented as taking place. Luke's narrative might even gain some support from the provision in Mishnah Sanhedrin, that that body could only meet as a court in the hours of daylight. Appeal to the Mishnah will hardly help, however. For the same passage also lays down that a capital trial could not be held on the day preceding a Sabbath or a festival day (4.1). Even disregarding the insoluble question of whether the Mishnah preserves any veridical conception of how justice was exercised before the destruction of the Temple, the notion that an arrest, an examination in the house of an *archiereus*, perhaps also a formal meeting of 'the Sanhedrin', the production of a prisoner before the Roman *praefectus*, popular demands for execution, and the crucifixion itself could all have taken place on the night of Passover and on the following morning must give rise to serious questions. It is time to turn to John's accounts.

D. *John*

As is well known, the overall structure of John's narrative differs fundamentally from that which is common to the Synoptics, and those details which do reappear in John mainly do so in a quite different narrative context.

It was mentioned before that the preceding narrative of the Last Supper explicitly locates the event before Passover (πρὸ δὲ τῆς ἑορτῆς τοῦ πάσχα, 13.1), and the lengthy account of it is consistent in betraying no trace of its having been a Paschal meal (13.1-17, 26).

This location in time is to be fundamental to the logic of the story, as we shall see. Further differences also appear immediately. For the armed band which Judas leads out to arrest Jesus in the garden beyond the Kedron is composed of the *speira* and attendants of (or sent by) the *archiereis* and the *Pharisaioi* (18.3). *Speira* is the normal Greek translation of *cohors*, and the impression that this is intended to be understood as a Roman detachment is confirmed by the reference a little later to the *chiliarchos*, the normal Greek for *tribunus* (cf. the χιλίαρχος τῆς σπείρης of Acts 21.31, who turns out to be the Roman officer Claudius Lysias). No explanation is given by John of this Roman involvement, and indeed no comment is made on it at all. The combined Roman-Jewish group brings Jesus first to (the house of) Annas, a person not mentioned in any other Gospel in this context, but carefully identified here: 'he was the father-in-law of Caiaphas, who was *archiereus* of that year' (18.13). John further identifies Caiaphas by saying that it was he who advised the Jews that it was advantageous for one man to die on behalf of the people (18.14), explicitly referring back to 11.47-52, where the advice had been recorded in the context of a *synedrion* of *archiereis* and *Pharisaioi*, and Caiaphas had already been identified as 'the *archiereus* of that year'. If John meant to imply that the High Priesthood changed every year, he was of course wrong. But he was correct in that Caiaphas was indeed High Priest from about 18-36 CE. His father-in-law Annas or Ananus (the relationship is attested only here) had however also earned the designation *archiereus* by holding the High Priesthood from 6 to 15 CE.[30] The term is thus also applied (by implication) to him when Peter and another disciple follow Jesus into 'the *aulē* of the *archiereus*' (18.15), where Peter makes his first denial. A first examination of Jesus is then conducted by the *archiereus*, evidently Annas, leading to no clear answer, after which Annas sends him bound to appear before Caiaphas the *archiereus* (18.19-24). It is here that Peter is again described as warming himself, and making his second denial (18.25-27).

No examination in the house of Caiaphas is represented. There is thus a clear contradiction of all three Synoptic narratives, which represent Jesus as being brought to only one High-Priestly house, where the examination is conducted; and specifically of Matthew who names the *archiereus* as Caiaphas. No taking of counsel in the morning is recorded either, and instead 'they took Jesus from (the house of) Caiaphas to the *praitōrion*'. The time is indicated clearly, and with it both the crucial element in the whole account and a source of considerable difficulty: 'it was morning, and they did not enter into the *praitōrion*, so that they might not be defiled, but (be able to) eat the *pascha*' (18.28). The context is thus made quite clear, even if the nature of the defilement which would ensue on entering the *praetorium* of the Roman *praefectus* is not immediately obvious. It is however clear, though not explicitly stated, that the group which would otherwise have entered the *praetorium*, coming as representatives directly from the house of the *archiereus*, should be presumed by the reader to have included at least some *kohanim*; this indeed becomes explicit later (19.6). Whether an even more profound significance is to be attached to this precise moment in time depends on how we understand the exchange which then follows between 'them' (not identified in any way at this point) and Pilate. He comes out of the *praetorium* to meet them, and asks what charge they are bringing. They reply that, if Jesus were not a wrongdoer, they would not have handed him over. Pilate then replies, 'Take him yourselves and judge him according to your own law'. They (here defined simply as οἱ Ἰουδαῖοι) say, 'It is not permitted to us to kill anyone (ἡμῖν οὐκ ἔξεστιν ἀποκτεῖναι οὐδένα). John's authorial comment is that the purpose of this was to ensure the fulfilment of Jesus' own prophecy (as to how he would be executed): ποίῳ θανάτῳ ἤμελλεν ἀποθνῄσκειν (18.32). The comment repeats exactly what John had said at 12.32-33, referring to Jesus' prediction that he would be 'raised up' (i.e. on a cross).

Leaving aside for a moment the question of how we should understand the exchange between Pilate and the Jews, it should be stressed that the structure of the narrative which follows depends entirely on the physical separation of Jesus, under arrest in the *praetorium*, and the Jewish group outside. In this narrative Pilate now goes back inside and questions Jesus about his alleged claim to be a *basileus* (18.33-38), and then comes out again to offer the release of Barabbas. John relates the custom to Passover, but puts the explanation of it in the mouth of Pilate addressing the Jews: ἔστι δὲ συνήθεια ὑμῖν, ἵνα ἕνα ὑμῖν ἀπολύσω ἐν τῷ πάσχα. Barabbas is identified by John simply as a λῃστής, a brigand (18.38-40).

The episode of the mocking of Jesus, still in the *praetorium*, follows (19.1-3), after which Pilate comes out again and tells those outside that he can find no cause for accusation in Jesus. Jesus then himself comes out (or is brought out, as must be understood), wearing the mock royal crown and robe. When Pilate displays him to those waiting, they, described as the *archiereis* and the attendants, shout 'crucify! crucify!' Pilate then 'seeks to release him', by which it seems to be implied, though it is not stated, that he has gone outside to speak to the *Ioudaioi* again. For they then shout, 'If you release him you are not a friend of Caesar; for anyone who makes himself a king is an opponent of Caesar'.

At this point John's narrative again goes in for deliberate and emphatic detail as regards place and time. This has to be understood as a significant feature of it *as narrative*; no presumption can follow as to whether these details are or are not historically valid. Pilate's response to these shouts is to lead Jesus out again and take his seat on his *tribunal* (βῆμα) 'in the place called Lithostrōtos, but *Hebraisti* "Gabbatha"'. The time is given with equal precision: it was the day of preparation for the *pascha* (ἦν δὲ παρασκευὴ τοῦ πάσχα); the time was 'about the sixth hour'. The location is clearly understood to be a paved stone courtyard, out of doors, and immediately outside the *praetorium*; it was in this courtyard that the regular *tribunal* from which the governor gave jurisdiction and held audience was situated. Matthew also mentions the βῆμα/*tribunal* (27.19), but does not give its location; and the consistent separation of inside, with consequent impurity, and outside, in the open air, plays no part in the Synoptic narratives. Nor of course does this indication of the date.

Once seated on his tribunal, Pilate responds to shouted demands for crucifixion by asking 'Shall I crucify your king?', and the *archiereis* answer, 'We have no king but Caesar'. John then appears to say that Pilate handed Jesus over to them (παρέδωκεν αὐτὸν αὐτῷς) for crucifixion (19.16), and continues by saying that 'they' took him (παρέλαβον). But as the narrative unfolds it becomes clear that the execution, and the division of Jesus' clothing (fulfilling Ps. 22.18), is being conducted by Roman soldiers (19.23-4). John's detailed and concrete narrative style is demonstrated to the end, though he makes no reference to Simon the Cyrenaican. Jesus is brought 'to the place called (place of) a skull, or, as is said *Hebraisti*, "Golgotha"'; he thus reverses the equivalence stated by Mark (15.22). The element which is central to all accounts of the crucifixion, the inscription on the cross, is given here in much more detailed form. First, a longer version of the text itself is offered: Ἰησοῦς ὁ Ναζωραῖος ὁ βασιλεὺς τῶν Ἰουδαίων (19.19). John goes on to say that many Jews read the inscription (τὸν τίτλον) since it was written Ἑβραϊστί, Ῥωμαϊστί, Ἑλληνιστί. The use of the Latin loan-word (from *titulus*) is unique to John among the four Gospels. So is the indication of the trilingual character of the inscription (here as elsewhere it is not clear whether Hebrew or Aramaic is intended by ʿ Εβραϊστί). John alone concludes his narrative with an exchange between Pilate and 'the *archiereis* of the *Ioudaioi*', who complain that the appellation 'king' should have been set out as what Jesus had claimed to have been, and not as the actual truth.

A step-by-step analysis of the structure of John's narrative is essential if we are to avoid the trap of attempting to amalgamate the separate accounts, or of selecting convincing details from each, to make up a historical reconstruction of 'what really happened'. John's account is in no way compatible with those of the Synoptics. It is not only that there are many different details, or even that the sequence of events unfolds quite differently. It is that the overall setting of these events in relation to the Jewish calendar is different, and significantly different: the Last Supper does not have the character of a paschal meal, and the nature of the exchanges between Pilate and the Jewish leaders is entirely determined by their refusal to enter the *praetorium* in order to avoid pollution, and thus not be prevented from eating the *pascha* later that day.

It has to be admitted that no precise explanation can be offered as to why John should have presumed that entering the *praetorium* would (or might) have entailed defilement. All that we know of the period suggests that, with certain momentary exceptions, the Romans avoided bringing into Jerusalem images which would offend Jewish sensibilities. Nor is there any reason to suppose that appearing before the governor would have involved any hospitality by way of food or drink. The context does however clearly suggest the idea either that the location, indoors, itself might impart pollution, or that contact with gentiles, in a relatively confined space indoors, as opposed to the open-air courtyard, might do likewise. Nonetheless, however uncertain we may be as to the precise rules of purity involved, it is not impossible to find in earlier or contemporary Jewish writing expressions relating to fitness for Passover which might reflect a general awareness of the need for extra caution.[14] So for instance Ezra 6.19-22:

> The children of the captivity kept the passover upon the fourteenth (day) of the first month. For the priests and the Levites had purified themselves together; all of them were pure: and they killed the Passover for all the children of the captivity, and for their

brethren the priests, and for themselves. And the children of Israel, which were come again out of the captivity, and all such as had separated themselves unto them from the filthiness of the heathen of the land, to seek the Lord, the God of Israel, did eat, and kept the feast of unleavened bread seven days with joy: for the Lord had made them joyful, and had turned the heart of the king of Assyria unto them, to strengthen their hands in the work of the house of God, the God of Israel.

The notion of the need for purity as extending to all, not only to priests, is also expressed very clearly in a source directly contemporary with the crucifixion, Philo's *De specialibus legibus* 2.145-46:

After the New Moon comes the fourth feast called the Crossing-feast, which the Hebrews in their native tongue call *Pascha*. In this festival many myriads of victims from noon till eventide are offered by the whole people, old and young alike, raised for that particular day to the dignity of priesthood. For at other times the priests according to ordinances of the law carry out both the public sacrifices and those offered by private individuals. But on this occasion the whole nation performs the sacred rites and acts as priest with pure hands and complete immunity. The reason for this is as follows: the festival is a reminder and thank offering for that migration from Egypt. . .

Moreover, as J.A.T. Robinson pointed out,[15] the Mishnah seems to offer a conception of a possible context for the incurring, or non-incurring, of impurity which fits precisely with the presuppositions of John 18. For the tractate *Oholoth* states categorically (17.7) that 'the dwelling-places of gentiles are unclean', but goes on (17.10) to provide some exceptions, including 'the open space in a courtyard'. We can reasonably conclude that the notions embodied in John's narrative are at least not provably inapplicable to this period.

However, far more significance than that *may* attach to the much-discussed exchange between Pilate and the Jewish leaders, in which he says to them, 'Take him yourselves, and judge him according to your own law' to which they reply 'It is not permitted to us to execute anyone'. Their reply has sometimes been read as an allusion to a fixed and universal ban on the carrying-out of executions (and capital trials?) by the local Jewish authorities, in view of the equally established reservation of that right to the Roman governor.[16] Indeed it has often been quoted as one of the conclusive items of evidence for the existence of such a rule. If so, however, it must be regarded as reading very strangely. For the narrative must represent the Roman *praefectus* as being unaware of this rule, and as being informed of it by the High-Priestly group before him. Such a reading, however strange, is not however impossible, *if* we conceive of the exchange as a feature of John's narrative style, in which necessary explanations are sometimes given by speakers to respondents who in the 'real world' might be presumed not to have needed them. An example already referred to, occurs a few lines later, when Pilate says, '*You* have a custom by which I should release one man to you at Passover' (18.39).

Nonetheless, seeing the exchange as such an authorial device is not the most natural way of reading the passage; and it does have to be emphasized that what we are doing *is* reading a narrative; so how we understand what we read ought to be determined in the first instance by the nature of the information and interpretation which the author has already provided. In that light the most significant guidance and explanation provided by John is given only four lines before: that it was morning, and that they would not enter the *praetorium* because they wanted to avoid pollution and be able to eat the *pascha*. In that light the exchange reads quite naturally. Pilate tells them to *judge* him (he does not here say *execute* him) according to their own law. And they reply that it is not allowed to them to execute anyone. Not allowed by the Romans? Such an interpretation is possible, as we have seen, but very strained. Or not allowed by *Jewish* law? It immediately makes sense, for we are in the morning before Passover and an execution was surely not permitted. We hardly need the Mishnah (*Sanhedrin* 4.1) to tell us, as we have seen, that capital trials could not be conducted on the day before a Sabbath or a festival, because a capital sentence could not be pronounced until the day following the trial. It should be stressed that to emphasize the possibility of reading the text in this way is not at this point to make any assertion about 'what actually happened', or about the rules of capital jurisdiction which generally prevailed in the real world of first-century Judaea. It is to suggest a way of understanding what story John is telling; one to whose entire logic, as we have seen, the approach of Passover is fundamental. John reminds us of this at the moment when Pilate takes his seat on his *tribunal*: ἦν δὲ παρασκευὴ τοῦ πάσχα· ὥρα ἦν ὡς ἕκτη. So he does again immediately after Jesus' death, when the *Ioudaioi*, since it was παρασκευή, ask that the bodies of Jesus and the two robbers may be taken down so as not to remain on their crosses 'on the Sabbath', by which he perhaps means 'on the day of a festival': ἐκείνου τοῦ σαββάτου (19.31). If that seems doubtful, we should note that some lines later, when Mary Magdalen comes early in the morning, when it is still dark 'on the first (day) of the Sabbaths' (20.1), John surely means 'on the first of the festival days'.[17]

The structure of the narrative and its religious meaning and context are derived from its location on the day of preparation and the approach of Passover. It is surely suggestive that one reader who without hesitation 'read' 18.31, 'it is not permitted to us', as an allusion to the restrictions imposed by *Jewish* law was St Augustine: 'Non sibi licere interficere quemquam *propter diei festi sanctitatem*'.[18]

Conclusions

This discussion has not attempted to present firm conclusions, which are unattainable, but a series of approaches to the question of how we should attempt to understand our evidence on how Jesus came to be crucified. The primary suggestion is that in studying both the course of Jesus' life and the manner of his death, we must not proceed by amalgamating data from all four Gospels. That is illegitimate, because not merely the details, but the entire structure of the story as told by John is different from that in the Synoptics. Our evidence consists of coherent texts, and even where they contain common items, derived either from each other or from a hypothetical common source, or sources, any approach must respect the integrity of these texts as embodying different narrative structures. Any attempt to answer the inescapable question of 'what really happened' must therefore involve a choice. No arguments for any particular choice can be conclusive, but without such a choice our selection of elements to prefer must remain merely arbitrary. Given the necessity of choice, this paper offers the suggestion that, both as regards the narrative of Jesus' life and the culminating story of how he met his death, we should give our preference to John.

The expression of such a preference can in itself be no more than a hypothesis. That is to say that our position should be as follows: if, hypothetically, we accept John's Gospel as offering us the best account which we have of the steps which led to the crucifixion, what are the consequences?

First, the arrest, successive examinations and crucifixion of Jesus took place not on the first day of Passover, but on the day before, from evening to mid-day. The Last Supper was therefore not a Paschal meal at which the Paschal lamb was eaten, following the custom by which, by extension, a ceremony originally conducted solely in public in the Temple had become also a domestic ritual. Instead it was merely a meal on the night before. We would thus have to accept that it is the Synoptic accounts which have turned it, not very convincingly, into a Paschal meal.[19]

Second, we would have to accept the assertion, unique to John, that the arrest of Jesus was carried out by a Roman cohort under a tribune, guided by Judas and assisted by attendants sent by the *archiereis* and *Pharisaioi*. If so, that places him closer to the category of the long succession of popular religious leaders, all viewed as instigators of popular disorder, who are known from the pages of Josephus, and all of whom, with their followers, Jewish and Samaritan, were repressed by Roman forces. Jesus must by implication have been viewed as being more like these than like the solitary and apparently unbalanced pseudo-prophet, the other Jesus, arrested by the Jewish *archontes* at Tabernacles of 62 CE (see above).

Most important of all, however, is the fact that John's narrative, in which Passover has not yet arrived, gives Passover a much more fundamental relevance to what happened—and how—than do the Synoptics, which, while describing these events as occurring on the first night and morning of Passover, ignore the significance which we must presume to have attached to it in real life. For it is indubitable that Passover was the most important of the annual Jewish festivals in this period. Matthew and Mark, it is true, do not claim any more than that the Jewish authorities arrested Jesus on that night, examined him in the house of an *archiereus*, and accused him before the Roman *praefectus* in the morning, pressing on Pilate the necessity of crucifixion, to which he assented, and which then took place. Even that may seem incredible in view of the requirements of purity imposed during the festival. But Luke goes further, and represents the calling of a regular council in the morning, after the examination in the High-Priestly house, and before the accusation before Pilate. If such an event really occurred, it must have offended even more profoundly against the rules later propounded in the Mishnah—and more importantly against the underlying beliefs about the sanctity of the festival which gave rise to those rules.

In John, by contrast, Passover, which has not yet arrived,

dominates everything. It is because Jesus is brought before Pilate on the morning of the day whose evening will see the onset of Passover that Jesus' accusers will not enter the *praetorium*. It is, on this interpretation, because the sanctity of the festival prevents the holding of a capital trial even on the day before, that they tell Pilate, 'It is not permitted to us to kill anyone'. It is because they (unlike Jesus, who has no choice) remain outside the *praetorium*, that Pilate conducts the examination by alternating between questioning Jesus inside and confronting his accusers, and the crowd, outside, in the paved courtyard. This courtyard, identified only by John, has a regular *tribunal* (βῆμα) on which Pilate formally takes his seat when he finally brings Jesus outside to confront the Jewish crowd. Nothing is described here, however, any more than in the other Gospels, which could count as a formal trial by Pilate. There is no formal accusation and defence; no opinions are asked of the governor's *consilium*; and no formal verdict is pronounced. As with the other Gospels, in John the decision by Pilate to have Jesus executed is not represented as a verdict concluding a trial, but as a political decision taken as a concession to political pressure both from the Jewish authorities and from the crowd. The long-debated question of whether it was the Roman governor or 'the Sanhedrin' which had the legal right to try capital cases in first-century Judaea and to order the execution of those condemned on capital charges may be doubly misconceived, if it is thought to be directly relevant to how we interpret the Gospels. For, first, it has already been suggested that we should think rather of the pattern presented by Josephus' account of the execution of James, when the High Priest summons 'a *synedrion* of judges' (*Ant.* 20.9.1 [200]); that is to say, when the occasion arose the High Priest called together a group of citizens of his own choosing, just as a Roman official would summon a *consilium*.[20] Secondly, of the four Gospels, only Luke represents anything that we could think of as a meeting of 'the Sanhedrin', and does so in a context (the first day of Passover) which is highly improbable. For the rest, what we see is an examination in the house of an *archiereus*; or rather, in John's case, of the two successive *archiereis*, whose current roles are carefully (and correctly) specified; again the distinction between the *archiereus* currently in office (Caiaphas) and an ex-holder with the rank of *archiereus* is unique to him. Since no Gospel represents Pilate's decision as a formal verdict, there is a very clear sense in which the entire notion of 'the trial of Jesus' is a modern construct.

If instead it was a political decision, then it is again John who gives the clearest conception of its motivation. As Martin Goodman points out, Annas/Ananus was the first High Priest to be appointed by a Roman *praefectus* after the establishment of the province in 6 CE, and he and Caiaphas between them occupied the position for all but about three of the first twenty years of the province. They cannot but be seen as having collaborated successfully with the occupying power. That Caiaphas actually expressed the view that it was worth sacrificing one man to prevent Roman retribution on the whole people (Jn 11.50) cannot of course be known. But the thought would have corresponded well enough to the logic of the political situation. Moreover, *either* we know nothing whatsoever about the crucifixion *or* we can at least accept the one detail on which all four Gospels agree, that on the cross Jesus was described as 'King of the Jews'. Only John adds the detail that this inscription was called by the borrowed Latin term τίτλος (*titulus*), and that it was written in three languages. More important, it is he who represents Pilate's final dialogue with the crowd as turning on just this point: 'If you release this man, you are not a friend of Caesar; for anyone who makes himself a king opposes Caesar', 'Behold your king!', 'Take him and crucify him', 'Shall I crucify your king?', 'We have no king but Caesar'. Philo's *Against Flaccus* happens to provide a precisely contemporary analysis of the susceptibility to such pressure of a Roman governor who feels himself to be out of favour with the Emperor (*Flacc.* 3-4/8-23).

It was still the day of preparation for Passover (παρασκευή), about the sixth hour; there was still time for the crucifixion to take place, and for the bodies of Jesus and the two robbers to be taken down before the festival proper began (19.31), though the tomb where the body was laid had to be close because of the 'παρασκευή of the Jews'. By the next morning it was already of course the first day of the festival, or, as John puts it, 'the first day of the Sabbaths' (19.42-20.1). It is the approach of Passover which dictates every aspect of how the story unfolds, just as, in John's narrative, Jesus' life as a Galilean holy man is structured by the need to go up repeatedly to Jerusalem to the annual cycle of festivals. This necessity should, I suggest, be seen as of crucial importance. It is remarkable that, even in recent years, it has seemed possible to discuss the 'Palestinian Judaism' of this time as a purely personal religion, without giving a central (or indeed any) place to the communal worship and sacrifice at the Temple.[21] But John's narrative may precisely reveal the centrality of this communal sacrificial cult in the life of Jesus. If his portrayal gives us a Jesus who is less far from 'the historical Jesus' than the one whom the Synoptics represent, then we can at least perceive that their attachment to these festivals was one thing which Jesus and his accusers shared. It was not Roman law but their own which made them say, at that moment, 'It is not allowed to us to execute anyone'.

NOTES

1. I do not wish to enter into this question, but draw attention to the powerful converging arguments advanced for Passover of 36 CE by N. Kokkinos, 'Crucifixion in AD 36: the Keystone for Dating the Birth of Jesus', J. Vardaman and E.M. Yamauchi (eds.), *Chronos, Kairos, Christos; Nativity and Chronlogical Studies Presented to Jack Finegan*, 1989, p. 133.

2. I should note here the use I have made over the years of A. Wikenhauser, *Einleitung in das Neue Testament*[5], 1963, and D. Guthrie, *New Testament Introd␣ction*, 1970, and more recently L.T. Johnson, *The Writings of the New Tesťa␣␣␣␣* 198␣. On the specific question of the trial narratives see especially E. Bickerman, 'Utilitas crucis', *RHR* 112 (1935), p. 169 = *Studies in Jewish and Christian History*, III, 1986, p. 82; A.N. Sherwin-White, *Roman Society and Roman Law in the New Testament*, 1963; P. Winter, *On the Trial of Jesus*[2], 1974; O. Betz, 'Probleme des Prozesses Jesus', *ANRW* II.25.1, 1982, p. 565.

3. My use of, and emphasis on, John clearly owes much to C.H. Dodd, *Historical Tradition in the Fourth Gospel*, 1963, and to J.A.T. Robinson, *The Priority of John*, 1985. See now M. Hengel, *The Johannine Question*, 1989.

4. For the historical framework and datings, and above all the crucial question of the census of 6 CE, see Schürer-Vermes-Millar, *History of the Jewish People*, I, Edinburgh 1973, pp. 326f.

5. *P. Lond.* 904, ll.18-38; Hunt and Edgar, *Select Papyri*, II, 1934, no. 220.

6. See e.g. *BJ* 2.1.3 [10-13]; 2.12.1 [224-27]; 2.14.3 [280-83]; 6.9.3 [422-27]; *Ant.* 17.9.3 [213-18]; 20.5.3 [106-12].

7. See e.g. *BJ* 2.12.3 [232-33]; *Ant.* 20.6.1 [118-21].

8. Philo, *De Spec. Leg.* 1.189; 2.204-13.

9. I rely on the very interesting, if not always entirely clear or conclusive, discussion by J.B. Segal, *The Hebrew Passover from the Earliest Times to AD 70*, London, 1963.

10. For the conduct of the sacrifices in daylight, during the afternoon of 14th Nisan, see Segal, *op. cit.*, p. 233, using *Jub.* 49. For the process of sacrificing in groups, amounting to vast numbers of individuals in all, see

Josephus, *BJ* 6.9.3 [423-26]. On Josephus' account, at Passover of (apparently) 66 CE, 295,600 victims were sacrificed on behalf of groups (φ(ρ)άτρια) of 10-20 each, these sacrifices being carried out between the ninth and the eleventh hour, hence towards evening, but before sunset.

11. For this point cf. Segal, *op. cit.*, p. 245, which does not however cite any very clear evidence. The term παρασκευή is attested as meaning 'the day before Shabbat', e.g. Josephus, *Ant.* 16.6.2 [163], but so far as I know not elsewhere unambiguously in relation to a festival. But (see below) Jn 19.14 uses παρασκευὴ τοῦ πάσχα.

12. *BJ* 6.9.3 (426): καθαρῶν ἁπάντων καὶ ἁγίων. οὔτε γὰρ λεπροῖς οὔτε γονορροϊκοῖς οὔτε γυναιξὶν ἐπεμμήνοις οὔτε τοῖς ἄλλως μεμιασμένοις ἐξὸν ἦν τῆσδε τῆς θυσίας μεταλαμβάνειν. See S. Safrai, 'The Temple', *JPFC* 2 (1976), pp. 865ff., on pp. 891-92.

13. For the family see now D. Barag and D. Flusser, 'The Ossuary of Yehohanan Granddaughter of the High Priest Theophilus', *IEJ* 36 (1986), p. 39.

14. The quotations are borrowed from Segal, *op. cit.*, pp. 10 and 26.

15. Robinson, *op. cit.*, pp. 228-29.

16. See e.g. Sherwin-White, *op. cit.*, pp. 32f.

17. The interpretation of all these expressions seems to me extremely problematic, and I am not convinced that any of them clearly indicate what day of the *week* (as opposed to what day before, or of, Passover) John means to represent. In particular the Anchor Bible translation of 20.1 as 'the first day of the week' seems to me quite impossible. For in that case Shabbat, as the *last* day of the week, has disappeared.

18. The quotation comes from Augustine, *In Joh. Ev. Tract.* 114, 4 (*Corpus Christianorum, Series Latina* XXXVI, 641): 'Sed intelligendum est eos dixisse non sibi licere interficere quemquam, propter diei festi sanctitatem, quem celebrare iam coeperant; propter quem de ingressu etiam praetorii contaminari metuebant'. The same point is made very briefly by John Chrysostom, *In Joh. Homil.* 73, 4 (*PG* LIX, col. 452).

19. So e.g. Segal, *op. cit.*, p. 245.

20. For this suggestion see M. Goodman, *The Ruling Class of Judaea: the Origins of the Jewish Revolt against Rome*, 1987, pp. 113f.

21. So E.P. Sanders, *Paul and Palestinian Judaism*, 1977, Part I: 'Palestinian Judaism'.

BIBLIOGRAPHY OF THE WORKS OF GEZA VERMES

1949-1989

Books

Les manuscrits du désert de Juda (Tournai-Paris: Desclée, 1953), 216 pp. (2nd edn, 1954, 220 pp.).

Discovery in the Judean Desert (New York: Desclée, 1956), 238 pp.

Scripture and Tradition in Judaism: Haggadic Studies (Leiden: Brill, 1961), x, 243 pp. (2nd edn, 1973).

The Dead Sea Scrolls in English (Harmondsworth: Penguin, 1962), 255 pp. (2nd edn, 1975, 281 pp., 3rd edn, 1987, 320 pp. [hardback edn, Sheffield: JSOT Press, 1987]).

Jesus the Jew: A Historian's Reading of the Gospels (London: Collins, 1973), 286 pp. (New York: Macmillan, 1974; London: Fount Paperback, 1976; Philadelphia: Fortress Press, 1981; London: SCM Press, 1983).

The History of the Jewish People in the Age of Jesus Christ (175 BC-AD 135) by E. Schürer, vol. I, revised and edited by G. Vermes & F. Millar (Edinburgh: T. & T. Clark, 1973), xvi, 614 pp.

On the Trial of Jesus by P. Winter, revised and edited by T.A. Burkill & G. Vermes (Berlin: W. de Gruyter, 1974), xxiii, 225 pp.

Post-Biblical Jewish Studies (Leiden: Brill, 1975), x, 246 pp.

The Dead Sea Scrolls: Qumran in Perspective (London: Collins, 1977), 240 pp. (Philadelphia: Fortress Press, 1981; London: SCM Press, 1982).

Jesús el Judío (Barcelona: Muchnik, 1977), 306 pp.

Jésus le Juif (Paris: Desclée, 1978), 298 pp.

[Jesus the Jew in Japanese] (Tokyo: The United Church in Japan, 1979), 420 pp.

The History of the Jewish People in the Age of Jesus Christ, vol. II, revised and edited by G. Vermes, F. Millar & M. Black (Edinburgh: T. & T. Clark, 1979), xvi, 606 pp.

Los manuscritos del Mar Muerto (Barcelona: Muchnik, 1981), 240 pp.

The Gospel of Jesus the Jew (Newcastle: University of Newcastle, 1981), viii, 64 pp.

Essays in Honour of Yigael Yadin, ed. by G. Vermes & J. Neusner (Totowa: Allanheld, 1983), xvi, 600 pp.

Gesù l'ebreo (Rome: Borla, 1983), 283 pp.

Jesus and the World of Judaism (London: SCM Press, 1983; Philadelphia: Fortress Press, 1984), x, 197 pp.

Historia del pueblo judío en tiempos de Jesús, vols. I-II (Madrid: Cristiandad, 1985), 792, 798 pp.

Storia del popolo giudaico al tempo di Gesù Cristo, vol. I (Brescia: Paideia, 1985), 736 pp.

The History of the Jewish People in the Age of Jesus Christ, revised and edited by G. Vermes, F. Millar & M. Goodman, vol. III/1-2 (Edinburgh: T. & T. Clark, 1986-87), xx, 1015 pp.

Storia del popolo giudaico al tempo di Gesù Christo, vol. II (Brescia: Paideia, 1987), 724 pp.

The Dead Sea Scrolls Forty Years On: The Fourteenth Sacks Lecture (Oxford Centre for Hebrew Studies, 1987), 20 pp.

The Essenes according to the Classical Sources, by G. Vermes & M. Goodman (Sheffield: JSOT Press, 1989), xi, 103 pp.

Jesus der Jude (Neukirchen-Vluyn: Neukirchener Verlag, forthcoming).

Translation

The Essene Writings from Qumran by A. Dupont-Sommer (Oxford: Blackwell, 1961), xvi, 428 pp.

Papers

'Nouvelles lumières sur la Bible et le judaïsme', *Cahiers Sioniens* 3 (1949), 224-33.

'La secte juive de la Nouvelle Alliance d'après ses Hymnes récemment découverts', *ibid.* 4 (1950), 178-202.

'A propos des "Aperçus préliminaires sur les manuscrits de la Mer Morte" de M. A. Dupont-Sommer', *ibid.* 5 (1951), 58-69.

'Le Commentaire d'Habacuc et le Nouveau Testament', *ibid.* 5 (1951), 337-49.

'La Communauté de la Nouvelle Alliance', *Ephemerides Theologicae Lovanienses* 27 (1951), 70-80.

'Où en est la question des manuscrits de la Mer Morte?', *Cahiers Sioniens* 7 (1953), 63-76.

'Notes sur la formation des traditions juives', *ibid.*, 320-42.

'La cadre historique des manuscrits de la Mer Morte', *Recherches de Science Religieuse* 41 (1953), 5-28, 203-30.

'A propos des commentaires bibliques découverts à Qumrân', *La Bible et l'Orient* (Paris: Presses Universitaires de France, 1955), 95-103.

'La figure de Moïse au tournant des deux Testaments', *Moïse, l'homme de l'Alliance* (Paris: Desclée, 1955), 63-92.

'Quelques traditions de la Communauté de Qumrân', *Cahiers Sioniens* 9 (1955), 25-58.

'La littérature rabbinique et le Nouveau Testament', *ibid.*, 97-123.

'Deux traditions sur Balaam', *ibid.*, 289-302.

'"Car le Liban, c'est le Conseil de la Communauté"', *Mélanges A. Robert* (Paris: Bloud & Gay, 1957), 316-25.

'The Symbolical Interpretation of Lebanon in the Targums', *Journal of Theological Studies* N.S. 9 (1958), 1-12.

'Baptism and Jewish Exegesis: New Light from Ancient Sources', *New Testament Studies* 5 (1958), 308-19.

'The Torah is a Light', *Vetus Testamentum* 9 (1958), 436-38.

'Pre-Mishnaic Jewish Worship and the Phylacteries from the Dead Sea', *ibid.*, 10 (1959), 65-72.

'Essenes–Therapeutai–Qumran: Ancient Jewish Asceticism and the Dead Sea Scrolls', *Durham University Journal* 52 (1960), 97-115.

'The Etymology of Essenes', *Revue de Qumrân* 2 (1960), 427-43.

'Essenes and Therapeutae', *ibid.* 3 (1962), 495-504.

'The Targumic Versions of Genesis iv, 3-16', *Annual of Leeds University Oriental Society* 3 (1963), 81-114.

'Haggadah in the Onkelos Targum', *Journal of Semitic Studies* 8 (1963), 159-69.

'Midrash', *Enciclopedia de la Biblia* (Barcelona, 1965).

'Neglected Facts about the Dead Sea Scrolls', *Daily Telegraph*, 9 April 1966.

'The Use of *bar nash/bar nasha* in Jewish Aramaic', in M. Black, *An Aramaic Approach to the Gospels and Acts* (3rd edn, Oxford: Clarendon Press, 1967), 310-28.

'The Decalogue and the Minim', *In Memoriam Paul Kahle* (Berlin: Alfred Töpelmann, 1968), 232-40.

'Quest for the Historical Jesus', *Jewish Chronicle Literary Supplement*, 12 December 1969.

'*He is the Bread*: Targum Neofiti Exodus 16.15', in *Neotestamentica et Semitica: Studies in Honour of M. Black* (Edinburgh: T. & T. Clark, 1969), 256-63.

'The Qumran Interpretation of Scripture in its Historical Setting', *Annual of Leeds University Oriental Society* 6 (1969), 85-97 (German transl. 'Die Schriftauslegung in Qumran in ihrem historischen Rahmen', in *Qumran*, Wege der Forschung, CDX [Darmstadt: Wissenschaftliche Buchgesellschaft, 1989], 184- 200).

'Bible and Midrash: Early Old Testament Exegesis', in *The Cambridge History of the Bible*, vol. 1 (Cambridge: Cambridge University Press, 1970), 199-231, 592.

'The New English Bible', *Jewish Chronicle*, 20 March 1970.

'Ancient Judaism in the Light of the Dead Sea Scrolls', *Pointer* 7.1 (1971), 4-6.

'Hanukka and History', *ibid.* 8.2 (1972), 7-8.

'From the very excellent to the poor: The Encyclopaedia Judaica', *Jerusalem Post*, 11 August 1972.

'Hanina ben Dosa', *Journal of Jewish Studies* 23 (1972), 28-50; 24 (1973), 51-64.

'Sectarian Matrimonial Halakhah in the Damascus Rule', *ibid.* 25 (1974), 197-202.

'Jesus the Jew: The Claude Montefiore Memorial Lecture 1974', (Liberal Jewish Synagogue 1975), 15 pp.

'The Archangel Sariel: A Targumic Parallel to the Dead Sea Scrolls', in *Christianity, Judaism and other Greco-Roman Cults*, Part III, ed. J. Neusner (Leiden: E.J. Brill, 1975), 159-66.

'The Impact of the Dead Sea Scrolls on Jewish Studies', *Journal of Jewish Studies* 26 (1975), 1-14 (Reissued in *Approaches to Ancient Judaism: Theory and Practice*, ed. W.S. Green [Chico: Scholars Press, 1978], 201-14. Hungarian translation in *Évkönyv 1975/76* [Budapest, 1976], 389-403).

'The Impact of the Dead Sea Scrolls on the Study of the New Testament', *Journal of Jewish Studies* 27 (1976), 107-16 (Hungarian transl. in *Évkönyv 1977/78* [Budapest 1978], 421-34).

'Dead Sea Scrolls', in *The Interpreter's Dictionary of the Bible*: *Supplementary Volume* (Nashville: Abingdon, 1976), 210-19.

'Interpretation, History of, at Qumran and in the Targums', *ibid.*, 438-43.

'Manuscripts from the Judean Desert', *ibid.*, 563-66.

'The Present State of the "Son of Man" Debate', *Journal of Jewish Studies* 29 (1978), 123-34.

'The "Son of Man" Debate', *Journal for the Study of the New Testament* 1 (1978), 19-32.

'Jewish Studies and New Testament Interpretation', *Journal of Jewish Studies* 31 (1980), 1-17.

'The Gospels without Christology', in *God Incarnate: Story and Belief*, ed. A.E. Harvey (London: SPCK, 1981), 55-68.

'Leviticus 18.21 in Ancient Jewish Bible Interpretation', in the *Joseph Heinemann Memorial Volume* (Jerusalem: Magnes Press, 1981), 108-24.

'The Essenes and History', *Journal of Jewish Studies* 32 (1981), 18-31.

'Jewish Studies and New Testament Exegesis: Reflections on Methodology', *Journal of Jewish Studies* 33 (1982), 361-76.

'A Summary of the Law by Flavius Josephus', *Novum Testamentum* 24 (1982), 289-307.

'Jesus der Jude', *Judaica* 38 (1982), 215-28.

'Miriam the Jewess', *The Way: Supplement* 45 (1982), 55-64.

'L'ebreo Gesù', *Sefer* 23 (1983), 5-9.

'Vita egy könyvröl [Controversy over a book]', *Vigilia* 49.5 (1984), 344-49.

'La littérature juive intertestamentaire à la lumière d'un siècle de recherches et de découvertes'(with M. Goodman), in *Etudes sur le Judaïsme hellénistique*, ed. R. Kuntzmann & J. Schlosser (Paris: Cerf, 1984), 19-39.

'Methodology in the Study of Jewish Literature in the Graeco-Roman Period', *Journal of Jewish Studies* 36 (1985), 145-58.

'Scripture and Tradition in Judaism: Written and Oral Torah', in *Literacy and the Written Word: Wolfson College Lectures 1985*, ed. G. Baumann (Oxford: Oxford University Press, 1986), 79-95.

'"Jesus: the Evidence" and the British Press', *Lycidas* 13 (1986), 40-42.

'The Jesus Notice of Josephus Re-examined', *Journal of Jewish Studies* 38 (1987), 1-10.

'Jesus the Jew', in *Renewing the Judeo-Christian Wellsprings*, ed. V.A. McInnes (New York: Crossroad, 1987), 122-35.

'Jesus and Christianity', *ibid.*, 136-50.

'Biblical Studies and the Dead Sea Scrolls 1947-1987: Retrospects and Prospects', *Journal for the Study of the Old Testament* 39 (1987), 113-28.

'New Light on the Dead Sea Scrolls', *Jewish Chronicle*, 5 June 1987.

'Symposium on the Manuscripts from the Judaean Desert: Preliminary Remarks', *Journal of Jewish Studies* 39 (1988), 1-4.

'"Josephus's" Portrait of Jesus Reconsidered', in *Occident and Orient. A Tribute to the Memory of A. Scheiber* (Budapest: Akadémiai Kiadó/Leiden: Brill, 1988), 373-82.

'Jesus the Jew: Christian and Jewish Reactions', *Toronto Journal of Theology* 4 (1988), 112-23.

'Biblical Exegesis at Qumran', in the *Yigael Yadin Memorial Volume*, *Eretz Israel* 20 (1989), 184*-191*.

'Biblical Proof-Texts in Qumran Literature', in *The Edward Ullendorff Festschrift*, *Journal of Semitic Studies* 34 (1989), 493-508.

INDEXES

INDEX OF ANCIENT REFERENCES

OLD TESTAMENT

NEW TESTAMENT

APOCRYPHA AND PSEUDEPIGRAPHA

PHILO

Against Flaccus
3-4/8-23   379

De Abrahamo
56   185

De Plantatione
37   146, 147

De Sobrietate
65-66   185

De Specialibus Legibus
1.189   380

2.145-146   374
2.204-13   380
4.183   314
36.287   300

Legum Allegoriae
3.106   354
200   273

On the Confusion of Tongues
44   95
142-46   92

On the Posterity of Cain
89   98

Quaestiones in Exodum
1.23   150

Quod Deus sit immutabilis
50   145, 151

Vita Mosis
2.138   147

RABBINIC LITERATURE

Mishnah
'Abodah Zarah
2.6   231

Aboth
2.4   204
5.2   354
5.3a   133

Demai
1.3   202

Megillah
4.10C-D   220

Menaḥot
13.10   97

Oholoth
17.7   374
17.10   374

Sanhedrin
4.1   369, 375

Shabbat
1.4   208, 238
2.2   227

Sukkoth
4.9   186

Tosefta
'Abodah Zarah
3.19   220
4.8   234, 239

Kelim
2.2   300

Kippurim
5.17L-V   220
5.17L-V   222
5.17V   221

Megillah
4.36-37   220

Menaḥot
13   96
12-15   96

Moed
11.36-38   208

Sanhedrin
7.11   121

Shabbat
1.16   208, 210
15.9   293

Sotah
6.5   137
6.6   220

Babylonian Talmud
'Abodah Zarah
5a   212
10a   300
10b   203
17a   203
18a   93, 203
25b   300
27b   91
35b-36a   232
36a   243
37a   231

Baba Bathra
8a   202
14b   166
75   204

Baba Kamma
59b   204

Berakhot
20a   204
28b   144, 146, 147
31b   115
55a-57b   118

CLASSICAL LITERATURE

Digest (cont.)	
1.2.2.47-53	111
33.10.7.2	113
50.16	113
50.16.6	113
50.16.102	113
50.16.124	113

50.16.195	113
50.17	113
50.17.1	113
50.17.9	113
50.17.56	113
50.17.147	113

Quintilian	
Institutio Oratoria	
VII 8.3	116
Xenophanes Frag.	
11	122

EARLY CHRISTIAN LITERATURE

Acta Petri et Pauli	
35	353
81f.	353
Acts of Thomas	
10	151
156	151
Aphrahat (Syr.)	
Dem.	
XII.8	151
XIV.31	151
XXIII.3	151
Augustine	
Epistle	
ccxlv.2	190
Quaestionum in Heptateuchum	
I	190
In Joh. Ev. Tract.	
114	381
4	381
Epistle of Barnabas	
4.3	353
15.4	353
18	139, 143, 147
John Chrysostom	
Homily	
LIX.4	190
In Joh. Homil.	
73.4	381

1 Clement	
20	330
31.3	191
31.4–32.2	191
32	330
38	330
43	330
45	330
50	330
54	346
58	330
61	330
64	330
65	330, 331
Clementine Homilies	
VII 7.1-2	141
VII 7.1	147
XVIII 17.2	141
De Principiis	
III.1.6	141
Clement of Alexandria	
Stromateis	
4.39.1	150
6.8.7	150
Didache	
1-6	139
1	147, 150
1.1	139, 143
8.2	330
9.2	330
9.3	330
9.4	330
10.2	330
10.4	330

10.5	330
Doctrina Apostolorum	
1	147
Ephrem (Syr.)	
H. de Fide	
XX.14	152
de Nativitate	
VIII.4	151
Comm. Gen.	
II.7	151
Liber Graduum	
XV.2	151
Hermas	
Mandates	
VI. 2.1	150
Justin	
Apology I	
1.20	354
44.1	151
Apology II	
7	354
Apostolic Constitutions	
VII. 1.1	142

Origen
Comm. Matt.
15.23   150

*Dialogue with
Heracleides*
27.11   150

Tertullian
Adversus Judaeos
10   353

Adversus Marcionem
3.18   353

de Castitate
2.3   151

de Monogamia
14.7   151

*De praescriptione
haereticorum*
VII   120

Theodotus
Praeparatio Evangelica
9.22.9   191

PAPYRI

Papyrus Lipsius
34.8   337

P. Lond.
904   380

Select Papyri
II   380

P. Oxy.
221   106, 107

1086   106
1087   106

INDEX OF AUTHORS

DATE DUE

MAR 20 1997			